Travels in Persia 1673=1677

Sir John Chardin

With a Preface by N. M. PENZER
and an Introduction by SIR PERCY SYKES

DOVER PUBLICATIONS, INC.
NEW YORK

This Dover edition, first published in 1988, is an un-
abridged republication of the work as originally published by
The Argonaut Press, London, in 1927 in an edition limited to
975 copies. The title-page vignette, based on a Persian tile,
originally had blue as a second color. Some of the illustrations
have been moved to new places in the book. The costume
illustrations following page 212 originally appeared on two
foldouts.

Manufactured in the United States of America
Dover Publications, Inc., 31 East 2nd Street,
Mineola, N.Y. 11501

Library of Congress Cataloging-in-Publication Data

Chardin, John, Sir, 1643–1713.
    Travels in Persia, 1673–1677/by Sir John Chardin ; with a
preface by N.M. Penzer and an introduction by Sir Percy
Sykes.
        p.   cm.
    An abridged English version of the author's Voyages du
chevalier Chardin en Perse, et autres lieux de l'Orient.
    Reprint. Originally published: London: Argonaut Press,
1927.
    Includes index.
    ISBN 0-486-25636-7
    1. Iran—Description and travel.   2. Chardin, John, Sir,
1643–1713—Journeys—Iran.   3. Authors, English—17th
century—Journeys—Iran.   I. Chardin, John, Sir,
1643–1713. Voyages du chevalier Chardin en Perse, et autres
lieux de l'Orient.   II. Title.
DS257.C5 1988
915.5—dc19   87-34665
                                                             CIP

PREFACE

I SHALL confine myself here to giving a few bibliographical details about the works of Chardin, paying special attention to the practically unknown two-volume English edition, which is here reprinted for the first time.

After his second visit to Persia in 1669, Chardin returned to Paris, and in 1671 issued a work entitled *Le Couronnement de Soleiman Troisième*, of which he had been an eyewitness. In 1671 he again set out for Persia, and did not return to Europe until 1677. An edition of his *Travels* in four volumes was projected, of which only the first actually appeared. This was entitled *Journal du Voyage...de Chardin en Perse et aux Indes Orientales*. Londres, 1686. It included a reprint of the coronation of Solyman III, as issued in 1671. An English translation was published concurrently. The reason why no further volumes of this edition were issued is not clear, but Chardin appears to have been in correspondence with Jean Louis de Lorme, an Amsterdam publisher. Under his imprint there appeared in 1711 the three remaining volumes of the *Journal*, and also a ten-volume edition which was an enlargement of the four-volume composite edition, and included a reprint of his translation of *La Relation des Mingreliens* by J. M. Zampi, which in 1731 formed Vol. VII of J. F. Bernard's *Recueil de Voyages au Nord*.

We now come to the two-volume English edition. It seems to have escaped the notice of all bibliographers, and is not even mentioned in Westby-Gibson's article in the *Dictionary of National Biography*. As the title-page reproduced (p. xxv) shows, it was to have been issued in eight volumes, the first of which was dated 1720. As stated at the end of the Preface, the work was issued by subscription, and it seems quite obvious that the response did not merit its continuation. The publisher, Mr J. Smith, must have had a large number of these first two volumes on his hands, and tried every means to sell them. The first attempt was by erasing the word "eight" on the title-page and substituting "two." A copy so treated is to be found in the library of the Royal Geographical Society.

The next attempt on the part of Mr Smith was to invent a new title-page for the incomplete work, entitled: *A New Collection of Voyages and Travels, Never before Published in English. Containing a most Accurate Description of Persia, and other Eastern Nations....*

There is no mention of either Chardin or Lloyd on the title-page at all, and the date is 1721. The contents of the volumes are the same, and the quires of Volume II are marked "Vol. I," as was also the case in the original 1720 edition. There is a copy of this in the Bodleian Library.

It would appear that this scheme was also a failure, and that Smith sold the remaining copies to another firm, for in 1724 they were issued with still another title-page, bearing the names of four different publishers or booksellers. The title-page reads: *A New and Accurate Description of Persia and Other Eastern Nations containing the Natural History...*, 2 Vols., London, 1724. There is a copy of this edition in the Library of the British Museum the title-page of which is shown opposite.

In 1735 a four-volume edition was produced, which, while containing many fresh extracts from Chardin's MSS., omitted certain passages which are considered to contain a direct attack on the Calvinists.

The complete edition did not appear until 1811, when it was issued in ten volumes, with a folio of plates by M. A. Langlès. With regard to the omission in the previous editions we find some interesting information in *Biographie Universelle*, Vol. VIII, p. 74, Paris, 1813, from which I extract the following passage:

"Nous disons à peu près complètes, parce que le libraire Delorme, qui avait été précédemment mis à la Bastille, exigea de l'auteur la suppression de certains passages capables de déplaire au clergé romain, et conséquemment de compromettre la tranquillité du libraire, même en Hollande, et d'empêcher le débit de l'ouvrage en France. Ces passages ont été réintégrés, avec usure peut-être, dans l'édition de 1735, 4 vol. in-4°; nous ne serions pas même éloignés de croire que les entrepreneurs de cette édition ont mis sur le compte de Chardin plusieurs diatribes virulentes contre les papistes. Ces calvinistes, bien plus occupés des ressentiments de leur secte que de la gloire de Chardin, ont laissé à des protes ignorants le soin de cette édition, dans laquelle on remarque les erreurs typographiques et les

A New and Accurate

DESCRIPTION

OF

P E R S I A,

AND

Other Eaſtern Nations.

CONTAINING

The Natural Hiſtory of thoſe Countries; the Religion, Temper, Manners and Cuſtoms of their Inhabitants; their Apparel, Exerciſes and Games; Arts, Trades, Manufacture, and Commerce.

WITH

Genuine Copies of the Inſtructions given by the *Engliſh*, *French*, and other *European* Powers, to their Reſpective Embaſſadors at that Court, and at thoſe of *China*, *Japan*, and other Neighbouring Empires; no leſs Uſeful and Inſtructive for carrying on the Commerce in thoſe Parts, than Entertaining to the Curious.

Illuſtrated with a great Number of Cuts of Habits, Towns, Beaſts, Birds, Ruins, Proſpects at Sea, &c.

VOL. I.

LONDON:

Printed for *A. Betteſworth* and *J. Batley* in *Pater-noſter-Row*; *J. Brotherton* and *W. Meadows* in *Cornhill*; *C. Rivington* in *St. Paul's-Church-Yard*; and *J. Hooke* in *Fleet-ſtreet.* 1724.

Title-page of the 1724 edition
From a copy in the British Museum

omissions les plus graves; malgré ces imperfections, elle était montée, dans ces derniers temps, à un prix énorme. L'auteur de cet article ose croire que les imperfections qu'il a blâmées dans les trois éditions authentiques des voyages de Chardin ne se trouvent pas dans celle qu'il a publiée en 1811, 10 volumes in-8°, avec atlas in fol., renfermant toutes les figures des éditions précédentes, et une carte de la Perse, dressée avec le plus grand soin par M. Lapie."

There remains but to mention the method adopted in the reprinting of the 1720 edition. All obvious printer's errors have been corrected, but contemporary forms of typography and spelling have been retained. In some cases proper names are found to be spelt in several different ways. Here we have printed that most generally accepted as being correct. One of the chief errors in Vol. I was the omission of a heading for Chapter VIII, and that for Chapter VII was transposed to the head of Chapter VIII. This has necessitated certain changes in setting-up, but is now restored as it was obviously originally meant.

In conclusion I would mention reprints of Chardin's *Travels* as published in subsequent collections of *Travels*. The Journey by way of the Black Sea to Persia appears in Vol. II (*b*) of Harris's *Navigatium atque Itinerantium Bibliotheca*, and Vols. XV and XVI of the *World Displayed*, 1767–8. Abstracts of all his travels are included in Pinkerton's *Travels*, Vol. IX, 1808–14. See also *New Collection of Voyages*, 1767, Vol. VI.

I should like to express my indebtedness to the Librarian of the India Office for the loan of the 1720 edition of the English translation of Chardin here reprinted.

N. M. PENZER

CONTENTS

PAGE

INTRODUCTION   xiii

"THE TRAVELS OF SIR JOHN CHARDIN"

CHAPTER   FIRST VOLUME

I The Author's Arrival at *Ispahan*. Monsieur *D' l' Hay*'s Expedition to the *East Indies*, and his Miscarriage; with the Occasions of it. Wild Oxen at *Trinc-male*. The particular Qualities of the Flesh of that Beast. Cannonading and Taking of *Coromandel*.   I

II The Author employs his Time in receiving Visits from his Acquaintance, and advises concerning his Conduct since the late King's Death. Debauches of the present King, and his Outrages in those Fits of Drunkenness. Reinstatement of the late Prime Minister. Manner of entertaining the King.   6

III The Author sent for to the Nazir concerning the Commission of the late King for Jewels, Character of the Nazir. The Author reads the Contents of a *French* Letter, in *Persian*.   12

IV Letters from Mr. *Carron* to Mr. *d' Thou*, Count of *Meslay*, &c. *Director of the East* Company of *France*, with Instructions concerning the Commerce. Amplification on the foregoing Subject.   17

V The King of *France*'s *Letter* to the Emperor of *China*. His Instructions to his Envoy at the Cham of *Tartary*'s and Emperor of *China*'s Courts. His Voyage from thence to the *Indies*.   26

VI King of *France*'s *Letter* to the Emperor of *Japan*, in relation to Trade. Instructions to Mr *Carron*, Envoy at the Court of *Japan*. Manner of putting up and carrying the King's *Letter* to Court.   32

VII Three Envoys from the Company join the two Deputies, but without any Character. The *Letter* they were charg'd with to the King of *Persia*. The Faults wherein. Their Request granted through the Author's Means.   40

VIII (There is no rubric to this chapter.)   42

IX The Author pays his respects to the two Favorites of the King, who promise Services but do nothing. Visits to Persons of Distinction. He is sent for to the *Nazir*. His Jewels produc'd.   45

X The *French* Envoy has a House ordered him. Number of the King's Houses at *Ispahan*. The Author is sent for again to the *Nazir* about the Jewels; what pass'd between 'em concerning them. A notable Instance of *Eastern* Craft. Entrance of a *Muscovite* Ambassador. The *Persian* Manner of entertaining them.   50

XI Captain of the *Haram-Gate* Bastinado'd. Some young Noblemen got drunk, the King's Order thereupon. Another Conference about the Jewels. The Day for the Publick Entry of the *French* Envoy appointed. Petition of the Christian *Armenians*. The *French* Ambassador's Entry and Reception.   53

CHAPTER   PAGE

XII The Grand Vizier affronted by the King when drunk. Settlement of the
Ambassadors Table during his Stay at *Ispahan*. The King, in Drink,
affronts the Grand Vizier worse than before. Contract of the *Dutch* for
Silk consider'd, and their Abatement.   56

XIII Civilities shown the Author in his Illness. Damage done by an Earthquake. *Portugueze* Duties. The Envoy delivers a Petition in order to be
dismissed. The Chief of the *Armenians* turns Renagade; the Consequences
dreaded. Their Application thereupon to the Pope.   62

XIV The Author concludes his Bargain with the Nazir about the Jewels. His
Reasons for dwelling so long upon the Subject of them.   70

XV Marriage of the Nazir's eldest Son. Governor of a Province brought up
Prisoner to Town. An Order deliver'd to the Author, for his Money;
Poor piece of Roguery of the Nazir's.   73

XVI The Nazir entertains the King, a Description of it. The Envoy of the
French East-India Company desires Audience of the King. The *Armenian*
who turn'd *Mahometan* Circumcis'd. Visit to the Cedre or Great Pontiff,
civilly receiv'd.   77

XVII The Ambassador of the *Resqui*, and *Muscovy*, admitted to an Audience. A
Dispute between the *French* Envoy and *English* Agent about Precedency
examined and settled. The Manner of the Ambassadors being conducted,
with the Magnificence attending it.   81

XVIII The Ambassador's Presents, the Shews exhibited upon this Occasion;
Character of the *Persian* Courtiers.   86

XIX Some Jewels sold to the Nazir; His Extortion. A fine Present of Sweet-
meats made to the Author by the Great Pontif's Wife, and Aunt to the
King. The Envoy of the *French* Company, and *English* Agent, conducted to
their Audience; with their Presents. An Instance of the Pride of the
Persian Kings. The Presents valu'd.   91

XX An occasional Conversation concerning the two Audiences. A Molla or
Priest Bastinadoed, the Reason. The *French* Envoys Presents to the
Ministers. The *Muscovite* Envoy has a Conference with the Ministers.
Several Conjectures about his Negotiations. Exactness with which the
Great Men in *Persia* are obey'd. First Establishment of the *English* in
Persia.   97

XXI The first Minister's Resentment shown to the *English*. Blunders in the
Letters of the *French* Envoy. The King begins his Tour of *Casbin*. Superstition observ'd. The sumptuousness of his Travelling Buffet.   103

XXII A Bargain of a thousand Pistols concluded with the Pontif's Lady for
Jewels, the Value paid in Gold Plate. Contests concerning Fees due to
some of the Ministers. Conferences of the *French* and *English* Envoys, with
the Ministers of State. The Princess, the Pontif's Wife, shows her fine
Jewels to the Author.   106

XXIII The Mosque of *Metched* repair'd, which was thrown down by an Earthquake. Calaats delivered to all the Ambassadors and Envoys. The King
proceeds on his Journey. Translation of the King's Edicts. The *Persians*
Ignorance as to the *European* Parts of the World.   112

CHAPTER   PAGE

XXIV The King's Letter and the Nazirs to the *French* Company. The *English* dispatch'd afterwards. Punishment of the King's Officers upon the Road. The Author receives his Money for his Jewels sold to the King, his Acquittance, the Manner of it.   117

SECOND VOLUME

I Of Persia in General   125
II Of the Climate, and of the Air   131
III Of the Soil   137
IV Of the Trees, Plants, and Druggs   140
V Of the Fruits of Persia   154
VI. Concerning the Flowers of Persia   159
VII Of Metals and Minerals: to which is annex'd a Discourse of Jewels   162
VIII Of Animals Tame and Wild   167
IX Of the Tame and Wild Birds, and of Hunting   174
X Of the Fish   182
XI Of the Temper, Manners, and Customs of the Persians   183
XII Concerning the Exercises and Games of the Persians   198
XIII Of the Cloaths, and Household-goods   211
XIV Of the Luxury of the Persians   220
XV Concerning the Food of the Persians   222
XVI Of the strong and small Liquors   240
XVII Of mechanick Arts and Trades   248
XVIII Of Manufactures   277
XIX Of the Commerce or Trade; and also of the Weights, the Measures, and Coin   279

ILLUSTRATIONS

Title-page of the 1724 Edition   vii
Title-page of the 1720 Edition   xii
Sir John Chardin. From an engraving by David Loggan   ii
Persian smoking the "Callion"   145
The Pigeon-houses   175
Persian in usual sitting position   191
Persian Costumes   *facing* 212
Wooden Crane   265

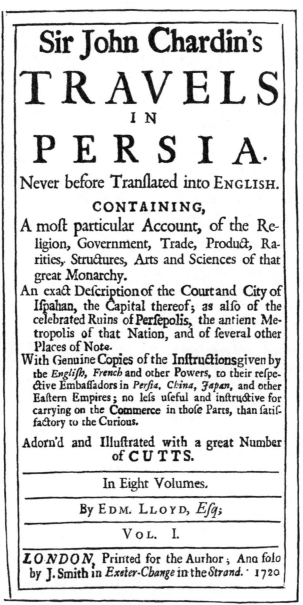

Sir John Chardin's

TRAVELS
IN
PERSIA.

Never before Tranflated into ENGLISH.

CONTAINING,

A moft particular Account, of the Religion, Government, Trade, Product, Rarities, Structures, Arts and Sciences of that
great Monarchy.

An exact Defcription of the Court and City of
Ifpahan, the Capital thereof; as alfo of the
celebrated Ruins of Perfepolis, the antient Metropolis of that Nation, and of feveral other
Places of Note.

With Genuine Copies of the Inftructions given by
the *Englifh*, *French* and other Powers, to their refpe-
ctive Embaffadors in *Perfia*, *China*, *Japan*, and other
Eaftern Empires; no lefs ufeful and inftructive for
carrying on the Commerce in thofe Parts, than fatif-
factory to the Curious.

Adorn'd and Illuftrated with a great Number
of C U T T S.

In Eight Volumes.

By EDM. LLOYD, *Efq*;

VOL. I.

LONDON, Printed for the Author; And fold
by J. Smith in *Exeter-Change* in the *Strand*. 1720

INTRODUCTION

BY BRIGADIER-GENERAL SIR PERCY SYKES, K.C.I.E., C.B., C.M.G.

I

THE travels of Sir John Chardin in the latter half of the seventeenth century mark the culmination of a remarkable period, during which Persia under the rule of the Safavi dynasty, attracted to her court Europeans of distinction.

¶ They were a notable band, which included Pietro della Vallé the Italian (1616–23), followed a few years later by our erudite countryman Sir Thomas Herbert (1627–8). Tavernier, the French jeweller, travelled both in Persia and in India from 1629 to 1675, while Olearius was Secretary to a Mission despatched by the Duke of Holstein, which reached Persia in 1637 and spent a year in the country.

¶ Chardin, greatest of them all, was born in Paris in 1643, the son of a wealthy jeweller of the Place Dauphiné. He felt the call of the East as a young man and, in 1664, he started on a journey to the East Indies, accompanied by a Monsieur Raisin of Lyons. Travelling by Constantinople, the Black Sea, Georgia and Armenia, he reached Persia early in 1666, and resided in the country for about eighteen months, during which period he commenced his studies in Persian and Turkish. He was fortunate to be at Isfahan when Abbas II died in the autumn of 1666. His eldest son, Prince Safi, had been immured in the harem, in accordance with the custom of the dynasty, and there was a widespread report that he had offended his father and been blinded.

¶ When the death of the Shah was reported secretly to the high officials of the Court, they met together to elect his successor. Swayed by their personal ambitions, they decided to accept the rumour that the heir had been blinded and was consequently incapacitated from ascending the throne, and elected his younger brother, a boy of eight, "a Prince whose blooming virtues promised something more than ordinary." But their plot to hold the reins of government during a long minority was defeated by a faithful eunuch testifying to the eyesight of the heir being intact and, after some hesitation, he was summoned to the throne. Informed of the change in his fortunes, he was brought out of the harem, and was immediately crowned. So promptly was the action taken that the citizens of Isfahan were awakened by music played in the palace at midnight to announce the coronation of the new Shah, before they were aware that Abbas II was dead.

¶ This was the theme of Chardin's first work, which he termed *The Coronation of Soleiman III*. With regard to this title, Shah Safi, as he was crowned, was constantly ill, mainly owing to excessive drinking and other excesses. His cunning physician, unable to remedy this unsatisfactory state of affairs, and fearing for his own safety, attributed the monarch's ill-health to the fact of his coronation having taken place at an inauspicious hour. This view was accepted by the superstitious Persians, and the young monarch was crowned a second time, assuming the title of Soleiman III.

¶ Apart from its considerable historical value, Chardin's first work affords a remarkable insight into Persian mentality, that is entirely new in the European writings of the period, being, in fact, the inside view. Chardin visited India in 1667, but returned to Persia in the spring of 1669, and left for Europe with "Letters Patents" from the Shah who "gave me in charge the making of several Jewels of a great value, of which his Majesty design'd the Models with his own Hands." The intrepid traveller reached Paris in 1670, and thereby successfully concluded his first journey.

¶ A man possessed of exceptional energy, Chardin set to work immediately after his return, to ransack Europe for the finest jewels that could be purchased, to ensure the success of his mission. This task occupied a year and, when every piece was completed to his satisfaction, he started off on his second journey to Persia, which he reached in 1672. On this occasion, he settled down in the country for a period of four years, and studied its literature, its customs and its resources with remarkable thoroughness. This is shown in the two volumes selected for reproduction, which are entitled *Sir John Chardin's Travels in Persia*. The great traveller explains in his preface that, in a previous volume, he deals with his journey from Paris to Isfahan, and I am giving some account of his experiences and reflections in this Introduction. Chardin not only travelled far and wide and studied Persia and its people profoundly, but he realised a handsome fortune by his dealings in jewelry; and when he decided to return home in 1677, he widened his experiences, by following the route *via* the Cape of Good Hope.

¶ Upon the conclusion of his travels, Chardin lived in France for some time but, owing to the persecutions directed against Protestants, which culminated a few years later in the revocation of the Edict of Nantes, he decided to settle in England. There he was well received by Charles II, who appointed him Court Jeweller and knighted him in 1681. Shortly after taking up his residence in England, he married Esther, daughter of a Rouen Councillor in Parliament, who was a refugee in London at the time. He continued to carry on his business and is referred to as "the flower of merchants," in the correspondence of his time. His journeys and works also brought him fame, as is proved among other things by the fact of his election to the Royal Society in 1682.

¶ For a while he resided in Holland as Agent to the East India Company, to which post he was appointed in 1684 but, after his return to England, he devoted himself mainly to his Oriental studies and other literary pursuits. He died in 1713 and, in the south aisle of Westminster Abbey, a tablet may be seen bearing the following inscription: "Sr John Chardin —*nomen sibi fecit eundo.*"

¶ I now propose to give some estimate of this great traveller and Orientalist. In the preface to the *Travels of Sir John Chardin into Persia and Ye East Indies*, the author writes: "And though I then provided my self of Observations, and all sorts of Materials for a Relation of it, in as great a Degree or perhaps greater than those that have visited those Countries before me (having Learn'd many things from the Turkish and Persian Languages, which have not been observ'd by any that have hitherto Writ of Persia), yet I did not then think myself sufficiently instructed for the Publication of so compleat a Work, as I intended. . . . And the earnest desire I had to improve my knowledge in that vast Empire of Persia, . . . induced me to undertake a Second Voyage thither . . . . Chiefly following the Court in its Removals, but likewise I made some particular Journeys, as well of Curiosity as Business, to prosecute my intentions, studying the Language, and assiduously frequenting the most eminent and most Knowing Men of the Nation, the better to inform my self in all things that were Curious and New to us in Europe . . . . In a word I was so solicitous to know Persia, that I knew Isfahan better than Paris (though I was Bred and Born there). The Persian Language was as easie to me as French, and I could currently Read and Write it."

¶ Such are the credentials of Chardin. That they are genuine and that his knowledge of Persia, its language and its people was profound, is proved by the eulogies of the great Orientalist, Sir William Jones, while the value of his work was acknowledged by Montesquieu, Rousseau and Gibbon[1].

II

By way of creating a background to Persia, as Chardin knew it, let us look back to the events which led such a fanatical people to desire intercourse with Europe.

[1] I would acknowledge my indebtedness to the *Dictionary of National Biography.*

¶ The rise of Islam early in the seventh century A.D. was one of the most important events in history. The warlike Arabs, united in fervent zeal for the teachings of their Prophet Mohamed, swarmed out of their deserts and overthrew the Persian Empire, that was ruled by the effete Sasanian dynasty. They also seized the most fertile provinces of the Byzantine Empire and expanded the bounds of their conquests until they created an empire which stretched from the Sir Daria, that great river of Central Asia, to the Atlantic Ocean.

¶ Persia remained a mere province of this vast empire for many generations, but the national spirit was never lost. Penetrated to the core with feelings of devotion to a royal family, the Persians adopted Ali, cousin of the Prophet, and husband of his only child Fatima, as their Patron Saint.

¶ Ali was an unfortunate Caliph who, after ruling for five troublous years, during which his rival Muavia held Damascus, was assassinated. His son Husein who, according to Persian belief, had married the daughter of the last Sasanian monarch, was invited by the inhabitants of Kufa to contest the caliphate. He accepted the invitation and started off from Mecca, with a little band of kinsmen and adherents, encumbered by women and children. Arabs are notoriously fickle and, upon Husein's arrival on the scene, hardly a man joined him, the message he received running "the hearts of the people are for you, but their swords are against you."

¶ On the plain of Kerbela, the little band, cut off from the water of the Euphrates and suffering from thirst, fought to the death with a heroism that challenges our admiration down the ages. From the first, the combat was hopelessly uneven, flights of arrows from hundreds of archers killing or wounding man after man. Husein was apparently spared for a while, but since he resolutely refused to surrender, he too was wounded, and a charge of mounted men, followed by decapitation, ended the fight. Not a man fled and seventy heads were duly counted before the Governor of Kufa, who callously turned them over with his staff, in order to identify them.

¶ Husein was thus slain, but his death brought him deathless fame and was considered to be martyrdom. This tragedy serves as the basis of a Passion Play, which is acted annually all over Persia. The streets are paraded by bands of men, who beat their naked breasts in rhythm, lamenting "Husein our Lord is slain on the plain of Kerbela. Dust be on our heads." These processions are headed by fanatics, clad only in their shrouds, with chains, locks and horse-shoes sewn on their bare skins.

Crying out, they cut their heads with daggers until their bodies and shrouds are stained with blood.

¶ In the play, the departure from Mecca, the arrival in the vicinity of Kufa, and finally the fight on the plain of Kerbela, during which women and children were struck by arrows, are realistically acted, while the death of the martyr Husein arouses such intense feeling that I, merely a privileged spectator, felt deeply moved. These sentiments of devotion for Ali and his descendants resulted in the formation of the Shia or "Separatist" sect, which is bitterly hostile to the Sunnis or "Traditionists," as the vast majority of Moslems are termed.

¶ The Safavi dynasty, which arose in the sixteenth century, claimed descent from Ali, and had long been regarded as a family of saints before aspiring to the throne. Thousands of warlike tribesmen were fanatically devoted to them, and when Ismail raised his standard in 1499, there was a wave of enthusiasm that bore him on its crest to the throne. Thus was founded a great national dynasty under a monarch who, like Melchizedek of Salem, was both priest and king.

¶ Ismail was a brave soldier, who won Persia by the sword and cut to pieces the Uzbegs of Central Asia, but he was defeated by Selim the Grim of Turkey, whose artillery killed thousands of the tribal horsemen. Ismail never recovered from this defeat and died in 1524, deeply regretted by his subjects.

¶ His successor Tahmasp, unable to hold Tabriz, the capital, retired to Kazvin, in the interior. This policy is referred to by Milton.

> "As when the Tartar from his Russian foe,
> By Astracan, over the snowy plains
> Retires, or Bactrian Sophy, from the horns
> Of Turkish crescent, leaves all waste beyond
> The realm of Aladule, in his retreat
> To Tauris or Casbeen."[1]

There is no doubt in my mind that the facts given in the above quotation were derived from Anthony Jenkinson, the first great English explorer by land. In 1561, Jenkinson sailed down the Volga and, hoisting the flag of St George, sailed across the Caspian Sea to the port of Shamakha, whence he proceeded by caravan to Kazvin. He was badly received by the fanatical Tahmasp, who even thought of sending his head as a gift to the Sultan of Turkey, with whom he was engaged in negotiations. But

---

[1] "Sophy" is the English corruption of Safavi, while Tauris and Casbeen are, of course, Tabriz and Kazvin.

the gallant Englishman escaped this and other perils, and finally returned home safely with good profits to show for his adventurous expedition.

¶ The Safavi dynasty reached its zenith under Shah Abbas, who reigned from 1587 to 1629. Upon his return from a successful expedition against the Uzbegs, Sir Anthony and Sir Robert Sherley presented themselves as English knights who had heard of his fame and desired to enter his service.

¶ Shah Abbas realised that he could not fight the Turks until he possessed an army trained on European lines. He consequently welcomed the Englishmen and entrusted to them the organisation of the new force. So successful were they that, four years later, Shah Abbas defeated the Turks decisively and regained the lost provinces of Persia.

¶ Sir Robert Sherley, who was wounded in the battle, was granted a pension for life. Later, he was sent as Persian ambassador to England where, as may be imagined, he created a great sensation. I have little doubt that there is a reference to him in *Twelfth Night* where Fabian remarks: "I will not give my part of this sport for a pension of thousands to be paid from the Sophy."

¶ Shah Abbas created a new capital at Isfahan, situated in the heart of Persia. There, on almost the only river of the interior, he built a fine city, approached by beautiful bridges and double avenues of plane trees, leading to the splendid pile of buildings which are still standing. This was the city so admirably described by Chardin. Shah Abbas worked incessantly to restore prosperity to Persia by putting down brigandage with an iron hand and by encouraging trade and agriculture. Unfortunately, like most Oriental potentates, he was afraid of his heirs and either killed or blinded his sons. He confined his grandsons to the harem, to be brought up by eunuchs and women, with the inevitable result that he had no capable successor and the dynasty rapidly declined and ultimately fell most ignominiously.

¶ His immediate successor Shah Sufi, reigned from 1629 to 1642, and this period was filled with a long series of executions, first of his relations and then of his father's most trusted councillors and generals. Shah Sufi was succeeded by Abbas II, during whose reign of twenty-five years from 1642–67, Chardin reached Persia. Apart from his devotion to the wine cup, he was not a bad ruler. Chardin relates that he was especially favourable to his Christian subjects and welcomed Europeans to his Court; and that his death was "look'd upon to have been a Judgment of Heaven upon that Potent Empire."

III

¶ Chardin left Paris for his second journey to Persia, in 1671. He resided at Constantinople for some months in 1672 but, owing to a quarrel that broke out between the French Ambassador and the Grand Vizier, which might have led to the imprisonment of all French subjects, he left hastily, bound for Caffa. There he changed ships and reached a port in Mingrelia, intending to travel to Tiflis through that country and Imeritia. He describes the country and its unfortunate inhabitants, who were habitually sold to the Turks by their cruel masters. Of one beautiful slave Chardin writes: "She had incomparable Features in her Face, and a true Lily-white Complexion, and indeed I never saw more lovely Nipples, and a sounder Neck, nor a smoother Skin; which created at the same time both Envy and Compassion."

¶ Owing to disturbances caused by a Turkish raid, the traveller was advised not to land but, after some hesitation, he hired eight carts for his property and proceeded to a monastery, where he was received most hospitably by its head, Father Zampi.

¶ Upon news of his arrival with rich merchandise reaching the Court, the Princess of Mingrelia promptly visited the monastery and demanded to see his wares. Chardin attempted to pose as a friar but failed to deceive the Princess who, furious at his refusal to unpack his bales, said to Father Zampi: "You have both deceived me, but 'tis my Pleasure that the Newcomer say Mass before me." Chardin, realising that trouble was imminent, buried or hid his most valuable effects and, scarcely had he done so, when the monastery was broken into by two nobles and their "assassinates." They searched high and low, and Chardin describes how he threw two bundles worth £6000 into some thick bushes, and then suffered agonies while the robbers were searching the garden. At last the band departed, taking off some articles of small value, but Chardin could not find the precious bundles which were, however, finally recovered by a faithful servant.

¶ Realising that he owed his escape to good luck and that his liberty, if not his life, was in danger, he hired a vessel and returned to Turkish territory. There he was fleeced to some extent by the authorities but, once inland, he travelled in perfect security and, crossing the Caucasus, arrived safely at Tiflis. At the capital of Georgia he was befriended by the Italian Capuchin monks and, through their devoted efforts, he was able to communicate with his comrade, whom he had left in charge of his property, and, after various narrow escapes from robbery, due to plots woven by a dismissed Moslem servant, he finally recovered his jewelry and money intact.

¶ Thanks to the letters patent of the Shah and other recommendations from Persian Court officials, Chardin was welcomed warmly by the Prince of Georgia who also appreciated the handsome gifts he offered, which included "a large watch with a Lunary Motion and a Surgeon's Case."

¶ He appeared frequently at the Court and was consequently able to give an excellent account of the history of Georgia and of the manners and customs of the people. The most important festivity which he attended was the wedding of the Prince's niece, and he notices that since Christian Georgia became subject to Persia, the women were kept apart from the men in the cities. The feast was gargantuan, the meat being served on silver dishes weighing five hundred ounces. There were three courses, each course "containing sixty of those large flat Dishes a piece." Chardin describes as an expert the gold bowls, cups, horns, flagons and jugs. The quantity of wine that was drunk was enormous, the feast lasting until the morning, by which time everyone was dead drunk. The traveller comments: "Had I Drank as much as my Neighbours, I had dy'd upon the Spot: but the Prince had so much kindness as to give orders not to carry us any Healths."

¶ Shortly after this banquet, Chardin received permission to continue his journey. He was anxious to leave Tiflis, as the Prince pressed him to show him the jewelry he had brought for the Shah. This he naturally declined to do and, equally naturally, he felt uneasy as to what the autocratic Prince might do, especially as his reputation was far from good.

¶ Leaving Tiflis on 1st March, he describes the wooded, fertile country he traversed, noting that the Georgians and Armenians, although inhabiting the same country, always occupied separate villages and were on bad terms with one another. On the pass leading into Armenia, which was covered with deep snow, Chardin suffered from "a terrible Dysentery, which forc'd me to alight altogether; and then two men held me up as I went." He crossed this range with much difficulty, cured his complaint by drinking hot coffee, and traversing the treeless plains of Armenia, reached its capital Erivan. Again he gives a valuable account of the country and of current events, while his description of the Governor is delightful.

¶ He refers to Mount Ararat, which he saw from a distance, and states that the Armenians have a tradition that the Ark still rests upon its summit and "that never any Body could ascend to the Place where it rested; and this they firmly believe upon the Faith of a Miracle."

¶ During his stay at Erivan, Chardin was again invited to a wedding and indulges in a dissertation on marriage, temporary marriage and concubinage, giving amusing stories to illustrate his theme. He sums up his opinion as follows: "Nay we may say in General, that the Matches are more happy in a Country, where the Men and Women never see one another, then when the Women are so frequently seen and courted. And the Reason is plain. For they that see not another Man's wife, lose less suddenly the Affection which they have, or ought to have, for their own."

¶ Chardin sold some of his jewelry, being bested in the deal by the astute Governor and, after spending the Persian New Year's Day (21st March) at Erivan, he continued his long journey to Isfahan.

¶ He refers to the ruined state of Nachivan. This was due to the deliberate policy of Shah Abbas, who sought to protect Persia against Turkish invasions by the creation of a desert area between the two countries, the population of this part of Armenia having been transplanted to Mazanderan, where it had been destroyed by malaria.

¶ Crossing the swift Aras, Chardin entered Persia proper and spent some days at Tabriz, which was then, as it remains to-day, the second city of the empire. He gives a detailed account of its buildings, many of which were in ruins, and of its sufferings in previous generations at the hands of the Turks, "who committed therein all manner of Inhumanity, even to an Excess unheard of before."

¶ Towards the end of April, the journey was resumed in the company of the Provost of the Merchants, and Chardin's description shows how he revelled in the short-lived spring greenery. Skirting Kazvin, the party made for Kum, celebrated as being the burial-place of Fatima, daughter of the *Imam* Musa. More fortunate than myself, Chardin was permitted to enter the precincts freely and to make sketches. His description of the tomb runs: "It is over-laid with Tiles of China, painted *alamoresca*, and overspread with Cloth of Gold that hangs down to the ground on every side. It is enclosed with a Grate of Massy Silver ten foot high, distant half a foot from the Tomb; and at each Corner crown'd as it were with large Apples of fine Gold. . . . Several breadths of Velvet hung about the inside of the Grate, hide it from the view of the People: so that only Favor or Money can procure a sight of it."

¶ Kum was also the burial-place of the two last Safavi monarchs and, with characteristic thoroughness, Chardin gives a translation of an

inscription in letters of gold which runs round the gallery of the tomb of Abbas II. It consists of eulogies of Ali, from which I cull the following:
"To speak something in thy Praise, we must needs say, that Nature is only adorn'd and enrich'd by thee.
Had not thy perfect Being been in the Idea of the Creator, Eve had been eternally a Virgin, and Adam a Batchelor."

¶ Kashan was the next city to be visited and Chardin comments: "There is not made in any place of Persia more Sattin, Velvet, Tabby, Plain Tissue, and with Flowers of Silk, or Silk mingled with Gold and Silver, then is made in this City." It still remains the "silk town" of Persia.

¶ The long journey was rapidly approaching an end. Rising from Kashan to the Koh Rud Pass, the route led through the mountains and, at last "drawing near that great city, that we thought our selves in the Suburbs, two hours before we got thither. We enter'd the City by five a Clock in the morning, all in good health, Thanks be to God."

¶ Upon reaching the convent of the Capuchin friars, where he lodged, Chardin received a bag of letters "from almost all Parts of the World." As a result he immediately indulges in a digression and gives a most interesting account of the French expedition to the East Indies, which the Dutch were able to ruin.

¶ He then turns to his main task, which was to secure payment for the valuable consignment of jewelry, which he was ready to hand over. The position was full of difficulty. Apart from the fact that the Shah was less wealthy than he appeared to be, the Prime Minister, who is described as "a mighty wise Minister, full of wit and of great Integrity," was a fanatical Moslem and bitterly hostile to Christians. Chardin gives an illuminating account of the disgraceful treatment that the drunken Shah inflicted on this devoted servant. When he steadily refused to drink the forbidden juice of the grape, it was flung in his face and he was ordered to "drink some Coquenard" or opium, and, of course, after obeying the royal command, "had no more motion than a dead body."

¶ Failing the Grand Vizier, Chardin, after much anxious consideration, decided to approach the Shah through the Nazir or Grand Steward, a typical Persian official, "an active Lord, Vigilant, laborious...and a most excellent Minister, but, if he were not restrained thro' fear of the King, the World could not have produc'd a greater Extortioner."

¶ This was no easy man to deal with, and Chardin's detailed account of the tricks and artifices to which he resorted gives an illuminating insight into Persian character, which reads like a play. Incidentally, it reveals the sterling character of the great traveller, who finally won by the display of those qualities on which European civilisation is based.

¶ Among many other events of interest, Chardin tells an amusing story of the manner in which a French Ambassador, "who made himself an Ambassador of his own Head, without Letters of Credence," reached Isfahan and was received with honour by the complacent Persians, who took Europeans a great deal at their own valuation.

¶ The reception of this ambassador and other envoys gives Chardin an opportunity for describing the magnificence of the Court, and here he is at his best. The Place Royal, as he terms it, was carefully swept and watered. After these preliminaries, on each side of the famous Ala Kapi Gate, six horses were "set out in the stateliest and most magnificent trapping the World can afford. Four of the said trappings were adorn'd with Emralds, two with Rubies, two with Stones of different Colours intermix'd with Diamonds." Four water cisterns, the horses' buckets and even the mallets for hammering in their heel-ropes, were all of pure gold. As it was in Jerusalem under Solomon, so also was it at Isfahan under the Safavi monarchs.

¶ The ambassadors were obliged to dismount at a distance of one hundred and fifty paces from the gate, and were separately escorted to seats. They were then conducted to an audience on the top of the gate, where the Shah sat in state. The Monarch of set purpose took no notice of the presents, when they "were order'd to pass along," nor of the ambassadors to whom he addressed no word of greeting, the idea in both cases being to exalt his majesty.

¶ Down below in the square, there were exhibitions of wrestling, of fencing and of lions attacking bulls, in which the latter made no effort to defend themselves. A more pleasing sight was an exhibition of the game we term polo, which we owe to Persia. Of this Chardin gives an admirable description and, reading it some thirty years ago, I was moved to take polo sticks and balls to Isfahan on the occasion of my first visit to that fascinating city. In the early morning, before the citizens were about, I hit the balls between the stone goal-posts, which still remain intact, although not used for perhaps two centuries, and thereby paid an act of homage to the greatest of games.

¶ The ceremony concluded with a banquet, at which the ambassadors were not served with wine, although both the Shah and his courtiers drank it freely. The reason for this lack of hospitality was that, on a previous occasion, the Muscovite Envoys had become disgracefully drunk. To quote once more: "There was a Buffet, one part of which was set out

with fifty large Flagons of Gold, filled with several sorts of Wine....And the
other Part was garnished with between three and fourscore Cups, and
a great many Salvers of the same Sort: Some of these Cups will hold three
Pints, they are large and flate-bottom'd, mounted on a Foot about two
Inches high only. No part of the World can afford any thing more
magnificent and rich, or more splendid and bright."

¶ For the Safavi dynasty in its decadence, pomp and pageantry had
succeeded to valour and virility, and on this note I may perhaps fitly end
this introduction.

¶ Not to mention the celebrated Mr *Bayle*; Mons. *Tournefort*, who has travell'd into those Parts where our Author form'd his Works, in his Sixth Letter to Mons. *Pontchartrin*, is pleas'd to give him the Character of an Author of great Exactness.

¶ As for my own Part, I hope that I have done him Justice in the Translation: And if it have the good Fortune to be an Amusement to your Grace, at your leisure Hours, I shall esteem my self very happy: That your Grace may enjoy an uninterrupted Course of Health and Happiness, is the sincere Wishes of

Your Grace's

Most Humble and

Obedient Servant,

EDM. LLOYD.

THE PREFACE

I AM not to inform the Reader, that the First Volume of Sir JOHN CHARDIN's Travels has already been publish'd in *English*, (I think in the Year 1686.)

⁋ That Volume relates to his Travels between *Paris* and *Ispahan*, where that Translation leaves him.

⁋ There I begin with him, and go through with the rest of his Works.

⁋ The many *French* Editions of them, are a sufficient Proof of the Reputation which the Author had Abroad; and who ever will consult the Celebrated Mr. *Bayle*, in his Months of *September* and *October*, 1686. call'd, his *News from the Republick of Letters*, will yet receive him with greater Pleasure.

⁋ And Mons. *Tournefort*, who travell'd by the late King of *France's* Order into *Turkey* and *Persia*, often makes Honourable Mention of Sir JOHN CHARDIN: But more particularly in his Sixth Letter to Mons. *Pontchartrin*, Secretary of State, wherein, speaking of the Country of *Georgia*, he says thus;

" Mons. CHARDIN gives a very Long and Particular Account how " *Georgia* fell into the Hands of the *Persians*, and to him I refer the Reader, " as being an Author of great Exactness."

⁋ But to return to my Subject, it must be observ'd, That our Author, from the Nature of his Employment, as a *Jeweller*, and one who had receiv'd so large a Commission from the Father of the King Reigning, at his Second Return into that Country, for Jewels; gave him Advantages superior to most others who have travell'd thither, of making the best Observations, having all the Opportunities requisite to such an End, from his constant Attendance on the Court, and Conversation with the Chief Ministers about it.

⁋ As for my own Part, I have (if that be not a Fault) been very faithful to our Author, in giving him as he is, without either adding or diminishing; I have even been so Conscientious as to insert a Paragraph as it is in the Original, which I must confess I cannot wholly give into, tho' as near as I can remember, it is the only Thing throughout his whole Work, (where he speaks, dead as I may say) that one may not readily give into it, a Thing pretty rare for a Traveller of a good Invention, it is this: In speaking of the Fruits in *Persia*, and among the rest of the Melons, he says, there are some People who will eat 35 Pound Weight of Melon at a Meal, without hurting themselves: and yet this may be an Error of the Press.

¶ But to proceed to the Order I have observ'd, with regard to the Translation; I was of Opinion, that to publish him in two large Volumes like the first, would not answer the Intention I had of Diverting, and not tiring the Reader; for which Reason I have follow'd the Method which has been us'd in *Holland*, where they have made ten, instead of three, Volumes of him, making each Subject a Book; as the History of *Persia* in general one; The Arts and Sciences another; The Political, Civil, and Military Government a Third, and so on: So that my Part of him will consist in Eight Volumes *Octavo*. As to the Method of Publishing them, I shall pursue that of the Author.

¶ I must observe one Thing more before I take leave of the Reader, *viz*. That I have put one of the Fronts of the Royal Palace of *Ispahan* before the first Volume; (which I have entitl'd, *the Introduction*, because it touches and gives a Light into all the Subjects that follow) not that this Plate comes in there, for it comes in with the rest in the Description of the City of *Ispahan*, but only to give an Idea of the Magnificence of that vast Palace, which is without doubt the finest in the World.

¶ *N.B*. The Expence being very Considerable from the many Plates which this Work will take up, the Author proposes to go through with it by way of Subscription, the Conditions. of which are in a loose quarter of a Sheet of Paper by the Title Page.

THE TRAVELS OF SIR JOHN CHARDIN

FIRST VOLUME

CHAPTER I

The Author's Arrival at Ispahan. *Monsieur D' l' Hay's Expedition to the* East Indies, *and his Miscarriage; with the Occasions of it.* Wild Oxen *at* Trinc-male. *The particular Qualities of the Flesh of that Beast. Cannonading and Taking of* Coromandel.

BEING arriv'd at *Ispahan*, my Companion and I went and lodg'd at the Convent of the *Capucin Friars*, which is almost in the Heart of the Town, and at a little distance from the Royal Palace. I met with a Bag full of Letters there, which were directed to me from almost all Parts of the World. Those from *Constantinaple*, gave me a Detail of the Campain which the *Turks* made in *Poland*; having the foregoing Year, with little or no Opposition, pass'd the Great River *Neister*, they ravag'd the finest Provinces, and took the famous Fortress of *Camineick*, which was the Bulwark of *Poland*. I was, among other things, inform'd, that the *Ottoman* Army had pass'd the *Danube*, over a Bridge five hundred Geometrical Paces long, built by the greatest Care and Diligence, and at the Expence of the Prince of *Moldavia*; and because the Fabrick did not please the Grand Seignior, he depriv'd that unfortunate Prince of his Principality, and Sentenc'd him to pay a Fine of a hundred and fifty thousand Crowns. ¶ My Letters from the *Indies* contain'd an Account of the Voyage of Monsieur *De la Hay*, Vice-Roy of *Madagascar*, who set out from *Rochel* with a considerable Squadron, in the beginning of the Year 1670. He was sent upon the Memorials of Monsieur *Carron*, Director General of the *French* Company, to put some great Designs in Execution, and among others, to Seize *Banca*, a little Island Scituated to the *East* of *Sumatra*, and pretty near *Batavia*. This little Isle of *Banca*, which is uninhabited, was not in any Body's Hands before that time. M. *Carron* judg'd it a Place proper to be the principal Magazine of the *French* Company in the *Indies*; and he had form'd a Design to seize it by Surprize: But the *Hollanders*, who were very vigilant and circumspect in regard to the Dominion which they had got in those Countries, hit exactly upon the Aim of the *French* Fleet, as soon as they saw it was equipping. They in vain gave out in *France*, that it was design'd for the *West-Indies*, they would not be bubbl'd under that Pretext. They dispatch'd three Advice-Boats one after another to *Batavia*, with Orders for the Council to take Possession of *Banca*, which was executed even before Monsieur *De la Hay* arriv'd in the *Indies*. His was a long Voyage, and to his great Misfortune, he put in at *Madagascar*, where he took it in his Head to make War with the People of the Island, at the Sollicitation of the *French*, who were Establish'd there. He lost six Months there, and near a thousand Men, who might have been better employ'd elsewhere; for he got nothing by quarrelling with the *Negroes*, but on the contrary, he enraged them to such a Degree, that they would never after be at Peace, nor keep up any Commerce with the *French*, and at last drove them quite out of the Island.

❡ Monsieur *De la Hay* went from *Madagascar* to *Surat*, and made a stay there till the beginning of the Year 1672; and then he set Sail from thence with Monsieur *Carron*, contrary to whose Advice he had receiv'd Orders not to Act. The Fleet at that time, consisted of six Capital, Ships and four Pinks; they put into Harbour at *Goa*, on the 21st of *January*, and met with the *Great-Britain*, another of the King's Ships, with two Pinks. These thirteen Vessels steer'd their Course towards *Ceylan*, and arriv'd on the 21st of *March* at the Bay of *Coti-ari*, commonly call'd the Bay of *Trinc-male*, which is a narrow, but good Bay, eight Degrees and thirty Minutes north Latitude, looking to the North East, and has a sound Bottom. The *Hollanders* had built a small Fortress about a League from the Shoar. There were but ten Men in Garrison, and they abandon'd it upon the first Sight of the *French* Fleet.

❡ Monsieur *De la Hay* having cast Anchor, sent some Deputies to the King of *Candy*, (the lawful Lord of all the Isle of *Ceylan*) who sent others back again to him; and after several goings and comings, they concluded a Treaty, by which that *Indian* Prince gave to the King of *France*, the Bay of *Trinc-male*, and the Fort which the *Hollanders* evacuated. The Contract of this Donation was regularly drawn up, and executed in due Form, and they took Possession of the Bay and Fort under several Salvo's of the Artilery, and with all the usual Ceremonies. A few Days after they began to build a Fort at the Mouth of the Bay, and another above the Shore.

❡ During these Negotiations a Sickness spread, and rag'd with great Violence among the Fleet. The Disease that reign'd most, was a burning Fever. The *Europeans* call the Distempers which they catch at *Ceylan*, the *Cinnamon Sickness*, because the strong Scents of that Wood inflame the Humours. Several dy'd of it, but the greater part of them recover'd, tho' they too found themselves in the midst of Penury and Want, as soon as they got rid of their Fevers; for the Victualling of the Fleet fell short in the Month of *April*, notwithstanding the good Management of the

Vice-Roy, who order'd all the Provisions to be bought up and sold amongst them again, not permitting any Person to deal with the Country People for Provisions, for fear of Waste. The most common Meat at *Trinc-male*, is Wild Oxen, yet they eat of it but seldom, and then sparingly, by Reason of a Property which the Flesh of that Animal has very particular to itself, and yet more strange and surprizing: It engenders Imposthumations in the same Parts, and as painful as those that are contracted from lewd Women. But that which is still more particular, is, that there is no other Cure, but abstaining from the Flesh which occasion'd them. They sent three Ships to the Coast of *Cormandel* for Provisions, but those Vessels being taken in their return by the Hollanders, the Fleet was reduc'd to so great a streight through the scarcity of Victuals, that although the two Fortresses which they were building, were not finish'd, they were compell'd to quit the Place, for fear of Perishing by Famine. They left behind them three hundred and fifty Men to go on with the Work, and a large Vessel for their Use, call'd the St. *John*.

❡ The Pretext which the *Hollanders* made use of, to give a colour of Reason to their taking the three Ships, was, that they carried Provisions to their Enemies, for so they esteem the King of *Candy*, and the Inhabitants of *Trinc-male*. They offer'd some time after to restore them, and even press'd Monsieur *De la Hay* to receive them, or to take his Choice of some others out of the *Dutch* Fleet in lieu of them. They did not know then in the *Indies* that *France* had declar'd War with *Holland*; but the News coming a little while afterwards to the *Hollanders*, those Ships were judg'd to be good Prize; and the *Dutch* Fleet sailing to *Trinc-male*, they Seiz'd the Ship, took the two Forts, and made all the *French* Prisoners.

❡ Monsieur *De la Hay* arriv'd the 22d of May on the Coast of *Coromandel*, within sight of St. *Thomas's* Island. It is a little Place belonging to the King of *Colconda*, which the *Portugueze* were in Possession of for near a Century and fortify'd it very well for that Country: The Walls are of Free-Stone, very high, and mighty thick, having regular Bastions about it, but no other Fortifications. The Vice-Roy sent to the Commandant of the Place, to desire Victuals for ready Money. He refus'd to sell any, excusing himself on the number of the Ships of the Fleet, which could not (as he said) be supply'd with Victuals, without leaving the Town itself quite destitute and unprovided. They did not know whether this Answer was sincere, or given rather at the suggestion of the *Hollanders*, who fac'd this Fleet every where, and follow'd it to all Parts with another. The Vice-Roy, who had no Provisions, seeing himself disappointed in that manner, caus'd the Town to be Cannonaded with that Violence, that in the space of four Hours they hung out a White Flag. He thereupon sent a Shallop on Shore, to demand whether they would deliver up the Town. The Commandant reply'd, that he did not think of doing that, but he was ready to let them have as much Provisions as they would for their Money. The Vice-Roy sent word back to the Commandant, That since he had been forc'd to compel him by dint of Cannon-Shot, to comply with what was so equitable and just, he expected to be reimburs'd the Charges thereof. The Commandant desir'd to know how often he had fir'd, and what the Price was of each Shot? They answer'd, that they had fir'd five Thousand three Hundred times, and would have twenty Crowns for each Shot. The Commandant, to gain time, and to have leizure to consider what Resolution he should take, answer'd, That he could do nothing without the Order of the Governor of the Province; that he was just then going to write to him, and would make his Answer known to the Vice-Roy.

¶ Monsieur *De la Haye* saw plainly this was only to delay time: He sent the Commandant Word, he would wait three Days for the Governors's Answer, but that if it did not come in that time, he would take the Town. He was as good as his Word: On the third Day in the Evening, he made a Descent with two Hundred Men, and two Field-pieces. He himself with about Fifty, Encamp'd over against one of the Gates of the Town, under some *Palm-Trees* that cover'd his Men, and sent an Officer with the rest, to the other side of the Town. Monsieur *Carron* stay'd without taking any Command upon him. The next Morning at break of Day, he order'd the Gate to be batter'd. All the Town ran to the Ramparts on that side. This was what Monsieur *De la Haye* desir'd: He gave the Signal to the Hundred and fifty Men who were on the other side, who immediately fix'd their Scaling Ladders and lodg'd themselves upon the Bastions of the Enemy, without meeting with any Resistance; and they went down into the Town, where the Inhabitants wonder'd to see them, as if they had fallen from the Clouds. The Garrison quite dismay'd, threw themselves from the Walls, there were such Crouds at the Gates: And thus the Town was Taken, without the loss of more than twenty Men.

¶ There is one remarkable Incident in this part of Monsieur *De la Haye's* Voyage. He had been inform'd, as I was assur'd from the King his Master's own Mouth, that he should declare War with the *Hollanders* in the Year 1671. The King told him so at his departure, in the Year 1670: And likewise, that he sent him to the *Indies* with no other Views than those of this War. But when he came to *Surat* at the end of the Year 1671, he found Letters there that inform'd him, the War had been deferr'd upon some important Reasons, but that it was only put off for a little time, and that Notice should be sent him shortly when the Declaration of War should be made. Accordingly two Packets were dispatch'd to him, in *August* and *September*, 1671; which brought him certain Advice, that War would be declar'd against the *Hollanders* the Spring following. I my self dispatch'd those Packets a little before my departure from *Paris*, which were brought me by Mons. *Berrier* from Mons. *Colbert*. Monsieur *De la Haye* was just gone from *Surat* when those Letters arrived there. They were of Opinion to send them to him by an Express-Boat, which they certainly ought to have done; But M. *Blot*, one of the Directors of the Company, imagining there was no pressing Business in them, said there was no need of being at that Expence; and that there was an *Indian* Vessel belonging to the Broker of the *French* Company, which was Sailing for the Coast of *Malabar*, and that they might be sent that way. The Spirit of Covetousness prevail'd, and the Packets were given to the *Indian* Vessel: But mark the fatal End of it. The Corsairs of *Malabar* met with the Vessel, took it, and after six Months time, the Packets from the Court of *France* open'd and torn to Pieces, fell into the Hands of the *French* Merchants on that Coast, and were sent back to *Surat* in *February*, 1673, which was above a Year after they had been receiv'd from *France*. There is no doubt to be made, but that, if they had been deliver'd in due time, M. *De la Haye* would have destroy'd the *Dutch* Fleet that cover'd *Ceylan*, which was the whole Force the *Holland* Company had, and would afterwards have Conquer'd all the Places which the *Hollanders* possess in that fine Island. He had an hundred times a desire to fall upon the *Dutch* Fleet, and he used to say from time to time, to M. *Carron*, *Sir, I know that we, at this present time, have a War in* Europe, *with the* Hollanders, *and you see we shall never have a fairer Opportunity to begin one in the* Indies. M. *Carron* put a stop to it, by saying, *As yet we have no Orders, we must wait for them, or at least till we have certain Advices that War is declar'd in* France. *It is true, you would destroy this* Dutch *Fleet, but then another would come immediately from* Batavia, *and be as much too hard for us.* M. *Carron* spoke very wisely according to his usual manner; but however he was mistaken on this Occasion, the *Hollanders* had no such thing as another Fleet at *Batavia*, and if that at *Ceylan* had been defeated, the *English* Fleet of ten Ships, which arriv'd near the Year's end on the Coast of *Coromandel*, and M. *De la Haye's* acting in concert, would have quite and clean overthrown the *Dutch* Company, especially in the Consternation they were in, upon the News they receiv'd from their own Country. But God had ordain'd it otherwise, and it was the *French* Fleet, that, with all its Enterprize, came to nothing.

CHAPTER II

The Author employs his Time in receiving Visits from his Acquaintance, and advises concerning his Conduct since the late King's Death. Debauches of the present King, and his Outrages in those Fits of Drunkenness. Reinstatement of the late Prime Minister. Manner of entertaining the King.

I SPENT the first Day of my coming to *Ispahan*, and all the next, in receiving Visits from the *Europeans* of the Place, from several *Persians* and *Armenians*, with whom I had contracted .a Friendship after my first Journey thither, and with whom I consulted about the Conduct and Management of my Affairs. The Court was very much alter'd from what it was the first Time I saw it, and in the greatest Confusion; almost all the Noblemen belonging to the late King were dead, or in Disgrace. Interest, and Favour, were in the Hands of certain young Lords, who had neither Generosity nor Merit. The Prime Minister, nam'd *Cheic Ali can*, had for fourteen Months past been under Disgrace; three of the chief Officers of the Crown discharg'd his Duty: But the worst thing of all for me, was, that they talk'd of restoring his Place to him, and reinstating him in the Royal Favour; for he being on one Hand a great Enemy to the *Christians* and *Europeans*, and on the other, inaccessible, by Recommendations and Presents, and having always made it apparent during the time he was in Office, that he had nothing more at Heart than to inlarge the Treasure of his Master; I had Reason to fear, that he would hinder the King from Purchasing the Jewels, which I brought by the express Command of the late King his Father, and made according to the Patterns which I had receiv'd from his own Hands: This Consideration made me come to a Resolution immediately of notifying my return to the King; my difficulty lay in the Choice of an Introductor to the *Nazir*, who is the great and supreme Intendant over the King's Household, his Wealth, his Affairs, and over all those who are employ'd in them; I mean, who I should pitch upon to give the first Admittance; I was advis'd by some to *Zerguer bachi*, or chief of the Jewellers, and Goldsmiths in *Persia*; others propos'd *Mirza Thaer* to me, the Comptroller General of the King's Household. I had done better to have trusted to the Conduct of the first, as I found afterwards, but because I had known the Comptroller General a long time, I resolv'd to put my Trust in him.

¶ On the 26th, the Superior of the *Capuchins* took the Trouble of going to visit him in my Behalf. I beg'd of him to tell him, that an Indisposition hinder'd me from coming to pay him my Respects, but that the Goodness he had shewn me six Years before, made me take the Liberty of Addressing my self to him, to be presented to the *Nazir*, or Super-intendant, for that I was sure I could not be introduced by a better Hand; that I most humbly intreated him, to represent to that Minister, the Order which I had receiv'd from the late King, to go into my own Country, and get him some rich Works of Jewels made there, and bring them to him my self, which I had accordingly perform'd in such a Manner, that I durst perswade my self it was not possible to do better. To this I added great Promises of Recompence, which I knew was necessary to be done in such Cases. The Answer I had from this Lord was, That I was welcome, that I might depend upon him, and that he would, to the best of his Power, answer the Expectations I had of his good Offices towards me; but that I might assure my self, the King had but little Inclination for Jewels, that the Court was very bare of Money, and that to my great Misfortune, the Prime Minister, who was a Man so averse to those sort of Expences, and so disingag'd from all Interest, was again coming into Favour; that he order'd this to be told me not to discourage me, but to dispose me to sell them cheap, to make a great many Presents, to take a deal of Pains, and have a World of Patience; that as for the rest, he would notify my Arrival to the *Nazir*, in the best Manner he could, and that I should place my Hopes in the Clemency of God. The *Persians* always conclude their Deliberations with these Words, being as much as to say, that God will give Overtures to those Affairs, which Men are in Pain to bring about with Success.

¶ I at the same time receiv'd a Piece of News, which confirm'd those Advices. This was, that the Day before, the King getting Drunk, as it had been his daily Custom almost for some Years, fell into a Rage against a Player on the Lute, who did not play well to his Taste, and commanded *Nesralibec*, his Favourite, Son to the Governour of *Irivan*, to cut his Hands off. The Prince in pronouncing that Sentence, threw himself on a Pile of Cushions to Sleep. The Favourite, who was not so Drunk, and knowing no Crime in the condemn'd Person, thought that the King had found none neither, and that this cruel Order was only a transport of Drunkenness, he therefore contented himself with Reprimanding the Player very severely, in that he did not study to please his Master better; the King wak'd in an Hours time, and seeing the Musician touch the Lute as before, he call'd to Mind the Orders he had given to his Favourite against the Musician, and flying into a great Passion with the young Lord, he commanded the Lord high Steward to cut off the Hands and Feet of them both; the Lord Steward threw himself at the King's Feet, to implore Mercy for the Favourite; the King, in the extream Violence of his Indignation and Fury, cry'd out to his Eunucks and his Guards, to execute his Sentence upon all three; *Cheic-ali-can*, that Grand Vizier who was out of his Post, happen'd to be there, as good Luck would have it, he flung himself at the King's Feet, and embracing them, he beseech'd him to show them Mercy; the King making a little Pause upon it, say'd to him, *thou art very bold to hope, that I should grant what thou desirest of me, I who can't obtain of thee to resume the Charge of Prime Minister. Sir,* reply'd the Suppliant, *I am your Slave, I will ever do what your Majesty shall command me.* The King being hereupon appeas'd, Pardon'd all the condemn'd Persons, and next Morning sent a *Calaat* to *Cheic-ali-can*: By that Name they call the Garments which the King presents great Men to do them Honour; he sent him besides the Garment, a Horse, with a Saddle, and Trappings of Gold, set with Diamonds, a Sword and Ponyard of the same kind, with the Inkhorn, Letters Patents, and other Marks, which denote the Post of the Prime Minister.

¶ This Lord had been, as I told you before, fourteen Months in Disgrace, and during that time, there was no Prime Minister at all, a thing without Precedent in *Persia*; three of the Principal of the Crown acted in his Room; he went from time to time to Court, the King having neither Banish'd, nor so much as forbid him his own Royal Presence. The Occasion of this Disgrace was, because he would not drink Wine, excusing himself always on Account of his old Age; the Dignity of Prime Minister, the Name of *Cheic*, which he bore, and signifies the same as a Religious, or Saint does with us and denotes a Man Consecrated to the strictest observance of Religion, and in fine, on Account of the Pilgrimage which he made to *Mecca*, whereby he stood engaged to a greater purity of Life. The King seeing him alone, firm in his Resolution not to drink Wine, us'd him often with very ill Language; he one time went even so far, as to strike him upon that Account, he has caus'd full Glasses of Wine to be thrown in his Face, pour'd down upon his Head, and over all his Cloaths, and in his Fits he us'd to offer him a thousand Indignities of this Nature; but when those Fits were over, he, in his cooler Considerations, had an infinite Esteem for him, on the Account of his so wholly dedicating himself to the Interest of the State, for his Virtues, and the vast Qualifications of his Mind: In Reality, he was a mighty wise Minister, full of Wit, and of great Integrity; his Religion is more to be blam'd than his Natural Temper, for the Hardships he deals to the *Christians*: 'Tis her we must accuse for his rigorous Practices against the *Christians*; were it not for the Transports of a blind Zeal, which she inspires into him, the *Christians* would have Reason, as well as the *Mahometans*, to bless his Administration: It is true, even these do not all bless it, because he hinders the King from going into Prodigalities, and from squandring his Treasure, like his Predecessors; and this is seldom pleasing to the Court, which is commonly Poor and Indigent, when the Prince is not Liberal. This Minister was fifty five Years of Age, he was of a good Stature, well Shap'd, and his Face Handsome, as well as his Make; he had the greatest Advantage of Physiognomy in the World, a perpetual Calm, and engaging sweetness reign'd in his Eyes, and throughout his Countenance, and far from perceiving in it any of those Signs of a Mind Occupied, and taken up, which appear in that of most great Ministers; one saw shine there all the Tokens of Tranquility, and of a Mind unperplex'd, and that possess'd it self perfectly; so that to behold him without knowing him, one would never have taken him for a Man of Business; those who have had the Honour to be more nearly acquainted with him, and to search into his interior Qualities, speak wonderful Things of his Moderation and Modesty; these Persons assure you, that he has little of Pride in his Mind, and of Presumption in his Heart, as there is of Fierceness in his Look, or of Vanity in his Comportment; this is so much the more to be credited, because he shows no Luxury in his Garb, no Pomp in his House, no Profusion or Prodigality at his Table.

¶ On the 27th, that Minister cloath'd in the Garment that the King had sent him, went to kiss his Feet, and receiv'd afterwards the Compliments of all the Court, upon his being re-instated in the first Employment of the Empire.

¶ On the 30th, he Entertain'd the King; the Entertainment lasted four and twenty Hours; the Prince went thither at eight a Clock in the Morning; all the way, between the Royal Palace, and the Palace of that Minister, was cover'd with Brocards of Gold and Silver, and lin'd on each Side by his Officers and Domesticks, who made a Lane, each of them holding a Piece of the magnificent Present which he made to the King, which consisted in Stuffs of Wool, Silk, and Gold; in Services of Gold, Silver, and China, in Bridles for Horses, Saddles, and Housings, and in Gold and Silver ready Coin'd. When the King was about six Spaces from the Door of his Apartment, the Prime Minister who waited there to receive him, caus'd some thousands of Livres, of Gold, Silver, and Brass, Coin'd, to be thrown at his Feet. This Pompous manner of receiving a Prince, is call'd *Pich endas*; *Pich* signifies before, and *endas* is the Verb, to spread, or to extend. They never make use of this kind of *Pageantry*, but for the Reception of the Sovereign, nor cover the Streets with Stuffs upon any other Occasion. However, 'tis not improper to observe, that they only cover one side of it; the other is well Swept and Water'd, and strew'd with Flowers, especially when the Place and Season will afford them. The Stuffs and the Silver which are thrown on the Ground, are for the King's Footmen. Sometimes the Lord himself, who makes the Feast, buys back the Stuffs: *Cheic-Ali-can* did the same, knowing very well, that they could not sell them for near so much, as he order'd to be given them. This Method of spreading Carpets in the Way for the Passage of Kings, and great Princes, is one of the ancientest Customs in the *East*, and most universally practis'd; they have a Precept or Command for this deliver'd in the *Porans*, which are the first Books, of the Religion, and Learning of the *Brackmans*.

¶ When any Grandee Entertains the King, he invites him singly, leaving to him the Choice of the Company, which he has a Mind to pitch upon. He comes at eight or nine in the Morning, to the Palace where he is invited, which is furnish'd in the most sumptuous Manner possible: As soon as he enters the Door, the Master of the House makes him a Present, which is always very considerable; the Room into which the King is introduc'd, is ready set out with a magnificent Collation of wet and dry Sweetmeats, of Biskets, Mass-Panes, Sherbets, and all sorts of Liquors, Tart and Sweet; they Place before his Person, and before the Principal Lords he brings with him, rich Perfuming Pans, that burn till they even offend the Head, and are order'd to be taken away; mean while the Musicians, and the Women Dancers belonging to the Court, are in a Place hard by, ready whenever the King pleases to be diverted by them; the King's Musicians are not only the most Skilful, either as to Singing and touching of Instruments, but are commonly the Ablest, and most ingenious Poets in the Kingdom; they sing their own Works, as it is related of *Homer*, and other *Greek* Poets, who liv'd in his time; they are for the most Part in Praise of the King, and on several Actions of his Life, which they are ingenious enough in Flattery to extol, let them be never so worthy of Blame, and Oblivion.

¶ The Songs, this Day were adapted to the Re-establishment of the Minister. I saw one that was full of fine and witty Turns, the Burthen of the Song was this.

> *Him set aside, all Men but Equals are;*
> *Even* Sol *survey'd the spacious Realms of Air,*
> *To see if he could find another Star.*
> *A Star, that like the* Polar *Star could Reign,*
> *And long he sought it, but he sought in Vain.*

¶ An ingenious Allusion to the Title of, *Ivon Medave*, attributed to the Prime Minister, which signifies the Pole of *Persia*. About eleven a Clock they serve up a light Dinner; all the Meats there are high Season'd, and consist of Pastry Work, Roast Meats, and delicate Ragousts; whatever is Roasted at these Feasts, is commonly stuff'd after the *German* Manner, as we call it; after Dinner, the King walks up and down the Apartments and Gardens of the House, or else he Reposes himself, or takes the Diversion of seeing the Horses, of Mounting some of them, drawing the Bow, and such like Exercises; he likewise if he takes a Fancy to it, goes into the Womens Apartments; when he goes there, the Master of the House does not follow him, without his express Order, only the Eunuchs of the House Accompany him, and the Master of the House is so far from being Jealous on that score, that he prides and glories in it extreamly: Such a Power have Prejudice and Custom over the Minds of that People, who being otherwise Jealous even of their own Brothers, and won't let them set a Foot within their *Seraglios*; yet are they of Opinion, that no greater Honour can ever happen to them, nor any higher piece of good Fortune, than when the King enters into that Place: The Reason they give for it, is, that the Persons of their Kings are Sacred and Sanctified, in a peculiar Manner above the rest of Mankind, and bring along with them wheresoever they come, Happiness and Benediction; you are not however to suppose, that when the King goes into those Places, any Obscenity is committed there; they assure on the contrary, that there never was one Example of this kind; but yet, sometimes the King taking a Fancy to the Beauty or Wit of some young Woman he sees there, desires her of the Master of the House; they are far from refusing him, for they look upon it to be a great Stroak of Fortune, to have a young Creature in the King's *Seraglio*, by whom they may back their Interest, and promote themselves.

¶ About four a-Clock they serve up a Collation of *Fruits*, and as soon as it is Night, they divert him with Fire Works, Fencers, and Dancers, who are prepared in great numbers. The House, and the Gardens the House looks into, are fill'd with illuminations that represent a thousand different subjects, and are so bright, that they exceed the Splendor of the finest Day in its full noon of Glory. They don't serve up Supper till the King bespeaks it, and his own Cooks always make it ready, and dress it to the King's taste, according to the orders given by the Master of the Household. *Abas* the great chang'd this custom, having discover'd too much roguery in it to be endur'd. The head Cooks were never satisfy'd, they never thought they had enough; and always caus'd twice as much to be brought into the Kitchen as was serv'd up to Table. That King settled it as a standing Rule that those who would entertain him, should give his first Master of the Houshold for preparing the supper only twelve *Tomans*, which amount to four and fifty *Pistoles*. The Master of the Houshold never sits down to the Feast, he is always standing near the Person of the King to wait upon him, and when he withdraws he reconducts him even to the Palace Royal, in the same manner as he before conducted him from thence. In the *Persian* they call these sorts of Feasts *Magele*, a word whose proper and primative Signification, is conversation.

CHAPTER III

The Author sent for to the Nazir concerning the Commission of the late King for Jewels, Character of the Nazir. The Author reads the Contents of a French *Letter, in* Persian.

THE first of *July* the Comptroller General sent for the Superior of the *Capuchins*; it was to ask him after me, and to let me know, that he had spoke of me to the *Nazir*, who desir'd me to come and see him as soon as I could, that he remembred me from the Time of my first Journey thither, and that he knew the occasion of this, and the Commissions the late King had given me, and that he wou'd use his utmost Power to procure me a happy success, as far as it was consistent with the King's Interest.

¶ On the 6th of July, all that I had brought being put in a proper order for being shewn, I went to the *Nazir*'s Palace a little before Noon; that was his usual hour of coming back from the King. I had a great desire to carry the Superior of the *Capuchins* along with me as an Interpreter; fearing least I should find a want of *Persian*, to express my self in a discourse of such Importance and likewise, because there are some things, which, in the *East*, are more proper to be deliver'd by a third Person than one's self. I beg'd him to do me that favour, and endeavoured to engage him by all the reasons I was Master of, but to no effect: He excus'd himself, saying, that he went no more among the Grandees as he us'd, because they had no farther regard for the *Europeans*: that otherwise he would gladly do me all the service I could desire, having done the same for Persons he had a less respect for. What this good Father said, was true in the bottom; however the true motive of his refusal was, that he believ'd the King wou'd buy nothing of me, I went my self, with only my Companion and two *French Men* the one a Goldsmith, and the other a Watchmaker to the King, who all three of them did not understand one single Word of *Persian*, but the *Turkish* only, which I understood my self too. I had the good luck to find the *Nazir* with very little Company, and in a mighty good Humour. After some compliments, the *Nazir* made us all sit down at the end of the great Parlour directly over against him, at about ten Paces distance, and a little after he sent his Secretary to me, to know if we were the Persons the comptroler General had spoke to him of, I sent him word back, we were the very same. He took notice I made use of no Interpreter to answer for me and he ask'd the Secretary if I spoke the Language of the Country, his Secretary answer'd him that I spoke to him in *Persian*. Thereupon he order'd me to be conducted singly towards him, and to be seated within two Steps of him; Immediately after, he sai'd you are welcome, which he repeated again two several times, not immediately one after another, but with intervals of about five or six minutes, during which he held a discourse with the Master Huntsman, who sat very near him. Within about a Quarter of an hours Time, he sent an Eunuch to me, to take the Paper I had in my Hand, they were the Patents and Passports of the late King, and the recommendatory Letter of the *Nazir* his Uncle, the translation of which I have set down above. After he had read them all he asked me what things I had brought. I had a Memorandum of them in *Persian*; he made his Eunuch come to take it of me, for in that Country one must keep in ones Place without stirring from it, and when any body stirs in the presence of a Nobleman, whether he be sitting or standing, they immediately say that's a *Fool* or a *Frenchman*, the reason of it is, because they have observ'd that the *French* or *Europeans* have naturally a motion or Gesticulation with them. The *Nazir* having perus'd the Memorandum, told me the King should see it, and that he would present him a Petition on my account: I rose up in order to retire, but he made me sit down again, and stay dinner with him.

¶ The *Nazir*, or *Superintendant*, is call'd *Negef-coulibec*. This is an active Lord, Vigilant, laborious, as dispatchful as can be, and a most excellent Minister. It is impossible sufficiently to commend the easiness of access to him, and the care he takes to dispatch all manner of Business with the utmost expedition. He was first Master of the Houshold, when his Uncle the late *Superintendant* died, who leaving no Children behind him, his post was confer'd upon his Nephew: His family is numerous; He has five Brothers, and as many Sons, all men grown, but as yet very indifferently settled in the World; which is some sort of an excuse for his insatiable desire after Riches. He takes every where where he can do it with privacy and safety; and if he were not restrain'd thro' fear of the King, the World could not have produc'd a greater Extortioner: Setting a-side that Spirit of avarice, he might be accounted a very honest Man.

❡ When I left that Lord's House I went to pay a visit to *Zerguer bachi* who is head of all the Gold smiths and Jewelers in the Kingdom, and intendant over all the Works of Gold and Silver, and precious Stones, that are made for the King. He puts the price upon every Thing that is Sold at Court, out of which he has a Right of two *per Cent.* brocage, and one *per Cent,* for what is sold of those kinds throughout the Town. It is easy to judge from hence, the indispensable necessity I was under, of obtaining his favour in this Affair. I asked his Pardon for not being so diligent as I ought to have been, in seeking the opportunity to pay my respects to him, telling him among other things, that I knew very well the success of my business depended upon him, he answer'd me, that I had done very well to have shewn him in private, what I had brought for the King, before I had seen the *Nazir,* because we might have talked about the price, by which means he could better have told how to have set the value. In the mean time that it was never the worse as it happen'd, for the *Nazir* and he were very good Friends, and repos'd a mutual confidence in each other. That for his part he had never given any cause for Merchants to complain of his proceedings, and that he would give me none, nor be any hindrance to me in selling the whole. I thank'd him heartily, assuring him at the same time, that I would not fail of making him some acknowledgments. That's a thing one must never forget to have at ones Tongues end in *Persia.* I take no present from any body reply'd he, for the services I do them, I am an honest Man, and am content with my right of two *per Cent.* out of what is sold. After he had said that, he caus'd me to be serv'd with Coffee, and some Flowers, and entertain'd me till it was pretty late at Night. The Grandees in *Persia* are, more ready and officious than in any Place of the World, to forward the Communication of those Things that will please the King; but you must be very careful who you choose for your Introductor; for if I had Address'd my self first to this Man for Example, the *Nazir,* who is the King's Overseer, that is to say his great Minister, Principal Agent, and Superintendant, would have highly Resented it, pretending that everything that was to be laid before the King, ought to come directly to him first.

❡ On the 7th, at three in the Afternoon, I ordered all my Jewels that were specified in a Memorandum I had given the *Nazir* the Day before, to be carried in a Box to his House; he was with the King, who had sent for him; and return'd about five a Clock; the President of the Divan, one of the Principal Officers of the Crown, the Head of the Goldsmiths, and several other Lords of the Court were with him; he view'd them all, Piece by Piece, and compar'd them with the Memorandum, and putting them all into the Box again, he affix'd his own Seal to the Lock, and sent it to his Wardrobe. All this he did with a negligent Air, and a very great Indifference; but that was affected, as well by Reason of the Company then Present, as that I might take no Advantage, by discerning in the least which he thought to be the Finest and best done: I was not at all discourag'd at his Acting thus, knowing the Manner of the *Persians* on such Occasions, and with what Ease and Address, they fashion, and comport themselves according as their Interest requires. After that Lord had dispatch'd some Affairs, he enquir'd of me, if I had brought no more than what he had seen; I answered him, that I had still some Jewels left by me, which I did not think worth the King's seeing; *bring me*, said he, *all that you have a Mind to sell in this Kingdom; His Majesty must have the first Sight of them, and if you act otherwise, you will create your self Trouble, and me to*; I answer'd, that what I had left, I would bring the next Morning without fail.

¶ Upon that Day, being the eighth, I went to this Lord's House at seven a Clock in the Morning, he was at that time gone abroad; one of his Officers attended, and conducted me by his Order, into an Apartment of the Royal Palace, which is call'd *Chiracone*, or the House of Wine; he was there in Council with the Prime Ministers and several other Grandees of the Court; I stay'd there near upon three Hours, walking up and down the Fine Garden, in the middle whereof this fine Apartment, is Scituated; after which, I was conducted into a Parlour, that lay open to the Garden, and was so low, that it lay almost level with the Ground; the Grand *Vizier* and the *Nazir* were sitting there and leaning upon the Rails; a Crowd of Officers and Servants were without, standing on one side, and ready at a proper distance, to receive their Orders; those who led me up to the Rails, bid me make my Bows, and go in; the Prime Minister as soon as I had Saluted him, ask'd me where I had learnt to dress so exactly after the *Persian* Manner, and to speak the Language; after those obliging Questions, they made me walk into the Parlour, and sit down near the great Lords, but in the Middle, and out of Rank; the *Nazir* ask'd me, if I understood how to read all the Languages of *Europe*, and at the same time presented me a Letter, folded and sealed after our Manner, with the Superscription in *French*, desiring to know if I could Interpret it to him; I returned for Answer, that I could give him the Sence of it clearly; upon that he bid me open it, I did so, and read it in *Persian*; the Prime Minister was very attentive to my reading; as soon as I had read it, he rose up and went away.

¶ The *Nazir* stay'd and asked me where the Jewels I had still left by me, were, I produced them to him, and he kept them, causing them to be set down on the Memorandum; he afterwards said to me with an Air of Chearfulness, *did you perceive the Favour I did you in presenting you to the Grand* Vizier? *I held him in Discourse on the Subject of your coming*, added he, *and have also mentioned you to his Majesty; you will by the Grace of God, meet with a favourable Reception.* He went out after having commanded a Secretary to take down in *Persian* the Letter I had been reading: It was from a Captain of the *French East-India* Company, who was by Accident, invested with the Character of an Ambassador, in the Affairs of that Company. I believe my Readers will not be sorry, if before, I relate the Subject thereof, I insert some Particulars concerning the Establishment of that Company.

¶ Few People are Ignorant of the Time, which was in the Year, 1664, a Time Memorable in *France*, for the many fine Constitutions for the Improvements of the Arts and Sciences, which the Bounty of the Prince had caused to Flourish more there than in any part of the World. Mounsieur *Colbert*, a famous, clear-headed, and vigilent Minister, whom the King made use of for this great End, had above all Things, the Manufactures, and Commerce, most at Heart: That to the *East-Indies* was resolved upon first, being the most Important; but because there was no setting it on Foot, without Foreigners, who were well Skill'd therein and had practis'd it upon the Places; it was resolv'd to engage the *Hollanders* as much as possible in it, cost what it would. Mounsieur *de Thou*, who had been some Years before Ambassador in *Holland*, was instrusted with the Affair, and made Director of the Company; several Subjects were engaged in *Holland*, who had served the *Dutch* Company in the *Indies*, but not in so great a Number, nor of so great a Capacity, as the largeness of the Salaries gave Room to hope for; M. *Carron* excepted, who was an illustrious Man, and had a deep Insight into Commerce. 'Tis from him I had the Pieces of History that I am going to Relate, and which I have Translated almost Word for Word, from the *Dutch*, the Language in which he wrote only at that Time, being then unacquainted with the *French*.

CHAPTER IV

Letters from Mr. Carron *to Mr.* d' Thou, *Count of* Meslay, *&c.* Director of the East *Company of* France, *with Instructions concerning the Commerce. Amplification on the foregoing Subject.*

To his Excellency Monsieur *d' Thou*, Count of *Meslay, &c. Director* of the East Company of *France.*

SIR,

' IHAVE with Admiration heard of the Enterprize of our Great Monarch,
' touching the Commerce of the *East Indies*, which is the same Design
' that *Harry the Great*, of glorious Memory, had concerted, and resolv'd
' upon, in the Year 1609, and which began to be put in Execution by
' a Merchant of *Amsterdam*, whose Name was *Isaac le Maire*, and who was
' a very Able and Mighty Experienced Man, when the Death of his
' Majesty put a Stop to it: It is much to the King's Glory, that he is
' desirous of executing a Design, form'd by his Illustrious Ancestors above
' fifty Years ago, which, if it had taken due Effect in those Days, had
' rendered *France* at present Mistress of those Places, where the Spices are
' gathered, and which are now in the Possession of the *Dutch* Company;
' but were at that Time, in the Hands of the Natives of that Country. It
' was in the Year 1615, that this *Dutch* Company appropriated to it self,
' the Island of *Amboyna*, where the *Clove* grows: They did the same with
' *Benda*, that produces the Tree which bears *Nutmegs*, and *Mace*, in the
' Year 1612, and it has since, in ten Years time, Conquered that part of
' the Island of *Ceylan*, where the *Cinnamon* grows, beginning from the Year
' 1635, to the Year 1644, inclusively. This Company, with these Spices,
' carry on such a Trade in the *Indies*, and in *Europe*, as brings in such
' immense Gains, that if it were to have no other Trade but that alone, it
' would be sufficient to keep and maintain it, as on the Contrary, if it
' were deprived of the Possession of those Spices, it could not even Subsist,
' much less Aggrandize it self, Experience shewing sufficiently in the
' *Portuguese*, and the *English*, that the Commerce of *Pepper, Linnen, Silks*,
' *Salt Petre, Indigo, Druggs*, and of all other Things which they bring into
' *Europe*, do not yield them any considerable Profit.
¶ ' This makes me conjecture (without Prejudice to the Opinion of more
' able and penetrating Persons) that the *French* Company will not be able
' to make any Profits that will be worthy it's Establishment: It will not
' be intirely deprived thereof, but far from being to be compared with

' those of the *Dutch* Company, they will be perhaps less than those of the
' *English* àt present, or even of the *Portuguese*. These two Nations have
' improved for a long Time their Trade in the *Indies*, out of their mutual
' Emulation, and that of the *Hollanders*, who deal with them both, where-
' soever they are: Now the *French* will come last, and make the fourth
' Nation in the Market; it will be forced to take the same way as the
' others in its Commerce, having no other, and so in all likelyhood will
' not succeed any better than they.

¶ ' There is another Inconveniency, which is, that the main part of the
' Trade must be carried on by Gold and Silver, carried Annually out of
' *France* to the *Indies*, unless there be a free and open Commerce to *China*
' and *Japan*, which is what I would chiefly and principally aim at. The
' Means of obtaining it, is to send an honourable Embassy in the Name of
' the King, to the great *Cham* of *Tartary*, and King of *China*, and afterwards
' to the Emperor of *Japan*. There is a great deal of Likelyhood, and much
' Room to hope, that that Commerce would be obtained of them, provided
' the Envoys carried themselves with Prudence and Sagacity; their
' Instructions ought to be drawn up with good Advice, and a great deal
' of Attention, and they must be very punctually followed, and Executed:
' The Trade in *Japan* should likewise be carried on by *Frenchmen* of the
' Reformed Religion (no Notice is taken of the Religion of the *Europeans*
' in any other Place of the *Indies*, excepting only in *Japan*) and if contrary
' Measures be taken, there is Reason to fear, that the Trade of *Japan*
' cannot be obtained at all, or at least not to be kept up: It has been seen
' already, what has happened to the *Spaniards* and *Portugueze*, for en-
' deavouring contrary to the Prohibitions made against them, to Plant
' and Propagate the *Roman* Religion, among the *Japoneze*: It was for that,
' they were Banished, the *Spaniards* in the Year 1616, and the *Portugueze*
' in the Year 1639, upon the Penalty of their Lives and Effects, never to
' return thither again; in Opposition to which, the *Portugueze* coming
' back, upon an Imagination of having that Arrest repealed by Instances
' and Intreaties, all the Embassy, and the Retinue were put to Death, to
' the Number of 95, and the Ship with all that was in it burnt, and this
' happened in the Year 1640: It is therefore necessary, that the Trade
' should be carried on by Persons who are not *Romans*, and likewise that
' the Vessels which go thither, should be free from all Marks and Tokens
' of the *Romish* Religion.

¶ ' If the *French* Company obtains the Commerce of *Japan*, she will do
' very well, and send home great Profits; and in that Case, a Cargo must
' every Year be sent to *China*, the greater part of which must consist of

' Silver. From *China* another Cargo must be taken, of Silks and Stuffs,
' according to the Quantities prescrib'd, which ought to be to the Value
' of between four or five Millions of *Livres*. This Cargo will be sold off at
' *Japan* for ready Money, at 60 or 70 *per Cent*. Profit; and out of this
' Product, a Fund must be drawn for a new Purchase in *China*, to the
' Value of four Millions, and the rest may be employ'd in the *Indies*, to
' purchase Pepper and Cloths, with other Merchandizes that are wanted;
' the Silks and Silk Stuffs of *Bengall* and *China*, may be bought up for
' *Europe*, for they yield at least *Cent. per Cent*. *China* can furnish what
' Quantity one will thereof, and *Japan* will consume as much of them as
' shall be carry'd thither; and this is the only Trade that can Enrich the
' *French* Company, provided it be freely granted them, wisely managed,
' and seconded with the Blessing of Heaven.

¶ ' The *Portugueze*, when they were in the Flower of their Commerce,
' carry'd away Yearly from *Japan*, ten Millions in Specie. The *Chinese* at
' the same time carried away twelve, and the *Hollanders* three. This, in
' all, amounts to twenty-five Millions, and yet, notwithstanding these
' vast Draughts and Exportations, money was not a whit the scarcer at
' *Japan*, nor the Silks a jot the dearer in *China*. It is true, that great
' Empire was ruin'd by the War and Devastations of the *Tartars*; But in
' my Opinion, it will be always very easy to lay out there four or five
' Millions from Year to Year more. This Trade would save the sending
' of Silver Yearly from *France* to the *Indies*, either for the Purchase of what
' must be Imported into *Europe*, or to supply what may be wanting some-
' times in the Gain of the three Millions propos'd to be got every Year
' at *Japan*; unless the Commerce of *China* increas'd in its Capital Stock
' in such a manner, that the Gain expected, always exceeded the Sum
' propos'd; and there would be no need of carrying Silver out of *France* on
' any other account than the *South Sea* Trade, which is not very consider-
' able. Till the Motion of this Wheel of Commerce can be compassed, the
' *French* Company ought to be very attentive to its Affairs in the beginning,
' and to have a great Capital Stock to carry on the Traffick from *China*
' to *Japan*, for the *South-Sea* Trade, for the Expences, and the Advances
' which are necessary to establish itself in the Places of Trade, and in the
' Staples. The Company has need of one near the Equinoctial Line, for
' the Trade of the *North*; and of one or two on the Coast of the *Indies* for
' the *South-Sea* Trade. As for that of the *North*, the Isle of *Banca* appears
' to be the most Commodious. It may be had by way of Purchase from
' the Great *Matram*, King of the Island of *Java*. An Ambassador should
' be sent to him on that Account. This Purchase would be a very advan-

' tagious thing to the Company, because in all Likelihood, the Pepper,
' Rice, and all sorts of Provisions for the Mouth, would flow in there from
' all Sides, and in greater abundance than to *Batavia*, whither all those
' Commodities have constantly been carried hitherto, and because the
' *Chinese* (a People so serviceable and so tractable) who inhabit the
' Territory of *Batavia*, would infallibly come, and fling themselves among
' the *French*, to free themselves from the insupportable Charges and Taxes,
' put upon them for some Years last past in that Place, by the *Dutch*
' Company, who treat them with extreme Severity and Rigour.

¶ ' The Staples, or publick Marts on the *Indian* Coast, for the *South Sea*
' Trade, might be on the Coast of *Malabar*, and the other on the Coast
' of *Coromandel*. There is upon this last Coast, a Place called St. *Thomas*,
' which may be had without any great Difficulty. In the mean time, as
' the establishment of Trade in the *South* is a great and important Enter-
' prize, and the Success of it depends on a wise and prudent Conduct, it
' is necessary to send out of Hand, a Deputation to the Great *Mogul*. This
' Deputation will settle things in those Quarters, and upon their Arrival,
' the Commerce will be free and open to *Surat*, to the Coast of *Coromandel*,
' and to *Bengall*, the three principal Places of Traffick. Pepper and
' *Cassalinga* will, without trouble be bought, and abundantly enough on
' the Coast of *Malabar*, especially if the Price thereof be rais'd ever so
' little.

¶ ' As for what remains, the Execution of all this must be committed to
' Persons who are already well Experienc'd, as well in the Mystery of
' Commerce, as in the Knowledge of those Countries: They will instruct
' the *French*, lessen the Labour to them, and put them in a Method, after
' which, these will be sufficiently able to carry on the Trade, with Pru-
' dence and good Conduct. One might speak or write more at large
' upon this Head, and set down the Places in particular, where it may be
' proper for them to settle and establish themselves; what I have here said
' being no more than a Project or Plan, upon which I think the *French*
' Company ought to build, and on which they may reasonably expect the
' blessing of Heaven; to whose Protection I recommend your Excellency,
' and remain, &c.'

Paris, May 29, 1665.

An Amplification on the foregoing Subject.

' Having had the Honour on the 31st of the last Month, to be enter-
' tain'd by M. *Colbert* and your Excellency, on the most proper
' Methods to set the Trade of the Company on Foot, I was told, among
' other things, what I had heard before in *Holland*, that the Company
' design'd to People the Island of *Madagascar* by the Assistance of His
' Majesty, to send a great number of Soldiers and Workmen thither, and
' make use of it as a Staple, and publick Mart: This in reality, is a well-
' concerted Design. The Ships that will be sent to the *Indies*, may readily
' and plentifully furnish themselves in that Island with Provisions, and
' in all likelyhood, the Company will reap the other Advantages which
' she promises herself therefrom, and which never having been look'd
' after by the *Dutch Company*, are neither known to them nor myself.
' However, with humble Submission to your Excellency's Opinion, the
' Island of *Madagascar* is a little remote from the Quarters of the *South*,
' to wit, from the Coasts of *India, Malabar, Bengall, Surat, Coromandel*, and
' *Persia*; and it seems to me, that a more proper Place might be found
' out towards those Quarters of the *South*, which might be better and the
' more easily Fortify'd, by reason of its being but a small Extent.

¶ ' My Lord *Colbert* gave me likewise to understand, that the Company's
' Design is to establish its Commerce first of all in the Quarter of the *South*,
' which is exactly my Opinion, and I believe they cannot take a better
' Method of beginning it, than by sending two little Vessels of 400 Ton
' each, to *China* and *Japan*, to desire the liberty of Commerce, and to set
' it on foot after they have got Leave, for that will take up two Years at
' least, if not more.

¶ ' These Ships, besides the King's Envoys, and the Presents for those
' Countries, should, for the opening of Trade, have a little Cargo, con-
' sisting of Cloaths, Shalloons, Tammins, Serges, Perpetuans, and of all
' other kinds of Serges, of Red, Purple, Carnation, Crimson, Sky-blue,
' and other suchlike Colours, with a few Black, a few White and Pearl
' Colour, to the Value in all of about 50000 *Livres*. They should be like-
' wise laden with about 25000 *Livres* worth of yellow Amber, and such
' Iron Ware as there is a demand for in *China* and *Japan*, and which the
' *Hollanders* have sent there for some Years; other 25000 *Livres* worth of
' Pepper, which the Vessels may buy on the Coast of *Malabar*; and
' 250000 *Livres* in ready Money.

¶ ' This Sum, which amounts to 350000 *Livres* shall be lay'd out in Silks
' and Silk Stuffs, that are proper for *France*, and not for *Japan*, because

' if it is not lawful to carry any Merchandizes to *Japan*, till after having
' had Audience of the Emperor, and obtain'd leave to Traffick. It is
' therefore proper, that the Vessel which goes first to *Japan*, should go
' empty, and serve only for His Majesty's Embassy, without being laden
' either with Merchandizes or Merchants. There is not a Place in the
' World where Policy and the point of Honour are more scrupulously
' observ'd. They are not so nicely kept up in the other parts of the *Indies*.
' The Liberty of Trading to *China* and *Japan*, will be a very good thing
' for the Company. That of *Japan* may be negotiated with all they
' shall bring to *China*, as the Silks, and Silk Stuffs of *Bengall* and *Tunquin*,
' and with a Stock of all kinds of Woolen Stuffs Manufactur'd in
' *France*.

¶ ' The King's Presents to the Emperors of *China* and *Japan*, shall
' consist of all sorts of Fire-arms, even the most curious the Arsenal can
' afford; of Superfine Cloaths, the most exquisite in their Kinds that are
' to be met with; the best of Serges, and some rich Brocaded Silks. They
' must be given to understand that all these are the Product of the Country.
' There may be also some things that are rare for their Use, and for their
' Invention. Among other things, there must be in the Present for
' *Ispahan*, three of the new invented Engines for the extinguishing of Fire.
' They may be had at *Amsterdam*, and will be lik'd at *Japan*, because
' the Houses there are very subject to Fires: Moreover three Marble
' Pieces made in the form of Basons, with the Arms of the Emperor of
' *Japan* carv'd on the Borders of them. The Bason should be white Marble,
' the other red Marble, and the third black and White Marble. They make
' use of such Basons as these in *Japan* to wash their Hands in, and they
' have no other sort of Marble there, but of a darkish green Colour, inter-
' mingl'd with a brown. They must be like the Figure that is in the Margin,
' and must be carefully cas'd up in Wooden Boxes, to prevent all Acci-
' dents: No Difficulty ought to be made in taking this Trouble, and being
' at this Expence for *Japan*, because Foreigners pay no Duties or Customs
' for all their Merchandizes, whether Imported, or Exported, let the
' Merchandizes be ever so Rich and Wealthy: They are only obliged to
' go once every Year and pay Homage to the King and his Ministers, and
' make them some Presents, little in themselves, but proportion'd to the
' Trade they have there. This Visit is an Honour to Foreign Nations,
' because the Ships of the Empire are oblig'd to do the same thing. But
' this Visit, and these Annual Presents, shall not be made in the Name of
' the King, but in the Name of the Subjects Trading to *Japan*.

¶ ' The Letters to these Emperors must be writ in Characters of Gold,

' not upon Parchment, but upon large thick Paper, the finest and smooth-
' est that can be got. The Letter must be put in a Gold Box set with
' Diamonds, and the Box inclos'd in a square Purse made of very rich
' Cloth of Gold, and stitch'd together with Gold Wire: The Purse must
' be put into a Silver Box of the same Form, made exactly of a right Size,
' to hold it, and Engrav'n on both sides with Chase-work. And this Silver
' Box at last, must be put into a little Box of Wood prettily Vein'd and
' Polish'd; in short, the finest that can be got. The Letter must necessarily
' be Embellish'd with all this Finery; and as to the Shape of it, it must
' be of a large Size, and the whole length of the Paper; and care must
' be taken not to fold it up, so as the Top and Bottom shall overlap.

¶ ' Ample and precise Instructions must be given to the Envoy, and he
' be ingag'd to follow them with utmost exactness, every thing wholly
' depending upon his Behaviour and Conduct. This may be observ'd in
' the Embassies made to *Japan*; one on the part of the King of *Spain*, by
' two Knights of the *Golden Fleece*, in the Year 1624; and the other on the
' part of the *Dutch* Company, in the Year 1628; and likewise in the
' Embassy on the part of the same Company to *China*, in the Year 1656.
' Audience was not given either to the *Spanish* or *Dutch* Ambassadors at
' *Japan*; and to these last mention'd, nothing was granted in *China*: The
' Cause of this was their own Wilfulness, in acting as their own Fancy
' led them, and departing from their Instructions. The Ecclesiasticks of
' the Romish Religion are much esteem'd and held in Consideration at
' the Court of *China*; they may give a great Helping-hand to the Business
' of the *French* Company, and put it in a good way. But to proceed; as
' on one Hand the Negotiation is difficult, and on the other, the Trade
' Winds must be exactly taken for the Voyage, the delay of a Month, or
' of twenty Days only in this Occurrence, carries with it the loss of a Year.
' And as it may moreover happen, that the Negotiation may flag, and be
' retarded in those Courts, by Accidents either of the Indisposition or
' Death of the King, and by others that are impossible to be foreseen, it
' is extremely necessary to be expeditious; and your Excellency, without
' doubt, sees very clearly, that the sooner the Work is undertaken the
' better, to the end we may Sow at leisure, in order to Reap afterwards
' the more plentiful Harvest; for before we can receive the expected and
' desired Fruit and Advantage, we must reckon that a great deal of time
' will slip away in spite of our Teeth. It is entirely my Opinion, that if
' the Trades of *China* and *Japan* succeed according to our wishes, they will
' yield a much greater profit, than that of all the *South*. There is a great
' quantity of Brass at *Japan*, which may be had at six Pence or seven

' Pence a Pound at most: This may serve for Ballast in the Ships ap-
' pointed to return, and be sold here at fifteen Pence a Pound.

¶ ' The Envoy who goes to *China*, should put into *Port*, in the River of
' *Nanquin*, Scituated between 30, and 31 Degrees of *North* Latitude; one
' may there Sail with a fair Wind and full Sails, within fourteen Leagues
' of the Town. It would be better to put into Port, in the River of *Pekin*,
' for it is higher and nearer to the Court, but then it is not so deep. The
' last Ambassador of the *Holland* Company not knowing where he had best to
' Land, went and cast Anchor at *Canton*, Scituated towards the twentieth
' Degree, but unluckily enough, because *Canton* is a Province that is full of
' *Tartars*: However, it is a Country, where, it seems, one may make a con-
' siderable Sale of Woollen-Stuffs, a Thing fit to be observ'd hereafter.

¶ ' To carry on this Trade of *China* and *Japan*, which is in Effect so
' Profitable and Necessary, and of the Countries of the *Malays*, and of
' all the *West*, and particularly of the *Molucchas* on the Coast of *Ceram*,
' and the Quarters depending thereon, and where grows the Pepper of
' *Bantum, Palibang, Jambay, Benjarmassing, Solor*, and *Timor*, with all Places
' Scituated to the *West*. To carry on this Trade, I say, it will be very
' necessary to pitch upon, and fix a general Rendezvous, or general Place
' of Meeting, which cannot be better chosen than in the Isle of *Bancha*.
' The *Dutch* Company has repented a thousand Times, their not having
' fortified this Island, and for not having made it the Capital of its Resi-
' dence, and of its Forces, and that by Reason of the great Wars, and
' Seiges which it has Sustain'd in *Batavia*, against the King of *Bantam*, on
' the one side, and against the King of Grand *Mataram* on the other, who
' will never be at Peace, or at rest. There are very fine and good Places
' in the Isle of *Banca*, for the bringing Ships to Anchor, and for building
' and refitting them; the Wood proper for that Purpose may be had from
' the Coast of *Java*; and from thence, and from several other Places, may
' be fetch'd all the Materials necessary for the Work-houses. It will be
' requisite to build Lodgments there, and a Fortress, in order to be in
' Safety. The Isle of *Banca* is almost covered over with Wood; it will be
' proper to cut down one part of the Wood, to grub up and clear the
' Ground, and Plant some Thousands of *Cocoa-Trees*; this *Cocoa-Tree* is
' extreamly useful, and brings in a great Profit. The Company will find
' in Time the Goodness of that Island, in regard of its Scituation, and of
' all Advantages that may be drawn from it. Experienc'd Officers, and
' Persons of Merit, should be establish'd there. There is at present at
' *Amsterdam* one *Vandermuyden* who was Counsellor in ordinary in the
' *Indies*, and Governour of *Ceylan*. Next Summer is expected there one

' *Coyet*, who likewise was a Counsellor in the *Indies* and Governour of
' *Farmosa*; these two Men would be of great service to the Company.
' Besides these, there is in *Holland* one *Dennis des Maitres*, who has serv'd
' the *Dutch* Company in Quality of a Merchant, and there are some Pilots
' very well skill'd in the *Indian Seas*, who know the Coasts and the Tides,
' and the dangerous Places; it is upon the Experience of such Men, the
' preservation of Ships frequently depends. It will be highly necessary
' to draw over some of these sorts of People, and to be furnish'd for that
' long Voyage, with People who have been it several times; because as
' one ought not to give a powerful Enemy Battle, without Courageous
' Soldiers and good experienc'd Officers; so neither must one go on so
' great an Enterprise, or hope for any good Success without one has
' Directors and Managers, endow'd with Capacity and Experience. I
' have been told some time ago, that the Company had taken into it's
' service one M. *de Ligne* a *Hollander*. He is mighty well acquainted with
' all the Quarters of the South, and is otherwise a very Able Man. It is
' much to be desir'd, That the Company would engage many such in their
' Service, for the advancement of their Affairs; because there are a great
' many Places in the *Indies*, and all of them of Importance too, where
' Settlements must be made. I flatter my self, that when they know I am
' in the Service of the *French* Company, they will more easily come to a
' Resolution of entring into it themselves.

¶ ' Great Care must be taken of the Merchandize and Victuals; and
' a diligent Inspection is requisite, that there be no defect in the Packing
' up, or in the Casks, otherwise both the one and the other will be spoil'd;
' and it sometimes happens, that Goods for being Damag'd, will yield
' no Profit at all; and that the Victuals for being spoil'd, cause Sickness
' among the Men, and is the Death of many of them; by which Means
' the Company falls into the inconvenience of a dismounted Horseman.
' A good Horseman takes particular Care of his Horse, and never grudges
' him Oats: The Company should do the same towards the Seamen and
' Soldiers, and the rest of the common sort who serve them. It is the
' Horse that draws the Plough, and there is no doing without him. The
' *Dutch* Company has learn'd this at its own Cost, and with great Losses,
' for above fifty Years, which were requisite to remedy the Defects of its
' Establishment, and to redress every thing. Men are dear in the *Indies*,
' because their Passage thither costs a great deal, and there are no fresh
' Men to be found there. The *Indians* are by no means proper to Navigate
' *European* Vessels, and they are the worst of Thieves and Murtherers.
' The *Holland* Company would never make use of them.

¶ ' It must be diligently observ'd to have all the Hogsheads and Pipes
' new to put the Water in, and they must be fill'd up and refresh'd with
' new Water once a Week, without which the Water turns black, and
' causes great Sicknesses. It must likewise be observ'd, that all Pipes of
' Water, Wine, Vinegar, Oil, Barrels of Beef, Bacon, and in general, all
' those that are shut up in the Hold of the Ship, be strong Casks, and
' bound firm with Iron Hoops. The Wooden Hoops are apt to burst in
' the Heats, and then all they contain is lost, of which there has been many
' prejudicial Proofs. Greater Care must be still had, that the Anchors,
' Cables, and Cordages, are not weak nor damag'd, or too much crowded
' in the trimming of the Ship. These Cautions seem of little Importance,
' but yet the want of a due Observation of them, may occasion great
' Delays and other Misfortunes, by reason that a small Accident often
' hinders a great Exploit. The Company ought to take this into their
' Consideration, and the rather because the Cargoes of these Ships will
' be Rich, and the Equipages Numerous. I am apt to believe, and there
' is a great likelyhood, that every thing that will be necessary for the
' Equipage of the Ships may be had in *Holland* with the greatest Con-
' veniency, and at the easiest Rates.
¶ ' I have made mention above of the Letters which the King will be
' pleased to write to the *Indies*: Here follows a Model for that, from His
' Majesty to the Emperor of *China*.'

CHAPTER V

The King of France's LETTER *to the Emperor of* China. *His Instructions to his Envoy at the*
Cham of Tartary's *and Emperor of* China's *Courts. His Voyage from thence to the* Indies.

To the Great Emperor of the Eastern and Western Tartaries, *King of* China,
a perpetual Increase of Happiness, and Long Life is wished, by the King of France
and Navarr.

' I HAVE been inform'd to my great Joy, of the Augmentation of your
'   Empire, and the Triumphs you have had over your Enemies for
'   some Years past. For me, who tread in the Steps of my Ancestors,
' Kings of my Kingdoms, ever Glorious Princes, Renown'd throughout
' the whole World, I have a peculiar inclination to enter into an Ac-
' quaintance with your Majesty, who are Famous in all the Parts of the
' Universe: It is this has led me to offer you my best Affections, and to
' let you know the Desire I have of giving all possible Content to Your

' Majesty. I send expresly for this End to Your Majesty, the Bearer of
' this Letter *N. N.* my Envoy, with the Presents herein set down, which
' are all Tokens of my hearty Affection: They consist in .... I do
' assure Your Majesty, I shall be extreamly pleas'd, that there is any
' thing in my Kingdoms, which may prove agreeable to you; and there
' is nothing which I would not willingly do, to keep up a long Corre-
' spondence and Alliance, between your Majesty's Kingdoms and my own.
' It is with this View, that I beg your Majesty to grant my Subjects free
' Access, and open Trade, with the Subjects of your Dominions, without
' any Hindrance or Molestation. I open, with all my Heart, every Port
' of mine to them, to the end that your Majesty may cause every thing
' to be transported which will be useful and proper for your Service.

Written in my Palace the Louvre.

At Paris,

(L. S.)   The Great Seal.   *The King*

LOUIS.

Instructions to N. N. *Envoy of the King of* France, *to the Great* Cham, *Emperor
of* Tartary, *and King of* China. *According To which he shall conduct himself
in the Execution of those Orders which have been given him.*

¶ ' His Majesty having accepted and approv'd the most humble Pro-
' posals, and most earnest Prayers, which have been offer'd him by
' the Directors of the *East-India* Company, to assist and favour their Com-
' merce with his Royal Protection; and these Directors having in particular
' represented the Desire they have to establish their Trade in *China*, if
' Liberty was granted them by the King of the Country; His Majesty has
' thought fit to cause it to be ask'd by an express Deputation, that it may
' the more easily be obtain'd of the King of *China*, and with greater
' Advantages; and likewise thereby to give more Weight and Credit to
' the Commerce of the Company. It is with this Design, His Majesty has
' made choice of your Person, to send you in His Name to the King of
' *China* with His Royal Letter, and the Presents which are mention'd in
' it. This you shall present with all sorts of Respect and Reverence, accord-
' ing to the Manner and Customs, which will be shown you, when you
' come to *China*.

¶ ' You shall make your Voyage from hence to the *Indies*, according to
' the Instructions that will be given you by the Company, and you shall

' from thence pursue it on to *China*, when they give you their Orders.
' Your shall do your endeavours to go to the Height of *Macau*, a Place
' belonging to the *Portugueze*, situated between the 19th and 20th Degree
' of Latitude under the Northern *Tropick*. You shall there make diligent
' Search after *Chinese* Pilots, and do all you can to win and draw into your
' Company, all those who know, by Experience, the Coast of China, and
' who shall be able to conduct you to the River of *Nanquin*. If it should
' not prove possible for you to meet with any such Persons, or not enough
' to be able to rely on them for the Success of your Voyage, you shall go
' higher up, as far as the 23d Degree, towards the River of *Chincheu*. The
' *Hollanders* will, in all appearance, be Establish'd there. You will in-
' fallibly meet in your way, with several *Dutch* Ships, and *Chinese* Vessels,
' who will furnish you with the Means of pursuing your Course with
' Safety to the said River *Nanquin*, for there are always People on Board
' those Ships, whom you may Discourse with about it.

⁋ ' It may happen, that before you get to the height of *Macau*, you may
' be met with by the *Ships* of that famous Pirate *Jacquun*. It is said, that
' he makes his retreat in the great Island of *Anyan*, and has newly got
' another powerful *Fleet* at *Sea*. You must take care not to sail in a straight
' line where you see many sail, or to wait for them if they are making
' towards you; you must avoid them as much as possible, still however
' continuing your Course. You must not be afraid of one, two, or three,
' Ships, but nevertheless you must be always upon your guard, and in
' a readiness to receive the Enemy in good order, upon all Occasions.
' If you meet with *Dutch* Ships and want Amunition, you may ask it of
' them, and say only we are going Northward to see what can be done in
' those Parts.

⁋ ' Being arriv'd by God's Assistance in the *River* of *Nanquin*, you shall
' sail with all possible circumspection, to avoid ill accidents. The Sands
' will stop you at about fifteen Leagues from the Town, and there the
' *Chinese* Fishermen will come in great numbers, you shall hire one of them,
' him you shall judge most proper, and send him with two of your common
' People, to the Governour of the Town, with a letter in *French*, and the
' translation of it in *Chinese*. You shall send him word, that in that Place
' there is an Envoy arriv'd from the King of *France*, with Letters and
' Presents for the great Emperor of *China*; and desire, that he would
' dispatch somebody to Court, to learn the State of Affairs, that you may
' afterwards study to acquit your self of your Embassy with all Care and
' Industry, and in a proper and suitable Manner. According to the Orders
' of the Emperor, you must wait your Answer with Patience, being always

' ready upon your Guard, never permitting too many People at a Time
' to come on board your Vessels: In the mean Time act with all manner
' of Courtesy and Civility imaginable towards every One of them; and
' let your People, who must go into the Town to buy up necessaries, do
' the same, keeping themselves at the same time secure from any surprize,
' or ill accident that might befall them, if there are, for example twenty,
' or thirty *Chinese* on board of one Vessel, that come either as Searchers,
' or out of Curiosity, and more desire to come in, you shall cause them to
' be told, that if they will be at the trouble of waiting a little, 'till the
' others are gone out, you will then receive them in very willingly: It
' may so happen, that the Governour of the Town, or the *Vice-Roy* of the
' Province, will deprive you of some Effects, and in that do you some
' Injustice, relying on this bad pretext, that you are not as yet under the
' Protection of their King. You must exert all your Prudence in these
' cross Accidents: Do not flatly deny them, nor on the Contrary, do not
' grant every Thing they ask. You must make a Virtue of Necessity, being
' always Content to get off of these Importunities, not as you would, but
' as you are able. You shall Daily and without Intermission Address and
' Petition the Governour, and the other Magistrates, to hasten the Arrival
' of your Dispatches from the Court, as much as lies in their Power, and
' to give you the necessary Passports for your going securely with your
' People to *Pekin*; which, is the Residence of the great *Cham*.
¶ ' The Governour of *Nanquin* will cause you to be conducted, and put
' into the Hands of the Chancellor of the Kingdom at *Pekin*. You shall
' then beseech him out of Favour, to permit you to go in Person, and
' carry to the Eyes of the Emperor, the Letter and Presents from his
' Majesty, with all the usual Solemnities, and to procure you a Favourable
' Audience. When the Day shall come, and you are before the Emperor,
' you shall declare to him that you are sent Expresly on the Part of the
' King your Lord, to know the State of his Health, and to wish him a Long
' and Happy Reign. You shall Present him afterwards your Services,
' and most humbly beseech his Majesty, to give a Favourable answer to
' the Letter of the King your Lord. It is not to be doubted, but that,
' before your Audience, you will have time enough to discourse with many
' Persons, from whom you must get the best Lights you can; you shall do
' this particularly with the *Roman Ecclesiasticks* who are at that Court,
' and are much esteem'd and consider'd there. You have Letters of
' Recommendation to them from the Prelates of *Paris*. You must engage
' them to the utmost of your Power, to assist you in your Design.
¶ ' After having deliver'd the Letters and Presents to the King, you shall

' make Presents to the Chancellor of the Empire, and to the other Ministers
' who will be able to serve you, giving each in Proportion to his Employ,
' and according to the Custom of the Country. You will not want People
' to advise you justly, to whom and in what manner you are to make these
' Presents; because all the *Chinese*, and particularly the Merchants, are
' overjoy'd at your coming, on account of the Profitable Trade, which
' they will be in hopes of having with the *French*, will Interest themselves
' in the Liberty you come to Sollicite for. They will Council you rightly
' what to do, to obtain it in the best and speediest manner, and seek your
' Friendship with a great deal of Sincerity. You must be Cautious, Civil,
' and Affable to all, according as your Experience shall have already
' taught you to be, and particularly to those People who use the Exchange,
' and to those who are appointed to Convoy you on the Roads and to be
' your guards at the Court; using your utmost efforts to oblige every body,
' to publish your Personal Merit, and have a good Opinion of the Nation
' you come from. And for this end you must keep all the Domesticks
' strictly to their duty, and all others who have any dependance upon you.
¶ ' After having had Audience of the Emperor, and made your presents,
' as also to the Court, you shall sollicit the Chancellor to obtain of his
' Majesty, the Grant and Liberty desired in your Letter, and particularly
' that of Vending the Merchandizes, and employing the Capital Stock,
' which the Company shall have given into your Hands. When you have
' obtain'd it, you must make good use of it and your principal care ought
' to be, to take exact notice, what Manufactures of *France* there is the
' greatest demand for, and what sort of Merchandizes sell best in *China*,
' and which bring in the greatest Profit. You shall afterwards imploy
' your Capital Stock in Merchandizes; to wit, two thirds in fine raw Silk,
' white and well sorted, informing your self diligently, if there is not a
' better kind than that which they shew you, for it is certain, that if they
' are not skillful People who are commission'd to buy, they will not at
' first let you see the best sort. The Province of *Nanquin* produces the best
' Silk in *China*, but it is not all of one Sort. You shall employ the other
' third in Silk-Stuffs, *viz*. Pelings, white, single, half double, and treble,
' almost all wrought, and a few Plain. The Stuffs of *Nanquin* are almost
' all sold in bundels all of a Sort, as well for the use of the Country it self,
' as for the Trade of *Japan*. They consist of Pelings, Linthees, Panghfills,
' Gielems, and Armosins. The *Hollanders*, import nothing of all this but
' the Pelings into their Country, because they yield the most profit. You
' shall however bring an hundred Pieces of the sorts named, to serve for
' a sample, and for the same purpose, fourscore or an Hundred Pound of

' the Silk of *Bogi*, of Mohair Silk, of sowing Silk, and of Silk to embroider
' with; and not any more of each, because your Cargoe will not be
' carry'd to *Japan*, but brought into *France*. There is neither Velvet,
' Brocards, Damasks, Sattins, nor Padesays, made in the Province of
' *Nanquin*. The *Portugueze* have erected Manufactures thereof in that of
' *Canton*, towards the *South*. It might be proper to bring some of them by
' way of Sample. The *Picol* of Silk, which is 125 Pound *Holland Weight*,
' sold in my Time in *China* for 200 *Piaster*. The first sort, is four Livers
' fifteen Pence per Pound, the second sort four Livers five pence, and
' the third sort three Livers ten pence *per* Pound. At these Rates the
' Silks of *Nanquin*, one with another costs four Livers *per* Pound, and
' sells at least for seven Livers in *Japan*. It is very requisite to buy the
' wrought Silks, and Silk Stuffs, by the Weight, for the goodness sake.
' Both the one and the other yielded formerly sixty and eighty *per Cent*.
' Profit in *Japan*. The Single Stuffs cost from four Livers ten pence,
' to five Livers the Piece; the whole ones between twelve and fifteen,
' all consists in having regard to the Weight and Quality of the Silk.
' There must be so much the more Circumspection us'd in this first Pur-
' chase, by reason it will be a Lesson in which the Company must
' study here that Commerce, and by which the *Chinese* will observe our
' Capacity.
¶ ' Your Commerce of Selling and Buying must be executed with all
' the Diligence possible that no Time be lost; and when that is done you
' shall get the Chancellor to ask leave of the Emperor for you to depart,
' You shall humbly intreat him to thank his Majesty, to assure him that
' the Agents of the Company will not fail to return the next Year, and
' all the ensuing Years, with a great Stock of Money and Merchandize,
' and humbly to implore in your Name his Majesty's Favour and Pro-
' tection for our Nation.
¶ ' In Fine, keep an exact and due Journal, of all that shall happen by
' Sea and Land, that shall be any whit Remarkable; give it to some
' capable Person to keep, who is curious and desirous to Learn, and will
' make all the Inquiries possible, and put the whole down in Writing.
' It would not be amiss, to leave at *Pekin* two or three Young Men of Wit,
' Prudence, and good Morals, to learn the *Chinese* Language. Leave must
' be had of the Chancellor for the same; the Terms of the Request, and
' the Time to make it are left to your Discretion.
¶ ' It will be much about the Month of *October*, before you have finish'd
' your Negotiation; that is the Time that the *North* Winds begin to blow,
' you shall make use of them to repair to the Place that shall have been

'specified to you, at your Departure from the *Indies* for *China*. God give
'a blessing to your Voyage and your Affairs.

¶ 'When the Commerce is granted in *Japan*, and is establish'd there,
'the Ships which shall be sent thither, ought to be about the middle of
'*May*, near the Line, that they be at the end of *June* in *China*, and set out
'from thence in the beginning of August for *Japan*, for that is the best
'Time; and if it is not laid hold of, the Navigation is liable to a great
'many Fatigues, and a great many Dangers.'

CHAPTER VI

King of France's LETTER *to the Emperor of* Japan, *in relation to Trade. Instructions to
Mr* Carron, *Envoy at the Court of* Japan. *Manner of putting up and carrying the King's* Letter
to Court.

To the Sovereign and most Mighty Emperor, and Regent of the Great Empire of
Japan, *whose Subjects are most Submissive, and Obedient; The King of* France
wishes a long and happy Life, and much Prosperity in his Reign.

¶ 'THE many Wars, which my Ancestors, the Kings of *France* have made,
'and the many Victories they have obtain'd, as well over their
'Neighbours, as over remote Kingdoms, having been succeeded by a
'great Tranquility, which I enjoy at present; the Merchants of my Do-
'minions, who Traffick all over *Europe*, have took the Opportunity to beg
'of me in the most humble manner, to open to them the way of Voyaging,
'and of Trafficking in the other Parts of the World, as the other Nations
'of *Europe* do. Their Supplication was by so much the more acceptable
'to me, as it is back'd both by the Desire of the Princes and Lords my
'Subjects, and by my own Curiosity, to be exactly inform'd of the Man-
'ners and Customs of the Great Kingdoms out of *Europe*, of which we
'knew nothing hitherto, but from the Relations of our Neighbours, who
'travel to the *East*. I have therefore resolv'd, in order to gratify my own
'Inclination, and comply with the Requests of my Subjects, to send my
'Deputies into all the Kingdoms of the *East*. The Person whom I have
'made Choice of to send to your High and Sovereign Majesty, is *Francis*
'*Carron*, who knows the *Japanese* Language, and has often had the
'Honour to pay his Duty to your Majesty, and have Audience from it.
'It is on that account that I have sent for him expresly into my Kingdoms;
'and because he is, as I know very well, of good Extraction, tho' decay'd
'in his Fortune it is true, by the fatality of War; But I have restor'd him

' to his first State, and rais'd him in Honour and Dignity, that he may be
' more worthy to approach your High and Sovereign Majesty, with due
' Respect. I moreover made Choice of him for fear another, for want of
' knowing the wise Ordinances, and Customs establish'd by your Majesty,
' should commit any thing contrary to their Intention, and by that means
' incur your Majesty's Displeasure; and that so my Letters and Request
' might be presented to you, by the said *Francis Carron* with the necessary
' Solemnities, and thereby be the better receiv'd by your Majesty: And
' to the End also, that he should make known to it, the sincere Desire
' I have to grant to your Majesty whatever it shall ask of me by way of
' Acknowledgement for the Concession of the Request I made to it; which
' consists in this, that the Merchants of my Kingdoms and States, In-
' corporated into a Company, may have a free Commerce throughout
' the Empire of your Majesty, without any Lett, Trouble, or Hindrance.
' I send you the Present here specify'd, although it be but of small Value
' ....I wish it may be acceptable to your Sovereign Majesty, and that
' there may be any thing within my Territories, that may be of Use to it,
' I very willingly leave all the Entrances thereof open and free to it.

Given at Paris *the* 24*th Year of my Reign*

L. S.   *The King*

LOUIS.

Instructions for Francis Carron, *Envoy from the King of* France *and* Navar,
to the Emperor of Japan, *to deliver to him His Majesty's Letter and Present;*
and according to which he must Govern himself in the Execution of the Projected
Affairs, which are committed to him.

¶ ' The Company will give you Instructions for your Voyage to the
' *Indies*, and for what you are to do in the *South*. When you have
' fulfill'd all their Orders, you shall set Sail with the Trade Wind, in order
' to be by the latter end of *April*, or the beginning of *May*, under the Line.
' From thence you shall Steer your Course to *China*, strait to the Place
' where the Company is settl'd; not to take in there any Merchandize,
' but only to be inform'd of the State of its Affairs, and that you may be
' able to make a Report thereof in *Japan*: For it is very necessary, that if
' the Freedom of Trade be obtain'd in *China*, the Ministers of *Japan*
' should be acquainted therewith.
¶ ' You shall from thence Steer *Northward* in quest of *Japan*: You shall,
' above all things, take care not to go on Shore at any Place without an
' extreme Necessity and Danger of Life: And you shall repair to the Bay

‘ of *Nangazaky*, scituated in 33 Degrees, 40 Minutes. You shall put in
‘ there without Fear, and advance to within half a League of the Town.
‘ It is certain, that before you arrive at the said Bay, some of the Barks
‘ belonging to the Guard of the Coast, will come on Board you: They will
‘ ask you from whence the Ship comes, and to whom it belongs. You
‘ shall answer that the Vessel comes from *France* with a Letter, and some
‘ Express Envoys from the King of *France*, to the High and Soveraign
‘ Emperor of *Japan*; and that they will be pleas’d to show you the Anchor-
‘ age, and afterwards go and acquaint the Governor with your Arrival,
‘ receive his Orders, and bring them to you, because you will govern
‘ your self thereby entirely. This will appear something new and un-
‘ common, and you will soon know what you have to do. If you are not
‘ immediately conducted to the Emperor’s Minister, establish’d in the
‘ said Place in the Quality of Agent, and Intendant of the Foreign Affairs,
‘ by reason you are the Envoy of a King, they will depute Persons of
‘ Quality as Commissioners, to come on Board you: These will have a
‘ great Retinue, and several Interpreters: You shall cause the Place you
‘ receive them in to be cover’d with Tapistry, and shall desire them to
‘ sit down thereon. These Commissioners will Interrogate you, and cause
‘ your Answers to be taken in Writing Word for Word, and likewise all
‘ your Discourse. Their Questions will be, what Business brings you
‘ thither? Whence you come? What Country you are of? What Kingdom
‘ you are come from? On what Design you are come? And what you
‘ have brought with you? You must Answer, that you are come from the
‘ Kingdom of *France*; that you are an Envoy from the King of *France*,
‘ having a Letter and Present to deliver, (after the necessary Permission
‘ obtain’d) to the most high and Sovereign Emperor of *Japan*: That you
‘ have brought with you only the Provisions necessary for your Voyage:
‘ That your whole Commission, and Orders, consist solely to ask accord-
‘ ing to the accustomed Manner of *Japan*, Audience of the Emperor, in
‘ order to deliver in the requisite Form, and with the usual Solemnities,
‘ the Letter and Present you bring from your King, to his High and
‘ Sovereign Majesty of *Japan*.
¶ ‘ These Commissioners will afterwards Interrogate you very amply
‘ on several things, and particularly on those they have Instructions for,
‘ and will cause your Answers to be put in Writing as before: Among the
‘ rest, What Country *France* is? What is its Extent? What are its Bounds?
‘ What grows there? Whether the King be Absolute Sovereign thereof?
‘ What Armies he maintains? Against whom he makes War? Who are
‘ his Allies? What is the Polity? What the Religion? What are the

' Customs of his Kingdom? and a hundred the like Questions. Moreover,
' who you are? You his Envoy? Of what Quality and Condition? And
' what is your Employment? Whether you have any Places? What sort
' of Letter is that of the Kings? How it is Writ? How it is Seal'd? how it
' is made up? And after what manner you keep it?

¶ ' Many the like Questions will be put to you as well from the Ministers
' of *Nangazacky*, as by those of the Court, and other considerable Persons.
' You must be sure to be very careful in your Answers, that they not only
' be always ready in your Memory, but you must keep a Register thereof
' for Uniformity sake, that there may not be found the least Variation
' in your Discourse. The *Japanese* naturally observe Strangers very narrowly,
' and especially since the Surprize that was offer'd them in the Year 1628,
' when a *Dutch* Embassador impos'd upon them. The *Holland* Company
' had sent him to Felicitate the Emperor on his Accession to the Empire.
' He said he was an Envoy from the King of *Holland*, and thereupon he
' receiv'd the Treatment and the Honours which are there done to the
' Embassador of a King, But this Man having ill kept up to his character,
' and being found to have Equivocated in his Answers; for in fine, Truth
' is not long disguis'd easily, he was found to be Embassador from the
' Company; so that he was sent back with Disgrace, and without receiving
' Audience. You must therefore act with a great deal of Prudence and
' Attention, that you may not fall into any of the Snares that will be laid
' for your Tongue; to the End the Respect due to the King your Lord
' may be maintain'd, and that his Requests may be granted.

¶ ' You shall answer to all these Articles frankly, and without Disguise:
' That *France* is the First and most Considerable Kingdom of *Europe*, the
' largest, and Situated in the happiest Climate, the most Fruitful, and
' the Richest, which supplies all *Europe* with many things, to each Part
' according to its Occasions: That it is bounded by *Spain* on one side, by
' *Germany* on another, and by *Italy* on the other; being flank'd by two
' great Seas, the one the *Mediterranean*, the other that which surrounds
' *England*.

¶ ' That *France* is so Powerful, that it curbs all *Europe*, and keeps all its
' Neighbours in a Ballance, without any extraordinary Trouble to itself
' in so doing: That it always maintains fifty Thousand Men well equip'd,
' in Horse and Foot: That she is able to raise three times the Number on
' pressing Occasions: That she is Govern'd by a Sovereign King, who
' has Power over the Lives and Fortunes of his Subjects, of what Quality
' soever; who from his very Infancy, has made divers Wars upon his
' Neighbours, chiefly against *Spain*, *Italy*, and *Germany*: That he has

'moreover, sent Powerful Armies of thirty or forty Thousand Men into
'Hungary, Poland, Muscovy and Sweden, some to Attack, and the others to
'Defend, according as the Interest of France requir'd: That this Great
'Prince is at present in Peace with all the World, having made and
'acquir'd it by the Power of his Arms, and his wise Politicks: That his
'Kingdom is a School of Sciences, of Arts, of Laws, and of Customs, to
'which almost all Europe conforms, and whither the Nobility is sent from
'all Parts to be Instructed and Educated.

¶ 'You shall say on the Article of Religion, that of the French is of two
'sorts; the one the same as that of the Spaniards, the other the same as
'that of the Hollanders: That His Majesty being inform'd, that the
'Religion of the Spaniards is disagreeable to Japan, he has Ordain'd, that
'those of his Subjects who are sent thither, be of the Religion of the
'Hollanders. That this shall be punctually executed. That the French shall
'never be convicted of acting contrary to the Commands of the Emperor.
'They will be apt to make an Objection, viz. Whether the King of France
'depends upon the Pope, as does the King of Spain, and others: You shall
'Answer, that he does not depend upon Him, the King of France acknow-
'ledging no Superior; and that it is easy to see the Nature of the Depend-
'ance his Majesty has on the Pope, in what happen'd two Years ago,
'for an Outrage done at Rome to the Person of His Majesty's Embassador.
'For the Pope not having soon enough made Reparation for the same,
'His Majesty sent an Army into Italy, which having put all the Princes,
'and even the Pope himself into a great Consternation, the Pope sent
'him a Legate a Latere, charged with humble and pressing Supplications,
'to which His Majesty having Regard, he recall'd his Troops, already
'Encamp'd in the Territories of the Pope: So that the King is not only
'most Soveraign and Absolute in his Dominions, but also prescribes Laws
'to several other Potentates, being a Young Prince of five and twenty
'Years of Age, Valient, Wise and Powerful, even beyond all his Ancestors;
'and moreover so curious, that besides the particular Knowledge of all
'Europe, he seeks with Avidity, to know the Constitution of the other
'Countries of the World.

¶ 'These are the most particular Questions which will be put to you, to
'which it is requisite, that your Answer should be always the same, and
'that all your Discourse, and all you shall do, be comformable thereto,
'without the least Variation in the Substance of your Words.

¶ 'You will be conducted on Shore, and lodg'd, during the Time
'the Couriers dispatch'd to the Court, shall carry the News of your
'Arrival. You must then have a mighty Care, that your People behave

' themselves wisely, civilly, and humbly towards the *Japanese*, and that
' the Conduct be in all things agreeable to what the Governour shall
' prescribe to you. If it should happen, that you should not be lodg'd
' nor treated altogether to your Mind, do not take notice of the Incon-
' veniency, nor express any Uneasyness thereat; and have always in your
' Thoughts, that it is from the Emperor you are to receive all your Ease,
' and conveniencies. You shall keep your finest Cloaths, and which you
' have never wore in *Japan*, as shall likewise those of your Retinue till
' you are brought to Court, and till the Day of your Audience. As soon
' as you shall arrive there, you shall cause your Retinue to provide them-
' selves with little Leather Pumps, and Slippers. The Floors of the Houses
' are cover'd with Tapestry in *Japan*, for which reason you must put off
' your Shoes when you enter them, and have some without Quarters,
' that you may quit them with the greater Ease.
❡ ' As soon as the first Orders shall come from Court on your account,
' and it may be before they will ask you to see the King's Letter, and will
' be for Translating it, and putting it down in Writing. You shall not
' deny this, but shall deliver a Copy of the rough-Draught which shall
' have been given you. The little Box, in which the King's Letter is, must
' be shut up in the finest Trunk you have, or some very fine Chest of
' Drawers. You shall place it in the upper end of your Chamber, on an
' Estrade, or some kind of Frame about a Foot high. You must never come
' near it but bare Headed. It is not the Custom in *Japan* to be cover'd
' before Persons of Quality, and Persons of Merit, as is frequently done
' in *Europe*. You must in this, follow the Custom of the Country, and
' especially when the Trunk or Chest shall be open'd, in which the little
' Box that contains the Letter shall be, when it shall be look'd at or
' remov'd. If the *Japanese* do not appoint a Person to remove and bring
' it to you, when you shall give your Orders for that Purpose, you shall
' make choice of two of the chiefest Officers of your Retinue, who bare
' Headed, and their Arms extended, shall take it with both Hands, and
' bring it where you shall direct. This little Box will be put into a Chest
' well pack'd up, and will be carry'd alone in a Palanquin, which is a
' Chair, or kind of Litter, when you are conducted to Court. Let this
' Litter always be before you, and follow it constantly; By so doing, you
' show the Respect you have for the King your Lord, and his Letter, and
' thereby excite the *Japanese* to do the same, as they never fail to do, to
' the Letters and Embassadors of Kings. If your Commission, and Letter
' were to felicitate on the account of a Marriage, about Affairs of State,
' to offer Assistance, or to ask it; or even for a simple Congratulation, as

' has been said the *Hollanders* sent for that purpose in the Year 1628.
' It would then be requisite to observe a great many other Ceremonies;
' to go with a much greater Retinue, and Appearance, than in all likely-
' hood, will be necessary on this occasion; because the Business here is
' only to obtain a Freedom of Commerce for a Society of Merchants; and
' the Merchants are much less esteem'd in *Japan* than in *Europe*: Not-
' withstanding which, according to all Appearances the *Japanese* will not
' receive you after so plain a Manner. But if nevertheless the contrary
' should happen, that your Entertainment was not to your Mind, nor
' splendid enough, you must in a particular Manner forbear giving any
' Hints thereof, and receive and take all things, with all possible Thanks,
' and with all the outward Satisfaction you are able to express: And at
' the same Time, you shall underhand cause to be bought, what you
' cannot be with out. Be careful even to a nicety, to show on all occasions
' the great Civilities and utmost Affability to the Comissioners who shall
' conduct you, and to those who shall guard you at Court. Always follow
' their Council, even when it is most contrary to your Humour, and to
' all the Maxims, and Lights of Reasoning in *Europe*. Their Manners and
' Customs have a Thousand things quite opposite to ours: They esteem
' them, and on the contrary despise what we approve and follow. The only
' Means to be respected and consider'd among them is to conform to
' their manners, as is manifest by a long Experience.

⁋ ' The King's Presents to the Emperor, are exactly specified in his
' Majesty's Letter to the Emperor. You will inform your self of those you
' are to make to the Ministers, and other Persons of Quality. You will
' find People enow who will advise you to a Nicety, what you must
' present to them: They will not tell you to do too much, because the
' Officers are alotted what to take of from Strangers, and never run the
' Risque receiving any thing over and above. These Presents shall consist
' of Woollen-Stuffs, which shall be given you for that purpose. When
' you shall be brought to an Audience of the Emperor, and shall draw
' near his Person, it will be well taken, and you will be much esteem'd,
' therefore, if you take off your Sword, and give it to one of your Retinue
' to keep, before you are bid to do it, as it would be certainly told you.
' You shall have nothing on your Head, not so much as a *Chalot*, or half
' Cap, all the time you behold the Emperor's Face. It will be one of the
' Chief Noblemen who presents you to his Maiesty, to wit, he who is
' upon the guard that Day. He will be on his Knees near the Presents,
' and Letter, in the middle of the Space that separates you from the
' Emperor. He will receive your Words, and will carry them to him. You

' shall tell him the Commands you have receiv'd from the King, to give
' an Assurance of his good Will, and Affection to his Imperial Majesty,
' to whom you wish a long and happy Life, and all manner of Prosperity
' in his Reign. You shall intreat his Majesty, that he will be pleas'd
' favourably to grant the Requests contain'd in the Letter of the King
' your Lord; and that he will vouchsafe to take into his Protection those
' of the *French* Nation who shall come to *Japan*. It may happen, that the
' Emperor may have some Discourse with you, it will be short without
' doubt, and if he has any Questions to ask you, it will be by the Inter-
' mediation of the Nobleman who conducted you to your Audience. This
' is their way to all sorts of Embassadors, not out of Contempt, but to do
' Honour, and it is so that they explain it. Your Audience will be given
' you at the Time of the New or full *Moon*, because then all the Kings,
' Princes, and other Grandees of *Japan*, come to Court, to see the Emperor;
' and pay their Reverence to him.

¶ ' After your Audience is over, you shall go and salute the Ministers of
' the Council, who have any Influence in your Negotiation. You shall
' make them Presents: You shall intreat them to assist you in the obtaining
' a favourable and speedy answer to his Majesty's Letter. This done, you
' will not be kept long in suspence. It will be brought you with presents
' from his Majesty. You shall receive the whole with a great deal of
' Reverence and Respect, and you shall cause his Majesty's Letter to be
' carry'd as you did the Letter of the King your Master. At your Return,
' you shall acknowledge by Reciprocal Presents, those which shall have
' been made you in the way, as you went to Court, and as here, you shall
' avoid all Profusion, so you must take care not to be behind hand with
' any body. You shall behave your self after the same manner towards
' the Governour of *Nangasacky*, at your return thither; and you shall most
' earnestly intreat him to favour those of the *French* Nation, who shall
' come to *Japan*, and bear with their Ignorance of the Manners and
' Customs of the Country: And cause them to be instructed therein as
' well as possible. Then you shall depart; and if time will permit, you shall
' pass by *China*, to see what the Company is doing. Do not however
' expose your self to the Winds and Storms that rise on the Coasts of
' *China*, during the Northern Monsoons. Go afterwards, supposing a free
' Commerce in *Japan* has been obtain'd, as it is hop'd it will, to the Coast
' of *Java*, Land at *Bantam*, in order to repair to the Great Mataram.'

CHAPTER VII

Three Envoys from the Company join the two Deputies, but without any Character. The Letter *they were charg'd with to the King of* Persia. *The Faults wherein. Their Request granted through the Author's Means.*

❡ Upon these Memoirs, the Company dispatch'd by Land, to the Court of *Persia*, and to that of the Great *Mogul*, three *Envoys*, who join'd themselves to the King's two Deputies, but without any Character, to prepare its Ways. Here is the Tenor of the Letter they were charg'd with for the King of *Persia*, as I took it from the Translation that was made thereof into the *Persian* Language.

Most High, *most* Excellent, *most* Powerful, *most* Invincible *Emperor of Persia,* Our most *Honour'd and most beloved* Friend.

' WE have taken a great deal of Satisfaction in seeing several of
' our Subjects resolv'd to make known to your Highness, the
' Establishment of Trade, which they design to settle in your
' Dominions, wherein a great many of the Nobility of Our Kingdom have
' interested themselves. We do not doubt, but that your Highness con-
' ceives, that it is an Undertaking, from which our Subjects, and your
' own may reap much Benefit. As to us, it is so much the more agreeable,
' by reason that it will be a Means of renewing that Friendship which
' subsisted in Ancient Times, between the Emperors of *Persia*, your
' Predecessors, and the Kings, our Ancestors. It is in order to make known
' to you, how much we esteem the Constitution of this good Friendship,
' and how much we have it at Heart, that you should favour the Merchants
' of this Company, that being inform'd that some Gentleman, curious
' to see your Court, go along with the Deputies the Company sends
' to your Majesty, to lay open their Intentions; we have charg'd them
' earnestly to intreat you on that Head, We perswading ourselves, that
' they will have favourable Access to your Highness. We conclude with
' our Prayers to God for the continuance of your Grandeur, and
' Prosperity.'

❡ To frame a Judgment of this *Letter*, according to our Idea's and Manners, there is certainly nothing that can be found fault with in it; but such is the Polite Civility of that other World to which it was address'd, that they found two Defects therein. The first was, its being Seal'd with a Common Seal. These Sovereigns of the *East*, have Seals of different Sizes; the largest about the bigness of a Crown-piece, the lesser about the bigness of a Sixpence, both the one and the other sort of different Figures, as square, round, oval; but the least of all are only put to Letters and Orders directed to Persons of a lower Rank, or else to Subjects. This has been known a long time ago at *Vienna, Venice, Rome*, in *Poland* and *Muscovy*, by reason of their mutual intercourses of Trade. All Letters likewise which they write out of those Countries to the King of *Persia* are under the Broad-Seal, and that Seal is inclos'd in a Box of Gold; for it is another piece of *Eastern* Civility, to put the Letters into rich Boxes, or into Purses made of Stuffs, more or less rich, in proportion to the Quality of the Persons to whom they are directed.

¶ The second Fault which the Court of *Persia* found with the King of *France*'s Letter, was, that it was sent only upon Occasion, or by a Friend's Hand, as the Trading People call it; that is to say, by two Gentlemen Travellers, whose Curiosity led them thither, and not by an Ambassador sent expresly for that purpose. However, an Excuse was found for all this, and for the first Point they alledg'd, That the King of *France* wrote with his Common Seal to the Emperor, the Pope, and to the Grand Seignior himself; and as to the second Point, that the King declin'd sending an Embassador, because it would have been necessary for him to have pass'd through the *Turks* Dominions, but that he would send one in a little time by Sea.

¶ These Excuses were taken. *Abas* the Second, who had a peculiar love for the *Europeans*, and had a mighty Inclination to enter into the strictest Leagues, and Bonds of Friendship with our Princes, to render himself the more formidable to the *Grand Seignior*, and *Great Mogul*, receiv'd those Deputies very favourably, and caress'd them after an extraordinary manner. The Particulars are to be met with in Mr. *Taverner's* Third *Volume*: But at the same time, that I refer the Reader thither; I am glad of this Opportunity of informing him, that I don't do it out of any Esteem I have for those Pieces, so far from that, I look upon the greatest part of them, to be a worthless Medly of the Debauches and Adventures of People of low Life, and those, for the most part, *Dutchmen*, publish'd from a Spirit of Flattery, and in compliance to the Animosity which they had in *France*, against that Common-wealth; just at that time when the *Rhapsody* was put in the Press.

¶ To return back to my Discourse concerning the Establishment of the *French* Company, I found two of the five Deputies at the Court of *Persia*, in the Year 1666. The one was from the Company; the other, whose

Name was *De Lalain,* came from the King; and I may say it was a piece of good Luck for them, because the Court of *Persia* not having had good Informations in favour of the Company, was resolv'd to wait for the arrival of their Ships, before they would grant the Deputies any one of their Requests: But what I represented to the King, and to his Ministers, was hearken'd to, and they obtain'd what they ask'd.

CHAPTER VIII[1]

THERE is room to believe, that the *French* Company knew nothing at all what the Trade of *Persia* was when they sent their Deputies thither: For the chief Directors thereof arriving in the Indies in the Year 1668, and having from thence, in the best manner they could, weigh'd and consider'd the Profits of the Traffick with *Persia;* they judg'd it not to be considerable enough to send their Ships thither, and they, in Fact, sent none at all. Other Directors being come to the *Indies* in the Year 1672, to wit, the Messieurs *Baron, Gueston,* and *Blott,* there was a talk of sending some. It is proper to observe, that out of these three Gentlemen, only the Person last mention'd understood Trade. Mr. *Baron* was pitch'd on, to go upon the Embassy to the Great *Mogul,* and had his Commission and Instructions accordingly; Mr. *Gueston* thinking he should gain neither Glory nor Profit at *Surat,* took a Fancy of making just such another Expedition. The *Capuchins* of *Persia* furnish'd him with an Opportunity, by renewing the Instances which they had for a long time made, that the Company would send an Ambassador and Presents into *Persia,* to disengage the Faith of the Promises they had made for these six Years to this Court, upon that Subject. The Agents of the Company at *Ormus,* and *Ispahan,* made the same Instances, representing that the Honour of the Nation was concern'd, and that it was requisite to make Presents to the King, and Ministers of *Persia,* in recompence of the exemption from the Customs, which he had granted to them, and which they had enjoy'd as the Occasions offer'd. Mr. *Gueston* believ'd that he had good Grounds enough to go upon, and to justify his Undertaking; insomuch, that contrary to the Advice, and Remonstrances of the Merchants of the Company, who represented to him, that the Trade of *Persia* was not

---

[1] There is no rubric to this chapter in the original edition. For this and other printer's errors in the "make-up" of the book see Editor's Preface, page v of the present edition.

worth the Charges. He made himself an Ambassador of his own Head, without Letters of Credence, and without Instructions, intending to draw them up himself, when he came upon the Place, because it never appear'd that he had ever come to a Determination of what he should ask, nor what he should Treat of in *Persia*.

¶ He Embark'd at *Surat* in the beginning of *March*, 1673, carrying along with him fine Presents for the King, and his Ministers, and a great Stock of Merchandizes to defray the Charges of the Voyage; but he took a small Train with him, and not so much as one Man in it, that was capable of any Negociation: In twenty Days he arriv'd at *Ormus*, from whence setting out with more Haste than good Speed, and without taking the necessary Provisions, for so long, and fatiguing a Journey, as that is from *Ormus* to *Ispahan*, which takes up at least a Month's Travelling; he and his whole Company fell sick in a very few Days: They begg'd of him to stay a little by the Way, and take a few Days' rest, but in Vain; he was re-solv'd to Travel more like a Messenger, than an Ambassador; the Gover-nours of the Places thro' which he pass'd, offer'd him Horse-Litters, but he would hear nothing of that kind neither, dreading the Expence, as well as the Delays, that would attend them. Another Unhappiness for him and his Attendance was, that he could not be perswaded to follow the Regimen of that Country.

¶ He came then to *Chiras*, more dead than alive, and all his People were in the same Condition, several of them never raising from their Beds any more. He had the Mortification of seeing his only Son die the first of all the Company, on the twelfth Day after his Arrival; and he died himself the last, at the Expiration of fifteen Days.

¶ The *Carmelite* Missioners, in whose Convent he died, pretending he had ordered upon his Death-Bed, that the Rest should be Ruled by their Counsel and Advice, were of Opinion, that this Troop of People so im-pair'd and lessen'd by the Fatigues of their Journey, among whom there was not one Experienc'd Man, or that could make a tolerable Appearance, should return Home, leaving the Presents Deposited at *Chiras* in safe Hands. They alledg'd for their Reasons, That among the Papers of the Deceas'd, no Credential Letters, no Instructions, no Memorandums, no Signs of an Embassy being to be found, it would be a downright Folly to go, and expose themselves, at so Polite and Wise a Court as that of *Persia*, and to spend five and twenty or thirty thousand Crowns, to make themselves the Laughing Stocks of the Nation. It was very good Counsel, but it was not follow'd: The Company's Interpreter, a *French* Merchant, born and bred at *Ispahan*, who in Truth was the End and Soul that

Animated the Embassy, not finding his Accompt in the Advice given by the *Carmelites*, over perswaded a Captain of a Ship, and a Clerk, who were the most considerable Persons of the Company, to oppose this Council; after several Debates, they came to a Resolution of referring the Matter to the Opinion of the *Capuchins* at *Ispahan*, though it would be three Weeks at least, before they could receive their Answer. These good *Capuchin* Fathers had taken too much Pleasure in the Thoughts of a *French* Embassy, to let it Vanish, or be deferr'd to another Time, Their Superior, a Man of good Knowledge and Conduct, Named Father *Raphael de Mans*, wrote them back Word, that they had nothing to do but to come, that the want of Credential Letters, Orders, and Instructions, signified but little; because that Deficiency should be Supplied, and that they would not have less Success, than the Deceased would have had, if he had been alive: These Encouragements were very pleasing to the little *French* Company at *Chiras*; the Heads, the Captain of the Ship, and the Clerk, of whom I made Mention, had already got a Custom of putting on the Cloaths of the Deceased, and being Treated like Ambassadors, and they found the Treatment too sweet to refuse the Present, Fortune had made them thereof; the Captain being the Nephew of Mr. *Berrier*, was Elected to represent the Ambassador; the Clerk was the Person who bore the Second Post. I cannot forbear relating a very Pleasant Incident in this Story, which is, that the Interpreter I have been speaking of, who was their Guide, and absolute Director, was just upon the Point of Constituting himself Ambassador, rather than to produce two such Personages to a Court, so Artful, and so Polite, as that of *Persia*.: It is true, he had a good Mein, and Wit enough to maintain the Character; but he durst not Presume to take it upon him, after he had reflected a while, what a Piece of Burlesque it would be to see him at the Head of an Embassy; him, who was a Subject of the Country, born among the *Armenians*, who are the lowest Class of Subjects, and who had Officiated for the Company from the Beginning, in the Quality of Interpreter, which is the Post of a Menial Servant. He has several Times protested to me, that the only Thing which hinder'd him from running the Risque, was, that he could not determine whether he should Dress after the *French* or *Persian* Manner: If I should go Drest, said he, in a *Persian* Habit, which is my own Country Fashion, it would be Absurd and Ridiculous to see a Native of *Persia*, in in a *Persian* Dress, appear as a *French* Ambassador, with a Train of *French men* Cloath'd after the Manner of their Country; and if I should Dress my self like a *French* Man, the Children would be running after me, and the whole Embassy would pass for a mere Masquerade.

¶ There are *Europeans* of all Nations, who frequently, in the *East,* give the like Examples of Imprudence, and Irregularity.

¶ When this Embassador was near *Ispahan,* he wrote a Letter to the *Nazir* or Superintendant, to give him advice of his coming, and that is the Letter which made way for this Digression. He sent word, that upon the arrival of the late Mr. *Gueston,* and himself at *Bander abassi,* they had dispatch'd an Express to inform him of it, and to beg of him to procure them, an Apartment in a Palace near the Court, to which, having receiv'd no answer, and being come near the Town, he renew'd his Instances, to know the Will of the King, concerning the Day upon which he should make his publick Entry, and touching the Place where he should first alight.

¶ In the Evening I was with the *Nazir,* and there I met with the *French* Company's Interpreter, I mean the same Merchant I was speaking of just now. The *Nazir* told him, he had presented a Petition to the King for the *French* Ambassador, and that his Majesty had order'd a Palace to be given him, and that all the Honours should be done to him, that are usually paid to Ambassadors. It is here to be observ'd, that the *Eastern* Nations call all those Ambassadors, who come on the behalf of a Sovereign, without any of those distinctions of Titles and Characters in use among us.

CHAPTER IX

The Author pays his respects to the two Favorites of the King, who promise Services but do nothing. Visits to Persons of Distinction. He is sent for to the Nazir. *His Jewels produc'd.*

ON the 9th I went and pay'd my respects to *Mira-li-bec,* and *Nisr-ali-bec,* the Favorites of the King, Sons to the Governour of *Armenia,* and to deliver to them the Letters of Recommendation, which I had receiv'd from their Father. They promis'd me all the Assistance in the World, but did not do the least thing in Nature for me, as I came to understand afterwards. Then I went and payed other Visits on that same Day, and the Day following, to several Persons of great Quality, whom I knew at the Time of my first Voyage, and particularly those for whom I had Letters of Recommendation.

¶ Upon the 11th the *Nazir* sent me several Horsemen, to conduct me to his Palace when he should be come back from the King. He had there got an assembly together, of the most Skilful Jewellers in the City, *Mahometans, Armenians,* and *Indians,* to the number of Eighteen or Twenty.

The Head of the Goldsmiths sat at the upper end of the *Mahometan,* Jewellers. The *Armenians* and *Indians* were in another Hall, separated from this, by a row of Balisters with Glass Sashes.

¶ The *Nazir* coming in caus'd all my Jewels to be brought forth; what the King had made choice of were in a large Gold Bason of *China* fluted. I was in a manner Thunderstruck when I cast my Eyes on what the King had set apart, which was not one Quarter of what I had brought. I became Pale and without Motion. The *Nazir* perceiv'd it, and was touch'd thereat; I was just by him, he therefore leaned towards me and said in a low Voice; You afflict your self that the King has lik'd only a small Part of your Jewels. I protest to you that I have done more than I ought, to create in him a liking to them all, and to make him take at least one half of them; but I could not succeed therein because your large Pieces, as the Sabre, the Poynard and the Looking-Glass are not well made according to the Fashion of the Country. However compose your Mind you shall sell them if it pleases God. These Words pronounc'd with Tenderness, brought me out of the Consternation, into which I had been cast without perceiving it my self: I was much surpriz'd, and very much afflicted that the *Nazir* had been sensible thereof. However I recover'd my self as well as I could, without disguising at the same time too much, the Displeasure I had, and which was so well grounded seeing that the great Pains which I had taken for four Years together, instead of making my Fortune, and heaping Honour upon me, as the late King of *Persia* had promis'd me, were like to afford me nothing but Losses and fresh Labour.

¶ The Chief of the Goldsmiths took before him the Bason, in which was what the King had set apart, and beginning with the little Pieces, he asked (whispering) the Price of each Jewel, one after the other, and then he caus'd it to be valu'd by the Jewellers, first by the *Mahometans,* then by the *Armenians,* and afterwards by the *Indians,* each Corps separately. The Merchants in *Persia* who treat upon any Bargain before People, never make use of Speech to tell one another the Price: They signify it by their Fingers, by giving their Hands under one end of their Garment, or under a Handkerchief, in such manner, that the Motions they make cannot be perceiv'd. To shut the Hand one takes hold of, is to say a Thousand: To take the Finger extended marks a Hundred, and bent in the Middle Fifty. The Number is express'd by pressing the end of the Finger, and the Ten by bending the Finger: And when they will signifie several Thousands, or several Hundreds, they repeat the Action, and the Management of the Hand, or of the Fingers. This way is easie and safe to express ones

Thought, without being understood by any, but those who it is intended should know it. It is made use of every where in the *East*, and principally in the *Indies*, where it is universal.

¶ At One a Clock Dinner was serv'd up, which was very noble, and nicely drest, and that being over, the *Nazir* dismiss'd the Appraisers, having taken their Valuation in Writing: then making me sit near him, he told me, that there was so great a difference betwixt the Price I ask'd, and that which the Valuers had set, that it would be impossible to conclude any thing, unless I abated at least one half: That he had told me himself, and caus'd me to be told, to consider the low Rate to which Jewels, and precious Stones were fallen, by reason the King did not mind them, and the Poverty of the Court, which was not in a Condition to buy any of me: That the Times of the late King were over, and that, had it not been for his Sollicitations with the King, he would not so much as have looked at my Jewels; so that I could not expect to make any great Gains, as I might have done formerly: That he was altogether surpriz'd at the excessive Rates I set upon my Things, and that according to what the *Armenians* (who are constantly going to, and coming from *Europe*) had valu'd them at, (and they could not but know very well the current Price of precious Stones) he found I had a mind to gain two for one. The *Nazir* season'd his Discourse with so many Civilities and Protestations of good Will to serve me, that to tell the Truth I fell into his Snares, and took all those dexterous Fetches, for Openness and Sincerity of Heart. I therefore began to talk to him very ingenuously likewise. I first thanked him for all his Favours, protesting I would for ever remember them, and then told him, that tho' intruth I did not find my Account in losing by my Jewels, after so long and fatiguing a Journey, attended with so many Dangers, and so great an Expence, and undertaken by the special Order, and for the service of a Great King; yet I did not flatter my self with the hopes of any great Gain, and that to be plain with him, I would be contented to let them go at five and twenty *per Cent*. Here he took me at my Word, and so quickly that I found immediately I had been too forward. He said, that five and Twenty *per Cent* was too reasonable a Gain to be refus'd me, that I should therefore declare frankly, and upon my Faith, the Prime Cost of each thing, and it should be pay'd me with that Profit. I would have been glad to have recall'd my Words, apprehending some Cheat, but I did not see which way I could do it. I made answer, that, if good Assurances were given me, for the Performance of the Agreement, I would declare what they cost me, even upon my Oath, if it was requir'd. The *Nazir* told me he had Knowledge enough of me, to believe me without my Swearing, and that for his Part he swore by *Aly*, (he is the great Saint of the *Persian* Sect) by God, and by his Religion, he would keep his Word with me. Here the Chief of the Goldsmiths interrupted him, and said that I was in the wrong to require an Oath from a *Nazir* of *Persia*. Other Lords who were also present exclaim'd likewise against it. I told them I did not require any such thing, and that his bare Word would satisfy me. Hereupon I was forc'd to declare the true Price I had given for each Thing, in a new Memorial. I was advis'd not to be so very exact therein, but I rejected the Proposition.

¶ When the Chief of the Goldsmiths, and the *Nazir* had seen this new Memorial, they exclaim'd strangely against one Part of the Articles, and told me that I over-valued several of the Jewels, this Discourse surprized me and made me grow warm. I could not forbear saying, that it was very wrongfull. They call'd my Oath in Question, after they had sworn to believe my bare Word. The *Nazir* put an end to the difference by saying, he would present a Petition to the King about this Affair, making at the same Time great Protestations, that it should not be wanting to his Indeavours, if I did not sell, but that I should think of lowering the Price of my Jewels. I then got up, and gave many Thanks to this Lord for his kindness, and especially for his having vouchsaf'd to be Eight Hours taken up with my Business, which I look'd upon to be a mighty Favour. He seem'd to relish that Part of my Thanks, which was exactly true, for it was then above five a-Clock in the Evening.

¶ On the 12th, the *Nazir* sent for me very early. I made haste, thinking it was about my Jewels I was sent for, but I was mistaken; it was to see a rough Diamond of seventy Carrats, that the King had a mind to buy. It was rough cut, and had already all its Form. The *Nazir* told me that the King fancy'd that Diamond, and had order'd him to show it me, to know if there was any defect in the Water and Clearness. I told him I had not Skill enough in Diamonds to give my Opinion on so large a Stone, but that my Companion was a very knowing Man in those Things. He Judged it to be of the first Water, and perfectly clear. It belong'd to the Prevost of the *Armenians* of *Julpha*, which is that Part of the Suburbs of *Ispahan*, where they are settled. The King bought it for three Thousand one Hundred and fifty *Tomans* ready Money, which amounts to about fifty Thousand Crowns! this Stone would have been worth in *Europe* a Hundred Thousand Crowns, and is the finest Diamond that can be seen of that weight.

¶ In the Afternoon I went again to the *Nazir*; He told me he had not dar'd to speak to the King about my Business, by reason of the excessive

Price I set my Jewels at. He then renew'd his Protestations, and the same Remonstrances which he had made to me the Day before. I was provok'd beyond measure at such a Procedure, which seem'd to me to be so unworthy and mean, as not to be express'd. However I did not draw from thence any ill Omen, as knowing the Genius of the Country. I told the *Nazir* for Answer, that I was in dispair to find that he would neither believe my Word nor my Oath. He flew in a Passion at these Words, and very sharply ask'd me, whether I was a Prophet, that People should be under an Obligation to believe my Word? I was seized with so strong an Inclination to laugh, at that pleasant Repartee, that I could not forbear. The Nazir turning to the Company, with an Air of Anger, said, pointing to me, *By God the* French *are altogether Extravagant; they pretend their Word should pass for an Oracle, as if they were not Men and Sinners.* I made answer, without being startled, *that in Reality we were Men, but that in our Countries, as it was knavish to give false Words in Point of Commerce, so a greater Affront could not be put upon a Merchant than to accuse him thereof.*

¶ On the 13th I went again to this Lord, he had commanded me to come every Day to see him; and indeed he had every Day some Business or other with me, some Jewel to Buy, or to Sell for himself, or for his Friends. He propos'd to me to truck all that I had brought for Diamonds or Silk. I refus'd it, saying, that being obliged to go to the *Indies*, the Country for Diamonds and Silk, Money would be more advantageous to me. It behov'd me to be very cautious, that I might avoid falling into the Snares of the *Nazir*, who did not fail to lay some fresh ones for me every Day. Among the Diamonds which he offer'd me, there was a Stone of Six and Fifty Carrats, which the King had made a Present of to his Mother, who had taken a distaste to it, and had a Mind to sell it. I valued it at Forty Thousand Crowns.

CHAPTER X

The French *Envoy has a House ordered him. Number of the King's Houses at* Ispahan. *The Author is sent for again to the* Nazir *about the Jewels; what pass'd between 'em concerning them. A notable Instance of* Eastern *Craft. Entrance of a* Muscovite *Ambassador. The* Persian *Manner of entertaining them.*

As Dinner was taking away, the *Prevost* of the *Armenians*, and the *Interpreter* of the *French* Company came to speak with the *Nazir*. He told the Prevost, that the King had given Orders to pay him ready Money for his Diamond, and to give him a *Calaat*. Such are call'd the Garments which the Sovereign gives to do Honour to those, for whom he has a Mind to show some extraordinary Esteem; and he told the Interpreter, that the King had order'd a House to be prepar'd for the Envoy of the Company: That he might chuse one himself in that Quarter he lik'd best, and it should be furnished out of the King's Wardrobe. The Interpreter made Answer, that the Envoy desired only the House, having wherewithal to furnish it himself sufficiently. The *Nazir* immediately commanded two of his Officers to go with the Interpreter, and let him see all the King's Houses in that Quarter, where the Envoy desired to be. He made choice of that where the *Capuchins* are, that he might have the Superior of the Convent, (who was his chief Councellor) always near him, for the Regulation of his Conduct.

¶ The King has above three hundred Houses in *Ispahan*, which are properly his own, having devolv'd to his Predecessors, and to himself either by Right of Succession, by Confiscation, or by Purchase. These Houses which are all large and fine, as it is easy to conceive, the King having no Controversy with little Folks, are almost always empty, and run to Ruin, for want of being kept up in sufficient Repair. These they give to Embassadors, and Strangers of Consideration, that come to *Ispahan*. The Commissioners of the Quarters where they are scituated, have the Keys of these Houses, and are charg'd to keep them Clean and Neat.

¶ On the 13th, by break of Day, one of the King's Goldsmiths came and told me from the Chief of the Goldsmiths, that the *Nazir* would send for me the same Day or the next Day after, and would give me back whatever we had bargain'd for, for the King himself, or his Friends, but that I should not show any Surprize or Displeasure thereat, but put on a good Countenance; because it was a feint to make me lower my Price, and that it would not be eight Days before they were all retaken back again. I sent my hearty thanks to the Chief of the Goldsmiths, for the Obligation I had to him, for so particular a Favour; but I was much more obleig'd to the *Nazir*, because it was he that caus'd the Advertisement to be given me, as I was afterwards inform'd. This may serve for a good Pattern of the Fidelity of the Ministers of State in the *East*. One may say in one Sense, that all that is done in those Countries is a reciprocal Cheat.

¶ About ten a Clock I went to the *Nazir* as I us'd to do. After Dinner he made me sit near him, and told me with a loud Voice, (that all the Company which was very great might hear) That the Night before, the King being inform'd from his Mouth, that I held my Jewels at so high a Price, was very angry, and had commanded him to give me them all back again; whereupon he had most humbly intreated his Majesty to vouchsafe to take into his Consideration, that I had brought them by the express Orders of the late King his Father; that that great Prince having had so much Kindness for me, His Majesty, who was the Heir of his Generosity, as well as of his Crown, might, if he thought fit, give me some Token of his. That it was a small Matter for the greatest King in the World, to buy of a Stranger some few Pieces of Gallantry, at one or two Pistoles more than they were worth: That he had moreover represented to him that it would become his Majesty to do so, if it were but for his Glory; and that he had alledg'd many the like Reasons: But the King was so far from granting the Favour which he ask'd in my behalf that he was angry with himself, and had forbid him speaking about my Affairs: That he was sorry for his vexatious Alteration, but that I my self was the Cause thereof; that all he could now do for me, was to buy himself my Jewels, and to pay me for the same, partly in Money, partly in Merchandizes, Brocards, *Turkish* Stones, Silks, or Diamonds, at my Choice, I speak frankly to you says he, and the Affection I have for you is so great, that it induces me to discover it in this naked Manner to you. It is not to be express'd with what a Serious Air the *Nazir* said all this. I should have thought it a Crime to have suspected any thing, if he had not himself let me into the Secret. I tried therefore, to play my Part well likewise, more especially having before my Eyes so many Lords, most of them as Subtile and Cunning as the *Nazir*.

¶ I Answer'd him, with abundance of thanks, for exposing himself to the King's Anger for a Foreign Merchant. That his Affection was a fresh Motive for me to deal plainly with him; but that I did Protest to him, I had told the Truth, and that I look'd upon the King to be a Prince of too much Equity, to desire that the Dangers, the Pains, and the Expences of a Seven Years Journey, should afford me nothing but Losses. That in a Word I could not part with my Jewels for less than what he had been pleas'd to promise. That after all, he would give me leave to tell him, that the King would without doubt, have taken them, if he had let him know that they were Cheap, and a Pennyworth, as they were in Effect. *How*, reply'd he, raising his Voice, *could I do less? Must I tell the King Lyes to oblige you? And shall I eat his Bread like a Profidious Servant? Moreover, have I not a Head to lose? And if I don't acquaint the King with the dearness of Things, can he fail of knowing it? And when inform'd thereof, will he not send to have it taken off of my Shoulders?* I was two Hours before this Minister arguing the Matter, but without any Success, and I could not but wonder that so great a Minister, who had such Business upon his Hands, and of so much Importance, could spare so much Time in playing a Part, so little suitable to his Dignity; But all is Gesture and Fiction, thorough Artifice and Cunning in those Oriental Courts, as I have frequently observ'd.

¶ On the same Day an Ambassador from *Muscovy* made his Entry at *Ispahan*. Every body judg'd, at the Sight of his Retinue, that he was a meer Merchant, who came chiefly to buy, and sell, as there often comes from *Muscovy*, *Tartary*, and several other Neighbouring Countries, considerable Merchants who have the Character of Ambassadors, that they may be free from the Customs, travel with the greater Safety and Ease, and carry on their Commerce more advantagiously: But several things were afterwards discover'd, that made it reasonable to believe, that this was also come to negotiate some Affairs of State. He had to the value of about two hundred and fifty thousand Crowns worth of Merchandize, which consisted in Cloaths, yellow Brass, Quick-Silver, Gold coyn'd, and in Furrs: His whole Retinue was compos'd of Nine sorry *Muscovites*, of so indifferent a Mein, and so wretchedly clad, that one would have taken them for some of the Poor belonging to an Hospital. The Pretext of his coming, was, to deliver a Letter of Civility from the Great Duke, to the King of *Persia*, and to acquaint him, That the Czar intended, in a little time, to send an Ambassador Extraordinary to his Majesty. These Merchant-Ambassadors, are treated and consider'd, as all other Ambassadors are, without Distinction; their Merchandize passes for their Baggage; they are defray'd and lodg'd, and conducted as they come, and when they return, at the Expence of the Publick: But then in Return thereof, they are oblig'd to make Presents, not only to the King and his Ministers, but likewise where-ever they come, which amounts to little less than their Expences. The Master of the Ceremonies went, by the King's Orders, to receive this *Muscovite* Ambassador at the Head of Fifty Horsemen well clad, most of them belonging to the Court. The Provost of the *Armenians* of *Julfa* was also there, followed by seven or eight of the chief Merchants of his Nation: He was lodg'd in their Quarter, in a House fitted up on purpose: He was treated there Three Days by the King, and afterwards was order'd Sixty Abassis *per* Day for his Entertainment, which makes Eighteen Crowns of our Money.

CHAPTER XI

Captain of the Haram-*Gate Bastinado'd. Some young Noblemen got drunk, the King's Order thereupon. Another Conference about the Jewels. The Day for the Publick Entry of the* French *Envoy appointed. Petition of the Christian* Armenians. *The* French *Ambassador's Entry and Reception.*

ON the 14th, the King caused Two hundred Bastinado's to be given on the Backside of the Captain of the Gate of the *Haram*; This is that Part of the Royal Palace, where the Women are kept, and which the *Turks* call Seraglio, the Access whereof is forbid to all Mankind, except the Sovereign. This Captain, who was already in Years, a Man of Quality and Reputation, was us'd after this Manner, for having suffer'd some Footmen belonging to the Eunuchs, who have the guard thereof, to come so near as within Sight of the Third Gate, which is what no Man is suffer'd to do. The First Gate of the Seraglio, is guarded by the King's Porters; whoever has any Business at the Palace, and with the Persons of Quality, passeth it freely. The Second is guarded by the Captain of the Gate, with several Domesticks, and a number of Guards, and none but the Officers of the King's Houshold are permitted to pass it, unless they are expresly sent for. The Third is guarded by Eunuchs, and none must come within Sight of this: In Reality, one must be quite upon it to see it; for it is scituate in the corner of a Turning, contriv'd on purpose, that it may not be discover'd.

❡ On the same Day, the Prime Minister having acquainted the King, that some young Noblemen, being drunk, had caus'd some Disturbance near the Royal Palace; he immediately dispatch'd Orders to all the Soldiers and Officers, to rip open the Belly (on the Spot) of every Man they should find drunk in the Streets, excepting such as should have Permission to drink Wine, seal'd with the little Seal. And the King caus'd forthwith these Permissions to be delivered to all the Grandees, that were us'd to be his Companions in his Debauches.

❡ They say in *Persia*, open the Belly, as we say among us, to Hang, or cut off the Head, because the most common Kind of Punishment is to rip open the Belly; which is done by plunging a large Poniard into the Belly, on the Left Side, and drawing it round to the very Back; a Punishment that is not of so quick a Dispatch as is that of Beheading.

¶ On the 15th, having din'd at the Nazir's according to Custom, with several Persons of Quality, he sent for all the Jewels he had of mine, and having made me sit down near him, he said, *There is your Merchandize; if you will sell it, put a reasonable Value upon it; the whole that the King has set apart has been valued at a thousand and eighty-seven* Tomans *only, and even at that Rate you have been favoured: If you will part with it for Eleven hundred,* (which is about Fifty thousand Livers) *I will petition the King to take it at that Price: You shall kiss his Sacred Feet, you shall have a Royal Garment, a Horse, and a Passport to travel, and trade throughout the Empire, without paying either Customs or Duties: If not, take them away, but think well on the Resolution you shall take, for the thing deserves it: If you would follow my Advice, you would not waver in the giving it.* All the Company then spoke and told me, That I ought to please the King, and the Nazir, and that on other Occasions, I might insist upon a greater Gain. There must have been a great many of the like Speeches to move me. I made Answer, *That the Nazir having obliged me to give my Jewels at five and twenty* per Cent. *Profit more than what they cost me, by which I suffer'd already a great Loss, considering the Expence of so long a Journey, and having thereupon engaged the King's Word to me, I hoped it would be kept with me: That the King and the Nazir might dispose of me, and all that I had, as they pleas'd, but that I could not fall lower, than what was agreed upon.* The Nazier, who had only in view, with all these Gestures, to impose on those who were about him, and by their Means, on the Court, and particularly upon his Master, flew into a Passion at my Answer, so far as even to abuse me; He said, I was not worthy of the good Disposition he had for me, nor of the Kindness he intended me. But seeing, that in whatsoever Tone he spoke, it was the same thing, he bid me take all away; and at the same time fell a tearing the Memorials with a Spite, so apparent, so deceitful, and so well imitated, that I had all the Difficulty in the World to forbear laughing. I took back my Jewels, I put them into a Box, which I sent away, and then fell a thanking that Nobleman for his Favours, in the Application he had bestow'd upon my Business, and I told him several things, that were proper for those who heard us; after which he dismiss'd me.

¶ As I was going out, the *Mehemander Bachi*, who is the Introductor of the Ambassadors, enter'd. The Nazir told him, he had sent for him, to tell him the King's Pleasure, in reference to the Envoy of the *French* Company, which was, That he should, on the Eighteenth, about Nine a-Clock, go and receive him at the Place where he was without the Town, and conduct him to the House which had been prepar'd for him, taking along with him Fifty Horse, the Prevost of the *Armenians*, and seven or eight of the principal Merchants of the Nation.

¶ On the same Day, the Clergy of *Julfa*, that great Suburb of *Ispahan*, the Dwellingplace of all the Christian *Armenians*, and is on the other side of the River, to the South, went with the Patriarch at the Head of them, to present a Petition to the Chief Minister, that they might be discharg'd of the Taxes laid upon the Churches within that Place. They flatter'd themselves, that that Minister would give a favourable Answer to their Petition. But they were mistaken; for he told them, They must either pay the Taxes which had been put upon their Churches, or else pull them down. This Tax is Six thousand Crowns a-Year for Ten Churches. The present Vizier caus'd it to be laid two Years ago.

¶ On the 18th, the Envoy of the *French* Company made his Entry: His Retinue consisted in Twelve Guards, with their Captain, clad in a Livery, and Six Officers: That which set off the Train, was a good number of Footmen, People of the Country, but very well cloath'd. The Introductor of Ambassadors went and receiv'd him, attended by Twenty *Persian* Horse, the Prevost of *Julfa*, and the most considerable of the *Armenian* Merchants. All the *French* at *Ispahan*, and a great many other Strangers, accompany'd him in their Coaches, to the very House which had been prepar'd for him, where, for three Days, he was treated by the King's Officers. They serv'd up the Dinner after this Manner: There were spread before all the Company, Cloaths of Gold Brocard, and upon them, all along, there was Bread of three or four Sorts, very good, and well made; This done, they immediately brought eleven great Basons of that sort of Food call'd *Pilau*, which is Rice bak'd with Meat: There was of it, of all Colours, and of all sorts of Tastes, with Sugar, with the Juice of Pomgranates, the Juice of Citrons, and with Saffron: Each Dish weigh'd above Fourscore Pounds, and had alone been sufficient to satisfy the whole Assembly. The four first, had twelve Fowls in each; the four next had a Lamb in each; in the others there was only some Mutton: With these Basons, were serv'd up four Flat Kettles, so large and heavy, that it was necessary to help to unload those that brought them. One of them was full of Eggs made into a Pudding; another of Soop with Herbs; another was fill'd with Herbage and Hash'd Meat; and the last with fry'd Fish. All this being serv'd upon the Table, a Porringer was set before each Person, which was four times deeper than ours, fill'd with Sherbet of a tartish sweet Taste, and a Plate of Winter and Summer Sallets: After which, the Carvers began to serve all the Company out of each Dish, in *China* Plates. As for us *Frenchmen*, who were habituated to the Country of *Persia*, we eat heartily at this Feast, but the fresh Comers fed upon the Admiration of the Magnificence of this Service, which was all of fine Gold, and which (for certain) was worth above a Million. The Introductor of the Ambassadors would neither eat nor drink, and at every Instance that was made him thereto, he always answer'd, That as he was there only to take care that the Envoy should want for nothing, it was not decent for him to eat. After Dinner this Nobleman discoursed with me about my own Affairs, and after a pretty long Conversation, he told me, That with the Help of God, I should in the end have Satisfaction from the Court. He withdrew as soon as the Clerks of the Kitchin had carry'd away all the Plate, earnestly entreating the Envoy to let him know whatever he should have occasion for, that he might readily supply him therewith. He likewise presented to him a Mehemander, or Waiter, to attend him, that he gave him to him by the King's Order, that he might serve him in every thing he should command him.

CHAPTER XII

The Grand Vizier affronted by the King when drunk. Settlement of the Ambassadors Table during his Stay at Ispahan. *The King, in Drink, affronts the Grand Vizier worse than before. Contract of the* Dutch *for Silk consider'd, and their Abatement.*

ON the 21st, in the Night, the King being in a Debauch, and as drunk as it was possible to be, caus'd some Wine to be presented to the Grand Vizier, *Cheic-ali-can*: This Minister refus'd, as he had always done, at the Peril of his Fortune, and even of his Life. The King seeing his Obstinacy, bid the Cup-bearer fling the Wine in his Face: This was done as soon as said. The King getting up at the same time, went and stood close to this Minister, and looking at him with a jeering Air, told him; *Grand Visier, I can no longer bear, that thou shouldst here preserve thy Senses, while we are all drunk: A drunken Man, and a Man that does not drink, do not pass their Time very agreeably together; if thou wilt divert thy self with us, and let us have any Satisfaction with thee; thou must drink as much as we have done.* *Cheic-ali-can* hearing this Command, flung himself at the King's Feet. The Prince seeing he had a mind to excuse himself upon the Injunctions of their Religion, told him; *It is not with Wine that I pretend thou should'st make thy self drunk, drink some Coquenard.* This is an Infusion of the Juice of

Poppies, much more heady and intoxicating than Wine. The Minister here could make no Defence: He therefore drank several Cups thereof, which did his Business for him quickly: He flung himself on some Cushions, and the King fell a laughing to see him in that Condition, and for two Hours together, did nothing but make Game of him, with his Favourites, as drunk as himself. He then commanded one of them to carry a Cup of Wine to that Minister, imagining that he would drink it without knowing what it was. They rais'd him on his Seat, but he had no more Motion in him than a dead Body. The King, laughing, cry'd out to him; *Grand Vizier, there is what will bring thee to thy self.* This Minister being informed the next Day of the Indignities his Master had put upon him, and of the abominable Condition he had been forc'd to fling himself in, would see no-body, but kept retir'd all the Day, to digest his Confusion and Grief. The King, who knew it, sent him a Royal Garment, and his Commands, to come to the Palace according to Custom.

¶ The same Day, the Introductor of Ambassadors went to see the Envoy of the *French* Company, to offer him from the King, the usual Entertainment during his Stay at *Ispahan*; that is to say, all that is necessary for his Table, and Stable. This is what is done to all Ambassadors and Envoys, and it is at their Choice, to have their Subsistance either prepared in the King's Kitchin, or Raw and in Kind, or else the Value in Money. The Envoy thank'd the King for this Offer, as all the *Europeans* are us'd to do out of a Spirit of Generosity, according to the Practice of their Country. It was upon that Model, that the Envoy Regulated his Behaviour.

¶ On the 23d, the Nazir sent him on the King's Part, an Order to Receive of the King's Purveyors, at once or at several Times, as he himself should think fit the following Provisions.

> Sixty Quintals of *Rice.*
> Sixty Quintals of *Flower.*
> Twelve Quintals of *Butter.*
> Twenty *Sheep.*
> Two hundred *Fowls.*
> A Thousand *Eggs.*
> A Hundred and twenty Quintals of *Wood.*
> Sixty Quintals of *Barley.*
> Four hundred Sacks of *Chopp'd Straw.*

¶ They that have ever so little read the Relations of the Eastern Parts, know that chopp'd Straw, and Barley, are there the common Food for Horses, as Oats and Hay are in *Europe*; and also, that all Provisions are reckon'd by Weight, and not by Measure. The Envoy was obliged to accept of this Present, which was worth about an Hundred *Louis D'ors*. The Purveyors ask'd his People, if he had rather have the Value thereof in Money: But he had commanded them to take the Provisions in Kind, one Part whereof was given to the Capuchins.

¶ On the 24th, the Nazir sent me word by a Domestick, to come to him, and to bring along with me all the Jewels which he had given me back. I made as if I did not understand the Order: I went to his House; he was at the Palace with the King, from whence being return'd at Noon, he made me sit down pretty near him, and dine with him; He afterwards asked me, where was what he had given me back. I made answer, That they were at my Lodging. He turned himself, without saying a Word more to me, and fell a talking of other Affairs with Persons that were about him. A quarter of an Hour after, he turn'd to me in a negligent Manner, and as it were without Design, and fixing his Eyes upon mine, he ask'd me if I was return'd. I would not give him the Trouble of any farther Explication, but got up, and went in haste, and fetched all that I knew he had a mind to have. He receiv'd it, and after having left me above an Hour in Expectation, he bid me come the next Day, and he would think of me.

¶ On the 28th, being at Court, I was told, that the Grand Vizier had there receiv'd a greater Affront the Night before from the King, than all the rest. It was in his Wine, as usual. I have already taken notice that this Minister is quite white, and very venerable: He wears short Whiskers, and the Beard on his Cheeks, and Chin pretty long, because he makes Profession of a strict Observance of the *Mahometan* Religion, which teaches, That Decency so requires. But the Original *Persians* of *Georgia*, especially those who frequent the Court, and the Men of the Sword, on the contrary, wear the Beard of the Cheeks and Chin very short, and their Whiskers so long, that they may, for the most part, tuck them under their Ear. The King seeing his Minister only following another Mode, and the Fumes of the Wine disturbing his Brain, he immediately ordered his Beard to be shav'd after the Mode of the Court. The King's Barber was preparing to execute this odd Command, but the Grand Vizier whispered him, not to cut the Hair so near the Skin that it might be seen. The Barber was unhappy and weak enough to obey him. This cost him his Hand. The King caus'd it to be cut off immediately, because he had not exactly enough executed his Orders; nay, it had like even to have cost him his Life. The Prime Minister was struck to the very Heart at so gross an Affront. He was disorder'd, and could not govern his Passion, his

Patience, and Moderation were quite worn out; so that he went from the
King's Presence without asking Leave, as is the Custom, and retir'd
home, oppress'd with the sharpest Grief he was capable of feeling, as he
himself told his Friends.

¶ The King being come to himself the next Morning, and not seeing
that Minister attend at the usual Hour, judged presently what was the
Reason thereof: He remember'd the Injury he had done him: He there-
fore sent for him. But the Prime Minister had not as yet digested the
Bitterness of the Affront; He answer'd the Officer who brought him the
Message, and was a Man of Quality, thus; *It would be much better if the
King would send for my Head, than for my Person; not that I am weary of suffering,
but because the Affronts he offers to me reflect upon his Majesty himself, and dis-
honour him, and it is properly that Shame which grieves me, and even pierces my
Heart: His Glory, for which alone I am concern'd, engages me against my self,
and I even hate my self, because his Majesty abuses me, and that I am the Occasion,
that his Subjects, his Neighbours, and the Foreigners, who cannot fail to hear of the
continual Affronts he is loading me withal, will have less Veneration and Respect
for his Person, than I would have them have: These Regards, my Lord, have
render'd my Life a Burthen, and tedious to me, and if the King would be pleas'd
to send, and put an end to it, I would bless the Order, and the Moment.* All this
Discourse was carry'd back to the King, Word for Word. He weigh'd
the good Sense and the Truth thereof; and having sent a Second time for
this Minister, he reach'd his Hand out to him, and promis'd to make
Reparation for the Injuries he had done to his own Dignity, in affronting
his Person. The Minister improving this favourable Opportunity, flung
himself at the King's Feet, and his Heart being still full, told him, That
he was his Slave, and his Creature, and so entirely devoted to his Majesty,
that he could not, without the utmost Concern and Grief, see his Majesty
sully his own Glory, destroy his Health, and hazard his Life in the Excesses
of Wine, as he constantly did. He carry'd on the Discourse with so much
Force and Tenderness, that the King promis'd him, upon Oath, not to
drink any more, as he had done.

¶ On the first of August, the Agents of the Dutch Company prevail'd so
far, as to get it self Discharg'd of one half of the Silk, She was oblig'd by
Contract, to take of the King every Year. That my Reader may the better
know, in what this Contract consists, I shall in a few Words give a Relation
of the Establishment of this Company in *Persia*.

¶ They who have read the History of the last Centuries, know the great
Views, which the Illustrious Princes of *Orange* stir'd up in the *Hollanders*
to go to the *Indies*, the Chief whereof was to Fight the *Spaniards* at the

Spring head of their Power, thereby to take from them, those immense Riches, by the means of which they oppress'd the United Provinces, and sent Forces every Year against them. The Undertaking was Glorious, Wise, and of great Utility: It show'd plain enough, that Money was the plain Nerve of War; for as soon as *Spain* saw it self assaulted in those Country's, where she neither entertained Armies nor Fleets, nor suspected she should ever be attack'd, she was confounded, and her Strength impair'd. The great Advantages that accrue from the Commerce in the *Indies*, engaged the *Hollanders* very Strongly in this Enterprize. This People who are Naturally Cunning, and Understanding, born to Trade, and have the most Favourable Dispositions for Trafick, considering the mighty Profits they would reap from the *Indies*, if they settl'd there, either by Contract, or Conquest, employ'd all its Care, and exerted its utmost Efforts therein. One may say, that they have succeeded even beyond their own Expectation; for in all likelyhood, they did not imagine at first, nor indeed for several Years, they should ever become the Masters of what is most exquisite in the *East-Indies*. This was the Reason, that they did not at first Form a Company. They let particular Persons who have a mind to send Ships thither, act the best they could; but when they became thoroughly acquainted with the Commerce of the Country, and that they saw themselves take Root in the *Indies*, they united themselves, and form'd that Body of associated Merchants, which was call'd the *East-India* Company. It settled it self in *Persia*, in the Year 1623, and for many Years, its Trade was for the most Part, only a Trucking or Barter, with the King. The Company unladed its Ships into the King's Magazines, who took the greatest Part of their Merchandize, and gave them in Payment Goods of the Country, as amongst other Things, Wool, Tapestry's, Silks, and Brocards. This interchanging became very Burthensome to the *Hollanders*. Their Merchandize was continually falling in its Price, while the King's was always rising. They would put upon him Things that were not good, and most commonly the best Part of what they had was such. In fine, as every Year they underwent some new Oppression, they sent in the Year 1652, one of their Counsellors of the *Indies*, whose Name was *Cuneus*, Embassador into *Persia*, with fine Presents for the King, and for the Ministers. The Grand Vizier had among other Things, eleven Hundred Ducats of Gold, several Rarities, and variety of *European* Stuffs. Notwithstanding which, this Embassador made a disadvantageous Treaty for his Company. It contain'd; That the *Hollanders* should every Year Import to the value of a Million in Merchandize free of all Duties, to what Part of the Kingdom they had a Mind, but if they brought more, they should for the Overplus, Pay the usual Duties, and that in Consideration hereof, they should be obliged to take of the King every Year, six Hundred Bails of Raw Silk, each Bail to weigh two Hundred Pounds, at four and twenty Tomans, which amount to about eleven Hundred Livers per Bail, and the whole to about six Hundred and fifty Thousand Livers. This is the Treaty of Commerce, that is between the King of *Persia*, and the *Holland* Company; a Treaty which this Company has always complain'd of, as being Detrimental and Burthensome, because the Silk they receive, is not worth upon the Place, one half of what they Pay for it. On their Side they return the like usage to the *Persians* as much as lies in their Power, Importing frequently above two Millions of Merchandize, which they pass off to be worth but one. They gain the Officers by dint of Presents, to let Cloves pass for Pepper, fine Cloth go for Course, two Bails be reckon'd but one. This is no hard matter in *Persia*, where Knavery is a common Distemper. The Company sent in the Year 1666 another Embassador into *Persia*, whose Name was *Lairesse*. He had no other Commission than to assure the King of the Respects of the Company, to desire the continuation of his Favour, and to Complain of the Governour of the Province of *Persia*, who acted very unfairly with their Agents, and Carriers. The General of *Batavia* Order'd the Director who was at *Bander-Abassi* to draw up the Embassadors Instructions. This was done, the Presents he made to the King, and to the Ministers, were worth about ten Thousand Crowns. They consisted of two Eliphants, of rare Birds, of Cloaths, Brocards, *China*-Ware, of Jewels, of Cabinets of *Japan*, and of Gold Coyn'd a little of each sort. This Embassador was received and treated perfectly well, and dispatch'd with all possible Expedition.

¶ The late *King*, who was then living, could not conceive that a Company of Merchants would send him an Ambassador with such considerable Presents, without having some particular Design. He inform'd himself several times, what the Ambassador's Demands were, and for what he was come. When he found that in Reality it was only to notify the Respect and Gratitude of his Masters; that generous Prince was so well pleas'd therewith, that if the Ambassador had had all the Wit and Assurance, that such an Employment requires, he might, in that lucky Moment, have obtain'd very considerable Advantages for his Masters. He was quickly dispatch'd, and with a great deal of Honour, and besides the usual Presents of Garments and Stuffs, had that of a Horse, and a Sword set with *Turkish* Stones, to the Value of Four hundred Pistoles.

¶ To return now to the Subject of this Digression, the *Hollanders* of *Persia*, considering, in the Year 1673, that no Ships had come to them for the last two Years, by reason of the War, and apprehending likewise, that possibly there might none come this neither, were of opinion, that they ought not to clogg themselves with so much Silk, but on the contrary, keep all the Ready Money they could. They therefore represented to the Ministers, that they could not take any Silk this Year; and that indeed they were not oblig'd to it, because the Purport of the Treaty was, That they should take Six hundred Bales, against a Million of Merchandize, which they were to bring thither Custom-free: That it was therefore self-evident, that as they had receiv'd no Merchandize, they ought not to take any Silk. They moreover said, That they could not do it, not having wherewith to pay for it. After great Debates upon the Matter, it was agreed, they should take but Three hundred Bales.

CHAPTER XIII

Civilities shown the Author in his Illness. Damage done by an Earthquake. Portugueze *Duties. The Envoy delivers a Petition in order to be dismissed. The Chief of the* Armenians *turns Renagade; the Consequences dreaded. Their Application thereupon to the Pope.*

THE 7th, I being fallen sick, the Nazir did me the Honour to send his Secretary to visit me; who told me very civilly from him, That if I desired to have any of the King's Physicians come to me, he would send me which of them I pleas'd: He farther added, That his Master had particularly charg'd him to tell me, to send to his House for whatsoever I had occasion for.

¶ The Days following, I had the Honour to be visited by several Persons of Distinction, and among the rest, by one of the Brothers of the High Steward, by that of the Governor of *Candahar*, and by the Chief of the Arsenal of *Ispahan*. This last, seeing I drank Sallow-Water, sent me a large Bottle thereof, which held about twenty Pints.

¶ On the 11th, there arriv'd two Expresses, one upon the Heels of the other, with bad News, to-wit, That two thirds of *Metched*, the Capital of the *Corasson*, which is the *Choromithrene*; one half of *Nichapour*, another great Town of the same Province, and a little Town near *Nichapour*, had been over-thrown by an Earthquake. That which most sensibly touched the *Persians*, and particularly the Devout Part of them, was the Damage that had happened to the Mosque of *Metched*, in which is the Tomb of *Iman Reza*, and is a Magnificent Mosque, and Famous throughout all the *East*. The Dome thereof was quite broke down, but the rest of the

Edifice remain'd as was said, pretty entire. The King immediately sent Post, a Person of Quality, to take a more particular Account of the Damage; and soon after, he dispatch'd two other Lords, with his Orders to the Officers of the Province, in so great a Calamity.

❡ On the 15th, the Introductor of Ambassadors, and the Receiver of the Presents that are made to the King, came to the Lodgings of the Envoy of the *French* Company. The First, to be thoroughly inform'd, by the Order of the Chief Minister, of the Subject of his coming, and of the Demands he was charged with. The Second, to see the Presents he had brought for the King, examine them, and take an Inventory thereof. The Receiver of the Presents is called *Peskis Nuviez.*

❡ On the 16th, arrived an Envoy from the Bashaw of *Basra*, under the Title of *Salem Chaoux*, that is to say, Herald of Peace, or to translate it more exactly, Usher of Peace; with an *Arabian* of Quality, named *Mirgahez*, which is to say, according to the Sense of the Word, Prince of the Sanctifyd. That Name is given to the Chiefs of those great Caravans of Pilgrims, who go to *Mecca*, a Town in the Stony *Arabia*, which, with the Territories round about it, to the distance of twenty Leagues, makes the Holy Land of the *Mahometans*. The Commission of these Envoys was, to intreat the King to repeal the Prohibition he had publish'd against any body's going to *Mecca* by the way of *Basra*. It was upon the account of the Vexations and Oppressions with which the *Arabians* loaded the *Persian* Pilgrims on that Road. The Bashaw of *Basra*, and this *Mirgahaz*, suffer'd very much by this Prohibition; the Duties which the Pilgrims are us'd to pay being very great, and the Number of Pilgrims amounting sometimes to Ten thousand Persons in a Year. The Bashaw's Letters imported, That he had caused those who had molested the *Persians*, to be chastised after an exemplary Manner; and that he had given such Orders for their good Treatment for the Time to come, that they would be thoroughly satisfy'd therewith. *Mirgahez* came himself to confirm these Assurances, to enroll the Pilgrims, and to treat with them concerning all the Duties they should pay, from *Basra* to *Mecca*, both going and returning. Indeed, as soon as he had obtain'd his Request, he caus'd a great Tent to be set up in the old Market-place of the City, and had a Proclamation made, That all Persons of either Sex, who had a mind to go that Pilgrimage, should come and be enroll'd, and that he would agree with each of them at a very honourable Price.

❡ On the 18th, finding my self in good Health, God be thanked, I got on Horseback, and went to thank the Nazir for his Goodness towards me. I had had Seven Fits of the Ague, Three very violent ones, and Four gentle enough. I made use of no other Medicines than two gentle Purges, and two Remedies: I was ty'd up to so strict a Diet, that in four and twenty Hours, I took only three or four Ounces of boil'd Rice, in some Almond Milk. They let me drink what I pleas'd, and I drank prodigiously. My Drink was Barley-Water, and Sallow-Water mixt together.

¶ I ascrib'd my Cure to the Sallow-Water, for it is mighty refreshing, and very agreeable to drink; It is call'd *Arac-bid*: *Bid* signifies a Sallow, and *Arac* signifies a Liquor extracted by an Alembic; and it is the Name they commonly give to Brandy, and to all other Extracts. In *Persia* they give this Sallow-Water to drink in all Fevers, either alone or mix'd with common Water. The *Europeans*, skill'd in Physick, who know the Temperature of that Country, say, That it is a most excellent Remedy to cure them.

¶ About this time, News was brought of the Arrival of the *Portuguese* in the *Persian* Gulph, with a Fleet, but which consisted only of small Ships. They gave out they were come to besiege *Mascate*, a Town in *Arabia*, near *Ormus*, with which they have been a long time at War, which one may say is on both sides carry'd on, as between the *Turks* and the *Moors*; but their Fleet was far short of being able to undertake such a Siege. All they did, was to cruise up and down, and intercept the Barks, and other small Vessels of the *Arabians*, of which 'tis said, they took to the Value of Forty thousand Livres. They went afterwards to the Port of *Congo*, where they had several Contests with the *Persians* about some *Arabian* Ships which were in that Port: They there receiv'd the Present which is commonly made them every Year, for the Right they have to one half of the Customs of that Port. They went from thence to *Bahrim*, a celebrated Island in the Gulph of *Persia* for the Pearl-Fishery. This Fishery was formerly in the Hands of the *Portuguese*, who, on that Account, have ancient Pretentions on all those who fish there. They got a small Present there, and afterwards resum'd their Course to *Goa*. A Rumour was spread about, that they would also go to *Basra*, where they have the like Pretentions, and of as old a Date, but they did not do it: They knew very well, that, to get any thing from thence, a great deal of Courage would be requisite, and a greater Strength than they had.

¶ The *Portuguese* have been for some hundred Years the Masters of almost all the *Indies*. They did not only possess all that is possess'd by the several People of *Europe*, who, for the Security of their Commerce have made Conquests in those vast Countries; but also many Islands, and several Sea-Coasts, a great many Towns, and a great many Forts, which have been re-taken by the ancient Possessors. The Islands of *Ormus*, of *Kichmiche*, of *Areque*, and of *Bakrin*. The *Persian* Coast of the Gulph, the

Ports and Fortresses of *Abas*, and of *Congo* upon that Coast, are what they once were Masters of, and what they have lost: And notwithstanding they had no other Right over them, than that of Conquest, and Possession, yet they maintain still that Right, and make it good upon Occasion. It is between the 10th and 25th Years of the last Century, that they lost the Isles and Ports we last mention'd; and as they for a long time after kept *Mascate*, a Maratime Town of *Arabia* forty Leagues from *Ormus* and that to preserve the same, they stood in great need of a Trade with *Persia*, they made an Agreement with the King in the Year 1625, by which they restor'd all that they still kept on the Coast of his Kingdom, upon Condition to have the Right of the Pearl-Fishery at *Bahrin*, and one half of the Customs of *Bandor-Congo*, which is a Port three Days Journey from *Ormus*. The *Persians*, in granting such advantageous Conditions to the *Portuguese*, managed them Politickly, that they might draw Succours from them when Need should require, against the *English* and *Dutch*, if they should chance to fall out among themselves. This Agreement was kept up to, as long as the *Portugueze* preserv'd *Mascate*; but as soon as they had lost it, which happen'd in the Year 1649, the *Persians* kept their Promise with them no longer. They deprived them of almost all their Right; and gave them only what they pleas'd themselves, which often did not amount to Five thousand Crowns a Year, for above Sixty thousand which they ought to have had. In fine, these last Years, the Vice-Roy of *Goa* having sent an Ambassador to the Court of *Persia*, it was agreed, that Fifteen thousand Crowns *per Annum*, should be paid to the *Portuguese* in the Port of *Congo*, and in consideration of that yearly Sum, they should renounce all their Pretentions on the Coast of *Persia*. However, as the Article of the Pearl Fishery is not mention'd in that Treaty, the *Portuguese* still pretend to be Lords thereof, and that those who fish there, are obliged to take their Passports, for which they make them pay about a Pistole for each, but very few Barks take them. It is computed that there are about a thousand of them employ'd in this Fishery.

¶ On the 20th, the Envoy of the *French* Company presented a Petition to the Divan, the Tenor of which was as follows.

GOD—

(a) *The Petition of the most humble of your Servants* (b) *the Envoy of the General Chamber of the* French *in the* East-Indies.

¶ ' (c) He most humbly entreats, with all the Earnestness imaginable,
' that Consideration may be had of the long time that has elaps'd since
' his Arrival within the (d) Seat of the Monarchy, and that a favourable

' Regard may be had thereto. The Ardent Desire of this humble Servant,
' is, that he may be admitted to Audience, that he may have the Honour
' and Glory of kissing the Feet of the most Noble Lieutenant of the
' (e) Prophets, that he may make known the Subject of his coming, and
' that he may afterwards be dismiss'd. The proper (f) Time to go from
' *Persia* to the *Indies* by Sea, approaches. The Ships that brought the
' Petitioner to the (g) Holy Port *Abas*, remain there useless: They lose
' a great deal in waiting for him: So that the sooner he is dispatched, the
' better will it be for his Affairs, and the greater will be his Master's
' Gains thereby. This is the Petition, that his urgent Business has obliged
' him to present. (h) your Commands are above all.'

EXPLANATION.

¶ (a) IT is the Custom in *Persia* of treating by Petition with the King, and
with the Great Ministers. These Petitions are called *Arzé*, or *Arizé*, which
is to say, *Proposition*.

¶ (b) I have observ'd elsewhere, that the Oriental People give the Title
of Ambassador to every Person that is sent from one Sovereign to another,
tho' his Commission were only to deliver a Letter, and the Reason thereof
is, in my Opinion, to make the People believe, that their King is reverenc'd
throughout the Universe, and that from all Parts, Homage is pay'd him,
by Ambassadors and Presents.

¶ (c) In the *Persian* Language, they speak always in the Third Person,
when they will speak civilly, and instead of the Pronoun Relative, they
use Terms of Submission, such as *Bendé*, which is to say, Servant, Slave;
and *Douagou*, that is to say, a Prayer, to signify one who is always praying
for you.

¶ (d) That is to say, at *Ispahan*; and the *Persians* give this Epithet to all
the Cities where the Kings make their Residence.

¶ (e) The *Persians* hold, that it is the Will of God, that the World be
govern'd by Prophets, or by their Lieutenants, or Vicars, in their Absence;
and it is in this Sense that their Kings stile themselves by the way of
Honour, Lieutenants, or Vicars of *Mahamed*, of *Aly*, and of the Prophets
in general.

¶ (f) *Mausson* is the *Persian* Word, which I have translated, the time
proper to go from *Persia* to the *Indies* by Sea: It is the Word that the
Oriental People make use of to signifie the Seasons proper to navigate
from one Place to another.

¶ (g) Those who have read the Topography of the *Indies*, know that the
Winds blow there constantly from certain Points for six Months together:

Thus, from *October* to *May*, for Example, they blow favourably for those who have a mind to go to the *Eastern* Coast of the *Indies*; but during the other Months they are contrary to them.

¶ (*h*) All the Requests, Petitions, and Memorials that are presented in *Persia*, are always concluded with these Words *Amrala*, the Sense whereof as the *Persians* give it, is, the Answer you shall make to my Petition, shall regulate my Desires.

¶ The 24th prov'd a Day of Affliction to all the Christians at *Ispahani*, more especialy to the *Armenians*, by the Revolt of their Head, or Governour, whose Name was *Aga Piri Caleu ar*, that is to say Prevost of that great Suburb of *Ispahan* where they Inhabit. He was a sort of half Scholar, who having read *Avicénne* and other *Arabian* Philosophers, and some of the *Mahometan* Controvertists, had not been able to resolve their Objections, so that it was blindness of Understanding, and the Spirit of Error that seduc'd him, rather than the love of the World or Voluptuousness. His Friend said that it was the *Opprobium of Jesus-Christ*, according to the Scripture's Language, that is to say, the Contempt and Repulses annex'd to the Profession of Christianity within the *Mahometan* Dominions. A Fortnight before his Apostacy, he went to the Nazir: and having intreated him to hear him privately; he Presented him with a Purse of Six hundred Ducats of Gold, and told him, that having been a long time a *Mahometan* in his Mind and Heart, he was desirous of making a publick Profession of *Mahometanism*; but as he had reason to dread the Aversion of his whole Nation, and the despair of his Family, if he abjur'd their Religion of his own meer Motion, as also that the Factors he had in *Europe* with a great deal of Goods, should take Occasion therefrom, to keep them, and never return; he thought it necessary, and desir'd with all his Heart, that the King would command him to turn *Mahometan*, to the end that his change might pass for Violence. Hereupon the Nazir Embrac'd him, and promised him every thing. This is what his nearest Relations have told me; be that as it will, his change happened after this Manner. He had a Year before made the King a fine Present of Fruits, for which he had sent him a Royal Garment Eight Days ago, and when he went Clad in this Habit, (being attended out of Honour, by the most considerable Persons of his Nation) as is the Custom to Thank the King for that Favour, the King Order'd him to draw near, and told him; *Aga Peri*, I understand thou hast read our Books of Learning, and Religion. How comes it to pass that knowing the Truth as thou now dost, thou dost not become a *Mahometan*; He stooped his Head with his Face towards the King; Then the first Minister came up to him, and said to him with a loud Voice, The King commands you to turn *Mahometan*: You must please him. This was the Signal this prefidious Wretch waited for. He boldly Answered and without the least concern: The King's Will be done; I declare my self a *Mahometan*. Upon this he was immediately conducted to the Feet of the Prince, and after the three customary Prostrations, They made him pronounce aloud the Confession of the *Mahometan* Faith. The King afterwards bid the great Pontif, who was there present, to make him *Sunnet*, which means to Circumcise him; and for Conclusion, he commanded the Nazir to order him a Royal Garment, of that sort which is given to Governours of Provinces, with a Horse, and the Trappings set with precious Stones.

¶ The Advantages of the Mind, and the Benefits of Fortune, with which God had favoured this unhappy Apostate, render'd his Desertion still the more Criminal; for he is one of the richest Merchants of the Country, being worth above two Millions of Livers, without having either Children or Brothers. The *Mahometans* triumph'd in the Conquest of him, saying that his Conversion could not be attributed to any human Motive, nor to Ignorance, but to the mighty work of Truth alone. As for his part, he would fain have made his Relations believe, that the King had threatned him with Death if he did not abjure, but there is nothing more false, and indeed no body gave Credit to his mean Excuses.

¶ All the *Armenians*, the Clergy, and the Patriarch who were then at *Ispahan*, were in a great Consternation at this unfortunate accident. They feared least some Violence should be offer'd to them, which might carry off the weak ones of the Flock; but Thanks be to God none was offer'd to them. The first Minister sent for them, and told them, that the King had a great Zeal for their Conversion, and that for his Part, he should esteem it the greatest happiness of his Life, if during the Time of his Ministry, they would embrace the true Religion. They trembling made Answer, that his Majesty having a World of *Mahometan* Slaves, his Goodness might permit to live in the Religion of the Prophet *Jesus Christ* the humblest of his Slaves, and let them have their Churches, where they did nothing oftener, and with more Fervour, than Pray to God for his Majesty's Life, and that of his Ministers. They likewise insinuated that their Factors who were gone to *Europe*, would not return, which would be the Loss of immense Riches to the State; moreover that the Christian Princes would not suffer them to Traffick in their Dominions any longer. This said, no further urgences were made to them on that account.

¶ The *Missionaries* being inform'd of all these Proceedings, insinuated to the Patriarch, that he ought to implore the Assistance of the Christian

Princes in Favour of his Nation, to which he lent an Ear. I was asked my advice. I would not dishearten him in the hopes he had on that Side. I contented my self with telling those who enter'd into that Design; that they ought to have a special regard to the Consequences of their Deputation, in case it should come to be known, whether by the Interception of their Letters, by the treachery of some false Brother, or indeed by any good Offices the Christian Princes might endeavour to do them with the King of *Persia*, either by Letters, or by Ambassadors, which might even do them more Prejudice than Service. The *Missionaries* caus'd the Envoy of the *French* Company to signify to the *Armenians*, that if the Pope desired the King of *France* to protect them, he would not fail to do it: So that the main Matter was to procure the Pope's Recommendation; but the Patriarch was given to understand, that to obtain this, it was requisite he should acknowledge the Pope's Soveraign Authority, and submit himself thereto. To which the Patriarch made answer, that if that were all that was wanting to save his Nation from *Mahometism*, he would make no Scruple to Submit himself thereto. After several Conferences, it was resolved that the Patriarch should write to the Pope, to the Congregation, *de propaganda Fide*, to the King of *France*, and to the Father Confessor, all which was executed some few Days after.

¶ The Patriarchs Letters were very urgent, and moving. He therein set forth in very plain terms, that he acknowledg'd the Pope's Monarchy, and submitted his Person, and his Flock, to the Authority of the *Roman* Church; but begg'd in the Name of God, that speedy and effectual Succours might be procur'd him. The Deputation procur'd nothing for the *Armenians*; for the *Augustins*, and the *Carms*, being jealous and provok'd, that they had no Share therein, writ to *Rome*, that they could perceive nothing but human Motives in all this Contrivance. The great Merchants of the Place having learn'd all that had pass'd, were very much incens'd thereat, fearing least the Court coming to be inform'd thereof, it should revenge it self upon them. In Reality they have reason to dread every Thing under the Ministry of the Grand Vizier *Cheic-Alican*; for he is an exasperated *Mahometan*, who mortally hates the Christian Religion: Nay, he looks upon the Country to be polluted, and in a State of Impurity by the Residence of the Christians there, for which Reason he would willingly drive out of it all the Christian Inhabitants, without excepting even the Strangers.

¶ The principal Merchants of *Julfa* laid hold of this Occasion to make pressing Instances to their Patriarch, that he would labour in the Reformation of the Clergy, and more especially in restraining the loose Manners,

and dissolute Life of the Nuns, whose enormous Irregularities were become notoriously Publick and Scandalous, for they were not contented
to Prostitute themselves, but made it their Business to corrupt others, and
to carry on the most infamous Intrigues. The Disorder was found to be
too General, and too deeply Rooted, to admit of a Remedy; for which
Reason, the Nuns were sent home to their Parents, and the Monastry
was secularis'd. It had been founded sixty Years. The *Carms* assur'd me,
that they had drawn the Plan thereof, and regulated its Constitutions.

CHAPTER XIV

*The Author concludes his Bargain with the Nazir about the Jewels. His Reasons for dwelling so
long upon the Subject of them.*

ON the 25th, I at last concluded my Affair, (thanks be to God) with
the Nazir. The chief of the *Goldsmiths* settl'd the Bargain. I shall
not say any Thing of the Deceipts, Tricks, Wiles, Disputes, Threats
and Promises, with which I was plagu'd for ten Days, and particularly
on this, to make me lower the Price of that little the King had a mind to
have. I was so weary of all the indirect Means the Nazir made use of to
compass his Ends, that I was even asham'd of 'em for his own sake, and
often doubted whether he counterfeited or acted seriously. I at last told
him, that rather than see him spend his Spirits in Clamours, Transports,
and Anger at me, I begg'd he would give me back my Jewels. What will
you do with them, said he hastily again? I can easily hinder you from
selling any of them, or from carrying them to the *Indies*. I made Answer,
that I fear'd nothing like that from his Equity. What provok'd him the
most, as he said, was, that I kept firm to my first Agreement, without the
least Abatement. He had put himself into so violent Passion, an Hour
before we concluded, that one would have thought he was going to devour
me, and indeed I should have dreaded some bad Consequences from so
vehement an Indignation, if I had not been well acquainted with the
Persians' manner of acting on the like Occasions.

¶ What I had most difficultly to bear, was the Reproaches of the Courtiers
who were there present, who imagining, that according to the Practice
of the Oriental Merchants, I had not spoken the Truth at first, found it
very strange, I should stick so stifly to my first Word; some of them ascrib'd it to my first Obstinacy, and others to an over-greediness of
excessive Gain. The Nazir finding he could not prevail upon me by any

means whatever, made a shew as if he would give me all back again. He sent for my Things, and deliver'd them to me. As I was receiving them, he was sent for to the King, He went away, Whispering something to the chief of the *Goldsmiths*. This Man, who, as I have already observ'd, was an honest good old Man, taking me into a Chamber apart, said to me, it is time to put an end to this Affair; I am my self weary of these extravagant Feints. Yield up something of your Right, how just soever it may be, and do not push the Nazir to an extremity. Consider that it is in his Power to make you sell more of your Jewels. If your largest pieces are left you, whether will you carry them? What other King besides ours, can buy them of you? Believe me, and let me terminate the Difference, by dividing it betwixt you. You must have according to your Account, about seventeen hundred Tomans: The Nazir will give you but twelve hundred. Now I will conclude the Bargain at fifteen hundred (this is about seven thousand Pistols). I had so great a mind to make an end, that I was ravish'd with the Proposition; but it was requisite to contain my self, and to seem not to be pleas'd. I answer'd the chief of the *Goldsmith's* with my Thanks, for the Pains he took for my Interest; but told him the Nazir had very bad ways with him, suffering himself to be transported to that Degree, as to call me Names. Take no notice of that, said he, with an Air of Rejection and Contempt, *Poc y edy*, that is to say, fairly translating those Words, he has eaten a Sirreverence, and that signifies, that one has spoken very ill. The Action, and Answer of that Lord, gave me a great mind to Laugh. I reply'd, that what he was for abating, was one half of the Profit I had been promis'd, and that the other would go in Duties, five *per Cent* to the Treasury when I receiv'd the Money, two *per Cent* to himself for his due, and what must be given to the Nazir, which would amount to above two *per Cent*. Hereupon the chief of the *Goldsmiths* made answer, that I should be exempted from the five *per Cent*, so that in fine, after some Repartees on both sides, I yielded.

¶ In an hours time the Nazir return'd. The chief of the *Goldsmiths* began to intreat him aloud, that he would rise to a reasonable Price, and sacrifice a thousand Pistols in Consideration of the Pains I had taken, which deserv'd a great deal more. The Nazir, who still play'd the counterfeit Part, flew into a Passion at him, and ask'd him, if he would insure my Jewels to be worth that, and why, having valu'd them but at fifty thousand Livres, he now bid him give me seventy Thousand. I have apprais'd the Merchandize, said the chief of the *Goldsmiths* according to the Rate it bears at this present in the City, and not according to its true Value. The decay of Commerce since the Death of the late King, has lower'd the

Value of Jewels one half. I acted on the foot of that Diminution, without having any regard to the Beauty, the Choice, or rare Collection, and well sorting together of the Stones, all which I leave to your own Consideration. There were some few Words more on both sides, concerning the Present which I pretended to from the King. At last the chief of the *Goldsmiths* took me by the Hand, and looking at the high Steward, told him; I give your word to *Aga Chardin* for fifteen hundred Tomans, with a Royal Garment, (it has been often observ'd that it is so they call those Habits which the King gives) and a Horse, which Things he accepts as a full and just payment for the Jewels which the King takes of him.

¶ The Nazir immediately caus'd two Pieces of eighteen Sous each to be given me by the way of Earnest, and beckoning to me to come near him, he told me with a chearful and serene Countenance, as different from that he put on before, as White is from Black, as the saying is; all ground of Contestation is now remov'd. We will for the future live in an open and undisguis'd Friendship; I was oblig'd to act as I did with you, for the King's Advantage, whose Wealth I have the Honour to manage. If I acted otherwise, I should rob him of the Bread I eat. Besides, I have a Head to loose: But I love you, and you shall be sensible thereof hereafter. Having spoken to me in this obliging Manner, he ask'd me, whether I would have an Order upon the Farmer-General of the Customs of the Gulph of *Persia*. *You will reap great Advantage thereby*, says he, *since you design for the* Indies, *for this Money shall be all carry'd to* Bander Abassi *and you will have nothing to do but to put it on Shipboard*. I had already reflected on the Assignment I was to ask: Indeed it would have been very advantageous at *Bander Abassi*; but I apprehended that when I should be there at the distance of Fifty Days Journey from the Court, I might meet with some Cavils, or Extortions, either to retard the Payment of the Money, or else to procure a Present. I therefore desired my Assignment might be made upon the *Hollanders*, which the Nazir presently granted without Reply; for which I thought my self very much obliged to him. I went away from him pretty late, very well satisfy'd with my Success, and praising God, that I had not been so unhappy, as most People thought I should be. The Nazir said to me as I went out, That notwithstanding we had bargain'd, he would have me come to him every Day, especially about Dinner-time.

¶ Perhaps I may have been tedious in relating so at length my Negotiation with the Nazir; but I chose to do it, because Narratives of this Kind, are better to inform the Intelligent, of the Genius of the Country, than the most exact Descriptions that can be given thereof. The Procedure of all the Oriental States is full as sordid and niggardly; nay, I have seen a great deal worse at the Court of the Great Mogul, altho it be, as one may say, the Center of all the Riches of the World.

CHAPTER XV

Marriage of the Nazir's eldest Son. Governor of a Province brought up Prisoner to Town. An Order deliver'd to the Author, for his Money; poor Piece of Roguery of the Nazir's.

ON the 26th, the Nazir began to solemnize the Wedding of his eldest Son, (who was first Steward) with a Daughter of *Divanbeghi*, or President of the Divan, which is one of the greatest Places in the Kingdom, his Name was *Mahamed-Hassen*; he was a Man very greedy of Wealth, and a great Tyrant. He was a great Plague to the Christians, Jews, and Gentiles, that had to deal with him, and there was not that Right, however clear and well-founded, that he would not oppress for Money. As for the rest, he had a great deal of Wit, and Fire, and was very handsome in his Person.

¶ The Wedding lasted Fourteen Days. The Three first, the Parents only, were treated: Several Lords of the Court were treated on the Fourth: The King's Favourites on the Fifth, and the Generals of the Army on the Sixth: The Pontiffs, and the most considerable of the Clergy on the Seventh. The first Minister was treated on the Eighth, and the King, the next Day after. The Tenth, was for the Chancellor, and the Secretaries of State. The Eleventh, for the principal Men of Letters. And on the three last Days, other Persons of Note were invited; so that there was not any Person of Consideration, either at Court or in the City, who was not at the Wedding. It is said to have cost the Nazir Four hundred thousand Livres, the greatest part in Presents to the Guests. Those he made to the King, were worth Twenty thousand Crowns. That very same Day he had the Goodness to think of me; he sent me a Present of Flowers, Sweetmeats, and Fruits, the finest that ever I saw.

¶ On the 31st, *Zael Can*, Governour of the City, and Province of *Candahar*, was brought to *Ispahan*; he was accus'd of having been an Accomplice in the Robbery of a Caravan, which was going to the *Indies*, and was worth several Millions. He was deliver'd up to the Kelonter, or Prevost of the Town, who is, as it were, the Lord Chief Justice for Civil Matters. The Prisoner had only one Servant; He himself was in the Carcan, which in *Persia* is made of three Pieces of Wood square, put in a Triangular

Manner, one Piece whereof is twice as long as the other two; the Criminal's Neck is enclos'd in the Triangle, having his Hand at the extream end of the longest Piece, in a Semi-Circle of Wood that was nail'd thereto.

¶ On the 1st of *September*, the Nazir delivered to me an Order for my Ready-Money, upon the Hollanders, which was compris'd in these Terms.

GOD.

¶ ' THE Command of the King of the World, directed to his Guests of
' the *European* Nation, bearing an Injunction to them, to pay upon Ac-
' count, and upon the so much less of the Silks, which have been sold and
' deliver'd to them, (*a*) in the Year of the Hog, the Sum of Fifteen hundred
' Tomans, (*b*) Money of *Tauris*, to the Lords *Chardin*, and *Raisin*, Mer-
' chants of *Europe*, the Flower of Merchants, and of the *Europeans*, in
' Payment for Jewels and Precious Stones, endors'd on the back of this
' Sublime Command. These Jewels and Precious Stones, having been
' presented by the Intermediation of the most High, and most Excellent,
' the Seer of the King's House, to his Majesty, whose Looks have the
' Virtue of Chymistry, he was pleas'd to like them, and has commanded
' by a sublime and absolute Order, that they should be bought. In Execu-
' tion therefore of this Holy Command, the Flower of Nobility, the
' Favourite of his most High Majesty, the Head of the Goldsmiths, was
' commanded to make an Estimate of these Jewels and Precious Stones,
' with the Advice of the best Jewellers, and the most skilful in the Royal
' City of *Ispahan*. They have accordingly apprais'd them at Eleven hundred
' Eighty-six Tomans, and Twenty-eight Abassis; but as the said Aga's,
' *Chardin* and *Raisin*, were not satisfy'd with this Valuation, and rejected
' it, making it appear, that upon the foot of the Prime Cost, and an honest
' Profit, they could not afford the Jewels for less than Fifteen hundred
' Tomans; It has been determin'd, by vertue of an Order from the most
' High King to that purpose, that without having Regard to the Valua-
' tion of the Jewellers, that Sum should be paid to the Sellers, to the End
' they might be fully satisfy'd. It has been since ordain'd, that these
' Jewels and Precious Stones should be carry'd to the Royal Treasury,
' and deliver'd to the High and Majestick Lord, Sublime and Honourable
' beyond all Comparison, accomplish'd in the Duties of Friendship, the
' Favourite of the most Great King, the Prop of the most Glorious Throne
' of the Earth, Pilgrim of the Noble and Sacred (*c*) Holy Places, the
' (*d*) Chief and Superintendant of the (*e*) Palace of the Women of the
' most High, and most Excellent Monarch, to the End he may receive

' them, and be answerable for the same, according to the Endorsement
' of this present Order. It ought to be known, that all this has been
' executed very exactly, and that the Expence of this Purchase has been
' approv'd of, and passed in Account. Done in the Month of *Gemadi*, the
' first, in the Year One thousand Eighty four.'

¶ On the Back of this Order, which was writ upon a Sheet of large Paper,
in the middle of the Sheet, was the Memorial of the Jewels, the Quality,
and Price at the Top, and on the Sides were the Counter-signs of the
principal Ministers who have the Charge of the King's Wealth. That of
the First Minister was the First, in these Terms:

GOD.

¶ *By Order of the most Great King.* ⸺ *Countersign'd with the Endorsement of
The most High, most Happy, and most* (f) *Beloved Lieutenant of the State,* Cheic-
ali-can, *most Excellent, most Glorious, most Bright, and most Eminent Con-
fident of the King of Kings, most Merciful and most Good; the Prop, and First
Minister of the greatest Kingdom of the Earth, rais'd above all Grandure.*

¶ Under the Signature, just by, was the Seal and Flourish of the First
Minister. This Flourish is call'd *Togra*, as is that of the King. It is a Knot
of several *Arabick* Letters, which compose Five Words in that Language,
which signify, *It is necessary to arm one's self with the Assistance of the most
High God, in all Temporal Affairs.*

¶ The Second Signature was that of the Nazir, in these Terms, *Counter-
sign'd with the Endorsement of the most High, most Happy, and most Beloved
Lord* Negef-couli-bec, *Supreme Intendant of the Royal Riches, Lieutenant of the
King, Favourite of his Majesty, and Great Overseer of the Royal House.*

¶ About the middle of the Page, in the Margin, on the Right-hand, was
the Seal, and Counter-sign of *Mirza Kebir*, Comptroller-General of the
Demesns, in these Words; *This Order has pass'd the Pen of the Comptroller
of the Finances.*

¶ On the left Side, likewise in the Margin, was the Seal, and the Counter-
sign of *Mirza Casem*, Comptroller of the Registers of the Chamber of
Accounts in these Words: *This Order has been seen.*

¶ Under these Countersigns there were three others. The first of *Ismael-
Bec*, Nazir or Comptroller of the Chamber, in these Terms, *this Order has
been ratify'd in the Office of the Nazir.* The other of *Mahamed Jafer*, first
Officer of the Chamber of Accompts, in these Words, *this Order has been
inserted in the Registers of the Demesn.* The Third was that of *Mirza-aboul
Hassein*, Receiver-General, and runs thus: *This Order has been enter'd.*

¶ (a) It is one of the twelve Years, that compose the *Epocha*, which they make use of in *Persia* in all the Offices of the Finances. The *Tartars* have introduc'd it in all the Countries where they have carry'd their Learning or their Arms, as it shall be more amply explain'd in the following Volumes, in the Treatise of the *Persian* Astronomy.

¶ (*b*) It is always specify'd in the Contracts, that the Payments shall be made in the Money of *Tauris*, because that great City has the Reputation of making the several Species more exactly to the Standard than all the rest; but this is only a Formality, the Money coyn'd in the other Cities of *Persia*, having the same Currency.

¶ (*c*) The *Mahometans* holy Places, are the Cities of *Mecca*, and *Medina*, they call them *Haramjuvé Cherefin*, that is to say, Sacred and Noble.

¶ (*d*) The Original Term is *Richs-sefid*, which signifies White-beard. They make use of that Figure all over *Persia*, to denote the Principal, and most eminent Person of a Place, that who governs the rest, as the Father of a Family in his House, a Captain in his Company, a Bailif in the Borough where he Commands, and the Leader of a Caravan. What there is absurd in this Custom, is their giving this Title to People who neither have, nor can have a Beard; as for Instance, the Person that is here mention'd, who is an Eunuch; but Use leads them still further, for it is given also to Women, and Maidens of Quality. This Figure is taken from the great deference the Eastern People have ever paid beyond all the rest of the World, to old Men.

¶ (*e*) The Apartment of the Women in *Persia* is call'd *Haram*, which is to say, a sacred Place, the entrance whereof is interdicted and forbid.

¶ (*f*) The Word which I have translated Well-beloved, properly signifies a Person who discharges his Office to the King's Satisfaction.

¶ The Nazir deliver'd this Order to me compleatly dispatch'd. Had I been to sollicit its passing through the several Offices my self, I could not have effected it in a Months time, nor for fifty Pistols. As he made me sensible on several Occasions, that he would not lose his Favours, I gave him to understand I was highly affected with this. He did me another the same Day, for he help'd me to sell seven thousand Crowns worth of Jewels to the Grandees he had invited. He had kept all that I had of a low Price, and by a piece of Villany not to be imagin'd in a Man of his Quality, he sent them to be sold in my Name in the great Houses; and when he had a good Price offer'd for any Jewel, he would immediately buy it at a lower rate, than what he had been bid for it. This was the true Reason that made him so often tell me, not to sell any Thing of what the King had seen, for fear he should ask for it again; but I soon found out his Cunning.

CHAPTER XVI

The Nazir entertains the King, a Description of it. The Envoy of the French East-India *Company desires Audience of the King. The Armenian who turn'd* Mahometan *Circumcis'd. Visit to the Cedre or Great Pontiff, civilly receiv'd.*

ON the 3d, which was the Day he entertain'd the King; I went to his House early in the Morning, to see the Preparations that were made. His House is just by the Royal Palace. The Way the King was to come, was finely gravell'd, and one Side thereof was cover'd with Brocards and Silks spread, and the other was strew'd with Flowers. There can be nothing neater, nor more Magnificent, than the Apartment where he treated the King. It gives upon a Garden that is not very Large, but very Fine; in the Middle thereof is a great Bason of Water, lin'd with white transparent Marble, the Borders whereof are bor'd for Spouts, four Fingers distant one from the other. Round about the Bason were spread Tapstries of Silk and Gold, on which were plac'd Cushions of very rich Embroidery to sit upon. The great Hall (in the middle of which is another square Bason, the Center whereof is distinguish'd by four Water-Spouts) was cover'd with the rich Tapistry of Silk and Gold, the finest that can be seen, with Cushions all round it of the same sort, but rather of richer Stuff, and finer Work. On the four Sides of the Bason, were four perfuming Pots of an extraordinary Bigness, finely embellish'd with Vermillion guilt, between eight little square Boxes of Ivory, adorn'd with Gold enamell'd, and full of Sweets and Perfumes. The whole Hall was cover'd with large Basons of Sweet-meats, and round the Basons were scented Waters, Bottles of Essences, Liquors, Wine and Brandy of several Sorts. At Night there were fine Fireworks play'd off in the middle of the Garden. No Body ever entertains the King of *Persia*, without giving him the Diversion of an artificial Firework. The King pass'd the whole Night at the Feast in Drinking, drawing the long Bow, and in other Exercises. His Favourites praising him on the Strength of his Arm, he took so much Pleasure in those Commendations, that to convince 'em the more how much he deserv'd them, he took some Cups of Gold enamel'd of the thickness of a Crown-piece, and squeezing them with one Hand, would make the Sides meet. This is almost Incredible; but this Prince really has the Shape and Presence of as strong a Man as any is. He was carry'd away about the break of Day, not being able to Ride or Walk, through Weariness and Merry-making. The Nobles who had been of the Feast, were so tir'd, and so drunk, that most of them not being able to sit their Horses as they return'd Home, caus'd themselves to be laid down upon the Stalls in the Way. The Nazir, who was presently inform'd thereof, order'd Centinels to be plac'd round them, that no Body might come near them, nor see them in so beastly a Condition, and so unbecoming their Quality.

¶ On the 4th, the Envoy of the *French East-India* Company presented a Petition to the Nazir, in order to obtain Audience of the King; and on the Sixth, by the Advice of that Minister, he presented such an other to the Grand Vizier, which I have thus translated.

GOD.

The Petition of a Person, who offers up his Vows for you with all his Heart, the Envoy of the French East-India *Company.*

¶ ' He with all earnestness represents to the most high Lord, magnificent
' in Titles, the unshakable Basis of the Kingdom, most worthy supream
' Lieutenant, Excellent, Noble, and Magnanimous; the Elect of the
' Crown, the Favourite of the most High, and most powerful Master of
' the World; That since his arrival in the Royal City of *Ispahan*, he
' receiv'd extream Favours and Liberalities from your Grandeur, and
' from the other high and powerful Lords of the Court, particularly the
' Nazir, and great Superintendant of the King's Houshold, who has
' caus'd him to be supply'd with all that is necessary for the (a) Sub-
' sistence of a Stranger of his Quality. As his most high, and most powerful
' King is at War with the King of (b) *Holland*, which renders Navigation
' dangerous, and the Suppliant having several Requests to make to this
' Court, which is the Basis and Prop of Heaven; he humbly beggs he may
' be brought into the Royal Assembly of Audiences, which is the Image
' of Paradise, and that his Condition and Requests may be made known
' to the most High, and most noble Monarch, to whom the Heav'n serves
' as a (c) Footstool. The Suppliant promises himself from the goodness of
' your Grandure, that he shall soon deliver the Letters and Presents with
' which he is charg'd for him, whose Looks have the same Force and
' Virtue as Chymistry has; that he shall have a favourable Reception of
' him, and that afterwards he shall acquaint your Grandure, (who is the
' true Source of Nobility) with the Subject of his coming.'

¶ *The Commands of your Grandure, shall regulate his Desires.*

¶ (a) The *Persian* Words signify, the Sustenance of this *Atom*, has been given on the part of the Ministers. Hospitality, in *Persia*, is called, the Nourishment of the Stranger.

¶ (b) The Republican Government is unknown in *Persia*, and further on, to the Extremity of the World. None but the Despotick Government is known there, and they cannot conceive the Administration of the Sovereign Power, by a Plurality of Persons of equal Authority, nor even that holy and happy Power of the Laws, which serves as a Barrier against Tyranny. They are accustom'd throughout the East to the Yoke of one Man, whose Caprice is a Sovereign Law, and who does and undoes as he himself pleases, without either Reason or Sense. The *Hollanders*, that they may not offend these Manners, speak always of their Country as of a Monarchy, after the Way of other Countries; and when they 'send an Ambassador into *Persia*, the Letters are made in the Name of the Governor of *Batavia*, or in the Name of the Prince of *Orange*. The first Embassies they sent to the *Indies*, were always in the Name of the Princes of *Orange*, and with their Letters.

¶ (*c*) *Sepeher recab*, which I have translated, *to whom the Heaven serves for a Foot-stool*, signifies also *mounted on the Heaven*, *Recab* properly signifies a Stirrup.

¶ The first Minister was somewhat displeas'd with the Envoy, whom he observ'd to apply himself wholly to the Nazir, without addressing to him. However, that did not hinder him from giving a favourable Answer to his Petition; he told the Interpreter, That he would employ his good Offices with the King in Favour of the *French* Company.

¶ On the 9th, the Nazir, with one of his Brothers, and one of the King's Favourites, went in the Morning to the Prevost's of *Julfa*, who had turn'd *Mahometan*. A great many of the most considerable of the Clergy had likewise repaired thither; it was in order to Circumcise him. One of the Domestick Chirurgions of the Great Pontif performed the Operation in a Closet adjoining to the great Hall, where the Assembly was. They gave him the Name of *Mahammed Peri* at his Circumcision; after which he was immediately put into a Bagnio; when he came out of it, he was cloathed with white Garments that were new. While this Ceremony was performing, the Assembly offer'd up their Thanks to Heaven for the Conversion of so illustrious a Neophyte, and a thousand Vows for that of all the Christians of *Persia*, and for the Exaltation of *Mahometanism*. Two Hours after, the Company was entertain'd at a great Dinner, which was brought from the House of *Aga Zaman*, Intendant to the King's Mother, because the Family of the new Convert not being yet become *Mahometans*, whatever had been provided therein, would have been polluted. This *Aga Zaman* gave him his Daughter in Marriage a Month after. Circumcision is very painful to those that are advanc'd in Years, who are commonly a Fortnight or Three Weeks before they can walk.

¶ On the 14th, I went to see the Cedre, or great Pontif, who had sent for me several times, to come to the Princess, his Wife, who had a mind to buy some Jewels. There are two great Pontifs in *Persia*; the one is appointed to look after those Legacies that are bequeath'd by the Kings, and is called the Pontif of the Demesne; the other supervises those that are bequeath'd by private Persons, and is call'd the Pontif of the Kingdoms. It was the Pontif of the Demesne who had sent for me, and with whom my Business was.

¶ This Lord having, with Pleasure, look'd over Piece by Piece, all the Jewels I had brought him, caus'd them to be plac'd one against another in a great Bason of Silver, and went and carry'd them himself to the Princess, his Wife, in the Seraglio. I would have taken my leave, and have retir'd, but he order'd me to stay; and that I might not be uneasie, he commanded two Officers to show me the Palace: They were about finishing the Structure thereof: Two hundred Workmen were still employ'd continually about it; but it was easie to discover that it would be one of the finest Edifices of *Ispahan*. According to the Computation of the Architects, it was to cost but Four hundred thousand Livres, but I have since been inform'd, that it cost a great deal more. I speak only of that part that is inhabited by the Men, for the other part, which is the Apartment of the Women, cost still more, being larger, and more magnificent. While I was viewing the Lodgings, they brought me Sherbet, Coffee and Sweetmeats, and I was treated in every thing with an Excess of Civility; I mean even for the Country it self, where they know better how to caress and flatter, than in any Country of the World. I was mightily pleas'd thereat, not so much on the account of the nice Treatment, as for the Hopes I had conceiv'd, that the Princess would buy some of my Jewels; for in *Persia* they do nothing but with Design, and out of Self-Interest. In about two Hours, the Eunuchs brought me back in two Basons, all that I had shown to the Pontif; one of them contain'd what the Princess had a mind to have, which I left in their Hands, after I had given them a Memorial of the respective Prices. As I was getting on Horseback the Pontif caus'd me to be call'd back, and having order'd me to sit near him, he fell on discoursing with me about *Europe*, and particularly concerning our Sciences, and our Mechanick Arts. At one a-Clock in the Morning he dismissed me, and order'd some of his People to conduct me.

CHAPTER XVII

The Ambassador of the Resqui, *and* Muscovy, *admitted to an Audience. A Dispute between the* French *Envoy and* English *Agent about Precedency examined and settled. The Manner of the Ambassadors being conducted, with the Magnificence attending it.*

ON the 15th, by break of Day, the Place-Royal was clear'd of all the Shops, and of all the Retailers who commonly there expose their Goods. This was done in order to render more magnificent the Audience and Entertainment which the King was to give the next Day to all the Ambassadors and Envoys who were at Court. It was swept, and all the Avenues thereof were shut up that no body might pass that Way. The First Minister notify'd at the same time to all the Ambassadors, by the *Mehemander Bachy*, or Guest-Keeper General, who is the Introductor of the Ambassadors, to prepare themselves, with their Presents, to receive Audience. The Envoy of the *French* Company, or to speak more properly, his Council, was very much surpriz'd at the King's Design, to give Audience to all the Ambassadors at once, and more especially, having been inform'd, that an Agent of the *English* Company, who was then at *Ispahan*, was likewise to have Audience; and that he had for some time been dealing secretly with the Ministers about the Precedency. He therefore immediately presented Petitions to the Nazir, and to the Grand Vizier, in order to prevent his receiving that Affront. He therein represented, That it was a Right due to the *French* Nation, to have the Precedency of all the Christian Nations, as well in the East, as in the West. These Petitions having been examin'd by the Ministers in Council, were answered to the Satisfaction of the Envoy. The Nazir told me so, at his coming from the King, and charg'd me to go from him, and acquaint the Envoy therewith, and to let him know, that he alone had stood firm in his Favour. The *Muscovite* Ambassador alledged, for Reasons of his having the Precedency; The vast Extent of his Master's Dominions, whom all the Christian Princes call'd Great, by Excellency, in which they show'd, said he, that they acknowledged him to be above them. The *English* Agent said, that he having a Letter to deliver from the King of *England* whereas the *French* Envoy had only a Letter from the *French* Company; the Letter of a King ought to be preferred to that of an incorporated Society of Merchants. I found all the Family of the *French* Envoy busy in delivering to the Burghers of that Quarter, the Presents he was to make: I shall here set down the Order in which that is done. The Piskis Naviez, or Receiver of the Presents, notifies to the Great Prevost, and Governor of the City, that he must have such a Number of Men, such a Day, in such a Place, to carry the Presents of such an Ambassador. The Governor sends for the Commissary of that Ward or Quarter, and gives him his Orders accordingly, and the Commissary delivers them to the principal Burghers of the Quarter. The *Persian* Word for Burgher, is *Ket-Koda*, which signifies *the Image of God*, because a good Head of a Family represents in his House, the Conduct of God in the Universe. These Burghers, to the Number of Eight or Ten, take a Man out of each Shop of the Quarter, or as many as are necessary, and repair, with a Clerk of the Receiver of the Presents, to the Ambassador's Lodgings, where they receive his Presents according to the Memorial, and deliver them to these Bearers. Each Man takes a Piece, and goes away. Fifty Men very often are employ'd to carry to an Audience, what one Man alone might easily carry. This Practice, is to do Honour to the Person who makes the Present, because it makes him appear the more considerable; and likewise for the Grandure of the King, by reason that the People seeing the Presents that are brought to him, conclude that he is highly esteem'd by Foreign Nations. The Present is thus kept by the Bearers till the next Morning, when they repair to the place which was appointed them, each with that Part that was deliver'd into his Hands. It sometimes happens that the Present remains even eight or ten Days in their Hands. One would think that in the Confusion that is caus'd by a Crowd of five or six hundred Men of the meaner Sort, (for sometimes there are so many employ'd to carry a Present) something should always be lost; yet that never happens, and the Account is always found exact. It is a thing impossible in *Persia* to rob the King; and, as the *Persians* say, the Sea it self is obliged to restore what it takes from him.

¶ The *English* were presently inform'd of the Resolution that had been taken in favour of the *French*. Their Interpreter, (who was a Man of Intrigue, had an easie access to the Ministers, and who spar'd nothing on such Occasions) wrought so much by his Goings and Comings, that the Grandees being assembl'd at Night in the King's Palace, the Affair of the Precedency was again started, and very strongly debated: At last it was resolv'd, that Audience should be given the next Day to the *Muscovites*, and that the *French* and the *English* should be put off to that Day eight Days. The first Minister caus'd the Difference to be regulated after that manner, saying amongst other Things; *The* Muscovite *is our Neighbour, and our Friend, and the Commerce has been a long time settled between us, and without Interruption: We send Embassadors each to the other Reciprocally almost every Year, but we hardly know the others. The Power of their Kings may be as*

Great as it is Represented, but it is so remote from us, that it is with Difficulty we receive any News of it. It is therefore necessary to have a regard to our Neighbours at any rate.

¶ The 16th, about eight a Clock in the Morning, the Place Royal appear'd water'd from one end to the other, and adorn'd in the manner I am going to relate. On the Side of the great Entrance to the Royal Palace, at twenty Paces distance, were twelve Horses, the finest in the King's Stables, six on each side, set out in the stateliest and most magnificent Trapping the World can afford. Four of the said Furnitures or Trappings were adorn'd with Emralds, two with Rubies, two with Stones of different Colours intermix'd with Diamonds, two with Gold enamell'd, and two others with fine smooth Gold. Besides the Trappings, which were of this Richness, the Saddle, that is to say, the fore and back Part, the Pommel and the Stirrups, were cover'd with Stones suitable to the Trappings, These Horses had large Housings that hung down very low, some of Gold Brocard, rais'd with Pearls, and others of Gold Brocard very fine, and very thick, encompassed with Tufts, and Balls of Gold beset with Pearls. The Horses were made fast with Tresses of Silk and Gold, to Nails of fine Gold. The Nails are about fifteen Inches long, and of a thickness Proportionable, having a large Ring at the Head, through which the Halter passes, or the String belonging to their Shackles. In Reality, there can be nothing more Stately, nor more Royal than this Equipage, to which must be added twelve covercloaths of Velvet and Gold friz'd, or high napp'd, which serve to cover the Horses from top to bottom that were in Parade before the Rails, which run along the front of the Royal Palace. It is impossible to see finer, whether one considers the richness of the Stuff, or the Art and Delicacy of the Work.

¶ Between the Horses and the Rails were four Cisterns, three Foot high, and large in Proportion, much like those that are made use of in *Paris* to preserve the Water in the Houses. Two of these were of Gold plac'd on Trevets, which were also of massy Gold; the other two were of Silver, plac'd on Trevets of the same Metal. Just by were two large Buckets, and two great Mallets, the largest that are to be seen; all these were likewise of massy Gold even to the very Handles. The Horses are water'd in these Buckets, and the Mallets serve to drive into the Ground, the Nails to which they are made fast. At the Distance of thirty Paces from the Horses, there were wild Beasts train'd up to fight with young Bulls. Two Lyons, one Tyger, and one Leopard which were made fast, each of them lying extended on a large piece of scarlet Tapistry, with their Heads towards the Palace. On the borders of the Tapistry were two

Mallets of Gold, and two Basons also of Gold of the Diameter of the largest Cisterns for a Dining-Room. These are to give Food in to these fine Beasts, when they are shown in Publick. Here you must observe, that all the Gold Plate that is in the King's Palace, is Ducat Gold, as I have found by tryal. Right against the great Portal, were two Coaches after the *Indian* Fashion very pretty, with Oxen put to them, after the manner of that Country, the Coachmen whereof were *Indians*, and clad likewise after the Mode of their own Country. On the Right were two Antelopes, (this is a sort of Hind, having white Hair, and whose Horns are strait like an Arrow, and very long;) and on the Left were two great Elephants cover'd with Cloaths of Gold Brocarde, having Rings at their Teeth, and Chains and Rings of Silver at their Feet; and one Rhinoceros. These Animals were near the one to the other, without shewing the least Aversion or Unesiness, notwithstanding what the Naturalists say to the contrary, *viz.* That the Elephant and the Rhinoceros have an invincible Antipathy, that keeps them constantly at War. At the two ends of the Place, they walk'd up and down in Leashes, the Bulls and the Rams that were train'd up to fight; and there were likewise Companies of Gladiators, Wrestlers and Fencers, all ready to engage at the first Signal that should be given them. In fine, there were in eight or ten Places of the Square, Brigades of the King's Guards drawn up, and under their Arms.

¶ The Hall that was prepar'd to give the Audience in, was that fine and spacious large Hall, built over the great Portal of the Palace, and is the finest Hall of that sort that I ever saw any where. It was rais'd so high, that when one looks down into the Place, Men seem to be but two Foot high, and when on the contrary one looks upward from the Place to the Hall, there is no knowing of any Body. I have given the Figure thereof in the Description of *Ispahan*. The King being come thither about nine a Clock, and all the Court, to the Number of above three hundred Persons, there came into the Place from the Eastern Corner, the Ambassador of the *Lesqui*. This is a tributary Nation to *Persia*, and inhabits a mountanous Country on the Confines of the Kingdom towards *Muscovy*, and near the *Caspian* Sea. The Ambassador was a young Nobleman, very handsom, and very well dress'd. He had only two Horsemen to follow him, and four Footmen who surrounded him. An Assistant or Under-Master of the Ceremonies conducted him. He caus'd him to dismount at the Distance of about an hundred Paces from the great Portal, and led him very fast to the large Hall where the King was. The Captain of the Gate, who is call'd *Jehic agasi bachi*, receiv'd him there, and conducted him to the kissing of the King's Feet. Thus they call the Salutation which his Subjects pay him; and all those Strangers who have the Honour to approach him, of what Quality soever they be. *Pabous* is the *Persian* Term, which signifies to kiss the Feet. It is also call'd *Zeminbous*, that is to say, to kiss the Ground, and *Ravi Zemin*, which implies, the Face upon the Ground. This Salutation is perform'd after this manner. The Ambassador or other Person, is conducted to within four Paces of the King, and right against him where they stop him, and make him kneel, and in that Posture he makes three Prostrations of his Body and Head to the Ground, so low, that his Forehead touches it. This done, the Ambassador rises and delivers the Letter he has for the King to the Captain of the Gate, who puts it into the Hands of the first Minister, and he presents it to the King, who puts it on his right Side without looking into it: After this, the Ambassador is conducted to the Place appointed for him.

¶ The *Muscovite* Ambassador appear'd in a quarter of an Hour after. He enter'd from the same Side, having the King's Horses, and being conducted by the Introductor of the Ambassadors; for this Ambassador was so sordid a Wretch, that he did not so much as keep one Horse. The Introductor light off his Horse about a hundred and fifty Paces from the Palace, and bid the Ambassador dismount likewise. I can't tell whether the *Muscovite* had been inform'd, that the Ambassador of the *Lesqui* did not alight from his Horse, till he was much nearer to the Entrance; or whether out of Grandure, and for the Honour of his Master, that he would needs ride further on, be it as it will, he made a Resistance, and clapping Spurs to his Horse, he made him go on three or four Paces, notwithstanding the Opposition of the Introductors Footmen, who had laid hold of his Horse's Bridle in order to stop him. Thereupon they stop'd him short, and as he made still a Resistance, and was for going forward, the before-mention'd Servants with their Sticks hit the Horse across the Nose to make him fall back, and then the Ambassador was forc'd to alight. He therefore dismounted with two of his Retinue, who follow'd him on Horseback, *viz.* his Interpreter, and his Steward. His other Servants, which were nine or ten in Number, march'd on Foot in a poor Equipage enough for so solemn an Occasion. The Ambassador was clad in a Robe of yellow Satin, over which he had a large Vest of red Velvet lin'd with *Marten* Furrs, and reach'd down to the Ground. His Cap was also of the same Furr, cover'd with crimson Velvet, and very high imbroider'd with small Pearls before, with two Tresses of Pearls that hung down his Back to his Wast. He was an old Man quite Gray, of a handsome Mean, and very Venerable. His Interpreter march'd on his Left, carrying the Letters from the Great Duke in a Velvet Bag seal'd up. He was conducted to the

Place call'd the kissing of the King's Feet, as the Ambassador of the *Lesqui* had been before, and was plac'd right against him on the Left. Next came the Envoy of *Basra*, they made him dismount at the entrance of the Royal Place, and he was conducted in the same manner to the King's Audience. *Besra*, which the *Europeans* call also *Balsura*, is that famous Town at the extremity of the *Persian* Gulph, where the *Tigris* and the *Euphrates* discharge themselves into the Sea.

CHAPTER XVIII

The Ambassador's Presents, the Shews exhibited upon this Occasion; Character of the Persian *Courtiers.*

THE Presents of these Ambassadors were all this while at the end of the Place, near the Royal Mosque, that is the Staple or Place of Rendezvous to which they are brought, and from whence the Bearers set out, when the King gives Audience in the great Hall that faces the Royal Place. The Godly say, that in making the Presents be brought from the East Side, and before the Mosque is given to understand, that God is the Source, and the Doner of all temporal Goods, insomuch that whatever Men receive, it is a Present from him. These Presents were order'd to set forward, about a quarter of an Hour after the Ambassadors had taken their Seats. The *Muscovite* Ambassadors past first, carry'd by seventy four Men, and consisted of the following Things.

A large Lantern of Christal painted.

Nine small Looking-Glasses of Christal, the Frames painted.

Fifty Sables.

A hundred and twenty Yards of red and green Cloth.

Twenty Bottles of the Brandy of *Muscovy*.

¶ *That of the Envoy of* Basra *was*;

An Ostridge, a young Lyon, and three fine *Arabian* Horses.

¶ There had like to have happen'd a pleasant Mistake, which was this; those Persons who had the Day before been charg'd with Presents of the *French* Company, as has been said, not knowing that the Audience of that Envoy had been put off to another time, had brought it to the Place, and were set out after the rest; but the Receiver of the Presents perceiving the gross Mistake, caus'd the Bearers to be well Can'd, and order'd them to carry the whole back till that Day eight Days.

❡ As soon as the Presents had pass'd by, the Drums, Trumpets, and several other Instruments began to play. This was the Signal for the Diversions, and the Combats; and at the same Instant the Wrestlers, the Gladiators, and the Fencers, fell to their respective Engagements. The Keepers of the wild Beasts let them loose upon young Bulls, which were held pretty near, and they who manag'd the Rams and the Bulls train'd up to fight, set them together. Indeed it may be esteem'd rather a Slaughter than a Fight, this Engagement between the wild Beasts and the Bulls. Thus it is perform'd; two Men hold the wild Beasts by a Leash fasten'd about its Neck. The Bull no sooner perceives him coming, but he runs away; the Beast persues him, and that so swiftly, that in three or four Leaps, it fastens upon him and brings him down; then the Keepers of those Beasts fall upon the Bull, and with Hatchets chop off his Head, and give his Blood to the Beasts. The Reason why they do not suffer the Beasts and the Bull to fight till they kill one another, and that they rush in upon the Bull, is because the Lyon being the Hieroglyphic of the Kings of *Persia*; the Astrologers and the Soothsayers say, it would be an ill Omen, if the Lyon that is let loose upon the Bull, did not intirely vanquish him soon after he had attack'd him. The Show of these different sorts of Fights lasted till eleven a Clock. Those that ensu'd were more Diverting and more Natural. The first consisted of three hundred Horsemen, who appear'd at the four Sides of the Square very well mounted, and as richly and finely Clad as one could wish; they were for the most part young Noblemen of the Court, who had all of them several led Horses, they exercis'd themselves for an Hour at the *Mall* on Horseback. At this Exercise the Gamesters divide themselves into two equal Bodies; several Balls are cast into the middle of the Place, and every one has a Mallet given him. To win, the Balls must be made to pass between the two opposite Pillars, which are at the ends of the Place, and serve as Passes. This is no easie Matter, because the adverse Party stop the Balls, and drive 'em towards the other end. They are laught at, that strike while their Horse is upon a Walk, or stop'd. The Game requires it should be struck only on the Gallop, and those are reputed the best Gamesters, who riding upon full Speed, know how to send back the Ball with a dry Blow when it comes to them.

❡ The second Spectacle was that of the Casters of Darts and Javelins; It is called *Girid-Bas*, that is to say, the Game of the Dart or Javelin, and they Exercise it after this manner. Twelve or fifteen Cavaliers single themselves out from the rest of the Troop, and riding in close Order upon full Speed, with their Darts in their Hands, challenge an Engagement, the like Number detach themselves, to go and meet them. They cast their

Darts one at another, and then repair to their main Bodies; from whence another Detachment is made like the first, and so after that Manner as long as the Game lasts. Among this fine Body of Noblemen, there were fifteen young Abyssines, about eighteen or twenty Years of Age, who excell'd all the Rest in the Dexterity of casting the Dart or Javelin, as well as in the skilful managing of their Horses, and in the Swiftness of their Career. They never quitted their Horses to take up their Darts from the Ground, neither did they stop them for that purpose; but in a full Career they flung themselves on the Side of their Horses, and gather'd up the Darts with that Dexterity and Gracefulness, that even charm'd all the Beholders.
¶ All these Exercises, which are the *Carrousels of the *Persians*, concluded at One a Clock in the Afternoon after which the Ambassadors were dismissed. The King did not say one Word to them, nor did not so much as look at 'em. He pass'd the Time in beholding the Games, the Fights, and the Exercises, that were practising in the Square; in hearing the Symphony that was performing in the great Hall, and which was composed of the best Voices, and of the best Hands that were in his Pay; in discoursing with the Grandees of his State, who were then present, and in drinking and eating. As soon as the Ambassadors were enter'd, the whole Assembly was served with a Collation of Fruits, both green and dry'd, and of all sorts of Sweet-meats, wet and dry. These Collations are commonly serv'd up in Basons, much larger than those which are used in our Countries; they are made of Wood lacker'd, and painted very delicately, and will hold five and twenty or thirty *China* Plates. Each Person has one of these Basons set before him, and sometimes two or three, according as it is intended to do him Honour. At the upper end of the Hall, right against the Entrance, there was a Buffet, one part of which was set out with fifty large Flagons of Gold, filled with several sorts Wine; some of these Flaggons were enamell'd, and others were thick set with Precious Stones, and some were cover'd with Pearls: And the other Part was garnished with between three and fourscore Cups, and a great many Salvers of the same Sort: Some of these Cups will hold three Pints, they are large and flate-bottom'd, mounted on a Foot about two Inches high only. No part of the World can afford any thing more magnificent and rich, or more splendid and bright. The Ambassadors drank no Wine; only the *Muscovite* was served with some of his own Country Brandy. I was surprised they gave no Wine to that Ambassador, being the King himself drank largely, as well as most of the Grandees. I ask'd one of the Noblemen there present the Reason thereof. He answered me,

* *An Exercise perform'd on Horse-back on solemn Occasions by Persons of Quality.*

That it was out of Grandure, and the better to preserve the Respect due to his Royal Majesty; and then smiling, he told me further, That it was still kept in Memory, what one of his Country-men had done in a solemn Audience, which he had of the late King. I presently desir'd to be inform'd, what that was. He told me, That in the Year 64 two *Muscovite* Extraordinary Ambassadors, at the Audience the King gave them, drank so excessively, that they quite lost their Senses: The King drank their Master's Health, and would needs have them pledge it in a Cup that held about two Pints: The second Ambassador not being able to digest so much Wine, had a pressing Inclination to vomit, and not knowing where to disembogue, he took his great Sable Cap, which he half fill'd. It is well known, that the *Muscovites* wear large and high Caps. His Collegue, who was above him, and the Secretary of the Embassy, who was below him, enrag'd at so foul an Action, done in the Presence of the King of *Persia*, and of the whole Court, reprimanded him, and jogg'd him with their Elbows, to remind him of going out. But he, being very drunk, and not knowing either what was said to him, nor what he himself did, clap'd his Cap upon his Head, which presently cover'd him all over with Nastiness. The King and all the Assembly broke into a loud Laughter thereat, which lasted about half an Hour, during which time, the Companions of this filthy *Muscovite* were forcing him by dint of Blows with their Fists, to rise and go out. The King was not at all angry; he only broke up the Assembly, and said, as he went away, That the *Muscovites* were the *Yusbecs* of the *Francs*. He thereby intimated, That as among the *Mahometans*, there is no Nation so nasty, so meanly educated, nor so Clownish as the *Yusbecs*, (who are the *Tartars* along the River *Oxus*) so among the *Europeans*, there was not any that equal'd the *Muscovites* in those foul Qualities.

¶ At noon Dinner was served up; each Guest had only one Bason set before him, but of a much larger Size than those that are made use of in our Countries. These great Dishes contain'd Pilaw, dress'd after five or six different Ways, with Capons, Lamb, Chickens, Eggs, Meat, Herbs, Salt-Fish, and over that a great quanty of several Sorts of roasted Meats. Fifteen Men might, without Exageration, satisfie the sharpest Hunger with one of these Dishes. The Dish that was serv'd up to the King, was brought and plac'd before him on a Hand-barrow of Gold. A large Porrenger of Sherbet was serv'd up with each Dish, as also a Plate of Sallet, and two sorts of Bread. The King withdrew without saying any thing to the Ambassadors, and without so much as turning his Head on their Side. The Ambassador of the Lesqui went out first, and found his

Horses at the same Place where he had dismounted. The *Muscovite* Ambassador follow'd him so close, that he saw him take Horse: Thereupon he insisted on having his Horse brought to the same place: But the Introductor of the Ambassadors, who re-conducted him, told him, He had Orders to make him take Horse at the same Place where he had alighted, and that it was the Custom so to do. The *Muscovite* alledg'd the Example of the Lesqui, and protested he would resent the Affront that was put upon him: He threaten'd and storm'd for a quarter of an Hour, stamping and cocking up his Cap in a strange Passion; but after all, he was forc'd to walk on, and go and take his Horses where he had left them. This is the Practice of the *Persians*, thereby to do Honour to their Religion, and to show the Regard they have to those who make Profession thereof. They had sacrific'd to. a Muscovite, (who seem'd to be no more than a simple Merchant, and to have no other Concerns in *Persia* than those of a small private Commerce) the Envoys of the *French* and *English* Companies, and that, upon Politick Views, as has been already observ'd; They, out of the same Regard, sacrificed the Rank of the *Muscovite*, to the Envoy of the Lesqui, who are Tributaries to them, a Mountainous People, and half wild. They were careful, however, in the Honours done to these Envoys; for they caus'd the *Muscovite* Ambassador to be conducted by the Introductor of Ambassadors, while the other was conducted only by an Assistant of the Ceremonies, and made the Presents of the *Muscovite* to pass first. But it is easie to perceive, that in the Distribution of these Honours, the Lesqui had the most Essential; for he was plac'd on the King's Right hand; and when the *Muscovite* Ambassador complain'd thereof, he was answer'd, That the Righthand was given to the Lesqui, because he came first. But to speak the Truth it was upon the account of his being a *Mahometan*.

¶ Towards Night, the introductor of Ambassadors pay'd a Visit to the Envoy of the *French* Company, to assure him, That in a few Days the King would give him Audience. He immediately sent for the Superior of the *Capuchins* to speak for him. This Father represented the Wrong that was done to the Envoy, in preferring to him, on the one side, a *Muscovite*, a Lesqui, and a Deputy of *Basra*; and on the other, in bringing into Dispute, the Right of Precedency which the *French* Nation has over that of the *English*. To all which the Introductor answered, with abundance of fine Words, after the Manner of the Country; for the *Persian* Courtiers never fly into a Passion or Heat, whatever Occasion may be given them. This made a *Portugal* Ambassador say pleasantly enough, speaking of 'em, That the *Persians* never give you ill Language, nor never do you any Good.

CHAPTER XIX

Some Jewels sold to the Nazir; His Extortion. A fine Present of Sweet-meats made to the Author by the Great Pontif's Wife, and Aunt to the King. The Envoy of the French *Company, and* English *Agent, conducted to their Audience; with their Presents. An Instance of the Pride of the* Persian *Kings. The Presents valu'd.*

ON the 18th, I fixed the Price for Eleven thousand Livres worth of Jewels, with the Nazir. I reckon'd to give him Three thousand, as well for his Right of two *per Cent.* for what I had sold to the King, as by way of Acknowledgment of his good Offices; but I was mightily surpriz'd to find, that he pretended to have Eight thousand. This he signify'd to me by his first Secretary, and by the Chief of the Goldsmiths. He observ'd, from the Place where he was, with what Air I should receive the Proposition. I therefore told these Gentlemen, with all the usual Exagerations of the Country, That the Nazir might, if he pleas'd, take all that I was worth, because it was impossible for me to make a sufficient Acknowledgment of all his Favours to me; but as I had lost a great deal in the Bargain I sold to the King, it was impossible for me to give him what he requir'd, without ruining my self entirely. These Figures are used in *Persia*, in the common way of speaking, and on the most trivial Occasions; and it is customary for a Man from whom you take a Penny, to cry out immediately, that you set his House on Fire. The Chief of the Goldsmiths, shaking his Head at this Answer, whisper'd to me thus; *It is in vain to think to get off with Words; the Person with whom you have to do, will not be paid with them: He is a Man that, for a Penny, would strip a Beggar in the Streets, more especially at this present, he having been lately drain'd by the vast Expences he has been at for his Son's Wedding. For which Reason, strain your self a little; reflect, that the Nazir has serv'd you, and that it is in his Power to do you further Kindness, in what you have still left to sell.* It is easie to judge how much this Speech perplex'd me. I not only seriously consider'd, that this Nobleman might do me great Services, but also that it was in his Power to do me as great Diskindnesses, if he should take a fancy to it. I desir'd the Chief of the Goldsmiths therefore to intreat the Nazir to accept of Four thousand Livres, which I would give him with all my Heart. He would not be satisfied therewith, but caus'd me to be spoken to again, to perswade me to take Five thousand Livres, for the Eleven thousand worth which he had of mine in Jewels. As he saw that I oppos'd it, he told me very coolly, That he could not, nor would not force me; and that I might take back my Jewels, and dispose of them as I pleas'd.

¶ I was very much troubled, to resolve what I should do in this Critical Juncture, being on the one side spurr'd on by Acknowledgment and Fear; and on the other, not being able to determine my self, to make such large Presents. While I was in this doubtful State, the Chief of the Gold-smiths took me aside, and told me, not to lose the Friendship of the Nazir for a hundred Pistoles, he being in great Favour with the King. In fine, I resolv'd to be a Loser, and therefore desir'd the Chief of the Goldsmiths to accommodate the Matter, at a Five thousand Livres Present. This was accordingly done, and the Nazir sent for Two thousand Crowns, which were paid me down before him. He caress'd me very much afterwards, and invited me to follow the King in the Progress he was going to make to *Casbin*, which is the Antient *Arsatia*, promising, that the Prince should allow me a Pension, and defray my Charges. After this, he bid me go to the Envoy of the *French* Company, and tell him from him, That he had read to the King the Petition which he had presented, in order to obtain the Precedency of the *English* Agent; and that he had back'd it with such strong Reasons, that the Prince had made Answer, that he would give Audience to the *French* first; however the Success did not agree with the Promise, for he gave it to both the Envoys at the same time, as shall be seen hereafter.

¶ On the 19th, the Princess, the King's Aunt and Wife to the Great Pontif, sent me by six Men, four large Basons of Sweet-meats, with Pots of Sherbet, some Loaves of amber'd Shugar, Marchpanes, and other sweet Things of the like Nature. I was agreeably surpriz'd at this fine Present, which was so genteel and curiously Perfum'd; but I was very much perplex'd, what Thanks I should return to the Princess. The next Day after, the Eunuch she employ'd to speak to me, took upon him to do it for me: I made no doubt but he discharg'd the part very well, for the Eunuchs have most commonly fine Tongues, Smooth, Flattering and Insinuating, and know wonderfully well how to find the way to the Heart.

¶ On the 20th, I went and paid a Visit to the chief of the *Goldsmiths*, and carry'd him five hundred Crowns for his Right of two *per Cent*. He was contented therewith, and told me amongst other Things, that for his Part, he hated the cheating Tricks of the *Persians*; that he took what was his due, and did not desire any more.

¶ On the 21st, the Envoy of the *French* Company had Audience of the King at the same Place, and almost in the same manner, as it had been given on the 16th to the other Envoys. He was brought about eight a Clock by the Introductor of Ambassadors, who made him dismount at the Distance of a hundred and fifty Paces from the Royal Palace. The Introductor walk'd before him. He had his Second, his Chirurgeon, and his Interpreter at his Side; this last holding with both his Hands, in a Purse embroider'd with Gold, the Letter which had been Counterfeited in the Name of the *French* Company, to the King of *Persia*. Then follow'd two of his Domesticks, his twelve Guards, and several Footmen, People of the Country cloath'd after their manner, in a very fine Equipage. The Envoy was conducted to a high-rais'd Seat under the Great Portal on the left. The Introductor went afterwards and fetch'd the Agent of the *English* Company, whom he brought after the same manner; he was follow'd by his Second, and by two Clerks, four Interpreters, and by ten Footmen, all well clad after the Fashion of the Country. He was led to the Seat that was opposite to that where the *French* were, and right against it. *Mirhagez* the *Arabian*, and Captain of the Caravans of the Pilgrims that go to *Mecca*, by the way of *Basra*, was introduc'd afterwards by one of the Assistants of the Ceremonies.

¶ About two a Clock, these Envoys were conducted to Audience; the *Frenchman* first, each having his Interpreter, and two Persons to follow him; and about a quarter of an Hour after, their Presents were order'd to pass along. That of the *Frenchman* consisted of the following Things.

A Chain of Emeralds and Diamonds.
An Emerald Ring.
A Ring, with a Balass Ruby.
A pictur'd Box set with Diamonds and Emeralds, with the King's Picture enamell'd, the back Part being of inlaid Work.
Two large Branches of Christal.
Four Looking-Glasses of Christal five Foot high, three with a Frame of Brass guilt, the other with a Christal Frame.
Picture of the King of *France* at full Length, in a Frame of Wood guilt.
A Bag of Ambergreese weighing 58 Ounces.
Two Bottles of the Essence of Cloves.
Four Pieces of Gold Brocard, twenty Yards in each Piece.
Three Pieces of Sattin.
Five *Marcs of Gold and Silk Lace.
Seven Pieces of white Cloth, of the finest that is made in *India*, each Piece containing four Yards and a half.
Six Pieces of Tapistry of Silk and Gold.

* *A Weight of Eight Ounces.*

Two thousand thirty three Yards of the Cloth of *Paris*.
Four Telescopes, each three Foot long.
Three hundred and six Pieces of *China* Ware of different Sizes.
Seventy Pounds of Tea.
Four large Basons fill'd with Wax-Candles of *Goa*.
Four Guns Damas'd, of a fine and neat Work.
Two Pair of Pistols of the same.
Four Cannon of a new Invention upon their Carriages.
Two Culverins finely Engraven, with the Arms of the Company on the Embrasure.
Fifty Bales of Pepper, each weighing a hundred and thirty Pounds.

¶ The Present of the *English* came after, and consisted of the following Things.

Twenty Pieces of *English* Cloth.
Forty Caps or Turbants of Silk and Gold of different Prices.
Forty Pieces of Sattin of different Sorts.
Thirty Pieces of Taffaty.
Twelve Pieces of Taffaty strip'd with Gold and Silver.
Twelve Pieces of Damask.
Forty Cases of Knives and Forks with Amber Hafts.

¶ The Present of *Mir-hagez* follow'd, consisting of five fine *Arabian* Horses of a compleat Furniture of Vermillion guilt, with a Caparison of Cloth of Gold.
¶ After these Presents came two others, the one with the Governors of *Jaron* presented by his Son. It consisted of six fine Horses, thirty Pieces of the finest printed Callicoes, and twenty Pieces of Gold Brocard.
¶ The other Present was from the Governor of *Guenja*, which is a Town in *Armenia*, and consisted only of Hounds.
¶ From ·the Place whence the King look'd into the Square, it was impossible for him to discern any Thing of these Presents. The Kings of *Persia* are so accustom'd to receive Presents, that they don't vouchsafe to look at them. The Ministers tell him from what Place the Present comes, and of what it consists; and when the King ask to see any particular Thing, it is sent into the *Seralio*, or to the Place the King appoints.
¶ To speak the Truth, it is out of Pride that they receive the Presents at so great a Distance, and with so much Indifferency; for they mean thereby, that they are not worthy to be brought before their Eyes. After the Presents had pass'd by, the Envoys were entertain'd as the Ambassadors

of *Moscovy*, and of the *Lesqui* had been the Week before, with the like Spectacles and Diversions, and with a Feast altogether of the same kind excepting that they had no Wine or Brandy. A little before Dinner, the King sent for the Son of the Governor of *Jarron*; he enter'd into the Hall, Saluted the King after the *Persian* manner, and presented his Father's Letter without saying one Word, neither did the Prince say one Word to him. The King does this out of Grandure, and to make his own Subjects and Foreigners pay him the greater Respect. The late King his Father was more affable both to the one and the other, he would cause the Ambassadors and Envoys to approach him several times, during the Entertainment at their Audience, and would Discourse with them about their Affairs, or at least of indifferent Things. Every time I had the Honour to approach him, and I had that Honour five times in the ten Weeks that I was at his Court in the Year 1666, he always did me the favour to speak to me; it is true, it was not directly, for he would impart his Thought to the Nazir, the Nazir would bring it to my Interpreter, and my Interpreter would signifie it to me; and having receiv'd my Answer, it pass'd to his Majesty thro' the same Channel. If I had at that time understood the *Turkish* or *Persian* Language, as I have since learnt the last, that good Prince in all likelyhood would not have made so much ado.

¶ Upon the 22d, a Price was set on the Presents of the Envoys; it is the Custom in *Persia*, to carry the Present that is made to the King, into a large Apartment of the Royal Palace, which is call'd *Chiracone*, that is to say, the House of Wine, because it is the Buffet, and the Magazine where all the Wine for the King's drinking is kept. The Presents are consign'd to the chief of the King's Buttery, who is the Superintendant of that Apartment; the Price is set thereon some Days after according to the Valuation of the Merchants, and those that are best skill'd therein. Each part of the Present is afterwards distributed to those of the King's Officers, who have the charge of Things of the same Nature. The Tapistry for Example is delivered into the Magazine of the Place, where the Royal Manufacture thereof is practis'd; the Arms and Cannon are put in the *Arsenal*. The Jewels are laid up in the Treasury, and so of the rest. The particular Intendants of each respective Apartment, enter the same into their Books. The Present is likewise Register'd in the Chamber of Accompts belonging to the Demesn; and it is enroll'd in so many Registers, that it is impossible that any part thereof should be lost. If they had a mind to know one by one, all the Presents which have been made to the Kings of *Persia* for these two hundred Years, nothing would be easier, and the detail thereof would be readily found.

¶ I was sent for by the Nazir's Order to the Valuation of the Presents; I went accordingly, having first acquainted the Envoys therewith, and ask'd them, whether they desir'd their Things should be apprais'd according to their just Value, or whether at a higher or lower Rate. I ask'd this Question, because the Presents which are made to the King, pay a Duty of five and twenty *per Cent.* ready Money to the Officers of his Houshold, which is taken according to the Valuation that is made thereof; and let that be well or ill done, the Person who made the Present is obliged to acquiesce, and to pay the five' and twenty *per Cent.* On this Consideration it is really a Damage to an Ambassador, to value his Present at a high Rate; but then in another Respect, the Loss so sustain'd is again Recover'd; because as the King and the Ministers cause an Information to be given them of the Value of the Presents, in order that a due Regard may be had thereto, in the Requests that are made them; there one finds one Account to have a Present over-valu'd. I went to the Assignation about nine a Clock, where I found the Prevost of the Merchants, a Comptroler from the Palace, the chief of the *Goldsmiths,* the Intendants of the Manufactures of the Stuffs of Gold and Silk, the great Master of the Artillery, the chief of the Painters, and ten or twelve of the most considerable Merchants of *Ispahan.* They had begun the Appraisement. The Presents of the Envoy of the *French* Company, without comprising the Cannon, were valu'd at near twenty thousand Crowns. Those of the Envoy of the *English* Company, were esteem'd at three thousand five hundred Crowns. This being done, each Thing was set in its proper Place, according to what has been already said; the Looking-Glasses, the Branches, the Pistols, the Picture, and the Telescopes, were carry'd to the common Treasury, which is in the Castle of *Ispahan,* where all these Things will be consum'd and destroy'd by Time and the Dust, with a multitude of other Pieces of the same Nature, which the *Europeans,* and among the rest the *Muscovites,* the *Turks,* and the *Armenians,* have presented to the Kings of *Persia* within these two hundred Years. The Reason thereof is, that those Things not being us'd in that Country, they let them go to decay in some corner or other, not thinking it Consistant with the Honour and Grandure of the King, either to have them sold, or give them away. The Pepper, the Tea, the Amber, and the Oil of Cloves, were carry'd to the *Cherbet-Cane,* (this is the Magazine of Liquors.) The *China* Ware remain'd in the *Buffet,* and the Stuffs in fine were distributed into several of the King's Ward-Robes, there being one for each sort of Stuff.

CHAPTER XX

An occasional Conversation concerning the two Audiences. A Molla or Priest Bastinadoed, the Reason. The French Envoys Presents to the Ministers. The Muscovite Envoy has a Conference with the Ministers. Several Conjectures about his Negotiations. Exactness with which the Great Men in Persia are obey'd. First Establishment of the English in Persia.

THE same Day I being at Dinner with the Nazir, the Conversation fell upon the two Audiences, which we have related, upon the *Europeans* in General; and in fine, on the Contents which had happen'd between the Envoy of the *French* Company, and that of the *English* Company about the Precedency. I was ask'd whether in *Europe*, those trifling empty Subjects were very much insisted on; I smiling made Answer, that they had good Reason in my Opinion to speak so of Disputes of that Nature; but that however in *Europe*, they were not counted so. That there they were looked upon as essential Things, and that not only the Kingdoms fought for the Precedency, but that there was hardly any private Person but who had an Attention thereto, and was chary of his Rank, as of his chiefest Interest. The Master of the Horse, who was present, said then, That the *Mahometans* were very happy, in their being cur'd of those Infirmities, and in their not having plac'd Honour in such troublesome and dangerous Chimæra's.

¶ They thereupon related, amongst other things, That the First Minister had that Morning caus'd Two hundred Strokes to be given on the Soles of the Feet to a Molla, or Doctor, because some Inferior Officers of the Ordnance had presented Petitions to him, which this Doctor had written, and where the Sense was so confus'd and perplex'd with Compliments, and old Canting Stuff, that it was a difficult Matter to penetrate into the Meaning thereof, with ever so great an Attention. After this miserable Wretch had receiv'd so severe a Punishment, the First minister caus'd him to be brought before him (for he was not in a Condition to walk). *A Great Vizier,* said he to him, *has other Business to do than to read thy sorry Compliments, and to unravel and disintangle the Chaos of the Petitions thou writest: Use a more simple and clear Style, or else do not write for the Publick; for otherwise I'll cause thy Hands to be cut off.*

¶ On the 23d, that Minister delivered to the *Portuguese* Renegade, who was the King's Interpreter, the Letters which the Envoys had presented to the King, and to the Nazir. This Renegade, who made the *Persians* believe that he understood all the Languages of *Europe*, tho' he really knew no other than his Native Tongue, went and carry'd the Letters to the *Portugueze* Augustins, Missionaries at *Ispahan*, believing they would be able to explain them to him, but he found them as incapable of it as he was himself. They sent for the Interpreter of the *Hollanders*: He is an *Arabian*, who had been a long time in *Europe*, and has a great Talent for Languages: He was glad to have those Letters in his Hands, that he might be able to give a Copy thereof to his Masters, who are very curious to know the Affairs of other People, but more especially those which have any relation to theirs, and any-wise concern the Commerce; but however, he could not translate the King of *England*'s Letter, as not understanding *English*: He render'd the other two into *Persian*.

¶ On the 24th, the Envoy of the *French* Company sent to the Ministers, the Presents which he had prepar'd for them; To wit, To the *Etmadulet*, or Grand Vizier.

Seventeen Ounces of *Ambergrease*.
Two *Chals*, or *Indian* Sashes, which were very fine.
Six *Turbants* of Silk, Gold, and Silver.
A small *Clock*.
A *Watch*.
Twelve Pounds of *Tea*.

¶ To the Great Master, or High Steward,

Seventeen Ounces of *Ambergrease*.
Three *Turbants*, of Silk, Gold and Silver.
Three *Sashes*.
Three *Watches*.
Twelve Pounds of *Tea*.
Fifteen hundred *Crowns* in Ready-Money.

¶ To *Mirzataher*, Comptroller of the King's Household,

Two *Turbants*.
Four fine *Indian* Pieces of *Printed Callicoe*.
Thirty-four Pieces of *China Ware*, of different Sizes.
Three Pounds of *Cloves*.
Three Pounds of *Cinnamon*.
Three Pounds of *Tea*.
Three Pounds of *Cardamum*.
Fifty *Nutmegs*.
Thirty Pounds of *Pepper*.
One hundred and fifty *Crowns* in Ready-Money.

❡ The same Day, about Ten a-Clock in the Morning, the *Muscovite* Ambassador was brought upon the King's Horses to an Apartment of the Royal Palace, whither the Grand Vizier and the other Principal Ministers of the Council being come soon after, he was two Hours in Conference with them: He was entertain'd afterwards: The Feast was sumptuous in Meats and Liquors, but there was neither Wine nor Brandy.

❡ The Negotiation of this Ambassador was kept secret enough. The Ministers gave out, That his Commission was to make known to the King of *Persia*, that his Master would send an Ambassador Extraordinary to him in a little time. But it was known afterwards, that he came to propose to the King, to enter into the League which the Great Duke had lately made with the *Polanders* against the *Turks*, The King of *Persia* would not hearken to it: He nevertheless promis'd, That if the *Muscovites* and the *Polanders* were once heartily engag'd in a War against the *Turks*, and would afterwards give Sureties not to make a Peace without him, he would then take to his Arms, and fall upon *Bagdad*. This was the Answer which was given to the Ambassador, and upon which he was dispatch'd. He press'd hard to have a more precise one, but the First Minister stopp'd his Mouth, by telling him; That the Christians had often engag'd the Kings of *Persia* in a joint War with them against the *Turks*, and had afterwards made a separate Peace without their Participation.

❡ On the 27th, the First Minister sent for me very early in the Morning, and in great Haste. I was not yet up, and my Groom and Footman were both gone out. I therefore told the Messengers, That they might go back, and that as soon as my Servants came in, I would wait upon their Master. *How Sir*, said they, smiling, *don't you know that we dare not return without bringing you along with us?* In saying that, one of them ran to the Stable to saddle me a Horse; another offer'd to dress me, and I was oblig'd to suffer it. As I was going down Stairs, four more Horse-men came to bid me make haste. I was a little unwilling to go without a Footman, it being the Custom to have always one or two with one through the Streets of *Ispahan*, by reason of the Crowds of People. But they told me, That as I went, they would make way for me, and that at my Return, they would order me some Footmen. I observe this, that the Reader may know, with what Dispatch the Orders of the Great Men are executed in *Persia*. An Officer dare not tell his Master who has sent him to fetch any Person to him, that he has not found him, or that he was not at home, or that he can't come; he is obliged to find him, and bring him, or otherwise the Negligence of the Messenger is punish'd with a good Cudgelling. I went as fast as my Conductors pleas'd, as well out of Complaisance to them, as thereby to know the sooner what I was wanted for, which made me somewhat uneasie. The First Minister told me, He had sent for me to translate the King of *England*'s Letter, and that of the *French* Company. He deliver'd them into my Hands at the same time, and commanded two Secretaries to conduct me into a Closet, and to take the Translation of those Letters. I cannot tell whether the first Version he had caused to be made of them pleas'd him, or not, or whether he had a mind to have a Plurality of Translations for his greater Satisfaction. I put them into the *Persian* Language, the best I could, and took Copies likewise of each. That of the King of *England* was written in *English*, upon a large Sheet of Vellum, in Golden and black Letters, the upper Part, and the Sides, for the Breadth of about Six Inches, were painted in Miniature. The King's Picture, his Arms, his Motto, and his Cyphers, were there inchas'd in a Frize of Moresque-Work. Before I give a Copy thereof, I shall lay down a short Account of the first Establishment of the *English* in *Persia*.

¶ The *English* went for the first time into *Persia*, about the Year 1613. They were well enough receiv'd by the *Persians* at *Bandar-abassi*, but the *Portuguese* gave them a very bad Reception at *Ormus*, which is an Island but three Leagues distant from *Bandar-abassi*. The *Portuguese*, who were sole Masters of the Commerce throughout all the *Indies*, not being willing to share any thereof to these new Comers, but on the contrary, being resolv'd to oppose their Undertaking as much as they could; they thwarted them on all Occasions, and amongst other Hardships, they made them pay at *Ormus*, (where lay the main Traffick of the Gulph of *Persia*) more Duties, than all the other Nations. *Abas the Great*, the then King of *Persia*, who was very well inform'd of what pass'd among the *Europeans* in those Parts, caus'd an Offer to be made to the *English*, of the Trade in his Ports of the Continent. He sent them Presents: He allur'd some of them to his Court, where he caress'd 'em very much; and in fine, in the Year 1620, he engag'd them in a League with him, to drive the *Portuguese* out of the Gulph of *Persia*. He was not less incens'd against them, than the *English*, because they, on all Occasions, loaded his Subjects with Injuries and Affronts, and obstructed their Traffick. There was no passing safely to the *Indies* but in *Portuguese* Ships. Now when any *Persian* Merchants went to *Ormus*, to desire a Passage of the *Portuguese*, the Chief of them at *Ormus* would ask them, What they would go to the *Indies* to do? And what sort of Merchandize they wanted to buy? And when they had told them, they would lead them to the Magazine of the Place, and there showing them great quantities of those Goods, would say to them; there is what you want, buy that first, and then if you have any Money left to lay out, I'll order you a Passage to the *Indies*. With this Severity did the *Portuguese* oblige foreign Merchants either to return without doing any Thing, or else to buy the Goods they wanted of them, at what rate they pleas'd.

❡ *Abas* complain'd several times of this Usage to the Governor of *Ormus*, but all the Answers he receiv'd were so haughty and offensive, that they afforded fresh Matter of Complaint. This Great Prince therefore, resolv'd to ruin so insufferable a Power; he wanted Ships to transport his Troops to *Ormus*, which was the chief Fortress the *Portuguese* had in the *Persian* Gulph, and that which most annoy'd the Coasts of *Persia*; he propos'd to the *English* to joyn with him, which they accepted. The Treaty contained; ' That they should attack at their common Expences, what the ' *Portuguese* held in the Gulph. That the *English* should transport the ' *Persians* to the Isle of *Ormus*, and to those in the Neighbourhood thereof; ' and during the Siege, should hinder any Succours coming by Sea; that ' the Places which should be taken, should remain to the *Persians*, but ' that the Pillage, and all that should be found therein, should be equally ' divided. That the Traffick should be transferr'd to *Bandar-Abassi*, where ' the *English* should not only be free from all sorts of Duties, but should ' likewise have an equal Share with the *Persians*, of all the Customs and ' Duties laid on Goods imported, on Condition however, that they should ' maintain four Men of War in the Gulph, or two at least, in order to ' secure the Navigation to the Merchants.'

❡ This Treaty procur'd the taking of *Ormus* from the *Portuguese*, in the Year 1623, and of two other Islands just by, but since it has receiv'd continual Infractions on both Sides. The *Persians* who are not Sincere enough in the Observance of Contracts, and who slip no Opportunity that offers to Cheat and Trick, have not kept their Word with the *English*, whom they thought sufficiently paid for what they had Contributed to the taking of *Ormus*, by the rich Booty they there found, and by the Traffick which they could not obtain before; whereas they ought to have consider'd, that it was to the *English* that they ow'd the taking of those important Places, and the Liberty of their Coasts, and of their Commerce. They every Year defrauded the *English* of some part of their half of the Customs of *Bandar-Abassi*, and at last they proceeded so far, as to give them only eight or ten thousand Crowns for their half, notwithstanding the whole amounted to seven or eight hundred thousand Livres; and what is superlatively unjust, they oblige the *English* Agent to give them an Acquittance for one half of the Customs aforesaid, without which they wont pay him any Thing; the Pretext they make use of to palliate this Injustice, is, that the *English* have not maintain'd any Ships of War in the

Gulph, as they were oblig'd to do by the Treaty. They compel them also to pass under their Name, Goods that do not belong to them, and to transport great Sums of Gold and Silver out of the Kingdom, contrary to the Prohibitions made against so doing. The *English* were for a long time oblig'd to pass the same, whereever the *Persians* had a mind, not knowing how to do better; but reflecting on the Wrong that was done them, the *English* Company address'd the King of *England* in the Year 1670, and begg'd his Majesty would write to the King of *Persia* in favour of their lawful Pretentions. The Envoy of the *English* Company obtain'd Letters Patent from the King of *Persia*, to the Farmers of *Bandar-Abassi*, to pay five and forty thousand Livres *per Annum* to the *English*, besides their exemption from paying any Customs for any Thing that belong'd to them; but as the *English* Company was not satisfy'd with this Grant, it pray'd his Britannick Majesty afresh, to give it another Letter that might be still more pressing to the King of *Persia*, which was done, and it was that Letter I was ask'd to interpret. Here is a Copy of it.

¶ 'Charles' the Second, by the Grace of God, King of *England*, *Scotland*, 'France', and *Ireland*, Defender of the Faith; to the high and potent 'Monarch *Cha Soliman*, Emperor of *Persia*, *Media*, and *Hircania*, and of 'several other vast Countries and Lordships. We have been inform'd by 'the Directors of the *East-India* Company, of the Elevation of your Majesty 'to the Throne of your famous Ancestors, and of the Peace and Tran- 'quility which that great and mighty Empire of *Persia* enjoys under the 'Obedience of your Majesty; We thereupon with Pleasure Congratulate 'your Majesty, and most earnestly wish, that the Happiness and Pros- 'perity which it now enjoys may increase, and last as long as it is possible; 'and that the Omnipotent God will preserve and surround you with 'Glory, and heap upon you all the Blessings of Body and Mind. The said '*East-India* Company has in most humble manner represented to us, that 'about fifty Years ago, it made a Treaty with the famous *Cha Abas*, one 'of the most renow'd Predecessors of your Majesty, by which that great 'Prince in Consideration of the great and important Services this Company 'had done him at her own Expence, and particularly for the Assistance 'and Succour she supply'd him with to enable him to take the Castle 'of *Kichmich*, and the Castle, Town and Isle of *Ormus*, granted to her 'amongst other Priviledges and Advantages, one half of the Duties of 'the Customs which are paid by all the Merchants who trade on the side 'of *Ormus*, as well by Sea as by Land, as appears by the 3d Article of 'the said Treaty. Now this Company complains, that for several Years 'past your Majesties Officers deprive her Agents of the greatest part of

' the said Duties, and let them have so slender a Share of the Revenues
' of these Customs, that most commonly what they give them, is less than
' a Thousand Tomans, notwithstanding the Revenue thereof amounts
' to above thirty thousand Tomans yearly. We therefore desire, with a
' great deal of Affection, that a due Regard being had to the ancient
' Friendship, and good Correspondence that is between the two Nations
' as ought to be, the Exposition and Remonstrance which we make with
' a sincere Heart, of the Wrong and Damages which are done to this
' Company, will prevail with your Majesty to cause Justice to be done
' her; and that your Majesty will give Orders, that she may be satisfy'd
' and paid the Arrears of those Duties of the Customs, that is to say, what
' was wanting to what has been paid her heretofore to make up her just
' half. We also desire that your Majesty will make a firm and unalterable
' Settlement thereof for the future, and will give an absolute Command
' to your Officers and Ministers, that for the time to come they satisfie
' the Agents of the said Company, with one intire half of the Customs in
' a just Measure and Proportion, pursuant to the Tenor of the afore-
' mention'd Treaty; to the end, that sincere Friendship and good Cor-
' respondence which has endur'd so many Years between the two Nations,
' may continue without any Violation or Alteration. Hereupon we
' recommend your Majesty to the Protection of the Omnipotent.'

CHAPTER XXI

The first Minister's Resentment shown to the English. *Blunders in the Letters of the* French
Envoy. The King begins his Tour of Casbin. *Superstition observ'd. The sumptuousness of his
Travelling Buffet.*

THE first Minister was so vext to see the *English* were not contented
with what he had done in their favour two Years before, but
made fresh Application, that he could not smother his Resentment.
He told the Interpreter of the *English* Company one Day, when he
earnestly sollicited for a more favourable Composition than the first was;
It is thou that dost encourage the *English* to tire us with reiterated Demands; thou put'st two Ells of Scarlet with a little Tinsel, on the Back of
a Clerk, and mak'st him an Ambassador to us. *Persia* has paid the *English*
a thousand times over for the Service they reproach us with so much,
and which is the only one we ever have receiv'd from them. It was not
we who first began to infringe the Treaty, the *English* were the first who
did it, and we should be well grounded if we had not further regard at

all thereto. The *English* Agent could obtain nothing more, but that he might not be sent back altogether empty, he had a new dispatch of the Letters Patent of the Year 1670, and a Letter for the King of *England*, which was seal'd. To speak the Truth, there is no excusing the *Persians* on that Head, for Treaties ought to be always observ'd in their full Extent; but it must nevertheless be own'd, that they are to be commended for letting the *English* trade throughout their Empire free from all manner of Duties, and to pay them every Year fifty thousand Livres for a Service done fifty Years before; for which one may say, they were even then Superabundantly paid.

¶ As for the Letters of the Envoy of the *French* Company, to the King and the Nazir, they were Pieces too ill contriv'd to bear being made Publick. They bore Date from the first of *May*, 1671, yet nevertheless mention was made therein of the great Victories obtain'd by the King of *France* over the *Hollanders*, which did not happen till the Year following, and of their total Ruin and Destruction which was near at hand; those are the Terms, and thus it is that the *Monks* confound and lose themselves, when they intermeddle with the Affairs of the World; for it was the Superior of the *Capuchins* Missionaries at *Ispahan*, who had compos'd those Letters, and who directed the whole Embassy. The *English* and the *Dutch* made these Contradictions very sensibly plain, and the *Persians* themselves easily perceiv'd that those Letters were forg'd, and particularly by this, that they made mention of two Envoys equal in Quality and Collegues; and yet the Letter which Monsieur *Gueston* had writ to the Nazir at his arrival at *Bandar-Abassi*, and those of the Governor, and of the King's People from that Place, which gave Advice of his coming, made no mention but of him only as Envoy, so that it was a notorious Truth that he had neither Collegue nor Second. They knew very well besides, that after his Death all the Persons of his Retinue were a long time resolving what they should do, and that for some Days they told every Body, and even signify'd to the Governor of *Chiras*, that they would return back to *Bandar-Abassi*, as not having any Commission to proceed further.

¶ I have heard related at the Nazir's, a comical Thing enough concerning these Letters, which was, that as he was reading them to the King, a pleasant thought came into that Princes Head, upon the Names of the Envoy's of the Company; this was call'd *de Joncheres*, a Word which if pronounc'd ill in the *Persian*, signifies a young Lyon, and one of the three first Envoys was nam'd *Beber*, which signifies an old Tiger. The King hearing these Names repeated, stopp'd the Nazir, saying, what do they write, these *French* Merchants, that they first send an old Tyger, and that at present they sent a young *Lyon*? These Equivocations made him laugh heartily, and all those who were about him.

¶ On the 28th, I went and acquainted the *French* and *English* Envoys, that I had put their Letters into the *Persian* Language by the Order of the first Minister. The *English* Envoy show'd himself very glad thereat, and thank'd me, assuring me, that the *English* Company would hold it self very much oblig'd to me on that Account. In Reality, he had reason to be pleas'd that I had made the Translation thereof, because I had preserv'd to the Original all its Force and Energy, which is what the People of the Country dare not do, for fear of drawing upon themselves the Indignation of the Ministers, by saying something that might Displease, tho' they only do it in Obedience to Command. As for the other, I could discover through his Thanks, that he was very sorry I had seen his Letters, because it was impossible for the Forgery not to be plain and obvious to the Eyes of a *Frenchman*.

¶ Upon the first of *October*, the King left *Ispahan* at three a Clock in the Morning to begin his Journey to *Casbin*, which is the ancient *Arsatia*, and alighted at the House of *Hazar-gerib*, which is at the end of the Place where they take the Air at *Ispahan*, and about half a League from his Palace. The Astrologers made him rise at that early Hour, to go so little a way as half a League, by reason it was the lucky Moment of a favourable Constellation to begin so great a Progress. His Mother and his favourite Ladies set out at the same time.

¶ On the Second, I went in the Morning to the *Chiraconé*, which is the King's Side-Board, to see it pack'd up for the Journey. The Intendant or Overseer thereof, who is call'd in *Persia Chi-rachi-bachi*, which is to say, the chief of the Purveyors of Wine, was so kind as to show me all the finest Things that he had in his keeping. It consisted of several Sets of Dozens of Spoons, of Vessels, Cups, Salvers, Dishes, Basons, large Tankards, Water-pots, Boats, Bottles, Spitting-pots, all which were of Gold, either enamel'd, set with precious Stones, or curiously garnish'd with Pearls; there is nothing there but fine Gold, either delicately wrought, or finely set. It is incredible, the vast Quantity, and the Value of this Plate; there are Cups so large, that one cannot hold them in one Hand when they are full. There are also Drinking-Cups made like Ladles, which are frequently us'd at the King's Table, and are call'd *Azar-peché*, that is to say, a thousand Chimera's. This is to express, that one is so drunk when one had taken off some of them, that one's Head is all in Confusion. Some of these Cups hold only half a Pint, the largest hold three Pints, the ordinary ones hold a Quart. What seem'd most Royal to me, was a Dozen of

Spoons a Foot long, and large in Proportion made, to drink Broth out of, and other Liquors; the Bowl of the Spoon was of Gold enamel'd, the Handle was cover'd with Rubies, the end was a large Diamond of about six Carats. This Dozen of Spoons might be worth sixteen thousand Crowns. One must not wonder that the Handle of them is a Foot long, because as throughout the East, they eat on the Ground, and not upon Tables, one would be oblidg'd to stoop too low to take up the Broth, if the Spoons were not so long. The greatest part of all these Pieces are old fashion'd; without seeing ones self, the vast quantity there is of them, there is no believing what can be said thereof. I have try'd several times to know, to what Value the whole might amount in the Registers, for it is set down and exactly known, but I never could find it out; all the Answer I could get, was, that it was worth an immense Sum, and that the Account thereof was infinite. I am perswaded after what I have seen of it, that there is to the worth of several Millions. The head Butler told me one Day, that the King's Buffet contain'd four thousand Pieces, or Utensils, all of Gold, or embelish'd with Gold and precious Stones, as I have already said. This Lord gave me a Dinner, and made me drink of several sorts of Wine and Brandy, so much, that my Head turn'd round in a quarter of an Hour; for those Wines are mighty strong, and the Brandy's still more Violent. If the Brandy is not as strong as Spirits of Wine, it does not please in *Persia*, and the Wine that is most esteem'd there, is that which is most Intoxicating, and fuddles soonest. He treated me like a *Persian*, thinking it was entertaining me finely, to make me drunk presently. Wine in the *Persian* Language is call'd *Cherab*, a Term which in its Etemology denotes all sorts of Liquor. The word Sherbet, and that of Syrup, come from that of Cherab, which the devout *Mahometans* have in such an Abhorrence, by reason Wine Intoxicates, that it is a piece of ill Breeding to pronounce it in their Presence.

CHAPTER XXII

A Bargain of a thousand Pistols concluded with the Pontif's Lady for Jewels, the Value paid in Gold Plate. Contests concerning Fees due to some of the Ministers. Conferences of the French and English Envoys, with the Ministers of State. The Princess, the Pontif's Wife, shows her fine Jewels to the Author.

ON the 3d, I concluded a Bargain of a thousand Pistols, with the Great Pontif's Lady, who was Sister to the late King, as I have already observ'd. The Bargain being made, she sent me word, that as she was to go along with the Court, she should have occasion for her ready Money, but that she gave me my choice, either to take an Order to be paid in two Months, or to take Gold Plate. I accepted of the Gold, and I was put off till the Evening; but I was no sooner come according to the Appointment, than an Eunuch, who was the Princess's Steward, brought a flat Bason that weigh'd six hundred Ounces within a very little. I had taken along with me an *Indian* Banker, very well skill'd in Gold and Silver; he touch'd the Bason in several Places, and judg'd it to be Gold of three and twenty Carats and a half, and told me he would warrant it at that rate. I bargain'd for it at fifty six Livres *per* Ounce; I would have willingly bought the whole Bason at that Price, but they would not let me have any more than what my payment came to.

¶ At Night I went to Court to see several Noblemen who ow'd me Money; the King's High Steward, the Captain at the Gate, and the Receiver of the Presents who were of the Number, desir'd me to go to the Envoy of the *French* Company, and to tell him, that it was wonder'd at, at Court, that he would not pay the Fees of the Presents he had made to the King. That therein he was wrong inform'd of the Customs of *Persia*, since all Ambassadors, and generally all those who make Presents to the King, from what Place soever they come, pay those Fees which were an establish'd Duty, and the chief Perquisite of their Places, and of the other Officers who had a share therein. That it was in vain he struggl'd not to pay them, for he would certainly find he must. Those Noblemen told me this in a much loftier Strain than I relate it; others who had an Interest in the same Duty, charg'd me likewise with the same Message, so that I thought my self oblig'd to acquaint him therewith, that he might be the better able to take safe Measures. I found him prepossess'd in favour of his Conduct; he answer'd me, ' That he had given those ' Lords to understand, when he was first spoken to concerning that Duty, ' that he was come to make a Present to the King, but had not brought any ' Thing for the Officers, and that absolutely he would give them nothing, ' and pray'd me to carry them that Answer at my Conveniency. It was ' put in the Envoy's Head to speak after this manner, and it was suggested ' to him, that the Nazir would free him from this pretended Duty; that ' Lord made some Steps indeed in order thereunto.' He read to the King the Petition which the Envoy had presented to that Purpose. On the other hand, the great Men who were concern'd therein, preferr'd likewise their Petitions in opposition to his, this Difference made a Noise. The first Minister did not declare his Opinion; the Envoy alledg'd, that his Collegue who had a greater Liberty in his Orders, was dead, but as for himself, he had no Power to give any Thing, beyond what was prescrib'd in his Commission. The Nobles alledg'd in their behalf the Customs, and that this Fee was a part of their Salaries. At last the King's Council order'd, that the Matter should be examin'd into among the *English*, the *Portuguese*, and the *Hollanders*, and that if it appear'd that any Ambassador or Envoy of those Nations had at any time been exempted from paying that Duty, this Envoy should likewise have the same Favour. The Interpreters of those Nations were thereupon sent for, and the Registers of the Receiver of the Presents were likewise brought and search'd. At last they all agreed, that no *European* had ever been freed from that Duty and that the *French* Envoy must do as the rest had done; they show'd him however some favour, and he came off for ten thousand eight hundred Livres.

¶ This Duty is fifteen *per Cent.* by Constitution; but the Abuses that have crept into it, have made it amount to near five and twenty. The Lord High Steward has ten of it, which of Right he ought to share with the Yessaouls, who are like the King's Gentlemen in Ordinary, and are four and twenty in Number; but he gives them little or nothing out of it. The other fifteen *per Cent.* are for the Intendants of the Gallaries or Magazines where the Presents are laid up, as has been said: Thus the Duties on the Jewels which are presented to the King, are for the chief of the Treasury, and the chief of the *Goldsmiths*, and so of the rest.

¶ The same Day the High Steward sold to the *Armenians*, in the King's Name, a Diamond of three and fifty Carats, which belong'd to the Princess his Mother, for a hundred thousand Livres to be paid in eighteen Months. This Minister had endeavour'd to exchange it with me, for some part of what I had brought, but as I did not care to meddle with it, and the King's Mother had taken a Dislike to it, and was desirous to get rid of it at any Rate, the Corporation of *Armenian* Merchants were compell'd to buy it. They refus'd the Bargain as long as they could; but they were so strongly press'd and importun'd to gratify the King's Mother, that they were at last forc'd to comply. If at first they had made a Present of seven or eight hundred Pistoles to the Nazir, he would have secur'd them from this Oppression. They offer'd me, eight Days after, that Diamond at a third part Loss.

¶ On the 4th, the Envoy of the *French* Company had a Conference with the First Minister. He went at Ten a Clock to that Lord's House. The Nazir was there, and several other Ministers. They fell to discourse concerning the Letters he had presented, and the Memorial of his Diamonds; and they ask'd him, What it was that he offer'd in exchange for the Exemptions from the Duties, and for the other Favours to which he pretended? Here he was at a loss what to answer, and he desir'd the

Superior of the Capuchins might be sent for. This was granted, and the Capuchin being come, he answer'd in the Name of the Envoy, That he had no power at all to treat, and he was come on no other Account than to make a Present to the King, and to desire a Confirmation of the Privileges granted by the late King to the Company, and confirm'd by the King Regent. The Ministers made answer: ' That the first Deputies of ' the Company, who came in the Year 1665, had given their Word, upon ' their receiving those Privileges, that at the Expiration of three Years, ' the Company would send fresh Deputies, not only to bring Presents, ' but also to conclude a Treaty of Commerce with *Persia*; and that it was ' entirely upon that Promise that those Privileges had been granted them; ' and that the King had confirm'd them at the beginning of his Reign.' The First Minister moreover said: ' The *English* have the Exemptions ' which you desire, for having put *Ormus* into the Hands of the *Persians*. ' The *Portuguese* enjoy the same; for having yielded up to *Persia*, those ' Lands which they held in the Gulph. The *Hollanders* have them likewise, ' in consideration of Six hundred Bales of Silk, which they every Year ' take of the King, at a 3d Part dearer than they are in the Market. Now ' what is it the *French* will give us for the same Exemptions they enjoy? ' The Superiour of the Capuchins answered for the Envoy, ' That he had ' no Order to treat of any Conditions: That Monsieur *Gueston*, who was ' Plenipotentiary, would have treated thereof if he had come; but he ' being dead, the Envoy here present had no other Orders, than to make ' the King the Present which he had brought, and to desire a Continua- ' tion of the Privileges which had been granted to the Company.' Hereupon the First Minister, turning to the other Ministers, said to them, with an affected Gravity, ' That he believ'd it was really true, since, in all ' Likelihood, the Company would not have made Choice of so young ' a Person as the Envoy was, for a Negotiation of Importance.' He afterwards turn'd to the Superiour of the Capuchins, and ask'd him, how he reconcil'd the Answer he had just now made, with the Letter which the Envoy had deliver'd to the King from the Company; which contains, that the Sieurs *Gueston*, and de *Joncheres*, are equal in Quality, and in Power; and that she sends two Deputies, that in case the one should die, the other might fulfil the Deputation. The Father Capuchin found himself a little perplex'd with this Contradiction, and endeavour'd to clear it; but the Divan was so ill satisfy'd with his Reply, that it did not vouchsafe to answer it. The First Minister then made a long Enumeration, ' of the ' good Usage that had been dealt to all those that belong'd to the Company, ' and how their Traffick had been encourag'd, since its Establishment in

' the Year 1664. They having been suffer'd to trade without paying any
' Duties; whereas the Company, instead of making good the Promises its
' first Deputies had made, and given in Writing in the Company's Name,
' sent now to desire a Continuation of those Favours, without offering
' any thing in exchange for the same.' The Envoy's Counsel answer'd in
Promises and good Words. In fine, after a pretty long Discourse, the first
Minister told them, ' That the King should be inform'd of what had
' pass'd in the Conference; and that his Majesty, according to his usual
' Generosity, would not fail to give a favourable Answer to the Envoy's
' Petitions, and that he might hope for the same. He charg'd him also
' to write to the Company, That the King was altogether well inclin'd
' to promote its Traffick, as were likewise all his Ministers, and that
' whatever was Reasonable, should be done in its Favour.' The Negotiation being ended, Dinner was serv'd up, which indeed was very splendid,
and a quarter of an Hour after, the Envoy was dismiss'd.

¶ The next Day, the Agent of the *English* Company had a like Conference
with the Divan, or Council, concerning its Affairs. He represented, in
a long Discourse, ' The Injustice which was dealt for many Years past
' to the Company, in defrauding it of the one half it has a Right to, of
' the Customs of *Bandar-Abassi*, by a solemn Contract made with the late
' Kings of *Persia*. Next, the little Regard that was had to the *English* for
' some time past, and the Hardships they were made to undergo in several
' Custom-Houses, where their Portmanteaus were search'd, and their
' Goods visited.' To which the First Minister made answer, ' That that
' had been done without Order, and that he would cause Justice to be done
' thereupon, tho' it was not altogether without Reason they had that
' Usage, because the *English* were suspected to have carry'd away every
' Year large Sums of Ducates, contrary to the Laws of the Kingdom, and
' had been caught in the Fact.' He then answer'd to the main Point,
' That as for what regarded the Customs of *Bander-Abassi*, the Face of
' things was very much chang'd since the taking of *Ormus*; and that if
' the *Persians* had any way infring'd the Treaty, it was upon the Pattern
' set them by the *English* Company: That this was evident from the same
' Treaty, by which that Company was oblig'd to maintain a Squadron
' of Ships in the Gulph of *Persia*, to keep the Sea clear, and to secure the
' Commerce; notwithstanding which it was many Years since any one
' *English* Ship had been employ'd on that Account: That this was the
' Cause, that the *Portuguese*, and the *Arabians* strangely infested it to the
' great Damage of *Persia*; the first carrying away the Ships by Force, to
' other Ports than that of *Bandar-Abassi*, and loading them with a thousand

' Oppressions.' This Conference was long, and the Grand Vizier re-proach'd the *English* severely on the account of the passing under their Name, Merchandize that did not belong to them. The Envoy reply'd, ' That this was done unknown to, and contrary to the Orders of the ' Company; and that he would take effectual Care that no such thing ' should be practis'd for the future.' After this, he was splendidly enter-tain'd at Dinner.

¶ The same Day, the Princess, Wife to the Great Pontif, caus'd to be shown to me a Pearl Necklace, a Jewel, and a pair of Pendants, which very well deserve to find a Place in this Journal. It was on the account of my Jewels that she did me this Favour. She had caus'd me to be ask'd for the finest I had left; and I had a Pearl Necklace which I very much esteem'd, it was worth Ten thousand Crowns; I sent it to her. The Princess having seen it, and all my other Jewels, she order'd me to be thank'd, and sent me a String of Pearls. I never in my Life saw such fine ones, nor so large; It consisted of Thirty-eight Oriental Pearls, each weighing Twenty-four Carats, all well form'd, of the same Water, and same Bigness: It is not an Ornament for the Neck, but for the Face, after the *Persian* Manner: It is fasten'd at the Temples to the Head-band, or Fillet, and comes down the Cheeks, and under the Chin. The two Pen-dants for the Ears, which she likewise sent me, were two Rubies Ballass, of an ill Form, but clear and of a good Colour, each of 'em weigh'd about two Drams and half. The Eunuch told me, That an Ambassador who was sent from *Persia* to *Turkey*, by King *Sefi*, the Father of this Princess, had bought them at *Constantinople*, for a hundred and twenty Thousand Crowns. The Jewel was of Rubies and Diamonds, with Bobs of Diamonds: No finer can be seen, either for the Clearness, Beauty, or Liveliness of the Stones.

¶ The Jewels of this Princess were worth Forty thousand Tomans, which, of *French* Money amounts to eighteen hundred Thousand Livres. The Eunuch told me, That the Princess had so much Goodness for me, that she would have let me see them too, if they had not been fasten'd to her Cloaths, and most of them made up into Girdles; but that it was not customary in *Persia* for the Ladies to let their Cloaths be seen. This is true, and it would be counted an infamous thing. They say moreover, That by seeing a Lady's Cloaths, one may guess thereby at her Shape and Make, and by that means, use Witchcraft upon her Person. The *Persian* Women are surprizingly weak in reference to Witchcraft, for they believe them as they do the greatest Truths, and dread 'em more than Hell it self.

CHAPTER XXIII

The Mosque of Metched *repair'd, which was thrown down by an Earthquake. Calaats delivered to all the Ambassadors and Envoys. The King proceeds on his Journey. Translation of the King's Edicts. The* Persians *Ignorance as to the* European *Parts of the World.*

O N the 9th, I went to the House of the King's Goldsmiths, which is in the Royal Palace, to see them make some Gilt Plates in the Form of Tiles, which were to cover the Dome of the Mosque of *Iman-Reza*, at *Metched*, which an Earthquake had flung down, as I before related. A thousand Men, as was said, were employ'd in repairing this Mosque; and they work'd at it with so much Diligence and Application, that it was to be finish'd by the latter end of *December*. These Plates were of Brass, and square, Ten Inches in Breadth, and Sixteen in Length, and of the Thickness of two Crown-Pieces. Underneath were two Barrs three Inches broad, solder'd on Cross-wise, to sink into the Parget, and so serve as Cramp-Irons to fasten the Tiles. The upper part was gilt so thick, that one would have taken the Tile to have been of Massif-Gold: Each Tile took up the weight of three Ducates and a quarter of Gilding, and came to about ten Crowns Value. They were order'd to make Three thousand at first, as I was told by the Chief Goldsmith who was Overseer of the Work.

¶ On the 13th, in the Morning, Calates were carry'd to all the Ambassadors and Envoys that were at *Ispahan*. These are (as I have often observ'd) those Cloaths which the King gives to do Honour to those they are sent to. The First Minister sent them word, to put 'em on, and to come and receive their Audience of Leave, at the House of Pleasure, where the Court was, since its Departure from *Ispahan*.

¶ No Ambassador nor Envoy receives his Audience of Leave, but cloath'd with this Habit; and when it is sent to him, it is a certain Mark that he is going to be dismiss'd. These Calates are of different Sorts: Some of them are worth a thousand Tomans, which are Fifteen thousand Crowns; those are enrich'd with Pearls and Precious Stones. In a word, the Calates have no set Price, and they are given more or less rich, according to the Quality of the Persons. Some of them consist of a whole Suit of Cloathing, even to the Shirt and Shoes. Some of them again are taken out of the King's own Wardrobe, and from amongst the Garments he has worn. The common ones are compos'd of four Pieces only, *viz.* a Vest, an upper Vest, a Scarf, and a Turbant, which is the Covering us'd in that Country for the Head. Those which are given to Persons of Consideration, as Ambassadors, are usually worth fourscore Pistoles. The others that are given to Persons of a meaner Condition, are not worth above half as much. There are some given, that are not worth ten Pistoles, and consist only of a Vest, and Survest, In fine, the Quality of the Person is what regulates the Value and Quality of the Calates that are given to him. I saw one given in the Year 1666, to the Ambassador of *India*, which was valu'd at an Hundred thousand Crowns: It consisted of a Garment of Gold Brocard, with several upper Vests, lin'd with Marten Furrs, and enrich'd with a Clasp of Precious Stones; of Fifteen thousand Crowns in Money; of Forty very fine Horses, which were valu'd at an Hundred Pistoles each; of Trappings garnish'd with Precious Stones; of a Sword and Dagger which were cover'd over with the same; of two great Boxes, fill'd with rich Brocards of Gold and Silver; and of several Chests of dry'd Fruits, Liquors, and Essences: All this was call'd a Calate.

❡ It is not to be believ'd, the vast Expence the King of *Persia* is at in these Presents; the Number of Garments he thus bestows is infinite; his Wardrobes are therefore always kept full of them, and the Nazir causes them to be deliver'd according to the King's Pleasure. They are kept in separate Magazines according to their respective Sorts. The Nazir only marks upon a Ticket, what Magazine the Garment which the King gives is to be taken out of. The Officers of these Magazines and Wardrobes have a settl'd Duty paid them out of these Cloaths, which amounts to above half the value thereof. This Duty or Fee is the chief Perquisite of these Officers, and when the King commands any Habit to be given without taking Fees, (which very rarely happens) he makes them good to the Officers, so that they never loose them. It is the same in all the Presents the King makes; if it be in ready Money, the Super-intendant of the Treasury takes five *per Cent.* which is shar'd among several Officers of the King's Houshold. The Nazir has for his particular Share two *per Cent.* if it be of Horses, the Master of the Horse has the like Fee out of it; if it be of Jewels, the chief of the *Goldsmiths* has the same, and so of the others; to conclude, the King of *Persia* never dismisses any Stranger, till he has sent to him a Calate, and likewise one to each of the principal Persons of his Retinue, and to his Interpreter.

❡ The Calate of the *Muscovite* Ambassador consisted of a fine Horse, with Trappings of Silver guilt, the Saddle and Housing being embroider'd; of three compleat Suits of Brocard, the Ground of one of which was Gold, that of another was Silver, and that of the other was Silk; and of nine hundred Pistoles, half is ready Money, and half in Stuffs. That of the

Envoy of the *French East-India* Company was, a Horse without Furniture, four Suits of Brocard, two of which were Compleat, the Ground of the one being Gold, and that of the other of Silver; the other two were not Compleat, and had Silk Grounds; and five hundred Pistoles, half in ready Money, and half in Stuffs. The Agent of the *English* Company had for a Calate, a Horse without Furniture, as the Envoy of the *French* Company had; three Suits like those of the *Muscovite* Ambassador, and a Sword garnish'd with *Turkey* Stones, to the Value of three hundred and fifty Pistoles. These Gentlemen repair'd to Court in the Afternoon. The *Mahometan* Ambassador had been dismiss'd in the Morning in the Great Hall, which is at the End of the Garden of that fine Palace. The Halls thereof were very neat, the Cascades play'd, the Waters made a charming Murmur, and the whole Court was there in admirable Order, and pompous Splendor. The Introductor of Ambassadors conducted the *Muscovite* Ambassador to Audience. The Envoy of the *French* Company follow'd, being conducted by an Assistant of the Ceremonies. The Agent of the *English* Company came after, conducted by such an other Officer; they all three joyn'd at the entrance of the great Hall where the King was, and the whole Court. The Ambassador from *Muscovy* enter'd with his Second, and his Interpreter cloath'd in Calates. They advanc'd to within four Paces of the King, and there the Ambassador and his Second, falling on their Knees, bow'd their Heads three times to the Ground, and then rose up. At the same time, the Nazir took from the Hands of the first Minister, the King's Answer to the Letter of the Great Duke, and put it into those of the Ambassador. He would out of Honour have fix'd it on his Forehead like a Headband, if it would have stuck, but it fell off; he took it up immediately and carry'd it on the Palm of his Hands. This Letter was shut up in a Bag of Gold Brocade, very thick, a Foot and half long, and as broad as one's Hand, the Seal being affix'd to the Strings of Gold with which the Bag was ty'd. While the Ambassador withdrew, the Envoy of the *French* Company advanc'd to the same Place, and bow'd after the same Manner; his Second, and his Chirurgeon, who accompany'd him, did the like. Then the *English* Agent advanc'd as the others had done; but he made his Bow after the *European* Manner, as did his Second also, and then he withdrew. As he was bowing his Body the third time, the Nazir put into the folds of his Turbant, the King's Answer to the King of *England*'s Letter; it was folded up, put into a Bag, and seal'd like that which had been given to the *Muscovite* Ambassador. The Envoy of the *French* Company, was the only Person amongst them that was dismiss'd without an Answer; he was put off for some Days. The King look'd at him, and at all the other *Europeans* with a great Inclination to Laugh, seeing them wear the *Persian* Habit so awkwardly; in reality, one could not contain one self, that Dress so ill became them, and even disfigur'd them. After this, the King gave several Strangers, and several Persons of the Country who were come to Court, leave to depart, and receiv'd divers Presents.

¶ On the 14th, the King set out towards the Evening, and went and lay at a Country-House two Leagues from this, at the other end of the Town. He went on the outside of the Town, the Astrologers having found by the Motion of the Stars, that he must not go through the City. The *Armenians* waited for him in a Body on the Road, having their chief at the Head of them, in order to wish his Majesty a good Journey; and because there is no appearing before the King with empty Hands, they made him a Present of four hundred Pistols.

¶ On the 17th, the Nazir introduc'd me to the King; he was in a Night-Gown in a little Garden, leaning against a Tree hard by a Bason of Water. The King bid me procure him the Jewels mention'd in a Memorial which the Nazir would give me, and that I should be Satisfy'd.

¶ The 18th, the King proceeded on his Journey, and went to a great Borough two Leagues off, call'd *Deulet abad*, that is to say, the Habitation of Grandure.

¶ The King's Stages are never longer than that, and he finds at every one of them a House of his own, throughout all the Provinces of his Empire.

¶ On the 27th, the Interpreter of the *French* Company, who had follow'd the Court, return'd with Dispatches for the Envoy, which consisted of three Ordinances of the King in favour of some of the said Envoy's Demands in a Letter to his Majesty, and of a Letter from the Nazir to this Company; it was not one half of what he expected, they told him that he might assure the Company, that whenever he sent a Deputy to treat of the Commerce, he should be gratify'd in all his Pretentions. He had begg'd some small Favours for the Capuchins and Jesuits, but they were refus'd him with the rest. Here follow a Translation of the Ordinances and Orders.

GOD.

¶ ' Edict of the King of the World, directed to the Governor, the In-
' tendant, and other Royal Officers of the Town of *Chiras*, the Theatre
' of Sciences who ought all to hold themselves sure of our good Will, and
' of our Royal Favours. The Great Kings who have been taken up to
' Heav'n, after having been during their Lives the true Lieutenants of

' the true Prophet, who is in Paradise, to wit, the King our Father
' (whose Excuses at Judgment may God vouchsafe to hear) and the King
' our Grand-Father (to whose Royal Ashes may it please God to show
' Mercy) having permitted by their Letters Patent, the Companies of
' the *Dutch* and the *English* to transport every Year to the holy Port *Abas*,
' and to *Ispahan*, the Seat of the Monarchy, all the Wine necessary for
' their Use, the *French* Company has by most humble Petitions to us
' presented, intreated us to grant it the Favour to transport likewise from
' *Chiras*, to the sacred Port *Abas*, as much Wine as shall be requisite for
' their Drinking. Our most noble Majesty has therefore granted to them
' these honourable Letters Patent directed to you, to the end you permit
' the Commissaries of this Company to make Wine in their Houses, and
' that at all times, even when we forbid you to make any Wine within
' your Government, the aforesaid Prohibitions relating only to the Faithful.
' Take therefore special care, that no Body hinders the Commissaries of
' the said Company from making of Wine and transporting it where they
' please. You must also know, that this Edict is made on rigorous Penal-
' ties, and that there is no infringing it, without being expos'd to Capital
' Punishment. Done in the Month of *Rejeb*, in the Year of the *Hegira*, 1084.'

GOD.

¶ ' Edict of the King of the World, directed to the Governors and in-
' tendants of the celebrated Cities of *Lar*, and of *Jarron*; they are to know
' that at this present, the Envoy of the *French East-India* Company, has
' given to understand by Petitions dispers'd in our Royal Palace, which
' is a Copy of the Heaven of God, that as he came to *Ispahan*, the Seat of
' the Monarchy; certain Thieves between *Lar* and *Jarron*, have taken
' some Things from his Domesticks to the value of sixty Tomans, Money
' of *Tauris*; We therefore absolutely command the Regents, and all the
' other Royal Officers of those Towns, to cause an exact and diligent
' enquiry to be made of this Robbery, and to recover it by whatever
' manner it may be, and to take the Robbers, and punish them as the
' Crime shall require, after having made them confess it by earnest
' Solicitations or by Torments. In case the Things stoln, nor the Robbers
' cannot be found, the said Regents and other Royal Officers, are to be
' Responsible for the Robbery, and to pay the Value thereof, *&c.*'

GOD.

¶ ' Edict of the King of the World, directed to the Governor, Intendant,
' and to the Farmer-general of the Holy Port *Abas*. They are to know,

' that the Envoy of the *French East-India* Company has had his Audience
' of Leave. Now he hath desir'd by a most humble Petition, that the said
' Company may be permitted to transport every Year some Horses from
' *Persia* to *France*. We have therefore granted his Request, and have
' ordain'd, and do ordain by these present Letters, that the *French* be
' suffer'd once a Year to transport five Horses from the Holy Port *Abas*
' to their Country, without giving them any Trouble or Opposition, or
' offering the least hindrance, as also without asking, or showing Pre-
' tentions to any Duties for the foreign Exportation of those Horses. You
' are to know, *&c.*'

¶ The *Persians* have so little knowledge yet of the World, that they
frequently ask, if there be any Horses in *Europe*, seeing all the *Europeans*
carry from *Persia* as many as they can. They imagine that we transport
them into our own Country, whereas it is to make use of them in the
Indies, where there are only little Horses, and those ugly ones, as well as
few in Number.

CHAPTER XXIV

The King's Letter and the Nazirs to the French *Company. The* English *dispatch'd afterwards.*
Punishment of the King's Officers upon the Road. The Author receives his Money for his Jewels sold
to the King, his Acquittance, the Manner of it.

¶ *The King's Letter, and that of the Nazir to the Company, were these following.*

' To the most honourable Lord, *Colbert, Berrier, le Pelletier, Jabac,*
' *Chanlatte, Cadeau,* most Illustrious Chiefs of the Christian
' Merchants, Directors of the great Commerce of the *French:*
' Be assur'd of our Royal Favour and good Will, and know that the Re-
' quests and Presents which you have sent to our Court, (which is the
' Refuge of the Universe) by the Sieurs *Gueston* and *de Joncheres* your
' Deputies, are happily arriv'd there. This last who is the Flower of his
' Equals, has had the Felicity and the Glory to appear before the Eyes
' of our most high Majesty, and to have had a look from it. We, in Con-
' formity to the Letters Patent, which the late King of high and invincible
' Memory has granted you, and which our Majesty had confirm'd and
' renew'd with Honour to you some time ago, have absolutely com-
' manded, that Honour be done to, and Consideration had for the cele-
' brated Merchants of the Kingdom of *France*, who go and come into our
' Kingdoms, the best govern'd of all the Earth. Knowing therefore the

' Grace and intire Favour which is done to you by our most high Majesty
' which wants nothing, apply your self wholly to your Traffick and Mer-
' chandize, with all Hope and Expectation of a happy Success: Cause
' your Agents and Factors to go and come throughout the whole Extent
' of our vast Empire with a full Confidence in our Royal Benevolence,
' and an Assurance of obtaining all sorts of Favours. Depute also to us
' one of your Merchants, and send him to our High Court (which is the
' Refuge of Human Kind) upon all Affairs you shall have to treat there,
' cause Petitions to be presented to us, and hold your selves sure, that they
' shall be honourably answered, and that as far as Reason will permit,
' you shall obtain all things from the extreme Bounty and Clemency of
' our Majesty, the lively Image of God. As soon as the Mark of our most
' High Majesty shall be put to this Letter, and that our Paraph, and our
' Seal, most Noble, most Holy, and most High, shall have embellish'd it,
' and fill'd it with Lustre and Force, it is requisite that all Belief be given
' thereto, that an absolute Obedience be paid to the same. Done in the Month
' of *Rejeb the Great*, in the Year of the *Hegira*, One thousand Eighty four.'

GOD.

¶ ' Emminent and Puissant Lords, *Colbert, Le Pelletier, Berrier, Chapellier,*
' *Jabac, Chanlate, Cadeau,* Persons full of Honour and Magnificence,
' Illustrious among the People who follow the Law of JESUS, Directors in
' Chief of a powerful Company of Christian Merchants. After we have
' paid you our Civilities, and have assur'd you, that this Letter is a certain
' Token of the Good-will and Friendship we have for you; We make
' known to you, the Arrival of your Deputies, M. *Gueston,* and M. *des*
' *Joncheres,* to whom you had given a Commission to come to this Court.
' The first of the two being Dead, M. *des Joncheres,* a Person of Dignity,
' Capacity and Honour, took upon himself the whole Commission. He
' came hither in a good, happy, and favourable Time, with the Presents,
' and Requests with which you had charg'd him for this Court, which is
' the Refuge of the whole World: He, his Presents, and Petitions, have,
' by Favour, had a Look from our most High, most Noble, most Sublime,
' and most Holy Monarch, to whom nothing is wanting, being King of
' the Universe, and the Image of God; may my Soul, and that of all his
' other Slaves, be sacrific'd to the Dust of his blessed Feet. His Majesty
' has made known, how much all that was acceptable to him, by the
' Privileges which he has caus'd to be dispatch'd for your said Deputy,
' full of his usual Magnificence.

¶ ' Your first Deputies, who came here in the Reign of the late King,

' presented Petitions to him, and he caus'd Dispatches to be made for
' them, with an incomparable Generosity, of very honourable Letters-
' Patent, the Tenor whereof was; That the Farmers of the Customs, and
' the Receivers of the Duties and Tolls of *Persia*, should acknowledge your
' Factors and Agents, to be free from all Duties, of what Nature soever,
' during the time and space of three Years, taking special Care not to
' show the least Pretension of Duty on your Merchandize; only that an
' Account should be kept of all the Effects they should so bring during
' those three Years, but without pretending to any Custom for the same;
' and that because your said Deputies promis'd, that at the Expiration of
' that Term, you would send to this Court, the Refuge of the Universe,
' fine and rich Presents, as an Equivalent, and by way of Compensation
' for the Duties of the Customs and Tolls which they ought otherwise to
' have paid, and that at the end of three Years, the Behaviour on both
' sides, should be pursuant to what should be agreed to in a Treaty of
' Commerce. At the same time that this Regulation was finish'd and
' prepar'd, it was annull'd at the Request of your said Deputies, and out
' of an Excess of Bounty and Favour, other Letters-Patent, were very
' honourably dispatch'd for them, which imported an Injunction to all
' the Officers of the Customs, Duties, and Tolls of *Persia*, to acknowledge
' your Agents, and Factors to be exempt from all sorts of Taxes and
' Duties, and out of the Bounds of their Power and Authority, without
' any Limitation of Time; and to take special Care not to exact from them
' any thing whatever, provided they made such Use thereof as was con-
' formable to the Terms of the Obligation in Writing, which they deliver'd
' to the Officers of our Court, the Image of Paradise. These Letters-
' Patent, have, by Honour and Favour, been confirm'd and renew'd in
' the same Form and Tenor, by our most High, most Great, and most
' Noble Monarch, to whose Happiness nothing is wanting. It is near ten
' Years this Day, since that was done, and yet no-body is come on your
' Part. What perplexeth most, is, That this Obligation of your first
' Deputies is not to be found, for that *Macsudbec*, Nazir, (to whom God
' has given Absolution) into whose Hands it had been deliver'd, has
' quitted this Life: So that there is no telling for certain, what were the
' Clauses, Articles and Conditions thereof. We have had a Conference
' on all this with the Emminent M. *des Joncheres*. All the Answer he made
' us was, That he was neither your Agent, nor your Deputy, to know your
' Affairs. Upon this Answer, we propos'd to our most Great King, that
' you might have three Years time more, to send to this most High Court
' a Deputy, to make another Obligation, and another Engagement. My

' Proposition was luckily approv'd of, and agreed to: Fail not therefore,
' Emminent Lords, to nominate, and send to this most High Court,
' before the Expiration of that Term, one of your Commissioners, to give
' another Obligation, and present Petitions on all the Requests you shall
' have to make. The *English* Nation has done several important Services
' to *Persia*, in Compensation for which, a great many Privileges and
' Advantages have been granted to them. The same is expected from your
' Nation, and that we shall receive good Offices from it, in Payment
' of the Royal Favours, which you have receiv'd from his Majesty, and
' of the Exemption from all kinds of Duties which he has granted to your
' Commerce. As to the Eight Requests contain'd in the Letter which
' your Envoy has deliver'd to us, some of them have been granted, *viz.*
' A Confirmation of the Privileges which had before been granted to you,
' and fresh Letters-Patent have been dispatch'd for that Purpose: And
' as to the others, the Grant and Concession of them has been delay'd
' till the Arrival of a new Envoy. Be most assur'd and fully perswaded,
' that the Person you shall depute to the Foot-stool of the unshakeable
' Throne of our Monarch, shall obtain all his Demands, and shall return
' with a Success altogether answerable to your Desires. Do not delay
' sending him, and do not behave your selves so, that I may be in Confusion
' for the Accommodation I have procur'd, and of the Assurances I have
' given of your Gratitude and Acknowledgment. In all kinds of Affairs
' you shall have here, make your Intentions known to us, and be assur'd,
' that, with the Help of God, and by the Favour of our Great King, whose
' most exalted, and most solid Fortune, is not subject to Change, they shall
' have a Success, which shall fulfil, and even surpass your Expectation.
' In the Month of *Regeb the Great*, and Year of the *Hegira*, One thousand
' Eighty-four.'

¶ The *English* had their Dispatches a few Days after, which consisted of
a Confirmation of their Privileges; but they had no Satisfaction concerning
the Arrears of the one half of the Customs of *Bandar-abassi*, which they
desir'd, nor touching the Assurances of being paid the same punctually
for the future. The First Minister answer'd as before, That *Persia* was not
oblig'd to observe the Treaty of *Ormus*, on that Head, because the *English*
had broken it first, in not maintaining Ships in the Gulph, to keep it free
from the *Portuguese*, and other Enemies, and in not furnishing half the
Expence for the Support of the Castle of *Ormus*, and the other Forts of
Bandar-Abassi, as they were oblig'd by that Contract: Moreover, that the
Customs were no longer the King's: That his Majesty had let them out
to farm, and meddled no more with 'em; However, that he had com-

manded the Farmer-General of the Customs, to give every Year Fifteen thousand Crowns to the *English* Agent, and that he should be content therewith. Indeed he was forc'd to be contented, for he could not obtain any thing more. The First Minister appointed also an Officer, to accompany the Envoy from *Ispahan* to *Chiras*, and to make an exact Enquiry all the way, into the Insolences done to the *English* by the Officers of the Customs and Tolls, and to punish them very severely for the same. These Wretches had, for some Years past, us'd them with so much Rigour and Haughtiness, that they visited their Merchandizes on the Road, nay, even their Cloak-Bags and Portmanteaus, under Pretence of searching for Gold and Silver. The King's Officers went as far as *Chiras*, fined all the Officers upon the Road, and did not let one escape without being Bastinado'd on the Soles of his Feet, which is the usual Punishment in that Country.

❡ On the 5th of *November*, I receiv'd from the *Hollanders* the Seventy thousand Livres which the King had order'd me to take of them. After the Money was counted to me, they desir'd me to go along with their Interpreter to the House of the *Chiec-elislam*, which is the chief Civil Tribunal in *Ispahan*, there to give a lawful Acquittance; for in that Country Writings under Sign Manual are of no Validity in Justice, all must be done Juridically. The Great Judge asked me, if my Name was *Chardin*? If I was the Person that had sold to the King the Jewels specify'd on the Back of the Order? And whether I had receiv'd to my Satisfaction the Sum therein contain'd? I answered, Yes, to all these Questions; and as by good Fortune, the Great Judge knew me before, he was contented with my Answer: Otherwise I must have produc'd Witnesses, that I was the right Person. After my Answers, he order'd one of his Secretaries to draw an Acquittance, to which he put his Seal and Flourish; after which the Notary, two Witnesses, and my self last of all, put each our Seal thereto. Here is what it contain'd.

GOD.

❡ ' Before us, the Sieur *Chardin*, *European* Merchant of the Kingdom of ' *France*, the Flower of *European* Merchants, has confess'd and acknow-
' ledg'd what follows. To wit, that he was Creditor to the King most
' Noble, for the Sum of fifteen hundred Tomans, money of *Tauris* of
' good Alloy, of the Coin of the Invincible *Soliman* (We, with a full Cer-
' tainty, and intire Knowledge, do pronounce that (*a*) the half of that
' Sum makes seven hundred and fifty Tomans, Money of *Tauris* aforesaid)
' which Sum of fifteen hundred Tomans was lawfully due to him for the

' payment of some Jewels of Goldsmith's Work and precious Stones,
' visibly fine, entire, and in good Condition, which he sold to the noble
' Officers of the King most Holy. A Catalogue, the Price, the Number of
' those Goldsmith's Works and precious Stones, are distinctly and without
' Mistake endors'd on the Order of the Monarch, to whom all the Universe
' owe's Homage and Obedience, and whose Face has the Splendor and
' Brightness of the Rays of the Sun. This Order bears, that the said Sieur
' *Chardin*, shall receive the said Sum of the Commissioners of the *Dutch*
' *East-India* Company, on account of what they owe for Silk to them sold
' and deliver'd in the Year of the (*b*) Hog, as is more amply express'd and
' contain'd in the said Holy Order of the King most Noble. The said
' Sieur *Chardin* also confesses and acknowledges, to have receiv'd down
' upon the Nail to his Satisfaction, the said Sum of fifteen hundred
' Tomans compleat from the Sieurs *Bent* Chief, and *Casembroot* Second of
' the Counter of the *Dutch* Company in this City, the Flower of all those
' of their Quality, of which the said Creditor gives by these Presents,
' a judicial Receipt and Discharge to the said Debtors, so that the said
' Creditor has not, nor shall not have for the future any Right or Preten-
' tion on the said Debtors, for and by vertue of the said Sum of fifteen
' hundred Tomans, nor for any part thereof. Wherefore if the Creditor,
' or any other in his Name shall sue at Law, or produce any Instruments
' contrary to, or different from what is here contain'd, his Action is hereby
' declar'd false and null to all Intents and Purposes. This Acquittance
' has been drawn with the Knowledge, and by the Consent of the said
' Debtors for their Satisfaction, and to serve them as a Certificate. Done
' the eighteenth of the Month of *Rejeb the Great*, in the Year of the *Hegira*
' one Thousand eighty four.'

¶ At the Top, on the left of the Page was the Seal and Paraph of the
Great Judge, with these Words; *It is true, that the Parties nam'd in this
Acquittance have confess'd before me, all that makes the Tenor thereof.* Under this
Attestation, was that of the first Assistant of the Great Judge in these
Words: *I,* Mahammed Taher *do certifie, that the Parties have acknowledg'd
before me, the Sums herein contain'd in the Form they are çouch'd in.*

¶ At the Bottom of the Acquittance two other Witnesses, to wit, the
Comptroller and the Register of the Great Judge had put these Words.

¶ *Testimony of* David, *Son of* Mahammed Saïd, *Witnesses of the Truth of
what is contain'd in this Acquittance.*

¶ *Mahammed Mehdy*, who drew up this Acquittance, testifies, that its
Tenor is the sincere Truth.

¶ The *Chicane* of the *Persians*, is as perplex'd and intricate as ours, and the Terms it makes use of, are as difficult to reduce into a plain unequivocable Sense; nay, it is more, because their Law being writ in *Arabick*, their Procedures are full of *Arabick* Expressions, all particular to the Subject, and very hard to Explain. The Attestations or Testimonies are all compos'd in Terms, and in Characters as particular as Cyphers. There is this moreover, that the Letter of their Processes is quite different from the other; so that to learn it, costs the *Persians* as much Pains and Time, as to learn to read any Foreign Character.

¶ (*a*) It is the Custom throughout the East, in pecuniary Acts, (simple Notes as well as others) to put after the Sum ; that half of it is so much, and it is frequently added, that the quarter part is so much. The *Persians* say, this is done to prevent Frauds, it being easie to change one Word, or one Figure, but not many different ones.

¶ (*b*) One of the 12 Years of the artificial Period, which the *Tartars* make use of, I have amply treated thereof elsewhere.

¶ On the 9th of *December* it began to Rain in this City, the Rain continu'd four Days successively. It seldom Rains at *Ispahan*, even in Winter; but when it does, it Rains so hard, and so continually, that the Earth is penetrated therewith to above three Foot deep, and that is what moistens it so well.

¶ On the 23d, fell another Rain, accompany'd with such furious Storms, that I never saw the like. It lasted four and twenty Hours and fill'd with Water not only the Streets, but also the Houses and Gardens. It damag'd a great many Houses, and flung down several Walls. It so swell'd the River, that it overflow'd and beat down part of the Houses on the Key; it broke into that fine Alley, which is the Place for taking the Air at *Ispahan*, between the Bridge and the Borough of *Julfa*, and rose to the height of four Foot. The Gardens thereabouts were laid under Water, and the Houses of Pleasure were overthrown. As all the Walls of *Ispahan* are made of Bricks of Earth, work'd up with Straw cut small, and dry'd in the Sun, it is but laying Water to the Bottom of the Wall to make it tumble down; if it lies there only four and twenty Hours, the whole or part is sure to fall, unless it be very thick. The Damage caus'd by this Storm, amounted to above two Million; the King's loss alone came to a hundred thousand Crowns. Two Days after the Water was all gone off, and in two Days more there was no sign thereof. The Ground about *Ispahan* drinks the Water like a Sponge; four drops sokes it, and a quarter of an Hour's Sun or Frost, dries it up intirely.

The END *of the* FIRST VOLUME

THE TRAVELS OF SIR JOHN CHARDIN

SECOND VOLUME

CHAPTER I

OF PERSIA IN GENERAL

THE First Volume of my Travels is a Journal of my Adventures and Observations from *Paris* to *Ispahan.* In this I am going to give you a general Description of *Persia*, wherein I shall treat of the Nature, Morals, and Manners of the People, and of their Industry, in procuring for themselves all the Necessaries of Life.

¶ PERSIA is the greatest Empire in the World, if you consider it according to the Geographical Description given by the *Persians*; because they represent it to the full Extent of its ancient Boundaries, which are four great Seas; the *Black Sea*, the *Red Sea*, the *Caspian* Sea, and the *Gulph of Persica*; with Six Rivers almost as famous as those Seas, *viz.* The *Euphrates*, the *Araxes*, the *Tigris*, the *Phase*, the *Oxis*, and the *Indus.*. One can scarce more precisely point out the Limits of this vast Kingdom, which is not like the States of petty Sovereigns, whose Frontiers are marked out with a Brook or a Rivulet, or some little Monument of Stone. *Persia* on every side hath the space of four or five Days Journey for its Confines, which is uninhabited, although the Soil is the best in the World in many Places, as on the Eastern and Western Sides. The *Persians* look upon it to be a signal Token of Grandeur, to leave these Countries, like some spacious Desert, between great and mighty Empires; for this hinders, as they say, Contests about Limits of Dominion, and these uninhabited Tracts of Land, serve for Partition Walls between Kingdoms.

¶ These Rivers and Seas which I have set down here, are not at this time the Confines of *Persia*. Its Extent is mightily shrunk and diminish'd on the Side of the *Red Sea*; and *Persia* has, at present, the Possession of but a few Places in those Coasts. But the *Persian* Geographers cease not, however, to stretch their Empire out, in their most modern Descriptions, as far as those Boundaries, which it had of old, alledging, that they are still in Right and Fact, the Bounds of their Country; and that they are not to be look'd upon as abridg'd, by reason of the little Revolutions and Changes, which have happened on one or two Sides, because they may recover what they have lost, and they only want a Reign like that of *Abas the Great*, who liv'd but Threescore Years ago, to carry their Frontiers once more, as far as their ancient Limits.

⁋ *Persia*, in the State it was in, when I saw it, reckoning from *Georgia*, reaches from the 45th Degree of Latitude, which is the farthest Extent on the North side, as far as the 24th Degree along the River *Indus*, on the Southern Side, and from the 77th Degree of Longitude, towards the Mountains of *Ararat*, on the West, as far as the hundred and twelfth Degree over against the *Indies* and *Tartary* on the East. The greatest Length of it is, from the River *Indus* to the River *Phasis*, which is full five hundred and fifty *Persian* Leagues, or seven hundred and fifty *French*: This is the Length of *Persia*; in Breadth, it is less by near three hundred Leagues.

⁋ The *Persians*, in naming their Country, make use of one Word, which they indifferently pronounce *Iroun*, and *Iran*; an ancient Term invented by the *Tartars*, from whom the Modern *Persians* proceed. Their Histories tell you, That in the Time of the Ninth King of *Persia*, who is call'd *Effrasiab*, the Empire comprehended, besides what it contains at present, all the Countries between the *Caspian* Sea and *China*, on the North and Eastern Sides; and that this Monarch of theirs, divided his unparallel'd Empire by the River *Oxis*, calling that on the West, *Iran*, and that on the North, *Touran*, as one would say, on this Side the River, or on that Side the River. These Names of *Iran* and of *Touran*, are frequently to be met with in the ancient Histories of *Persia*; *Key Iran*, *Key Touran*, which signifies King of *Persia*, and King of *Tartary*, *Irandoct*, and *Tourandoct*, which is as much as to say, the Queens of those Countries; and even to this very Day, the King of *Persia* is call'd *Padcha Iran*, and the Great Vizier, *Iran Medary*, the Pole of *Persia*.

⁋ This is the Modern Appellation, the most in Use in that Country. That which they frequently make use of in the Second Place, is, the Term *Fars*, which is the particular Name of the Province; the Metropolis of which, in ancient Days, was *Persepolis*, and which gave its Name to all the Empire, because, under the second Race of Kings, it was the chief Province of the Kingdom, and the Seat of its Monarchs. This Word *Fars*, to signifie *Persia*, is very ancient; and the *Persians* still call the Old Language of their Country, which was in use before the Days of *Mahometanism*, *Saboun Fours*, the Tongue of *Persia*. Several learned Men deduce the Etymology of this Term from that of *Pherez*, which in the *Hebrew* and *Chaldaick* signifies to divide, because (say they) *Cyrus*, after his Conquests, divided the Empire of *Babylon* between the *Persians* and the *Medes*; and that *Persia* was in a manner divided and separated. They might have added likewise, that in the *Persian*, this Word signifies the same as *Fereston* to divide. But the *Persians* don't much care for allowing that Etymology, which gives *Babylon* the Antiquity of Empire, above themselves, who on the contrary maintain, that *Persia* is the oldest Seat of Dominion. But be that as it will, the Word *Fars* signifies a Cavalier in the ancient *Persian*, as well as in *Arabick*, from whence they still, in the Modern Tongue, call a Querry, *Farasch*. And that which makes me believe this Etymology the rather, is, that all the Kingdom, and particularly the Province which bears the Name of *Persia*, abounds in Horses; and in *Persia* they are thought to be the best Breed in the World. *Xenophon* says, that *Cyrus* was the first who made the *Persians* good Horsemen, having given the Example to the Nobility, by going always on Horseback, and ordering all People to do so, who could afford it; and it grew at last so common in the Country, that no Body but indigent People ever went on Foot. He adds, to confirm this Relation, that the Children in *Persia* are taught three Things, to tell Truth, draw a Bow, and mount a Horse. This is really their whole Practice to this very Day, in regard to the third Point. Every Body, even to the Shop-keepers, go on Horseback. Each Person keeps his Saddle-Horse; and there is such plenty of Horses in that Country, that before the last Age, there was no such thing as Infantry in the *Persian* Armies. All their Troops consisted of Cavalry: And there is no room to doubt, but that it was the constant Custom of the *Persians* to be always on Horseback, that the *Greeks* form'd their Fables of *Centaurs*, of the *Sagitary*, and of *Perseus*.

¶ The *Arabians* and the *Turks* call the *Persians*, *Agem*, and *Persia*, *Agemessaan*, a Word which imports a Stranger, as likewise a *Barbarian*. It is to give you to understand, that the *Persians*, altho' *Mahometans*, and a Learned and Zealous People, are not descended from the *Arabians*, the Source of Mahometism, and the Fountain of all Sciences; In the same Sense as the *Greeks* call'd all the Nations of the World barbarous: And it is in this Sense that the Grand Seignior stiles himself *Sultan Alaragh ve Al Agem*, to signify all Nations of the World; and that they call the Body-Guard of his Person *Agem Oglan*, Sons of *Barbarians*, to signify that they are not Natives of *Turky*. I will not here make mention of all the other Names, which the ancient Books, and among the rest the Holy Scriptures, give to *Persia*, some whereof are the Names of Princes, or famous and noted Personages, as that of *Elam*; others the Names of some Province in the Kingdom of *Cuth*; and others again are taken from those that were the most powerful Towns in the Country in ancient Times, when there were but very few Towns in all, as the Name of *Erec* or *Arac*, which is found in the Tenth of *Genesis*, a Word which signifies a Town inhabited upon the Banks of a River. The *Orientalists*, and among the rest the *Arabians* and the *Persians*, call to this very Day all *Persia*, *Araken* or *Yeraken*, the plural Number of *Arak*; they divide it into two Parts, *Arak Arab*, and *Arak Agem*, as who should say, the Towns of the *Arabians*, and the Towns of the *Barbarians*; and these Terms are sometimes us'd to distinguish the Lower from the Higher *Persia*; the last of which stretches it self even up to *Indus*. In fine, they now give three other Names to the *Persian* People, to wit, those of *China* and of *Raphesi*, when they discourse of their Religion, and that of *Kesilback*, when they are talking of their Conquests. But I will dwell no longer on this Subject at present, because I shall have occasion to treat of it hereafter.

¶ The *Persian* Geographers divide the Empire into four and twenty Provinces, counting for one of them, a Country which the *Turks* took from them, and have still in their Possession. They make mention of five hundred and forty four considerable Places, Walled ˙Towns, Cities ànd Castles and they compute that there is in *Persia*, some threescore thousand Villages, and forty Millions of Souls. I will likewise hereafter treat of the Mountains, and the Rivers of the Country, of which I shall content my self with only saying this at present. There is not in all the World that Country which hath more Mountains, and fewer Rivers. There is not so much as one single River that can carry a Boat into the Heart of the Kingdom, nor serve to transport Goods from one Province to another: Those which I mention'd as giving bounds to the Empire, run strait along upon the Frontiers, without branching themselves out, and carrying Streams into the Body of those Territories.

¶ The Country of *Persia* is dry, barren, mountainous, and but thinly inhabited. I speak in general, the twelfth Part is not inhabited, nor cultivated; and after you have pass'd any great Towns about two Leagues, you will meet never a Mansion-House, nor People in twenty Leagues more. The *Western* side above all the rest, is the most defective, and wants to be peopl'd and cultivated the most of any, and nothing is to be met with there almost, but large and spacious Deserts. This barrenncss proceeds from no other Cause, than the scarcity of Water, there is want of it in most Parts of the whole Kingdom, where they are forc'd to preserve the Rain-Water, or to seek for it very deep in the Entrails of the Earth. For in all the Places where there is good store of Water, the Soil is kindly, fertile, and agreeable: However *Persia* is in a manner one continu'd Country of Mountains, as I have been saying. There are so many, that the great Provinces are quite full of them, as that which is on the *East*, and is for that very Reason by them call'd *Koubeston*, that is to say, a Country of Mountains. It is in *Persia* that there are the highest Mountains in the Universe. Mount *Taurus,* which runs athwart the Kingdom, from one End of it to the other, towers up in such pointed Pinacles, that by Reason of their immense Height, the Tops and Summits of them are beyond the reach of the Eye of Man. The loftiest Parts of these Mountains, are the Mounts of *Ararat,* in Upper *Armenia*; the Row or Chain of Mountains, which separate *Media* from *Hyrcania,* that which is between *Hyrcania,* and the Country of the *Parthians,* and particularly Mount *Damavend,* the Mountains that separate *Chaldea* from *Arabia*; those which lie between *Persia* and *Caramenia,* where the most famous Place of all is the Mount *Jaron.* One of the great Defects in these Mountains is, that they are all dry and Sun-burnt; I mean generally speaking; for there are some Places where the Mountains are cover'd over entirely with Woods; such is *Kourdestan,* the greatest part of which is call'd also upon that account *Genguella,* that is to say, the Woody Country. But for one Woody Mountain that you shall meet with, there are three that bear nothing at all. But as I have just now been referring the Cause of Barrenness of the greater Part of *Persia,* to the deficiency of Water; and since in the sequel of my Discourse, it may be observ'd, that I say, that the *Persians* for Moistening Earth, make use of subterraneous Canals in the Earth, that run generally through their Countries, where they stand not in need of Water: I am very willing to explain my self, to avoid all appearance of a Contradiction, because all which I have recited hereupon, as above, is exactly true. The Water is the Cause of Fruitfulness in *Persia,* in all Places where it is to be had; and there is some, generally speaking, when People will be at the Pains of digging for it; but there are not People enough every where to look after it, and draw up a sufficient Quantity: Hence, the want of People does not proceed from the barrenness of the Soil, but the barrenness of the Soil from the want of People; just in the same manner as it fares with the greatest part of the Countries of the *Ottoman* Empire, which, altho' they are of their own selves, and by their Nature the best, and the finest Countries upon the Face of the Earth, are nevertheless as dry as Heaths for want of Hands. As for the Cause of the want of People in these vast Countries, it is very easy to comprehend. It proceeds on one Hand from the unmeasurable Extent of these Monarchies, and on the other from the Arbitrary Government that is exercis'd there. The People who are Conquer'd, not being able to support the being Govern'd by the Caprice of a Foreigner, whereas they were before rul'd by due and constant Laws, flowing regularly from their own Constitution, shake off the Yoke as soon as the Conqueror removes two or three hundred

Leagues from them. It was thought advisable, in order to maintain their Conquests, to banish the better Part of them, and to transport the other into distant and different Climates, where they perish'd little by little, like a strange Plant. This is what the *Persians* have practis'd, as well as the *Turks* for latter Ages. They have already remark'd in the *Indies*, which is a Country very Rich, Fruitful, and Populous, the dreadful Effects of this kind of Politicks; for in Proportion, as the *Great Mogul* extends his Empire, by the Conquest of *Indian* Kingdoms and Principalities, the People, and at the same time Plenty and Riches, decrease; one may add to this Political Reason, some other natural ones, for the Depopulation of *Persia*, and among the rest, these three. *First*, The unhappy Inclination which the *Persians* have, to commit that abominable Sin against Nature, with both Sexes. *Secondly*, The immoderate Luxury of the Country. The Women begin there to have Children betimes, and continue fruitful but a little while; and as soon as they get on the wrong Side of Thirty, they are look'd upon as old and superannuated. The Men likewise begin to visit Women too young, and to such an excess, that though they enjoy several, they have never the more Children for it. There are also a great many Women, who make themselves abortive, and take Remedies against growing Pregnant; because when they have been three or four Months gone with Child, their Husbands take to other Women, holding it for an Act of Turpitude and Indecency, to lie with a Woman gone so far in her Time. The *Third* Reason is, that within this last Century, a great many *Persians*, and even entire Families, have gone and settl'd in the *Indies*. As they are a handsomer, wiser, and more polite People, beyond all Comparison, than the *Mahometan Indians*, who are descended from the *Tartars*, in the Country of *Tamerlane*; they all advance themselves in the *Indies*. The Courts of the *Indian Mahometan* Kings are all full of them, particularly that of *Colconda* and *Vijapour*. As soon as any of them are well establish'd, they send for their Families and Friends, who go willingly where Fortune invites them, especially into a Country, which is one of the most plentiful in the World, and where Cloaths and Food are sold cheaper than any where else soever. They are not yet so well advis'd of this in the *East*, as to forbid the Departure of their Subjects: Every one is at Liberty to go where he pleases, and there is no need of a Pass, they having free Egress out of the Kingdom without it. You will likewise find in the Sequel of this Work, that when the Peasants in some Places, think themselves oppress'd, they will come crying in a Body to the Gates of the Governours, and even to the Gate of the King's Palace, that they will leave the Country, if they are not eas'd.

CHAPTER II

OF THE CLIMATE, AND OF THE AIR

I WILL begin this Chapter with this Remark, that there is perhaps nothing more memorable at this time of Day, in the Writings of the Ancients, than what *Xenophon* makes young *Cyrus* speak. *The Kingdom of my Father is so great, that there is no enduring the Cold on one side of it, nor the Heat on the other.* In effect, one may say with Truth, that there is a Winter and a Summer in *Persia* at the self-same Time; for on one Side, as on the *South*, there is no Winter, and on the opposite Side there is little Summer. As this Kingdom is of this prodigious Extent, it is easy to imagine, that the Air is different according to the Scituation of each Country. It is cold even up to *Chiras*, which is the Capital City of the Province of *Persia*; and it is warm from that City even up to the End of the Kingdom on the *Southern* Side. It is dry every where, where it is cold, but it is not dry in all Places where it is warm. It is warm and dry all along the *Gulph* of *Persica*, reckoning from *Caramenia* to the *Indus*; and in those Countries there are Places where the Heat stifles People, and is insupportable even to those that are Natives, and have never been out of the Country, They are forc'd to quit their Houses, during the four sultry Months of the Year, and retire towards the Mountains: And at that time, those who are forc'd to travel in the scorching Countries, meet with Villages quite deserted, except by a few miserable Creatures, that are left to take care of things, and those who are the Archers of the Provosts. The Air is not only insupportably hot in these Maratime Provinces, but also very unhealthful, and the People who are not accustom'd to it, seldom fail of falling sick, by reason of the badness of the Air, in the excess of the Heats, and it frequently proves mortal to them. All this I know too well, by my own Experience, and to my own Cost, having been infected my self by this malignant Air, by reason of my not going from thence before the Month of *May*, and so I fell into an Indisposition, that I could not shake off for a good while. The Places for Retreat are the Valleys, the Mountains, and the Palm-Tree-Woods, but these Woods themselves are not look'd upon to be very wholsome.

¶ The sultry Air of *Persia* is still more unwholsome, where it is attended with Moisture and Dampness, as it is along the *Caspian* Sea, and especially in that part which is counted to be the ancient *Comisena*, and which they call *Mazenderan*, which is very like our *European* Climate. To speak the Truth on't, the Country is in that part admirably fine, from *October*, even till *May*. I was there in the Month of *February*, at which time I was in a manner charm'd, and inchanted with it; for the whole Country is nothing but one continued Garden, or a perfect kind of Paradise, as the *Persians* call it. The Causways and Highways appear like so many Alleys of Orange-Trees, border'd on either side with fine Parterrees, and flowery Gardens. I have there also met with excellent Fruits, much of the same kind with ours, and of as delicate a Taste and Flavour as any we have in *Europe*. The Wine is good, and there is Plenty of it; Plenty of good Game; but particularly Wild-Boars, the finest in the whole World. But by observing the Countenances, and the Complexions of the Inhabitants, I could easily perceive, that it must be the worst Air that could be; for the People are more yellow, more defective in their Make, more weakly and sickly than ever I saw in any other part whatsoever. This Country of *Mazenderan* was almost grown a Desert, by reason of the bad Air, before *Abas* the Great's Time: But that Prince, a mighty Conqueror, and a vast Politician, transported thither a prodigious number of People from *Armenia*, and *Georgia*, as well to depopulate those Countries, where the *Turks* came every Year to encamp and make War against them, as because he believ'd that Soil to be of more Significancy and Importance, seeing among other things, that the Silk-Worms bred very kindly, and came to Perfection in those Parts. His Mother, who was of *Mazenderan*, which might of consequence be called his native Country, in as much as it produc'd the Person who gave him his Being, sollicited him on the other hand, to People again the Place, to which he ow'd his Birth. He transported thither a thousand Families of Christians, imagining that they would be very fruitful and increase there mightily: *It is*, say'd he, *a perfect right Country for the Christians*; *it abounds with Wine and Hog's-Flesh, two Things which they mightily like*; *they love to go to Sea, and they will traffick with their Brothers the* Muscovites, *by the* Caspian *Sea*. *Abas* caus'd Towns to be built, and magnificent Palaces to be erected, in several Places of that Country, and all this to encourage the Increase of the Colony; but the Malignity of the Air was so cross to his Designs and Projects, though laid and carried on with the utmost Care and Diligence, that when I was at *Mazenderan* with the Court about forty Years ago, the number of Christians was reduc'd to four hundred Families, from the thirty thousand that were there at first, as I was very credibly inform'd. The Bishop of *Ferackbad*, a good old *Armenian* Prelate, who was well enough acquainted with the Country, told me frequently, that if it was not for the Fertility of the Soil, which draws the Neighbouring People thither, the whole Country would be left like a Desert, by reason of the Unwholsomeness of the Air;

for about the end of *April*, they find it necessary to retreat to the Mountains, which are about five and twenty or thirty Leagues off, and to leave the Brooks and the Rivulets by reason of the insupportable Heats, which even dry up large and deep Rivers, insomuch, that all the Summer-time long there is none other but the worst Water in the Earth to be had. During my sojourning there, I found so prodigious a Dampness in the Air, that only hanging out a piece of Linnen over Night, I have seen it drop in the Morning, when no Rain has fallen. I must add to this Description, that the Air on the Coasts of the *Caspian* Sea is accounted so bad, that it is look'd upon as a Disgrace for any Person to be sent thither in Commission. And when the King makes any Person Governor of *Guilan*, which is the most considerable and profitable Post, that an Intendant can have, they inquire one of another, *Has he kill'd or robb'd any Body, that he is sent Governor of* Guilan? Rust is there so sudden and so active, that I have seen Arms rusted within four Hours after they have been oil'd and clean'd. Hence the People of the Country seldom carry any other Arms than Hatchets, because the Rust fastens the Swords in their Scabbords, and their Bows are by the Moisture, render'd very soft and slack. Hereupon they recount the following Story; That a Courier being one Day arriv'd from *Mazenderan*, at *Ispahan*, arm'd with a Bow and Sabre, a young Lord that was at Court at his first Arrival there, happening to take his Bow into his Hand, to make a Trial of it, as it is usual among them to do, found it so slack, that he said, smiling to him, *What is this Mounsieur Courier, you have a Bow a Child can bend? That may be, my Lord*, reply'd he, *but if you are so very strong, draw out my Sabre*. He meant, to signify by this, that the same Dampness which had slacken'd the Bow-string had fasten'd his Sabre in the Scabbord.

¶ However, as there are no Countries else so damp on the side of the *Caspian* Sea, but on the contrary, the other Places are almost all of them dry to the last degree; one may, generally speaking, say, that the Air of *Persia* is dry, its Drought proceeding from the few Rivers and Lakes that are to be met with in the whole Extent of that vast Kingdom; and one may, with equal Truth, alledge, that that Air is good, pure and wholsome. Such it is in all the Inlands of the Kingdom; which is plainly to be seen by the healthful Complexion of the People, who are strong, robust and sanguine, and commonly enjoy a constant Series of Health, and a good Disposition of Body. As to its Frontiers, there are none but the Countries I have been speaking of, that are unhealthful, and where the Air is contagious during the Heats of the sultry Season.

¶ The Air being dry, as I have been saying, it follows of course that

Persia cannot be very much subject to Rain: It is seldom Rainy Weather there, especially in the Summer-time, and in the Heart of the Kingdom; and at that Time you will scarce see so much as a little Cloud hanging in the Air, but all is calm and serene to Admiration. If in the Evening you should lay a Sheet of Paper in the Air, you will find it in the Morning as dry as you left it. Neither the Leaves on the Trees, nor the Herbage on the Ground, have the least Moisture in them. It is remark'd in some Countries, as in that, namely, of *Loureston*, the Capital City whereof is *Hamadan*, which was the Ancient *Susa*, that the very Sweat of human Bodies is suppress'd and repuls'd by this Drought; whereas at *Babylon* and in *Caramenia*, it runs pouring off the Body like Water through a Sieve. Hence they have taken further notice of two natural Effects it has, which are very different, but equally surprizing: The First is, That in the Provinces I have been naming, and in many others, altho' the Air is quite clear from Clouds all Summer-long, yet in the Evening Winds arise, which refresh the Climate, and last till an Hour and an half before Sunrise; and these are usually so fresh and sharp in the Night-time, that one must be forc'd to put on a great Coat to guard one against the Cold. The Second Effect it has, is, that altho' at other Seasons of the Year the Winds cease, so far as not to be perceptible, you will see the Sky over-cast with great Clouds, that pass off softly from East to West, without any Sign of Wind to drive them on; so that it is judg'd their Impulsion may proceed from some other Cause. There is such an exquisite Beauty in the Air of *Persia*, that I can neither forget it my self, nor forbear mentioning it to every body: One would swear that the Heavens were more sublimely elevated, and tinctur'd with quite another Colour there, than they are in our thick and dreary *European* Climates. And in those Countries, the Goodness and Virtue of the Air spreads and diffuses it self over all the face of Nature, that it enobles all its Productions, and all the Works of Art with an unparallel'd Lustre, Solidity and Duration; not to speak how much this Serenity of Air enlivens and invigorates the Constitution of the Body, and how happily it influences the Disposition of the Mind; of which I shall have occasion to make ample Mention in the sequel of my Discourse. I shall here only just set down one Remark more to make my Reader have a true Idea and just Sense of the Goodness and Purity of the *Persian* Air, in most parts of the Country, and amongst others at *Ispahan*: There is no need of stopping the Bottles, any further than just to hinder the Wine from running out: For this they make use of a Flower, as a Pink or a Rose, and put in the Mouth of the Bottle instead of a Cork, and after they have poured any part of it out, they never stop it afterwards. The Remnant of a Bottle that has been uncork'd for four and twenty

Hours, and which one would think should evaporate and pall, is so very little alter'd that 'tis scarce to be perceiv'd.

¶ The common Variation of Times and Seasons, to speak in general, and above all in the Heart of the Kingdom, are after the following manner: The Winter begins in *November*, and continues pretty harsh and violent even till *March*, with Frost and Snows, which fall in great Flakes among the Mountains, but do not come down in so great Quantities, among the Plains and regular Champain Countries. There are Mountains three Days Journey distant from *Ispahan*, on the West-side, that are cover'd by the Snow for eight Months together. They say, that among the Snow, you will meet with little white Worms, about the bigness of one's little Finger, that move up and down lively upon the Surface of it, and if you crush them, they are colder than the Snow it self. From the Month of *March* to that of *May*, the Winds are very high, the coming of which is a certain sign that Winter is quite gone. From *May* till *September*, the Sky is serene, being refresh'd by the Winds that blow in the Night, and just at the close of the Evening, and opening of the Morn. And from *September* to *November*, the Winds are just the same as in the Spring of the Year. Here you must observe, that during the Summer, in the Countries we are speaking of, the Nights are about ten Hours long, and there is but little Twy-light; which join'd to the constant Freshness and Sharpness of these Night-Winds serves very much to moderate the Heat of the Days: Insomuch that in Consideration of the Warmth, I had rather pass a Summer at *Ispahan* than at *Paris:* For if it is warmer there by Day-time, the Day, by way of Amends, is so much the shorter. There are divers Remedies against the Heat, and the Night is always sure to bring a fresh Gale; whereas there are Nights frequently at *Paris* that stifle one almost with Heat and Closeness. On some Days in Summer, I have known the Sun and Air so hot at *Paris*, from Twelve till Three in the Afternoon, that the late Mr. *Benner* and my self both agreed, that it was not warmer at *Ispahan*, nor even the *Indies*. I will speak more at large of the Air of this Metropolis of *Persia*, in the following Parts of this Work, when I come to give a particular Description of that famous City. All that I shall say more of it in this Place is, that the Air is dry there to the last degree, to which I don't know whether one may properly impute the Reason, that dead Bodies, as well Animal as Human, always swell, within an Hour after they are dead, to be half as big again as they naturally are. And another Thing which is very different, that the Conclusion of almost all Diseases, shews it self in a great and painful Swelling of the Legs, and which takes up a long time before one can get over it.

¶ *Persia* is rarely expos'd to Tempests, or Earthquakes; there is very seldom any Thunder and Lightning, or other Meteors; the Matter and Composition whereof arises from Vapours, because the Air is so dry, as I have already said: It only Hails now and then in the Spring; and as, at that Time, the Harvest is pretty far advanc'd, those Storms of Hail make terrible Havock and Waste among the Corn. The News of this never fails of coming where the Court is; for they send out of those Countries that are laid waste by the Hail, Deputies to the Ministers of State, to desire an Abatement of their Taxes; and those Deputies always represent the Damage to be much greater than it really is. As to Earthquakes, they happen very seldom in *Persia*. I would here be understood always to except *Hircania*; for they are on the contrary, frequent and furious there, especially in Spring; but they do nothing but frighten and terrify the People, and very seldom have any Tragical Effects. For the other Phænomena, they are likewise very seldom to be seen in *Persia*, particularly the Rainbow; because there is not abundance of watery Matter to compose it. You may see sometimes on a Summer's Night, little glimmering Streaks and Rays, that shoot athwart the obscure Parts of the Air, and look like falling Stars. These kind of Exhalations, like firing of Squibs and Rockets, fall sometimes strait downwards, sometimes obliquely, and seem to leave behind them little Streaks of Smoak, or black Vapours, which are nothing perhaps but Haloes or Heats round about the Moon; and the principal Planets, which the Eye, by a Deception of Sight, takes to be Smoak. I must add, that the Clearness and Serenity of the *Persian* Air, is so great, that the Stars alone give Light enough, for Persons to travel by, and know one-another.

¶ The Winds of *Persia* seldom rise so high as to come to the degree of a Hurricane, and are not frequently Stormy and Tempestuous. But there are some which are Mortal, and rage with extreme Violence along the Gulph of *Persia*; they call these deadly pestiforous Storms, bad *Sammoun*, that is to say, the Winds of Poison: But upon the Spot, where those Storms happen, they call them *Samyal*, a Word compos'd of *Yel*, which signifies Wind in the *Turkish* Tongue, and *Sàm*, which signifies Poyson in *Arabick*. It rises only betwen the 15th of *June*, and the 15th of *August*, which is the Time of the excessive Heats near that Gulph. That Wind runs whistling through the Air, it appears red and inflam'd, and kills and blasts the People; it strikes in a manner, as if it stifled them, particularly in the Day time. Its surprizing Effects is not the Death it self, which it causes; what's most amazing is, that the Bodies of those who die by it, are, as it were, dissolved, but without losing their Figure or Colour; insomuch that one would only take them to be asleep; but if you take hold of any piece of them, the Part remains in your Hand. In the Year 1674, a Chatir, or Footman, named *Mahamet Aly*, who had been in my Service, returning from *Basra* to *Ormus*, (during the time of these Winds that are so violent and mortal) with a Packet of Letters, found another Footman of his Acquaintance, who had the Charge of a Packet of Letters too, lay stretched along in the middle of the Road; he thought him to be asleep, and pull'd him by the Arm to awake him; he was very much surpriz'd to find the Man's Arm in his Hand; and afterwards taking him hold in several other Parts, that his Hands were buried as it were in so much Dust. In the Year 1675, in the Month of *May*, a little *Portuguese* Squadron being come to the Port of *Congue*, about three Days Journey from *Ormus*, to get their Customs paid, which the *Portuguese* pretended to be their Due, they arrested the Ships that were returning from *Mecca*, full of *Persian* Passengers, and detain'd them till the Month of *July*, at which Time, those poor People hastning to get out of the bad Air of that Country, several perished in the Manner I have mention'd, being catched in the way by the Wind. As soon as one finds this terrible Wind coming, which rises with a Vehemence like a Whirlwind; the only Remedy against it is, to cover one's Head up close, and throw one's self upon one's Belly to the Ground, and lie with one's Face press'd into the Dust of the Earth, till such time as the Whirlwind is past, and that lasts, as I have been told, about a quarter of an Hour.

CHAPTER III

OF THE SOIL

I MUST say of the Soil of *Persia*, as I did of the Air; That Kingdom being for its bigness, a little World, part whereof is burnt with the heat of the Sun, while the other part is frozen over with Cold. It is impossible but that there should be strange Varieties and Alterations in the Nature of the Soil: But *Persia* is, generally speaking, a barren Country, as I have observ'd already; and the Tenth part of it is uncultivated. I have likewise remark'd before, that *Persia* is the most Mountainous Country in the Universe, and most of its Mountains barren and dry to the last degree, consisting generally of bare Rocks without any Trees or Grass. But there are here and there between the Mountains, Valleys and Plains, that are more or less fruitful, and more or less agreeable, according to their Scituation and Climate. The Soil is gravelly and stony in some Places; in others, it consists of a white Clay, that is as heavy and as hard as the Stone itself. But both in one and the other it is so dry, that if the People don't water their Lands, they will produce nothing, not so much as Grass. It is not altogether an entire want of Water, but because there is not enough of it. It scarce rains at all during Summer, and in Winter the Sun is so hot, and so drying for the five or six Hours that it is high in the Horizon, that the Land must be water'd from time to time. But on the contrary one may say, that in every Place where they are water'd, they are fruitful in their Productions. Thus it is the Scarcity of Water that occasions the Barrenness; and after all, it is the Deficiency of Inhabitants, as I have already remark'd, which causes the Water to be so scarce, there being not in that vast Empire, the twentieth part of the Hands that are necessary to occupy and manure the Ground with any Ease. A Man would be strangely surpriz'd in *Persia*, who went thither prepossess'd with the Ideas given of it by ancient Authors, particularly *Arian*, and *Quintus Cursius*; for to read their Accounts of the Luxury, Effeminacy, Delicacy, and Treasures of the *Persians*, one would imagine 'twas a Country made up of Gold, and where the Conveniencies of Life were in great Plenty, and to be had for little or nothing. But whoever comes there, finds it quite otherwise: However there is no doubt to be made, but that *Persia* has been one of the most opulent, and sumptuous Countries, as those Authors have reported it, because the Holy Scripture confirms it. What way is there to reconcile these visible and seeming Contradictions? This I will do without much difficulty, by relating two Things, which I have found out to be the Causes of this strange Alteration. The first proceeds from the difference of their Religion; the second arises from the difference of the Government. The Religion of the Ancient *Persians*, who were *Ignicoles*, or worshippers of Fire, lay'd upon them the strictest Engagements to cultivate the Land; for according to their Maxims, it was a pious and meritorious Action, to plant a Tree, to water a Field, and to make a barren spot of Earth yield Fruit; Whereas the Philosophy of the Mahometans, tends only to the enjoying the Things of this World, while one is in it, without having any more regard to it than a High-way, through which one is to pass quickly. The Government of those Ancient People, was likewise more Just and Adequate. The Rights of Proprietors to their Lands and Goods, were inviolably Sure and Sacred. But at present the Government is Despotick and absolutely Arbitrary. What moreover induces me to believe, that all I have read of *Persia* in those Ancient Times is true, and that it was beyond comparison, more Fertile and Populous than it is at present, is, from taking a Review of what it has come to within these Sixscore Years, from the beginning of the

Reign of *Abas* the Great. He was a Just and Equitable Prince, and all his Endeavours had this one Tendency, to render his Kingdom flourishing, and his People happy. He found his Empire all torn to Pieces and Usurp'd, and the greatest part of it Impoverish'd and Pillag'd. But it is scarce to be believ'd, what Effect his good Government had, throughout his Dominions. To give the Reader but barely one single Instance of it; He brought into the Capital City a Colony of *Armenians*, who were a Laborious and Industrious People, and had nothing in the World when they came there; but in the space of thirty Years they grew so exceeding Rich, that there were above threescore Merchants among them, who, one with another, were worth from an hundred thousand Crowns, to two Millions, in Money and Merchandize. As soon as that Great Prince ended this Life, the Prosperity of *Persia* ended likewise. The People began by little and little to go over to the *Indies*, during the two succeeding Reigns; and at length, in the Reign of *Soliman*, which began in 1667, their Wealth and their Plenty were found to be excessively diminished. The first time that I came to *Persia*, was in the Year 1665, in the Reign of *Abas* the Second, and my last in the Year 1667 (*sic*), during the Government of *Soliman* his Son. Counting from that time to this, the Riches seem'd to be half diminish'd, within so little an Interval as twelve Years time only. Even the Coin itself was alter'd; there was no such thing as good Silver to be seen. The Grandees being impoverish'd, exacted upon the People, and peel'd them of their Fortunes. The People to ward against the Oppressions of the Great, were become Cheats and Sharpers; and from thence all the ill tricking Ways that could be, were introduc'd into the Art of Trade and Commerce. There are too many Examples throughout the World, which shew, that even the Fertility of the Soil, and the Plenty of a Country depends on the good Order of a just and moderate Government, and exactly regulated according to the Laws. If *Persia* was inhabited by *Turks*, who are still more slothful, and less engag'd in the things of this Life, than the *Persians* and cruelly severe in their manner of Government, it would be still more barren than it is; whereas, if it was in the Hands of the *Armenians*, or of those People call'd *Ignicoles*, one should quickly find it appear again in all its Ancient Glory and Primitive Splendor.

¶ To return to the Soil of *Persia*: It is however with these Defects, as good in some Places as any Soil can be; as for Example, in *Armenia*, in *Media*, in *Iberia*, in *Hyrcania*, in *Bactria*, which are called at present, the Provinces of *Corasson* and *Candahar*, in the Country of *Koureston*, which is between *Persia* and *Arabia*. In the Year 1669, when I was in that Province, they gave an Account to my Servants at an Inn, of the Price of things in the following manner. Barley at a *Denier* and a half a Pound, the Bread at four *Deniers*, (a *Denier* being the 12th Part of a *French* Penny) good Mutton for a Penny, Pullets for Two pence Half-penny, and large Turkeys for Four-pence. One may easily judge what all these were worth to the Peasant at first Hand. However, I have heard of better Penny-worths by half at *Candahar*: But on the contrary, the Borders of the Gulph of *Persia*, and the Desart of *Caramenia*, are more barren, Cattle are scarcer there, and every thing is got with greater Difficulty and Expence.

CHAPTER IV

OF THE TREES, PLANTS, AND DRUGGS

I SHALL treat in the following Chapter concerning those kind of Trees, which are usually distinguish'd by the Name of Fruit-Trees. As to what regards the other sort; the Trees that are most common in *Persia*, are the *Plantane*, the *Willow*, the *Fir*, the *Cornell*, which the *Arabians* call *Seder*, and the *Persians Conar*, from whence the Word *Cornus* evidently proceeds; and from that, in *English* we come to call it the *Cornell-Tree*. The *Persians* hold, that the *Plantane* hath a natural Virtue in it against the Plague, and all other Infections of the Air; and they affirm, that they had no more Contagion at *Ispahan*, their Metropolis, after they had planted them every where round about, as they did in the Streets, and Gardens: Several other Towns of *Persia* are stock'd with these Trees, and particularly that of *Chiras*.

¶ The Tree which bears the *Gall-Nut* is common in several Parts of *Persia*; but particularly in the Province of *Coureston*, where they grow in whole Rows together.

¶ The Trees that bear the *Gum*, the *Mastick*, and *Insence*, lie scatter'd up and down the different Parts of the Country, in great Quantities. The Tree which produces *Frankincense*, and very much resembles in its Form and Make, a great *Pear-Tree*, grows in a more eminent Manner, in the Desart of *Caramenia*, upon the Mountains. You may likewise find there, and in many other Places, the *Turpentine-Tree*, the *Almond-Tree*, and the wild *Chesnut*.

¶ The Tree that bears *Manna*, is likewise to be met with there. There are several sorts of *Manna* in *Persia*, the best is of a yellowish Colour, a large coarse Grain, and comes from *Nichapour*, a Country of *Bactriana*. There is another sort call'd the *Tamarisk*, because the Tree from which it drops, is call'd the *Tarmarisk*. They grow in great Quantities, in the Province of

Sousiana; especially round about *Daurac*, a Place by the *Gulph* of *Persica*, which is the *Aracas* of *Ptolmomy*. The third sort of *Manna* that I have taken notice of is Liquid; they gather it about *Ispahan*, from a kind of Trees that are of a bigger Size than a *Tamarisk*, the Rind of which is bright and shining. The Leaves of this Tree do in Summer drop this Liquid *Manna*, which they pretend is not Dew, but the Sweat of the Tree congeal'd upon the Leaf. In the Morning you may see the Ground that lies under it perfectly fat, and greasy with it. It is made use of in Remedies, the same with the *Manna* of *Tamarisk*, and 'tis as sweet as the rest.

¶ There are two kinds of little Trees or Shrubs in *Persia*, that are very remarkable for the dreadful Qualities and Properties that belong to them. Both the one and the other grow in the Desarts of *Caramenia*, near the *Gulph* of *Persica*; the first is call'd *Gulbad Samour*, that is to say, the Flower which poisons the Wind. The *Arabians* give it the Name of *Chark*, it bears a sort of *Lambriches*, full of tart and eager Milk, as thick as Cream. It is averr'd, that in the Places where many of these Shrubs grow together, the Wind in the most sultry Season of the Year, passing thro' these Trees, receives a deadly and mortal Quality, and kills all those who breathe in it, or whom it blows upon with any Violence. The other little Tree or Shrub, is call'd *Kerzebre*, a Name that signifies *Asses-Gall*, or the Poison of an *Ass*; and to which they attribute all that's bitter and mortal; because an *Ass*, as they account in the *East*, is a Beast of the most vigorous and healthful Constitution; or because *Asses*, and other Domestick Animals, that eat any of that Shrub, die in a little time after. They say likewise, that the Water which washes the Root or Trunk of that Tree, is Death to any Body. The Trunk of it is about the Bigness of one's Leg, and the Branches not so big as one's Arm, and it commonly grows to the Height of about six Foot. The Rind, which is generally pretty thick, is greenish, the Leaves are rather round than oval, with a Point at the End. This Tree bears a Flower, almost like our single Rose, and is of a Flesh Colour, like a Bryar-Rose; which is I believe the Reason why the *Greeks* have given this Tree the Name of *Rododendron*. The *Arabians* call it likewise as the *Persians* do, the *Gall* of *Asses*, and also *Felly*. They say, that it is the *Nerium* of the Herbalists; which in *French* is call'd *Rosage*, and is treated of in all the Herbals of that Country.

¶ The Herbage grows very kindly in *Persia*, particularly those that we call the Fine Herbs, which have a wonderful good Scent. The Roots, Greens, and *Roman Letuce* that grow there, are larger, of a finer Colour, and better Tasted, than in any Country of the World. They eat them raw, like Fruit, without perceiving any Harshness or Tartness in them. The

Europeans have found by Experience, that our Greens come to a great Perfection in *Persia*; and it is certain, the *Persians* would have greater Plenty of them, and better than we, if their Religion put them upon manuring them, as carefully as they do in other Countries, where Flesh is forbid so many Days in the Year.

¶ *Persia* is a perfect Country for Physical Druggs. Besides the *Manna* that comes from thence, which I have spoken of, there grows *Cassia, Senna, Antimony,* with which almost all the Fields are cover'd over, and *Fænu Grecum.* They call this *Simple Kambalack,* which is the *Persian* Name for great *Tartary;* because they say it Originally came from thence. *Nux Vomica* grows likewise almost every where, of the breadth of a Five-Penny Piece, and the Thickness of two Crowns, cover'd with a smooth Skin. The *Gum Armonick,* which the *Persians* call *Ousioc,* is very plentiful in the Confines of *Parthida,* towards the *South.* They take it out of a Plant which resembles the Stalk of an *Artichoke.* There is also in the same Places, and in all the Territories of *Ispahan,* a Plant which we in *Europe* are not acquainted with, and which is like the *Spanish Thistle,* they call it *Livas;* the Taste is somewhat sowerish, and very agreeable; it is at its growth in the Spring, which is the proper Season for it. The *Persian* Herbalists call it *Rivendayvoni,* as much as to say, *Horse-Rhubarb,* because they use it to purge the Beasts. They hold it to be a kind of *Bastard Rubarb,* and the *Rubus Arabicus* of our Herbalists. The *Rhubarb* grows in *Corasson,* which is the ancient *Sogdiana.* The best comes out of the Country of the *Eastern Tartars,* who are between the *Caspian* Sea and *China.* The one and the other is call'd *Rivend-Tchini,* the *Rhubarb* of *China.* They eat *Rhubarb* in *Corasson,* as we do *Red-Beet,* and it grows there just in the same Manner.

¶ The other remarkable Plants of *Persia,* are first, the *Poppy;* for tho' there are Plenty of *Poppies* in other Countries, yet they have in no other Place so much Juice, and so strong, as they have there. This Plant is four Foot high, its Leaves very white, it is ripe in the Month of *June,* and they then extract the Juice from it; they slice it in the Head, and the *Persians* by way of Superstition, always make twelve Slices of it, in Memory of the twelve *Imans,* three Incissions one just by another, all at one time, with a little Bill, that has three Edges, like the Teeth of a Comb. There comes out of it a kind of viscous or thick Juice, which they gather together at the dawn of Day, before the Sun appears; and this is so strong, that the People who gather it together seem like dead People, taken up out of their Graves, being livid, meagre and trembling as if they had the Palsie. There is something that happens when one goes near those who bruise it, and prepare it for drinking, which I shall let you know in the

Sixteenth Chapter. This Humour or Fume, gets into their Heads, and freezes up the whole Body. They make this Juice up into Pills, and in Proportion as it issues out, and the Head of the *Poppy* is drier and drier, it grows black, and so do the Seed and Stalk likewise. The *Persians* call the Juice *Afioun*, from whence our Word *Opium* is deriv'd. The best in the Kingdom is made in the Canton of *Linjan*, six Leagues from *Ispahan*, where the Fields are all cover'd over with *Poppies*. The Bakers sprinkle the Seed of them upon the Bread, because it is a provocative to Sleep, which they look upon to be very wholsome after Meals; and the lower sort of People eat the Seed between Meals. There are some who hold the *Afioun* of *Cazeron* in greater Esteem, which is towards the Gulph of *Persica*, than that at *Ispahan*, saying, that this engenders waterish Crudities, and the other does not.

¶ *Secondly*, There is Tobacco, which grows throughout all *Persia*, and particularly in *Susiana* at *Hamadan*, which is the Ancient *Susa*, and in the Desarts of *Caramenia*, in the Neighbourhood of *Coureston*, near the Gulph of *Persica*, where they gather the best of all. It is very easy to grow, and requires no more than the ordinary Tillage of the Ground. They dry it and transport it in the Leaf by Bundles and Parcels, as they do Beets. 'Tis a perfect dead Leaf in its Colour when 'tis dry'd. They neither dress nor bind it up together, for that would make it too strong, and like the *Brazil* Tobacco. But the *Persians* don't like to have it so, but had rather have it milder, that they may continue smoaking it all the Day long. They hate the Smoak and smell of the twisted Tobacco of *Brazil*, which they call *Tombacou Inglesi*, or *English* Tobacco, because the first *European* takers of Tobacco, with whom they had any Commerce, were the *English*. The *English* us'd to bring this Tobacco from *Brazil*, and sell it in *Persia*, about fifty Years ago. But the *Persians* finding it to be both too strong and too dear, they made use of it no longer. Some People who love to make themselves Drunk with Tobacco, mingle Hemp-seed with it, and that makes the Vapours mount into the Brain, and intoxicates them immediately.

¶ I remember to have heard it made a Point of Debate among some knowing Persons in *Europe*, whether Tobacco and Sugar were Originals of the New World, or whether they always grew in the Eastern Countries. I have endeavoured to find the Truth of this upon the Spot. But you would scarce believe how little Curiosity the Eastern People have in such Remarks and Observations. There's scarce a Person among their Learned Men, who keeps a Register of the Discoveries that are made in the Arts and Sciences. As for Tobacco, I could not learn in *Persia*, whether it was originally the growth of that Country, or brought thither from Foreign

Parts; and I found my Enquiries all in vain. One of the most curious Men in *Ispahan* told me thus much only, That he had read in a *Parthian* Book of Geography, that in taking up the Ruins of the Town of *Sultania*, they found among the Rubbish, a great Earthen Urn, in which were wooden Pipes, with Cups and Mugs, and Tobacco cut very small, just as the Turks cut theirs at *Aleppo*, which made him believe, that the Plant was brought from *Egypt* into *Persia*, and that it could not have been the natural Growth of that Country, till within these four Hundred Years. I have seen some Persons who are of Opinion, that the *Portugueze* were the first who brought it from the *Indies*, not above two Hundred Years since. But that is not credible, because it appears, that it is far less time since they began to cultivate it in the *Indies*. For by all that I have been able to learn, I find it has not been above fifty Years standing there; And even the best and greatest of Tobacco that is made use of in the *Indies*, is carry'd from *Persia*, and that is the Tobacco which is transported in greater Quantities from thence by Sea.

¶ As to Sugar, I believe there was always some in the *Indies*. I know very well it is a Point mightily contested, and the greater part of Authors hold, that Sugar is a product of the New World, and that the Ancients us'd nothing but Honey. But I am of a contrary Opinion, which I found upon this, that Sugar grows throughout all the *Indies*, in great Plenty, with great Ease, and to a great Perfection; and not like Products that are brought from remote Countries, that never came up so kindly, when they are transplanted so far from their own Soil. Another Reason that I have, which is stronger, than the former, is, that Sugar is to be found, nam'd, and prescrib'd in an hundred Places of the Ancient *Indian*, *Persian*, and *Arabick* Manuscripts of Physick.

¶ The manner of taking Tobacco in *Persia* is unknown to us, and a singular way, which the *Indians* and *Persians* have to themselves. As the Air is more warm and dry there than in *Europe* and *Turkey*, and the Animal Spirits of the People more subtile, the Tobacco would be too heady for them, if they took it as we do, because they are at it continually. They pass their Tobacco-pipes thro' a Bottle of Water, of which I have given you a Figure on the side. They call these sort of Pipes *Callion*. The Bottle is cover'd over with an Earthen or Metal Mug, to the height of the Conduit, which is put into the Water as you see.

¶ At the Bottom there is a Plate like that belonging to some Candlesticks, and the Cane or Pipe by which they draw the Smoak, is fix'd to that Conduit. When they would Smoak, they wet the Tobacco which is in that Cup, and mince it very small, that it may not burn away too fast.

They put two or three little Coals upon it, and draw the Smoak, which enters into the Water, circulates there, and is then suck'd back into the Mouth, not only cool and fresh, but likewise purg'd of all the unctious and gross Qualities of the Tobacco. You see some in taking it, that have good Stomachs, make great Bubbles, and cause great Murmurings in the Water, by the Attraction of Air. These Bottles are commonly fill'd

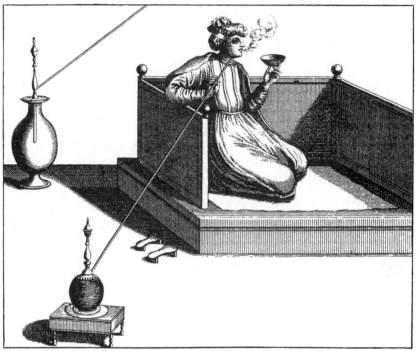

Persian smoking the "Callion."

with Flowers to give Pleasure to the Eye. They change at least once a Day the Water, which is all corrupted, and smells very rank of the Spirit of Tobacco. I have made an Experiment, and found that a Cup-full of that Water is a great Emetick, and would almost make a Man Vomit his Heart up.

¶ This mad Inclination to Tobacco, is an ill Habit, that has bewitched almost all the World. Our People in the West smoke it, snuff it, and chaw it, as every one knows: and some People, as particularly the *Portuguese*, have always a Nose full of Snuff. The Eastern People take it no other way, than smoaking, but with the same insatiable Greediness, most of them, especially the *Persians*, having always a Pipe in their Mouths. The People of Quality have their Pipe or Callion always carry'd before them by a Servant on Horse-back; and they often stop by the way to smoak, and sometimes smoak as they ride. They never go abroad without it, and where they go a visiting, there's their Bottle of Tobacco placed before them as soon as ever they are seated. It is true, that seldom is any Hindrance to Business, for they dispatch that as they smoak, and as well as if they don't. Go into the Colleges, and you will find both Tutor and Pupil very hard at their Studies, and both of them with Pipes in their Mouths. In a word, they had rather go without their Dinners, than their Pipes; and this is plain, because during the Fast of *Rhamazon*, which lasts eighteen Hours, when it falls in the Summer; in all which time they take nothing at all in their Mouths, not so much as Water, the first thing they break their Fast with, is Tobacco. The excessive Use of this Weed drys them up, makes them lean, and weakens them; and in this they all agree, as an undoubted Truth. But then if you ask them, why they don't leave it off? They answer, *Aded Chud, it is a Habit*; and they say further, *That there is no Joy, nor a cheerful Heart, without it.* *Abas* the Great, at the time when this Habit began to gain ground apace, try'd several ways to root it out, but all in vain, altho' he himself abstain'd from Tobacco at that time. They say, among other things of him, that having one Day all his Noblemen round about him at a Feast, he commanded, that the Bottles of Tobacco, which were to be serv'd up to them, should have the Cups belonging to them full of Horse-dung dry'd and pounded, instead of Tobacco. This was not perceptible to the Sight, the Tobacco being usually served up, bruised or minced very small, as I have said, and moistened a little, and then a Coal or two of Fire placed upon it. The King ask'd the Grandees from time to time, *How do you like that Tobacco? It was a Present from my Vizier of* Hamadan, *who, to reconcile me to the taking it, sent me the most excellent Tobacco in the World.* Each of them answered him, *Sire, it is most wonderful Tobacco; there is none that is more exquisitely good.* At length the King, addressing himself to the General of the Courtches, who are the ancient Militia of *Persia*, and who passed for a Lord more stayd, and freer to speak his Mind than the rest, said to him, *My Lord, I pray you tell me freely, and sincerely, What do you think of this Tobacco? Sire,* reply'd he, *I swear by your sacred Head, it smells like a thousand Flowers.* The King turn'd, and looking on them all with Indignation, *Cursed be that Drug,* said he, *that cannot be discerned from the Dung of Horses.*

¶ *Thirdly*, There is *Saffron*, and it is the best in Nature; it grows in several Parts of *Persia*; but they esteem that above the rest, which grows by the Side of the *Caspian*-Sea, and next to it, is that of *Hamadan*, which is the ancient *Susa* or *Suzan*.

¶ *Fourthly*, The *Assa-Fætida*, which is a Juice or Liquor that thickens, and grows almost as hard as the Gums: It drops from a Plant, which they call *Hiltit*, and is supposed to be the *Lazerpithium* or *Silphium*, of *Dioscorides*, which grows in many Parts of *Persia*, particularly in *Sogdiana*, and the adjacent Countries round about it. It is very good to eat, especially the White, for there are two sorts, one White and the other Black. The Juice which comes out of the White is not so strong, and for that Reason only, less esteemed by them. The *Orientalists* call *Assa-fætida*, *Hing*, and the *Indians* make a great Consumption of it: They put it into all their Ragouts, and most delicate Meats: It is a Drug that has the strongest Scent I ever smelt; Musk does not come near it; you may smell it at a vast distance; and if there is any of it put in a Room, the Scent will last for whole Years. The Ships in which it is transported to the *Indies*, are so very strong of it, that there is no putting any thing else there, for fear of spoiling the Goods, or altering them; of which I had the unhappy Experience in some rich Stuffs; for though they were all wrapped up close in Cotton, and Sear-cloth folded round about it in several Folds, yet the Gold was tarnish'd, and the Silver turn'd quite black.

¶ *Fifthly*, There is the *Mummy*, and there are two sorts in *Persia*: One is *Mummy*, commonly so call'd, which comes from Bodies embalm'd, and interr'd in dry burning Land, where, in the course of Ages, they petrify, as is very well known to all the Curious. This *Mummy*, which is nothing but the Petrifaction of a Corpse imbalm'd for two thousand Years, as they assure you, in *Persia*, is to be seen in *Corasson*, which is the Ancient *Bactria*. A Visier of the Province Named *Mirza-Chefi*, a very knowing Man, told me several times, that when they were working in the Sand to make Subterraneous Conduits for the carrying of Water, they have found some of these *Mummies* seven or eight Foot long, whether it is that the Bodies were larger at that time of Day, or that they took Pleasure to bury them, and stretch them out to a greater Length for the Admiration of Posterity: He added moreover, That when they found these Bodies, some of them had Heads of Hair and Beards, remaining, with Nails upon their Hands and Feet; and that their Faces were so little alter'd, that the Features of them might be plainly distinguish'd and discern'd. He thereupon told me, That our Bodies are like a Spunge, and that upon letting out the Blood, and those noble Particles of Life, which render the Body too moist, and then drying the rest well, one might keep them many Ages. The Soil of *Bactria* is a warm dry Sand, very proper to preserve and petrify Bodies after this Manner. The other *Mummy* is a precious Gum, which distills from a Rock. There are two Mines, or Springs, of it in *Persia*, the one in the Desarts of *Caramenia*, in the Country of *Sar*, and that is the best: For they avow, that let a human Body be never so much mill'd, broken, torn, and even minced all to pieces, one half Drachm of this *Mummy* will reestablish it in four and twenty Hours time. Of the Truth of this, no body in *Persia* makes the least Doubt, by reason of the Experience of miraculous Cures, which they perform daily, by means of this precious Drug. The other Mine is in the Country of *Corasson*, which is the Ancient *Bactria*, where I have told you, there are also *Mummies* of human Bodies, as there are in *Egypt*. The Rocks, from whence the true *Mummy* distills, belong to the King; and all that drops from them, is preserv'd for him. They are inclos'd, and lock'd up, and at the Entrance, are five Seals, of the principal Officers of the Province. They open the Mine but once a Year, in the presence of these Officers, and likewise several others, and all that is found of this precious Mastick, or the greatest part, is sent to the King's Treasury, from whence a Person that has occasion for it, may get it very easily, if he has but a little Credit and Interest. The Word *Mummy* is a *Persian* Word taken from *Moum*, which signifies Wax, Gum, Ointment. The *Hebrews*, and the *Arabians*, make use of this Name, with the same Signification. The *Persians* say, That the Prophet *Daniel* taught them the due Preparation and Use of the *Mummy*.

¶ Among the remarkable Plants of *Persia*, and that are at this time very well known, there is the *Hannah*, which is a Grain wherewith both Men and Women make a Colour to paint the Hands, the Feet, and sometimes the Face, in order to preserve the Skin, and the Complexion. The Sun has not the Power to tan a Face that is anointed with it, neither can the Cold penetrate it, as before, and chap the Skin. They likewise rub their Horses Legs over with it, for the same Reason. This Grain or Seed grows upon a little Tree, in Tufts, like *Pepper* or *Ginger:* There is abundance of it in the Countries of *Kirmon*, and at *Siston*: They say, it is the Shrub, which we call a *Pastel*. They also make use of the Leaves of it, for the same Effect. The manner of using them, is to beat 'em to a Powder, and then to temper them with Water in a Mortar; when that's done, they wet their Hands, and anoint them with *Hannah* so temper'd, and in a manner, enamel themselves over with it for the whole Night, that the *Hannah* may take place. This Tincture is nevertheless taken off by Water, which makes those, who have newly rubb'd their Hands with it, wash them very seldom for fear of the *Hannah*'s going off: It commonly lasts fifteen Days or more before it goes away of it self.

¶ The *Rounas*, which our Authors call *Opoponax*, is a reddish root, that is employ'd in colouring and dying: It grows very much in *Persia*, and from thence the *Indies*, which is the best Country for colouring and dying, receives it. The Cotton-Tree grows up and down all over *Persia*; you may see whole Fields full of it: It is a Fruit as large as the Head of a Poppy, but of a rounder Figure. They find in every Head seven little Grains, or black Berries, which are as it were the Seed of that Fruit. There grows also in *Persia*, in several Places, a little Tree, perfectly rare and curious, the Fruit whereof is large and long, like green Lambriches, which when they come to open, yield a downy Silk, as fine as Wadding. I have had Quilts and Cushions made of it for my own Use in *Persia*. They Card it as they do Cotton, without spoiling it.

¶ I must place among these Physical Druggs the *Bezoar*, which is that Stone, that is so famous in Medicine. It is a soft Stone, form'd with several little Coats and Skins, after the Manner of Pearls, or just like as Onions grow. They are found in the Bodies of He-Goats, and She-Goats, whether tame or wild, on the side of the Gulph of *Persica*, in the Province of *Corasson*, which is the ancient *Margiana*; and they are incomparably better than those which are got in the *Indies*, in the Kingdom of *Colconda*, and in the Countries most remote. They say further, that there are in those Countries of the *Indies*, great *Bezoars*, in the Bodies of the *Asses*, of the wild *Boars*, of the *Porcupines*, and in the Bodies of the *Geese*. I have seen some brought from *Colconda*; but because the Goats were driven three Days Journey out of the Country, there were *Bezoars* but in a few of them, and those were only little pieces. We kept some of those Goats Fifteen Days alive, and that with nothing but common Green Herbs; and when we came to open them, we found nothing in them. I kept them at that time to try the Truth of what was said, that there was a particular Herb, which by heating those Animals, produc'd this Stone in their Bodies. The *Persian* Naturalists say, that the more these Animals feed in dry Countries, and eat warm and Sun-burnt Herbs, the more efficacious, and wholsome is the *Bezoar* that they yield us. *Corasson*, and the Borders of the Gulph of *Persica*, are Countries by their own Nature dry and Sun-burnt, if there are any in the World. One may always in the Heart of these Stones meet with some piece of Bramble, or other Wood, round about which, the humid Particles coagulate, that compose and form this Stone. It is to be observ'd, that in the *Indies*, they are the She-Goats that bear the *Bezoar*; and in *Persia* the Sheep, and the He-

Goats; and this makes the *Persians* esteem most the *Bezoar* of their own Country, as being more hot, and better digested, and set but little Value on the others, which are sold at a much cheaper Rate. The *Bezoar* of *Persia* is sold by the *Kourag*, which is the weight of three Mesals; or to speak more plainly, Fifty Four Pound to the *Kourag*.

¶ The *Orientalists* hold, that the *Bezoar* is a Counter Poison, for which reason they have given it the name of *Pe-zaer*, which is as much as to say, the Conqueror of Poison; or a thing that has the upper-hand of Poison. Our Word *Bezoar* undoubtedly proceeds from thence, in the same Manner as the Word *Civit*, comes from the Word *Zabad*, which is the *Persian* Name. The *Bezoar* is made use of with great Success in Sudorifics; they give it in Purple Fevers; they more especially prescribe it in Cordials, Confections and Philtres. They say it warms and enlivens the Spirits, awakens Vigour, and confirms the Temperature of the Body. The *Eastern* Physicians prescribe this in the room of any thing else. The less knowing People, and the Quacks, cry it up to the Skies; but in the Bottom, it is a Drug that loses its Esteem in the *East*, and that will, in a short time, be entirely cry'd down, as I think it is already in *Europe*.

¶ The Manner of using it in *Persia*, is to grate it with the Point of a Pen-knife, or to make it into Powder on a Marble, and the usual Dose is two or three Grains, in a Spoonful of Rose-water. The *Bezoar* is very easily and commonly falsified. The greatest and most polish'd Pieces are the most to be suspected; because the Price of those Pieces being far above the Price of the common Pieces; the Falsifiers of it make more by the Drachm than any other way. I never saw true *Bezoars* that weigh'd above six Grains; and the true *Bezoar* is always lighter than the Counterfeit, which is one of the Marks the knowing Purchasers go by. There is another surer Mark still, which is to apply an Awl, made red-hot in the Fire; for if any Vapour issues from it, or if the Awl enters it, 'tis a certain Sign of its being a Counterfeit. Rosin and *Spanish* Wax, are the Materials which they commonly make use of, in falsifying the *Bezoar*. It must not be forgot, that the fine Polish of that Stone is Artificial; its Skin or Coat, when 'tis first taken out of the Body of the Animal, being Rough and Greenish, without as well as within.

¶ As I have had several Questions put to me since my return, concerning *Musk* and *Ambergrease*, I thought it would be very well done of me to set down here what I have observ'd in my Travels.

¶ I believe that all the World knows very well, that *Musk* is the Excrement and Corruption of a Beast, that resembles a wild She-Goat, excepting that her Body and Legs are smaller. It is to be met with in upper

Tartary, in South *China*, which is bordering upon it; and in *Great Tibet*, which is a Kingdom between the *Indies* and *China*. I never saw any of those Animals alive there, but I have seen their Skins in several Places. You may meet with Draughts of them in the Embassy of the *Hollanders* to *China*, and in the *China Illustrata* of Father *Kirchor*. They give it out as a common Opinion, that *Musk* is the Sweat of an Animal, which runs and gathers it self in a small Bladder near the Navel. The *Orientalists* say more exactly, that it forms it self in a recess of the Body of that Goat, near the Navel, the Humour whereof works and eats its way out, particularly when the Beast is in a Heat; that then by dint of rubbing it self against Trees and Rocks, the Vessel is broke and penetrated, and the Matter spreads it self into that part, between the Muscles and the Skin, and gathering together there, it forms a sort of Lump or Bladder; that the Internal and External Heat, warms the corrupted Blood, and 'tis that Heat which gives so violent a Scent to the *Musk*. The *Eastern* People call this the Navel of *Musk*, and also the Odoriferous Navel. The good *Musk* is brought from *Tibet*; the *Eastern* People esteem it beyond that of *China*, whether it be that it has a more strong or lasting Perfume, or that their own comes fresher to them; because *Tibet* is nearer to them, than the Province of *Xensy*, which is the part of *China* where they make the most *Musk*. The great Trade for *Musk* is carried on at *Boutam*, a celebrated City in the Kingdom of *Tibet*. The *Patans*, who go to make Purchases there, distribute it out about all the *Indies*, from whence 'tis afterwards Transported to all the Parts of the Earth. The *Patans* are Neighbours to *Persia*, and the upper *Tartary*, and are Subjects, or rather only Tributaries to the *Great Mogul*.

¶ The *Indians* make great Account of this Aromatick Drug, and esteem it, as well for its Use, as for the great Demand there is for it. They use it in their Perfumes, in their Medicinal Epithems, and Confections, and in all Preparations which they are accustom'd to make, in order to awaken the Passions of Love, and confirm the Vigour of the Body. The Women make use of it to dissipate the Vapours, which rise from the Matrix into the Brain, by carrying a Bladder of it at their Navel, and when the Vapours are violent and continual, they take the *Musk* out of the Bladder, and inclose it in a little piece of single Holland, made in the fashion of a small Bag or Purse, and apply it to the Part, which Modesty will not permit me to Name.

¶ The best Musk in a Bladder, is worth fourscore and ten *Roupies* a Pound; the inferior sort goes at forty-five or fifty. A *Roupie* is thirty Pence *French* Money. The *English* and *Portugueze* make many Purchases in the

Indies to sell again in *Europe*. The *Hollanders* buy theirs in *China*; the *Armenians*, the *Persians*, and the *Patans* carry theirs into *Persia* and *Turkey*, where there is a great consumption of them, for certain Reasons, that are very easy to Imagine.

¶ 'Tis the general Opinion, that when they cut the little Purse where the Musk is, there issues forth from it so strong a Perfume, that the Huntsman is oblig'd to stop his Mouth and Nose very close with Linnen folded in several Doubles; and that frequently, notwithstanding that Precaution, the excessive strength of the Perfume, forces the Blood to gush out with such Violence, that he bleeds to Death: I have appriz'd my self of this very exactly; and as, in effect, I have heard the same thing told by several *Armenians*, who had been at *Boutam*, I am my self perswaded of the Truth of it. My Reason is, because this Drug does not gain strength by Time, but on the contrary loses its Smell intirely at the long run. Besides, that Perfume is so strong in the *Indies*, that I was never able to bear the Smell. Whenever I trafick'd for Musk I always kept my self in the Air, with my Handkerchief held to my Nose, and stood at a pretty good distance from those who handled the Bladders, referring my self to my Broker's Opinion of it, by which I am well assured, that the Musk must be very heady, and perfectly insupportable, when 'tis taken just fresh from the Body.

¶ I add, that there is not a Drug in Nature, that is more easily counterfeited, nor more subject to Adulteration. There are several of these Bags or Purses, to be met with, which are no more than barely the Skins of the Animals, and fill'd with their Blood and a little Musk, to give it the Scent, and that are not the Purses which the Wisdom of Nature has plac'd near the Navel, to receive that wonderful and Odoriferous Moisture. As to the true and genuine Bladders themselves, when the Huntsman does not find them full, he squeezes the Body of the Animal, that the Blood may run into it, and fill it up; because 'tis a receiv'd Opinion, that the Blood of Musk, and even the Flesh it self, smells well. The Merchants afterwards put Lead, Bulls-blood, and other Things, into it, to add to the Weight. The Art which the Eastern People have to know when 'tis adulterated and when not, is first, to take and weigh it in their Hands. Experience has taught them, exactly to know by the weight, whether a Bladder be alter'd or not. Their Taste is the second Proof; the *Indians* never fail of putting into their Mouths the little Grains that are continually falling from the Bladders, when they are about buying them; The Third is, to take a piece of Thread soak'd in the Juice of Garlick, and draw it through the Bladder, in a Needle, for if the smell of the Garlick goes away quite, the Musk is good, but if the Thread retains that smell, it is certainly adulterated.

¶ *Ambergrease* is got in the *Indian* Sea, along the Coasts of *Africa*, which lie between the *Cape of Good Hope*, and the Gulph of the *Red Sea*: The Sea throws it out at times, so that it goes much farther, even up to the River of *Ceylon*, and the Coast of *Malabar*; but this happens very rarely. I have read in a *Persian* Author, that the *Arabians* believe *Ambergrease* to be a Matter produc'd by the Water of Springs and Fountains, which are at the bottom of the Sea, as the *Naphte*, which the Winds, and the force of the Currents drive into the River. They hold, among the generality of the People, on the contrary, that it is a Froth of the Sea, that's harden'd and congeal'd, or else the Seed that comes out of large Fish, which likewise grows hard and congeal'd. But this is an Opinion that does not carry along with it an Air of Truth; for why should not the Sea, which is frothy, and has vast Fish every where in it, produce this precious Aromatick in other Places of the *Indies*, where there is still more Warmth, and a greater degree of Drought? The most knowing *Indians* say, that *Ambergrease* is an Odoriferous Gum, as Incense, which grows in *Arabia*, and which being wash'd into the Sea, by the Rains, the Floods, and the Torrents, which are usually subsequent to these rainy Seasons, (and these happen much about the time of our *Autumn*) is carried by the Winds and the Currents of the *Monsoons*, towards *Africa*, and driven along upon those Coasts, even to the last great Point of Land, which we call the *Cape of Good Hope*, where it is again driven back by the Course of a contrary Sea, which runs to meet it from the Island of *Madagascar*. One of the wisest Men in *India*, and one of the greatest Lords, by Name *Miszar cheri felmole*, whom the late King of *Colconda*, out of a particular Esteem, sent for from *Ispahan*, to give him his Daughter in Marriage, and who, the last time I was at *Colconda*, had the largest Pieces of *Ambergrease*, and the finest I ever saw in my Life, was of Opinion, that it was Wax and Honey congeal'd: He told me, as he was showing me some Pieces, which were very porous in the inside, and almost like a Spunge; that the Bees in *Africa* made their Honey among the Rocks, and in the old Trunks of hollow Trees, as they do in the *East*, mostly in Countries that are thinly inhabited, and sometimes even in others that are very well Peopl'd, as I have observ'd in my first Volume, that they make their Honey so in *Mengrelia*, and *Circassia*; and that the Torrents of Rain, carry pieces of their rough Work into the Sea, where the Matter hardening, contracts at last that admirable Scent, for which it is so much esteem'd. He said, that the difference between *Ambergrease* and the black *Amber*, which is not worth so much as the other, proceeds from this, that one Honey is not so good as the other, and that one may perceive just as much difference in the *Ambergrease* as one may in the Honey in all the Countries where there is wild Honey. This precious Drug, which was unknown to the ancient Professors of *Pharmacy*, as well *Greeks* as *Arabians*, smells at first very ill to what they pretend it does, but afterwards in proportion as it hardens, it loses that Quality. I have remark'd, that the *Amber* which is fresh and newly fish'd up, hath a strong smell, which is both displeasing and injurious, but goes off in time: They assure you still further, that the Birds of the Sea are very greedy of it, and peck it up, which I believe to be very true; however I never met with the point of a Bird's Beak in any piece of *Ambergrease*, which, they say, is frequently to be met with.

¶ The *Persians* don't use a great deal of *Civet*, which they call *Zabad:* The Women rub their Hair with it, having first very well prepar'd it for that purpose.

¶ Over and above all these Medicinal Drugs, which I have told you grow in *Persia*, there are also the *Galbanum*, which grows in the Mountains at seven or eight Leagues distance from *Ispahan:* The vegetable *Alcali*, which grows almost every where; the *Sal Armoniack*; the *Orpiment*, which is used for Depilation, or taking away the Hair; this grows in *Media*, and round about *Casbin*, particularly the yellow sort.

¶ I shall say nothing here of these latter Druggs, because they are neither so extraordinary, nor so much enquir'd after, but yet are sufficiently known already.

CHAPTER V

OF THE FRUITS OF PERSIA

I BEGIN with the *Melons*, which are the most excellent Fruit in all *Persia*. They reckon in that Country above twenty different sorts of them; the first are called *Guermec*, as much as to say, the hot ones; they are round and small. This is a sort of *Melon* that the Spring Produces; it is very insipid, and melts in the Mouth like Water. The *Persian* Physicians advise People to eat plentifully of it; and they say it is necessary to purge one's self with it, in the same manner as Herbs are used to purge Horses, and at the same time. This is a thing which they never fail to do, as constantly as the Year comes about, in the Month of *April*. They will eat at that time a matter of ten or twelve Pound of *Melon* a-Day, for a Fortnight or three Weeks together; and this is as much for Health's sake as it is to please their Palates, for they look upon it as a great refresher and cooler of their Blood; and if a Man is fallen away, it will restore him again, and make him grow fat. They tell you a Story upon this Subject, of two *Arabian* Physicians, who coming to *Ispahan* in quest of Business, they came there exactly in the Season of these *Guermec,* and seeing the Street full of this kind of Fruit, they said one to another, *Let us go further on, don't let us stay here, there is nothing to do for us in this Place*; these People have a Remedy for all Distempers. However some wise People believe on the contrary, that 'tis the excessive Use of this Fruit which causes those Fevers, that are so rife there in *Autumn.* They say, that these *Melons* load the Stomach with Phlegm, and that the soft and Sugar *Melons,* which must of Consequence be very hot, and come after these first, concoct the Phlegm, and turn it into Cholar, and that from thence proceeds the Fever. After these *Guermec* or hot *Melons,* there come up different sorts every Day, and the later these Fruit are, the better. The latest of them all are White, and you would swear, that they were nothing but one entire Lump of pure Sugar. They are a Foot long, and weigh ten or twelve Pound. These are eaten in the Winter time. In those Houses where they keep a good Table, there is a Service of *Melons* all the Year round, because the old ones will keep till the coming in of the *Guermec Melons.* They keep them in Caves where the Air can't get in, and according to the bigness of the Place, they have always one or two Lamps lighted, which dispel the Cold, and hinder the Frost from getting into them. *Melons* in the common Season, which lasts full four Months, are the daily Food and sustenance of the poorer sort of People. They live upon nothing else but *Melons* and *Cucumbers,* the last of which they eat without paring them. There are some that will eat five and thirty Pounds of *Melon* at a Meal, without making themselves Sick. During these four Months, they come in such vast Quantities to *Ispahan,* that I can't help believing they eat more there in a Day, than they do in *France* in a Month. The Streets are full of Horses and Asses, that are loaded with them, from Mid-night till Morning, and all the Day till Sun-set. The best in the Kingdom grow in *Corasson,* near lower *Tartary,* in a Village call'd *Craguerde.* They carry 'em to *Ispahan* for the King, and for Presents to their Friends. They don't spoil at all in their bringing, tho' they come thirty Days Journey off. But this is nothing near so wonderful, as what I have seen at *Surat* in the *Indies*; for there I have eaten *Melons* my self, sent from *Agra,* which is forty Days Journey off, and they had been brought to *Agra* from the Frontiers of *Persia,* before that, which is forty Days Journey more. A Man carries them on Foot, and he can't carry above two at a time, they are so weighty, and so very big. He carries them in two Panniers hanging from a Beam-like Ballances, which he carries upon his Shoulders, and Shifts them every now and then to ease himself. These Porters will travel seven or eight Leagues a Day with one of these Burthens. They likewise bring the Seed out of *Tartary*, which must be renew'd every seven Years; for after that time, it degenerates intirely, grows insipid, and the Fruit retains nothing of its former Taste.

¶ Among all these sorts of *Melons*, there are *Water-Melons* or *Pateques*, that grow up and down throughout the Kingdom; but the best of these, as well as the others, come from *Bactria*. They have *Cucumbers*, one sort whereof, have few or no Kernels, which they eat raw, and without dressing them in any manner whatsoever; and they have likewise a Fruit, which they call *Badinian*, which is the Xanthium of *Dioscorides*, and the same with what we call the *Love-Apples*. It has a Taste that comes very near that of the *Cucumber*, is as big as Apples generally are, and as long again, and when 'tis Ripe the Skin grows quite black; it grows as *Cucumbers* do, it is very good in several different Sauces, and to be dress'd up in many Things; no Body eats them till they are Roasted: They are to be met with in the Southerly Parts of *Italy*.

¶ There is another Fruit in *Persia* that grows upon a Plant, it is round, and about as big again as a common *Apple*, but hollow and light, and not worth the Eating; they esteem it only for the Smell; it is call'd *Destembovié*, that is to say, the Perfume of the Hand, because they carry it in their Hands like a Nosegay.

¶ Next to the *Melons*, the most excellent Fruits in *Persia*, are the *Grapes* and *Dates*; there are at least ten or a dozen sorts of *Grapes*, Purple, Red and Black; the *Grapes* are so large, that a single one is a Mouthful; that which they make their Wine of at *Ispahan* is call'd *Kich-Mich*, it is generally a little white *Grape*, and better than our *Muscadine*; but if one eat too many, they rise in one's Throat, and are overheating when us'd to Excess; it is round, and without Stones in it, or at least, one cannot perceive there's any in them in the Eating; but when the Wine works, you may see the Seeds of that *Grape* float at Top, like little Filaments or Threads, that are as thin as the Point of a Needle, and very tender. In *Persia* they keep their *Grapes* all Winter, leaving them half the Winter hanging upon the Vine, each Bunch being folded in a Linnen Bag, to hinder the Birds from getting at them; they pick just the quantity they intend to eat; this is the Advantage of the dry serene Air, which the *Persians* breathe, that it preserves every Thing; whereas the Quality of our moist Climates spoil and corrupt all our Fruits. They make their *Raisins* dry, by hanging Bunches of them to the Ceiling, from whence they fall *Grape* by *Grape*. In the Country of

Kourdeston, and near *Sultania,* where there are abundance of Violets, they mingle the Leaves with the Raisins, and they say it is very good and wholsome for the Stomach. It is certain, it gives the *Raisin* a better Flavour. The best *Raisins* that are to be had round about *Ispahan,* are those which the *Guebres,* or Ancient *Persian Pagans* make; and especially those of *Negafabad,* which is a great Market-Town, four Leagues from *Ispahan,* where none but *Guebres* live; they dress their *Raisins* with more Care than the *Mahometans;* because they are permitted by their Religion, to drink Wine, as well as the *Jews* and *Christians.*

¶ As for the *Dates,* which I take to be the best Fruits in the World, they are no where so good as they are in *Persia.* They grow in *Arabia* in greater Quantities than they do in *Persia;* but besides, being much less in Size, they do not come near those of *Persia* for Goodness; that both at the Time you gather them, and a long time after, are cover'd over with thick Juice, like a Sirrop, which is clammy, and sticks to the Fingers, and is more soft, and more delicately sweet to the Taste than Virgin-Honey. The most exquisite *Dates* in the Kingdom, are gather'd in *Coureston,* in *Siston,* at *Persepolis,* upon the Borders of the *Gulph* of *Persica;* and more particularly at *Jaron,* a Market Town, upon the Road from *Chiras* to *Lar.* Some People Export them dry in Bunches, or loose; but most People keep them preserv'd in their own Juice, and export them in great Gourds, from fifteen to twenty Pound Weight. They prepare them likewise with *Pistachos* in Pots, as we do *Pickl'd Walnuts.* There is not more delicate Eating in Nature than they are. You must however, be moderate in the Use of this Fruit, if you are not accustom'd to eat of them; for in that Case, when People eat too much, they heat the Blood, even to the making Ulcers spread all over the Body, and to the Weakning of the Sight, a Thing which never happens to the Inhabitants of the Country, from whence this Fruit comes. The *Dates* grow in Tufts or Bunches, on the Top of the *Palm,* which is a slender Tree, but taller than any Fruit-Tree whatsoever, and it has no Branches but on the very Top of all. A Man climbs up by means of a Rope, which he fastens about the Knots of the Tree, from one to another, and so higher and higher, till he gets up to the Top; then in an Hours time, the whole Fruit of the Tree is gather'd; for that Fruit sticks together in Clusters, which will weigh from thirty to forty Pound. The *Date*-Trees will bear near two Hundred Mans of Fruit at a Time, which is the same with four and twenty hundred Weight: This Tree does not begin to bear till it is fifteen Years old, but it bears afterwards for near two hundred Years together.

¶ There are in *Persia,* all the same sorts of Fruits which we have in *Europe,* and many others that we have not; and certainly, if they understood Gardening as well as we, their Fruits would be still incomparably finer and more delicious than they are; but they have no knowledge at all of the Matter. They do not understand the Art of *Grafting*, *Inoculating*, of spreading Trees into *Hedge-rows*, and breeding *Dwarf-Trees*. All their Trees are commonly very high, and laden with Timber. They have excellent *Apricocks* of five or six sorts, and other Stone-Fruits that we have, whereof they have more than fifteen Kinds, that succeed and grow up one under another. You may frequently see in *Persia*, *Nectarins* of sixteen or eighteen Ounces, and *Peaches* near as large; but what you will find no where else, is a kind of *Apricocks*, which they call *Tocmchams*, that is to say, the *Seed* or *Egg* of the Sun, which are red within, and very delicious to the Palate. This sort of *Apricocks*, and the others likewise, are very easy to open, the Stones within them open at the same Time, and they contain a sweet Almond, that has an excellent Taste; they Export them when dry'd to a thousand Places, and when they are boil'd in Water, the Juice which is very pleasant, thickens the Water, and makes it a perfect Syrrop, as if you had put so much Sugar into it. I have been at some Entertainments in *Ispahan*, where they have had above fifty sorts of Fruit at Table, some of which grow three or four hundred Leagues off. *France*, or *Italy*, can't afford any Thing like it. Nothing is more common to be seen there than the *Pomegranate*, which is very excellent: There are several sorts, as *White*, *Flesh*-Colour, *Rose*-Colour, and perfect *Red*; there are some which have such tender Kernels in them, that you can scarce feel them in your Teeth, and others that have got a Membrane, or little Skin, between the Seeds. *Pomegranates* come from *Yesd*, which weigh above a Pound; the *Apples* and *Pears*, I mean the best, come from *Iberia*, and the Parts adjacent; the *Dates* from *Caramenia*, as I have observ'd; the *Pomegranates* from *Chiras*; and the *Oranges* from *Hyrcania*. *Quinces*, amongst the rest, are very good in *Persia*, having a soft and agreeable Taste; and among the Fruits for the Curiosity of them, they reckon the *Onions* of *Bactria*, that are as large and sweet as Apples. There are just such others grow at *Carek*, a little Isle in the *Gulph* of *Persica*. *Bactria*, beyond all the World, is one of the Countries that produces the best and finest Fruits; there are *Prunes*, as our *Prunes* of *Brignole*, but more agreeable and better for the Stomach; half a Dozen boil'd in Water make a gentle Purge, and if you only mingle with them as much *Sena* as one takes up between a Finger and Thumb, it makes a compleat Medicine; they call them *Alow Bocora*, that is to say, *Prunes* of *Bocora*, which is a Town belonging to the *Bactrians*, in little *Tartary*, situated on the River *Oxus*.

¶ The *Pistachos* grow at *Casbin,* and round about in the Countries of *Media,* and are larger than those of *Syria*; they grow no where in the World that I know of, but in those two Places: They have one sort of *Pistacho-Nuts,* that I never saw any where else, which are not so good as the others, and are as small as *Cherry-Stones*; the *Persians* eat them dry, fry'd with Salt: They give you some of them at all Collations, especially when there's any Wine at the Table.

¶ They have moreover, *Almonds,* great *Nuts,* little *Nuts, Filberds,* and *Figs,* that are excellent to the highest Degree. The greatest Exportation of Fruits is from *Yesd. Olives* likewise grow in *Persia,* on the Frontiers of *Arabia,* and in *Mazenderan,* near the *Caspian* Sea; but they don't know how to preserve them, nor extract Oil out of them.

¶ I shall not discourse in this Chapter of the Grain, which the Earth produces for the Nourishment of Men and Beasts, because I shall treat of them in the Chapter of *Mechanick Arts, and Trades* under the Article of *Husbandry,* or *Agriculture.*

CHAPTER VI

CONCERNING THE FLOWERS OF PERSIA

THERE are all sorts of Flowers in *Persia,* that are to be met with in *France,* and in the finest Countries of *Europe*; but they are not equally distributed in all the Provinces; for there are fewer sorts of Flowers, and a less Quantity, even of those, in the Southern Parts of the Kingdom, than in the others, an excessive Heat being as much contrary to the Nature of most Flowers, as extream Cold; from whence it happens, that there are not so many Kinds of Flowers in *India,* as in *Persia,* tho' they are alike in this, that they last all the Year round. But the Flowers of *Persia,* by the Vivacity of their Colours, are generally handsomer than those of *Europe,* and those of *India. Hyrcania* is one of the finest Countries for Flowers; for there are whole Forests, of *Orange-Trees,* single and double *Jessamins,* all the Flowers that we have in *Europe,* and several that we have not. The most Eastern Part of that Country, which they call *Mazenderan,* is nothing but one continu'd Parterre, from *September,* to the End of *April.* All the Country is at that Time cover'd over with Flowers; and it is likewise the best Time for the Fruits; as on the Contrary in the other Months, they cease to Flourish, by reason of the excessive Heat, and Malignity of the Air. Towards *Media,* and the Southern Parts of *Arabia,* the Fields produce of themselves *Tulips, Anemones, single Renun-*

culus's of the finest Red, and *Imperial-Crowns*. In other Places, as round about *Ispahan*, the *Jonquils* grow of themselves, and there are Flowers that last all the Winter. They have in the proper Season, seven or eight sorts of *Daffodils*, *Lilly Convallies*, *Lillies* and *Violets*, of all Colours, single and double *Pinks*, and the *Pinks* of *India*, which are of so gay and bright a Colour, that they dazle the Eye; single and double *Jessamins*, and those which we call *Spanish Jessamins*, that for Beauty and Fragrancy, far surpass those of *Europe*. They have a sort of *Mallows* too, that are of a very beautiful Colour. The *Tulips* at *Ispahan* have a short Stalk, not growing above four Inches from the Ground. Among the Flowers that grow, during the Winter-Season, are the white and blue *Somboul*, which is the same Flower with what we call the *Hyacinth*, the *Lilly* of the Valleys, little *Tulips*, the *Violet*, the *Liriconfancy's*, and the *Myrrh*. In the Spring-time, they have the like Plenty of yellow and red *Gilliflowers*, *Ambretts* of all Colours, and a Flower we have not, as I know of, that seems to me to be one of the finest in Nature; they call it *Gulmikek*, that is to say, a *Clove Gilliflower*, because it perfectly resembles a Clove; it is of an incomparable Scarlet Colour; there is nothing in Nature or Art to be seen, that has so lively a Look with it; every Sprig bears Thirty of these Flowers, rang'd in a round Form, and about the Bigness of a Crown Piece in Circumference. The Rose, which is so common among them, is of five sorts of Colours, besides its natural one, *White*, *Yellow*, *Red*, which we call the *Spanish Rose*, and others of two Colours, *viz.* *Red* on one Side, and *White* or *Yellow* on the other. The *Persians* call these *Roses Dou Rouye*, or Two Places. I have seen a *Rose-Tree*, which bore upon one and the same Branch, *Roses* of three Colours, some *Yellow*, others *Yellow* and *White*, and others *Yellow* and *Red*. They make great Green Flower-Pots in the Spring, which are very agreeable to the Eye; with these they adorn their Apartments, and their Gardens, by placing upon these Pots a Couch of sifted Earth, intermingled with the *Seed* of *Cresses*, and keeping it always cover'd with a wet Cloth. The first Rays of the Sun, make the Seed sprout out, and you see the Pot all over Green, just like the Rind of a Tree over-run with Moss: But there is nothing more beautiful to behold than the Trees in Blossom, particularly the *Peach-Tree*, because the Blossoms are so very thick upon them, that you can't look through them.

❡ I have made mention, among the other Flowers that grow at *Ispahan*, of the *Hyacinth*, which they call *Somboul*; whereupon, I must tell you, that *Pietro della Valle* speaks in his Relations, of a Root exquisite for its fragrant Smell, and Perfume, which he says, the *Persians* call *Somboul Catay*, or *Tartarian*; and as he said no more of it, than barely that it was an Odoriferous *Root*, several People ask'd me at my Return, what it was? I believe it can be nothing else but the *Spica Nardi*, mention'd in the *Gospel*, which in *English*, we call *Spikenard*; for *Somboul* in *Arabick*, signifies *Spike*, or *Ear* of Corn, from whence the *Arabick Astronomers* term that Sign of the *Zodiack*, which we call *Virgo, Somboul*, or Bearer of Ears of Corn, by reason of the Sheaf of Corn, which Painters place in her Hand: But I never heard any Body in *Persia* say, that such a Fruit grew there, and I will venture to say, that *Pietro della Valle* is mistaken in that, as he has been in many other Things, by taking a Compound for a Root. I have made it my general Observation in *Persia* and *Turkey* too; that they call many Things that are exquisite in their Kind, *Catay*, or *Tartarian*; not that they mean by this, that it came from thence, but only to express the Rarity, and the Value of the Things: As for Example, they call the *Brocards* of *Venice*, *Zerbaft Catay*, that is to say, *Tartarian* Cloth of Silver.

¶ After what I have said of the Number and Beauty of the *Persian* Flowers, one would be very apt to imagine, that they must of course have the finest Gardens in the World; but it is no such thing; on the Contrary I have found it to be a general Rule, that where Nature is most Easy and Fruitful, they are very raw and unskilful in the Art of Gardening. This comes to pass, by reason, that in those Places, where Nature plays so excellently the Part of a Gardner, if I may be permitted to use the Expression, Art hath in a Manner nothing to do. The Gardens of the *Persians*, commonly consist of one great Walk, which parts the Garden, and runs on in a straight Line, border'd on each side by a Row of Plantanes, with a Bason of Water in the middle of it, made proportionable in Bigness to the Garden, and likewise of two other little Side-Walks, the Space between them is confusedly set with Flowers, and planted with *Fruit-Trees*, and *Rose-Bushes*; and these are all the Decorations they have. They don't know what *Parterres* and *Green-Houses*, what *Wildernesses* and *Terraces*, and the other Ornaments of our Gardens are. The most particular Reason one can assign for this, is, that the *Persians* don't walk so much in Gardens as we do, but content themselves with a bare Prospect, and breathing the fresh Air: For this End, they set themselves down in some part of the Garden, at their first coming into it, and never move from their Seats till they are going out of it.

CHAPTER VII

OF METALS AND MINERALS: TO WHICH IS
ANNEX'D A DISCOURSE OF JEWELS

As *Persia* is very Mountainous, it is full of *Metals* and *Minerals*, which they have begun to draw out by Force in this last Century, much more than in the preceding Ages. It is to the great *Abas* that this Diligence of theirs is owing, and it was the great Number of *Mineral* Waters, which are here and there to be met with in all Parts of the Kingdom, which induc'd him to cause the Work of the Mines to be carry'd on with Vigour. The *Metals* that are the most usual to be met with in *Persia*, are *Iron*, *Steel*, *Brass*, and *Lead*. They have not as yet, found any *Gold* or *Silver* there. They are however very well assur'd that there must be some in the Mines, it being impossible that so many Mountains which produce all sorts of *Metals*, and *Sulphur*, and *Salt-Petre*, should not likewise produce those *Minerals* of the Sun and Moon: But the *Persians* are too slothful to make any Discoveries. Among them, if they have what others before them us'd to have, they stop there and sit down contented, and never trouble their Heads to seek further into Things: If they were as active, as restless, and as necessitous a People as we are, there would not have been a Hole or a Corner of these Mountains, but would have been rak'd into, and rummag'd several and several times. That which proves it still further, that there is *Silver* in those *Mines*, is, that the Refiners always find their Encrease in the refining of it, and this could never be, but from the *Silver* that is in the *Lead*, which they make use of in the refining of this Silver, and in the melting, this unites itself to the other. The principal Mine which they work upon of *Silver*, even to this Day, is at *Kervan*, in the Country of *Dendamon*, four Leagues from *Ispahan*, in a Mountain call'd *Chacouch*, or *Mount-Royal*. But as Wood and Coals are both very scarce at *Ispahan*, and in other Places, Mines are not to be met with that abound with *Silver*, the Expence always exceeding the Profit; from whence it is become usual to say by way of Proverb, for all vain and fruitless Undertakings, *It is the Mine of Kervan*; in that they lay out Ten for Nine: There are likewise *Silver* Mines at *Kirman* and *Mazenderan*. We have great room to believe, that the Luxury and Wealth of *Persia* formerly came from the Mines of the Country, which are quite exhausted, or that they neglected to keep them up, by reason of the plenty of *Gold* and *Silver*, which Trade and Commerce bring into that Kingdom.

¶ The *Iron* Mines are in *Hyrcania*, in Southern *Media*, in the Countries of *Parthia*, and in *Bactria*. There is *Iron* in Abundance, but it is not so smooth and tractable as that in *England*.

¶ The *Steel* Mines are to be found in the same Countries, and they produce a great deal, for the *Steel* there is not worth above seven Pence a Pound. This Steel is so full of *Sulphur*, that if you throw the Filings on the Fire, they will go off and make a Report like Gun-powder. It is fine, having a mighty thin and delicate Grain, a Quality which naturally, and without the help of Art, renders it as lasting as a *Diamond*. But on the other Hand, it is as brittle as *Glass*; and as the *Persian* Artificers don't very well understand how to temper it, they have no Method among them of making Wheels and Springs, and other minute and delicate Pieces of Workmanship. It however takes a very good Seasoning or Temper, by being thrown into cold Water; and this they do by wrapping it up in a wet Cloth, instead of putting it into a Trough of Water, after having made it very warm, but not red hot. This *Steel* can never be join'd with *Iron*, and if it is put into too hot a Fire, it burns, and becomes like the Dross of a Coal. They mix it with *Indian Steel*, which is softer, tho' it be equally full of Sulphur, and held in much more Esteem. The *Persians* call both the one and the other sort of Steel *Poulad Jauherder*, Wash'd Steel, which is that we call Damask'd Steel, to distinguish it from the Steel of *Europe*. They melt it down in a round form like the hollow of one's Hand, and in little square Sticks.

¶ Brass thrives principally at *Sary*, in the Mountains of *Mazenderan*. There is also some in *Bactria*, and near *Casbin*. It is rough of it self, and to soften it, they mingle it with the Brass of *Sweden* or *Japan*; proportioning one part of foreign Brass to twenty of their own: This is the Metal they make the most use of.

¶ The *Lead Mines* are near *Kirkman* and *Yesd*, and these last are those which have the greatest share of Silver in them.

¶ Minerals abound throughout all *Persia*; *Sulphur* and *Salt Petre* are extracted out of the Mountain of *Damavend*, which separates *Hircania* from *Parthida: Antimony* is found in *Caramenia*. But it is a Bastard sort, for that having melted it, they found nothing in it but fine Lead. *Emery*, which is near *Niris*, is pretty harsh, but it loses its harshness when it is pounded small; quite contrary to that of the *Indies*, which the smaller it is made, the more strong and sharp it is, for which Reason it is counted much better. As for the *Vitriol* and *Mercury*, those are things that they want in *Persia*, as much as they do Tin. They are forced to send for them to the *Indies*.

¶ Salt is made by Nature alone, without the least Art. *Sulphur* and *Alom* are made after the same manner. There are two sorts of Salt in the Country, that of the Earth, and that of the Mines or Rocks. There is nothing so common in *Persia* as Salt, for on the one hand there is no Duty laid upon it, and on the other you may see whole Plains ten Leagues or more in length, cover'd quite over with Salt; and so you will find others as much cover'd over with *Sulphur* and *Alom*. You pass by a vast Quantity of them in the Roads of *Parthida*, *Persida*, and *Caramenia*. There is a Plain of Salt near *Cashan*, which you must pass thro' to go to *Hircania*, where you will meet with Salt as neat and pure as any can be whatsoever. In *Media*, and at *Ispahan*, the Salt is taken out of the Mines, and cary'd in great Quarters like Free-stone. It is so hard in some Places, as in the uninhabited *Caramenia*, that they make use of it as Stones in the building of poor Peoples Houses.

¶ The *Marble*, the *Free-stone*, and the *Slate*, come from *Hamadan* particularly, which is the ancient *Susa*. There are several sorts of Marble in *Persia*, as *White*, *Black*, *Red*, and some vein'd with *White* and *Red*. It is brought from *Nair*, near a Market-Town of *Susiana*, call'd *Sary*; it breaks into Scales or Tables, just like Slate; but the most admirable of all, is that which comes from a Place hard by *Tauris*. It is almost as transparent as Rock-Chrystal, and you may see thro' Tables of an Inch thick, if not more. This Marble is white, mingled with a green palish Colour, like the *Jadde*, which is a precious Stone, of a pale Green: It is so tender, that a Knife will enter it, which makes many People think, that it is not a true Mineral, neither has the Consistence of Parts, and cement like a true Genuine Stone.

¶ The *Persians* don't make use of a *Flint* to their Guns, nor to strike Fire with. They have a Wood which serves them instead of a Steel and Flint, and has the same Effect, because if one is struck against the other, they inflame and fire immediately.

¶ Towards the Frontiers of *Arabia*, on the side of *Babylon*, there are whole Rows, from whence you may gather that sort of Pitch which we call *Bitumen*.

¶ In the Countries round about *Tauris*, you will find the Mineral *Azure*, but it is not so good as that which comes from *Tartary*; its Colour alters, becomes dark, and at length vanishes quite away.

¶ In *Armenia* and *Persida*, you may meet with abundance of *Bole-Armonick*, and a Marl which is like White Soap, and serves them for the same Uses as Soap. The Women use it, most especially when they wash their Heads at the Bagnio. There are also Mines of *Isinglass* discovered there.

¶ In *Hyrcania*, on that side they call *Mazenderan*, they have found the *Pretoleum*, or *Naphtha*: There is both white and black. It is used in varnishing and painting, and in Physick too, for the curing of raw cold Humours. There is a great deal of *Naphtha* to be met with in other Places, as in *Chaldea*, where the meaner sort of People burn the Oyl that is made of it.

¶ But the richest Mine in *Persia* is that of the *Turkey-Stones*; they have it in two Places, at *Nichapour* in *Coraston*, and in a Mountain that is between *Hyrcania* and *Parthida*, four Days Journey from the *Caspian* Sea, named *Phirous-Cou*, or, *The Mount of Phirous*, who was one of the ancient Kings of *Persia*, that conquered this Country, and built up Towns and Castles in it. *Pliny* calls this *Mountain* the *Caucasus*. The Mine of the *Turkey-Stones* was likewise discovered, during the Reign of that *Phirous*, and took its Name from him. So does the fine Stone that we get out from it, and call *Turkey-Stone*, because it comes from the true ancient *Turkey*, for they in the East call it *Phirouze*. They have since discovered another Mine of these sort of Stones, but they are not so fine and lively; they call them *New Turkey-Stones*, which is what we call the new Rock, to distinguish them from the others, which are old *Turkeys:* The Colour of it goes off in time. They keep all that comes out of the old Rock for the King, who after he has pick'd and cull'd the best, sells or trucks away the remainder. The Miners and the Officers overlook it, taking care to carry off as much as they can; and from thence it comes to pass, that one so often runs great Hazards in buying these *Turkey-Stones*.

¶ After these Mines of precious Stones, I must set down the Fishery of *Pearls*, which is all along the Gulph of *Persica*, but particularly round the Isle of *Baherin*. This Fishery has a prodigious Plenty, and produces more than a Million of *Pearls* a Year. I have seen a *Pearl* taken out of it, that weigh'd Fifty Grains, and round to Perfection: This was a great Rarity, the largest Pearls in that Sea weighing no more generally than Ten or Twelve Grains. The Fisher-men are obliged, under the severest Penalties, to present the King with the *Pearls* that are above that Weight; but still that is a Point in which they perform their Trust only when they have not an Opportunity to break it. The *Persians* formerly paid a Tax to the *Portugueze*, that they should not trouble them in that Fishery: But since the Power of the *Portugueze* is fallen in the *Indies*, and that 'tis so low as we see it at this time of day reduc'd, the *Persians* have pay'd little or nothing, and what they did was only by way of Present; but now they give them nothing at all.

¶ The *Pearl* has pompous Names every where throughout the East. The *Turks* and the *Tartars* call it *Margeon*, a Word which signifies a Globe of

Light. The *Persians*, *Mervarid*, that is to say, Offspring of Light; and *Loulou*, which signifies also *Luminous* and *Brilliant*; it is to express its Fineness to the Eye. And truly the Pearls of *Persia* have much more Splendor in them, and a higher Colour than the Pearls of the West. The Term of *Loulou* is very probably the Original of the *French* Word *Lueur*, that is to say, a glimmering Light, just as from the Word *Mervarid*, the People of the West of *Europe*, have fram'd the Name of *Margarites*, by which they us'd to signifie Pearls: They take them in very large Oysters, near the Isle of *Baherin*, where the Sea is made soft and sweeten'd, by the Intermixture of a prodigious number of Subterraneous Canals that carry their Waters thither. They say that these Pearl-Fishermen draw out sweet Water, by laying of Pipes to the Hole by which the Water discharges it self into the Sea. They even say, That when the *Portugueze* were Lords of *Baherin*, as they were almost of the whole Gulph, they provided their Ships with Water out of that very Place, drawing it up from the Deep of the Sea by Pumps. The Divers that fish for Pearls are sometimes near half a quarter of an Hour under Water, and shew an inconceivable Strength of Nature in these hazardous Enterprizes.

❡ I must add in this Place, that the *Persians* make a Distinction between *Emeralds* as we do between *Rubies*. They call the finest sort, the *Emeralds* of *Egypt*, the next sort, old *Emeralds*, and the third, new *Emeralds*. Before the Discovery of the New World, *Emralds* us'd to come to them from *Egypt*, which were higher colour'd, as they pretend, and harder than the *Emeralds* of the West. They have several times shewn me some of these *Emeralds*, which they call *Zemroud-Mesri*, or of *Mesraim*, the ancient Name of *Egypt*; and likewise, *Zemroud-Asvani*, of *Asvan*, a Town of *Thebaida*, call'd *Syena* by the ancient Geographers. But though they seem to me to be very fine, of a very deep sinking Green, and of a sprightly Lustre; yet I thought I had seen as good from the *West-Indies*. As for what belongs to the Hardness, I cannot say any thing to it, having never had an Opportunity of Tryal; and as it is certain that there has been no Talk this great while of any Mines of *Emeralds* in *Egypt*. It may very well be, that the *Emeralds* of *Egypt* were brought thither by the Canal of the *Red-Sea*, coming either from the *West-Indies*, by the *Philippians*, or from *Pegu*, or from the Kingdom of *Colconda* upon the Coast of *Coromandel*, from whence they daily got out *Emeralds*. The *Persians* will have it, that the Mines of *Egypt* yield likewise the *Oriental Ruby*, the *Topaz*, and the *Carbuncle*; that Stone merely nominal, which is to be met with no more, and was very probably never any thing else but an *Oriental Ruby* of a higher Colour than usual. They call this imaginary Stone *Icheb Chirac*, the

Flambeau of the Night, because of the Property and Quality it has of enlightning all things round it; *Cha Mohore*, Royal Stone, and *Cha Deva-cran*, King of the Jewels. They attribute to it Supernatural Virtues; and that their Relation should not fail of being fabulous enough, they tell you, that the *Carbuncle* was bred either in the Head of a *Dragon*, a *Griffin*, or a *Royal Eagle*, which was found upon the Mountain of *Caf*. The *Orientalist* gives this Name to the *Hyperborean* Mountains. As to the Ruby, they call it *Yacut Eeylani*; and *Yacut* is apparently the Radix or Root of the Term *Hyacinth*, a Name which we give to Rubies that are soft and tender. It is true, there are Mines of precious Stones in *Ceylon*, but then there are none of them but what are soft and tender. They likewise call it *Balacchani*, the Stone of *Balacchan*, which is the *Pegu*, from whence I judge might be deriv'd the Name of *Balays*, which they give to their Rose-colour'd Rubies. It is natural that the East, being the Source of the Mines from whence our precious *Stones* come, we should likewise have their original Names come from thence along with them. Even the Name of *Jeweller*, which is given to the Traffickers that way, came undoubtedly from thence; for in all the Eastern Countries, they call them *Jeuaery*.

CHAPTER VIII

OF ANIMALS TAME AND WILD

I MUST place the *Horse* at the Head of all Domestick Animals. The *Horses* of *Persia* are the finest of all the *East*. They are taller than the *English* Saddle-Horses are, strait before, a little Head, and Legs that are wonderfully thin and fine, exactly proportion'd, mighty gentle, good Travellers, and very light and sprightly. They carry their Noses to the Wind when they run a Course, and gallop with their Heads lifted high in the Air, and this as they are bred and taught: But lest their Heads should be thrown back upon the Horseman's Breast, they put them on a kind of Caveson, which is nothing but Leather, and like a Halter, but broader, and very finely embroider'd, which bridles in their Noses, and passing between the Legs, is fasten'd like the Breast-leather to the Girth under the Horse's Belly. The *Horses* wear a long Tail which they braid, and tie up sometimes. They are very gentle and managable, easy to feed, and do good Service till they are eighteen or twenty Years old. They know not what a Gelding is among all the Horses they have in *Persia*. I have told you they are the finest in the *East*; but they are not for that

Reason the best, nor the most sought after. Those in *Arabia* surpass them far, and are mightily esteem'd in *Persia* for their lightness: They are in their Make like perfect Jades, and being lean and wither'd, they make a wretched Figure. The *Persians* say, that to try the *Horses* which are sold for *Arabs* of a good Breed, which is in *Arabia Fœlix*, you must make them go thirty Leagues on end, and at a good rate, and afterwards lead them into the Water up to their Breasts, and then give them their Oats; if then they fall to their Oats greedily, they are true *Arabian* Horses. The *Persians* have several *Tartarian* Horses too, that are lower than those of *Persia*, and more burly and ugly, but will bear more Fatigue, are more lively and nimble for the Race. *Horses* are very dear in *Persia*; the fine ones are valu'd from a Thousand *Livres*, to a Thousand *Crowns*: The great Exportation of them to *Turkey* and the *Indies* is what makes them so dear; but they can't carry any out of the Kingdom, without a special Permission from the King.

¶ The best and commonest way of riding there, after the Horse, is the Mule; they have very good ones in *Persia*, that Pace very prettily, never Stumble, and very rarely Tire. The highest Price of a Mule is five hundred Livres.

¶ The other Beasts of Use, after these, are Asses, and they have two Kinds of them; The Asses of the Country, which are like ours, slow, and heavy, are employ'd for nothing but to bear Burdens; and a Breed of *Arabian* Asses, that are mighty fine Beasts, and the best Asses in the World; they have smooth shining Hair, they carry their Heads lofty, their Feet are light, and they move them gracefully as they go along; these are kept for Riding; the Saddles which they put on their Backs are round, like Pack-Saddles, but flat at Top, made either of Cloth or Tapistry, with Stirrups, and Furniture: They sit nearer towards the Crupper than the Shoulders. Some of them have all Silver Furniture, and their Masters love them for their Lightness and easie going. There are some of them valu'd at four hundred *Livres*, and there is no such thing as having one that is tolerably good under five and twenty *Pistoles*. They esteem them the same as *Horses*. The Church-men, that are not in any Post or great Benefices, affect riding upon Asses.

¶ They teach these tame Beasts nothing but to pace; and the Art they have of breeding them up to it, is by tying their Legs, the foremost to the hindermost with two Cotton Cords, which they proportion to the Step of the Ass that is to pace, and these Strings they buckle up to the Girt on each side, in the Place where the Stirrups usually hang. There are a sort of Grooms that mount them Night and Morning, and exercise them, till they have learnt perfectly how to pace. They learn it by being driven on by the Groom, and at the same time stopt by the Cord, when they step'd to such Distances as are proper to form the Pace. They commonly make a manag'd Beast or two go Side by Side with them when they are training them up, that they may take the Step the sooner: These Beasts go so quick, that there is no following of them without galloping. They likewise teach their *Horses* to stop short of a sudden, and fall back on their Breech in the middle of a Course.

¶ The *Persians* understand *Horses* very well, and have mighty good Jockeys. I have already spoke of the Food of Horses in the First Volume. They make their Litters of their own Dung dry'd and beat to Powder, with which they throw up their Beds two or three Inches thick. Every Morning they spread the Dung of these Beasts in the Stable-Yard, to dry in the Sun, and at Night, upon a little beating, it crumbles into Powder: Being spread out all Day to dry in the Sun, the Smell of it evaporates away, so that the Stables have no ill Smell. They use also another Expedient to prevent that Smell, *viz.* By mixing some Salt with the *Horses* Barley when they feed them. The Currycombs of that Country are made without Handles, the edges of them are dented, and serve instead of Rubbers; they rub them after that with a Felt: They keep their Stables very clean, so that they do not smell as ours do. There are no Mangers neither, as in our Country: The *Horses* eat their Oats and Barley in a Hair Bag ty'd about their Heads, the *Horses* Shoes are flat, without Heels, and thinner than ours; yet they last much longer, by the Reason, the *Persian Horses* Hoofs are much harder than ours, and much better and sounder, and bear Nailing every where, which is owing to the wholsomness of the Air. Those light and smooth Shoes make the *Horses* swifter in a Race. They do not Shoe their Horses in Winter, and in Frosty-weather, otherwise than in Summer, but they Nail on their Shoes with Nails of bigger and sharper Heads. Other Beasts are Shod in the same Manner as those are, except in Winter, in those Parts where it freezes. There is no fear of the *Horses* sliding in *Persia*, for the Streets are not Pav'd. They have a way also in Winter of Painting the *Horses* with *Henna*, that yellow Paint abovementioned, used likewise by Men and Women; they anoint their Legs, and their whole Bodies, up to their Breasts with it, and sometimes their Heads; they say that it keeps them from the Cold, tho' it is rather used for Ornament; for in several Parts it is done at all Seasons: They Paint on the King's Horses for distinction sake, a broad Tagged Lace, with Flourishes like those of Coronets.

¶ In *Persia*, none but the King can keep a *Stud* of *Horses*. The Governours and Lieutenants of Provinces, who have any of their own, keep them with his Leave. The King has very large *Studs* in all Parts of the Kingdom. In *Media*, and in the Province of *Persia*, and chiefly, near *Persepolis*, where the beautifullest *Horses* of the Kingdom are bred. There are Stables also in every Province, and in most great Cities, that there may be always *Horses* ready for the Troopers, the Trades-men, and all others in the King's Pay, and to the Officers; for they never deny a *Horse* to any of those Men, when they ask for one; but when once they have had one, they cannot return him, they must keep him. They send sometimes such vast Number of *Horses* to the King, either from his Studs, or by the Way of Presents, that his Stables cannot hold them; and then they are divided among the Wealthiest House-keepers, to every House one, and they are oblig'd to keep them, till they are sent for; they have in the mean while the Liberty of riding them. All the King's *Horses* are Mark'd with a large brown Tulip, on the near Thigh. All other People's *Horses* are Mark'd on the other Side. Those who have any of the King's *Horses* cannot sell them; but they may swap them between them; and when the *Horses* die in their Hands, they must cut off the Piece of Skin where the Mark is, with a little Flesh to it, and carry it to the King's Master of the *Horse* in that Place, who blots the *Horse* out of the Register, after they have taken an Oath, that the *Horse* died a natural Death, and not for want of Care, and then they have another given them, with asking for. They affirm, that the Officers of the Stables, by steeping that Bit of *Horse*-Skin in the Water for a few Hours, know what Distemper the Beast died of, whether of Hunger, or of hard Work, or whether it has been kill'd; for sometimes a Trooper when he can keep his *Horse* no longer, is willing to be rid of him; or he that has a bad one, wishes the same Thing, that he may ask for a better. They observe in *Horse* Bargains, the same Conditions as they do with us, and may return them three Days after Trial.

¶ I will pass by the Trappings and Saddles of *Persia*, which are the same as in *Turkey*, except perhaps the Saddles, which are a little higher, yet they never, or very seldom, hurt their Horses, because the Cushion being loose from the Saddle, the Groom sees presently whether it hurts the Horse; and every Morning he beats the Cushion with a Flint to soften it. These Cushions are richly Embroider'd on the Back-side, and a little on the Right-side. The *Persians* also ride with short Stirrups, as the *Turks* do, but their Trappings are richer.

¶ They slit the Asses, and sometimes the Mules Nostrils, that they may draw in more Air, and breathe more freely in running. They Purge all those Beasts in Spring, first with a light and juicy Plant, call'd *Kasil*, which works them violently for four or five Days; then they give them green Barley for five or six Days, which they blend afterwards with their chopt Straw for three or four Weeks: They do not ride the Horses for the first Fortnight, they keep them in the Stable; and also they give them no Litter for the first six Days.

¶ These Beasts are subject to many Distempers, most of them unknown in our Country; for Instance, when they eat too much Barley, they are troubled with swollen Feet, grow Weak, and in their Breasts rises a kind of Wen, which they cure, either with a hot Iron, and no Barley for some Days, or with launcing the Swelling which they keep open and running with a Willow twig run thro' it. There grow sometimes in the *Horses* Noses two Gristles, one on each side, which take away their Stomachs, and swell their Bellies, and make it as hard as a Drum, and cause the Horses to lie down Night and Day; and if they are not look'd after, they die of it in eight and forty Hours. They call that Distemper *Nachan:* As they presently know it, by squeezing the Beast's Nose, so they cut it open on each side speedily, and take out of it those Gristles as whole as they can, and immediately the poor Beasts recover, and are as sound as ever. Besides, they have another Gristle growing sometimes within the Flesh, on one side of their Eye, which exposes them to the hazard of their Lives, which they likewise draw out by making an incision in the Part, after they have cast the Horse down. Lastly, those Beasts lose again their Stomachs, by a swelling in their Lips, which is cured with running an Awl through a vein in the roof of their Mouths. They cure most other Distempers incident to Horses, either in their Legs, Feet, or Hoofs, with a hot Iron, immediately. 'Tis likewise the easiest and the safest Cure for the Men of the *East* Country, as I shall inform ye in its proper Place. I have seen in *Persia*, a receipt for fatning a Horse, tried very successfully; they knead some Snake-skin and Meal together, and make it up into Balls as big as an Egg, which they give their Horses.

¶ The Camel is a Beast much prized by the *Eastern* People; they call him *Kechty Krouch Konion*, i. e. a Ship of the Continent, upon the account of the great Load he carries, which is usually twelve or thirteen hundred weight for great Camels; for there are two sorts of them, Northern and Southern ones, as the *Persians* call them. The latter, which travel from the *Persian* Gulph to *Ispahan*, and no further, are much smaller than the other, and carry but seven hundred weight: Yet they bring their Masters as much or more Profit, because they cost little or nothing to keep. They lead them without Halter or Reins, grazing on the Road as they go, for all their Load. They shed their Hair so clean in the Spring, that they look like a scalded

Pig, and then they Pitch him all over, to keep the Flies from stinging him. The Camels Hair is the most profitable Fleece of all tame Beasts; they make of it very fine Stuffs; and in *Europe* we make Hats of it with a little Beaver mixed with it. They take notice when he is in Love, that they may encrease his Load, for otherwise he would be ungovernable; and sometimes also he must be *moraillé*. He flings and capers then about the Country like the nimblest Horse. They observe likewise, that his Love-fit continues always five or six Weeks, and then he eats much less than at other times. 'Tis remarkable, that when those Creatures couple together, the Females lie on their Bellies as when they are loaded. They are eleven or twelve Months a breeding; and when they have brought forth their Young ones, Grooms lay them on their Bellies with their Feet folded for fifteen or twenty Days and Nights in that posture, to use them to it. They never lie otherwise, and have nothing but a little milk given them, to teach them to be content with a little Food; and they are so well used to it, that they will be eight or ten Days without Drinking. As for Food, he is the least feeder of all Beasts by far; 'tis a wonderful thing to see such large Creatures kept with so small a matter. There are abundance of them in *Persia*, and they carry on a good Trade with the *Turks*, who buy great Numbers of them. The *Persian* Camels have but one Bunch, but the *Indian* and *Arabian* ones have two. They breed in the Southern and Eastern Parts of the Country, as towards *Arabia* and *Tartary*, towards the *Indies* and *Persian* Gulph, a kind of running *Camels*. They call them *Revahié, i. e.* going. They trot so swiftly, that they put a Horse to the Gallop to follow them; 'tis that kind of Camels which the *Hebrews* call *Gemela Sarka*, flying Camels. In some of these Provinces, and especially towards the *Persian* Gulph, they feed those Beasts with dried Fish and Dates; and the Asses also. They tell all the Beasts of Burden in the *East* Country by the Number of seven, called *Kater*, because say they, a Groom can look after so many. Another remarkable thing about Camels, is, that they are taught to go, and are led with a kind of a Tune, they order their Steps by cadence of the Voice, and go either quick or slow, according to their Leader's Musick: And likewise when they will have them perform an extraordinary Journey, their Masters entertain them with one of their favourite Tunes.

¶ The *Persian* Oxen are like ours, except towards the Borders of *India*, where they have a Bunch on their Back: They eat little Beef all over the Kingdom: They breed them up only for Carriage and Tillage: They Shoe those for Carriage, because of the stony Hills they travel on.

¶ There are no Hogs in *Persia*, but in *Iberia* and *Media*; in other Places they breed up a sort of small Wild-Boar like a Pig. And the *Armenians*, who inhabit the Country of *Ispahan*, bring them in Winter to sell to the Christians; the Skin of them is black and rough, like that of the Boar; the Flesh is red, lean, and dry, not so well tasted as the Pigs or the Boars Flesh.

¶ I shall speak of the small Cattle in the Discourse about Meats; and shall only say, that *Persia* abounds with Sheep and She-Goats: There are some of those Sheep which we call *Barbary* Sheep with great Tails, one whereof weighs about thirty Pounds. That Tail is a great Load to those poor Beasts, and 'tis the more troublesome, because 'tis small and narrow at the Top, and broad and heavy at the Bottom, and shaped like a Heart. You see some often that cannot draw it after them; to those they tie a little Cart with two Wheels to carry their Tails after them the more easily. The most plentiful Provinces of *Persia* in Cattle, are *Bactriana*, *Media*, and *Armenia*; I have seen there some Flocks of Sheep that cover'd five or six Leagues space. All *Turky* is supplied with Cattle from those large Flocks, as far as *Constantinople*.

¶ As to Venison, there is not so much of it in *Persia* as there is in our Country, because *Persia* is, generally speaking, an open Country: The Wood Countries, such as *Hircania*, *Iberia*, *Chaldea*, and next to those, *Armenia* and *Media*, have abundance of Bucks and Deer; in the hilly Countries are wild She-Goats, and almost all the Kingdom over one finds Rabbits and Hares, but in no great Plenty. The Antelope is a very common Beast all over the *East*: It is very pretty, and smaller than the Deer. There are so many of them in *Europe*, that it is needless to describe Him. It is supposed, that it is the Beast which the *Hebrews* call *Chets*, and which they write with two Letters *Caph* and *Trsadé*, frequently mentioned in Scripture.

¶ Wild Beasts are not very common in *Persia*, generally speaking, because 'tis no Wood Country, as I have observed several times: But in all Woody Countries, as in *Hircania* and *Chaldea*, there are abundancè of *Lions*, *Bears*, *Tygers*, *Leopards*, *Porcupines*, and *Wild Boars*. The Saying of the Ancients of *Hircania* on that Account is very true, *viz*. That *Hircania is the Country of the Wildest Beasts*. And when I was there, they hinder'd us from wandring out of the Towns, and of walking alone above five hundred Paces distance, lest we should be torn by some of those Beasts. Take Notice however, that there are but few Wolves in *Hircania*, and in the other Provinces; but you may see every where a Beast that roars hideously, called *Chakal*; he is very greedy of dead Bodies, which he digs up, except somebody watches the Grave. I have given a Description of them in my Journey from *Paris* to *Ispahan*.

¶ I have but a Word to say concerning the Insects of the Country, there being but a few of them, which is to be imputed to the Drought of the Climate. In some Provinces there is an infinite number of Grashoppers; you may see them fly along like Clouds, and so thick, that the Air is darken'd with them. I shall have an occasion to speak of them fully in the sequel of this Work. There are, in some Parts of the Kingdom, some large and black Scorpions, which are so venemous, that those who are stung by them, die in five Hours: And in some other Places Birds of a dreadful length, *viz.* An Ell long, and in bigness like a great Toad; they have a rough Skin, and as hard as a *Sea Dog.* 'Tis reported that they fall on Men sometimes, and Kill them. In the Southern Provinces there are abundance of Gnats, some with long Legs, like those we call *Midges*, and some white and as small as Fleas, which make no buzzing, but Sting suddenly, and so smartly, that the Sting is like the prick of a Needle. Among the creeping Insects, there is a long square Worm, which they call *Hazar-pag*, or a thousand Feet, because its whole Body is full of Feet, therefore it crawls very fast: It is longer and smaller than a Caterpillar, and its Bite is dangerous, and even Mortal, when they get into one's Ears.

CHAPTER IX

OF THE TAME AND WILD BIRDS, AND OF HUNTING

THEY have in *Persia* the same winged Fowl which we have in *Europe*, but not in such Plenty. The Turkeys are scarce there: About thirty Years ago the *Armenians* brought a great many from *Constantinople* to *Ispahan*, which they presented to the King for a Rarity: And to make them Amends, they were told, *That the* Persians *being unacquainted with the Way of feeding them, entrusted them with the Care of them:* And so they were distributed to several Houses, to each House one. The *Armenians* being tired with the Care and Charge of them, did let them starve almost in every House. I have seen some that throve pretty well, in the Territory of *Ispahan*, four Leagues off the City, at some Country *Armenians* Houses, but they had very few. Some believe that that Fowl comes from the *East-Indies*, because of its *French* Name, Cock of *India*; but, on the contrary, there are none at all. It must come from the *West-Indies*; except it was called Cock of *India*, because, being bigger than ordinary Cocks, it resembles in Bigness the *Indian* Cocks, which are bigger than the ordinary Cocks of all other Countries. The *Persians* fatten some

The Pigeon-houses.

Hens which grow as big as any we have of that sort. And the *Armenians* have Capons which grow so big and so fat, that they must be killed for their Fat.

¶ Tame and wild *Pidgeons* are to be found in all Parts, but the wild ones are in greater Plenty; yet they breed abundance of Pidgeons all over the Kingdom, upon the account of their Dung, which is the best for Melons. I don't think there are any finer Dove-Cots in any part of the World. I have given a Draught of them on the other side (p. 175). Those great Coops are six times as big as the biggest we have; they are built with Brick overlaid with Plaister and Lime, full within of Holes for the Pidgeons to breed in. All may build them that will, except those Inhabitants who are of a different Religion from the Natives, there being no Clause to exclude them from that Privilege, 'tis but paying the Dung Tax. They reckon above three thousand Pidgeon-Houses about *Ispahan*, all built for the sake of the Dung, more than for the sake of the Breed of the Pidgeons, as I have observ'd. They call it *Tehalgous*, *i. e.* enlivening: It is sold a Bisty, or Four-pence, the Twelve Pound Weight, on which the King lays a small Tax. One of the best Sports the Rabble can have, is to catch Pidgeons in the Country, and in the Cities also, tho' 'tis forbidden. They take the wild Pidgeons by means of the tame ones, which are bred up for that purpose, and which they cause to fly all the day-long after the wild ones; and all those they meet with they take in amongst them in their own Flock, and carry them to the Dove-Coat.

¶ Sometimes tame Pidgeons bring away likewise other tame Pidgeons from their Dove-Coats; so that all of a sudden a Pidgeon-House happens to be gutted and clear'd: No Satisfaction must be expected in that Case; the Pidgeon that flies into a strange Pidgeon-House, is accounted a wild Pidgeon. Those Pidgeon-Hunters are called *Kester-baze*, and *Kester perron*, *i. e.* Deceivers and Stealers of Pidgeons. Those Words, in a moral Sense, are scandalous, denoting an idle Fellow, and a Pick-pocket: Truly the Pidgeon-Stealers spend whole Days at that Trade, and are not diverted from it by the Severity of the Winter-Season.

¶ The Partridges in *Persia* are, I believe, the biggest Partridges in the World, and of an exquisite Taste; 'tis a common thing to find some as big as a Chicken. As to the Water-Fowls, such as Geese, Ducks, Plovers, Cranes, Herons, Dy-dappers, and Snipes there are some in all Parts; but there are greater Numbers of them in the Northern Provinces, as in *Armenia, Media,* and *Iberia,* In the Autumn and Winter-Season there are also some as big as *Turkey-Pouts*; the Flesh of them is grey, and as delicious as that of the *Pheasant*; their Feathers are long and beautiful,

and on their Head is a bunch of them, that looks like a Plume of Feathers.
¶ As to Singing Birds, they are the same in *Persia* as in *Europe*. The
Nightingale sings in all Seasons, but louder in Spring than at other times;
The *Chaffinch* warbles charmingly; The *Lark* sings continually, and learns
all sorts of Tunes; The *Martin* also learns all he is taught; And another
Bird like him, which they call *Noura*, twittles twattles all day-long, and
repeats comically what he hears others speak.

¶ Among the Wild Birds, the most wonderful is that long Bill Bird, call'd
in *English*, the *Pelican*. The *Persians* call it *Tacab*, *i. e.* Water-drawer, or
Water-carryer; and also *Misc*, *i. e.* Sheep, because in *Persia* it is as big as
a Wether; its Feathers are white, and as soft as that of a *Green Goose*; by
its Head one would take it for a Monster, it being so much less than its
Body, and its Bill so much longer proportionably, *viz.* from Sixteen to
Eighteen Inches long, and as big as one's Arm; under its Bill hangs a Skin
which it gathers up, and spreads out like a Fan, that holds a Pail-full of
Water; it commonly lays its Bill on its Back to rest it: That Bird lives upon
Fish, and it is wonderfully cunning in catching of it, watching it in
Streams, and taking it in its Bag, as in a Net; when it opens its Bill,
a Lamb might go through it: The Name of Water-carryer, given it by
the *Persians*, is because that Bird, in the Desarts of *Arabia*, and in other
Places where there is no Water, is observed to build its Nest far from the
Water, for Safety-sake; because there being little Water in *Arabia*, every
body takes his Station near the Places where they find any. Now they
affirm, that when its Young-ones want Water, it flies two Days Journey
from them, sometimes, to fetch Water, and brings it in its Bag. The
Mahometans believe, that God makes use of that Bird to supply the Pilgrims
going to *Mecca* with Water, when they find none in the Desart, as he did
make use of a Crow to relieve the Prophet *Elias*. 'Tis upon that account,
perhaps, that we have given that Bird the Name of *Pelican*, because it
really kills itself with the Care it takes of its Young-ones, as the Naturalists
have related of their imaginary Bird, that pecks open its Breast to feed
its Young-ones with its Blood.

¶ There is a kind of Bird in *Persia* that is curious and wonderful, by the
Effect Spring-Water has upon its Nature, for it smells it, and follows it
where-ever it is carry'd, with an unaccountable Fondness. It is as big
as a Chicken, and has black Feathers, and grey Flesh, and broad Wings,
and flies in Flocks like Starlings; they live on Grashoppers where-ever
they find them: And if a Country be plagued with those mischievous
Insects, one may be sure to rid it of them, if one can but bring thither
a company of those Birds. The *Persians* call them *Abmelec*, *i. e.* Water of

Grashoppers; intimating that Bird, which is allur'd by a certain Water, and eats Grashoppers. The Water which has that powerful Influence on them, comes from a Spring in *Bactriana*. They bring it in Glass-Bottles unstopp'd, and keep it always in a high and airy Place both on the Road and at Home: The Birds that follow it, tho' they don't taste a drop of it, always set near the Place where 'tis laid, and begin again to fly, when those that carry it set forwards again. I'll relate here upon that account, a Passage out of an old *Eastern* Relation, Entitled, *The Travels of* Villamont, in the 97th Page, where he confirms my Relation. In *Cyprus*, about Harvest time, the Ground breeds so many Grashoppers, that they darken sometimes the Light of the Sun, and where-ever they light, they burn and waste every thing without any possibility of preventing it, for the more you destroy, the more the Ground breeds. God raised them an Instrument to destroy them in this manner. In *Persia* near the City of *Cuerch*, is a Fountain, the Water whereof has the Property of destroying those Grashoppers, provided it be brought in a Flaggon, and comes not under any House or Cave, and be set on a rising Ground within sight of some Birds that follow it, and flie after the Men that bring it, and cry out continually. Those Birds are reddish and black, and go in Flocks like *Starlings*. The *Turks* and *Persians* call them *Mussulmans*. Those Birds were no sooner come to *Cyprus*, where the Grashoppers were, but they presently killed them with their Flight and their Singing; but if the Water be lost or spilt, those Birds disappear; as it happen'd when the *Turks* took the Island; for one of them going up to the top of the Steeple of the Cathedral of *Famagosta*, found the Flaggon of Water, which he broke, supposing it to be full of Gold, or some other precious thing, and so spilt all the Water. The *Cyprians* have been plagued with Grashoppers ever since.

¶ They catch Birds of Prey on the side of *Iberia* to the North of *Media*; and they bring so many from other Places, that I question whether there be as many in any part of the World. *Persia* is very well seated on that account, being near Mount *Caucasus*, *Circassia*, and *Muscovia*, from whence come the best Birds of Prey: They take also abundance of them on the Hills, fifteen and twenty Leagues off of *Chiras*, in the Province of *Persia*; and they say that the largest come from thence. They understand likewise extraordinary well there to teach them how to Hunt. The *Persians* teach the very *Crows* to Chase. There are eight hundred Birds of Prey constantly kept in the King's Bird-House, *viz. Spar-hawks*, *Hawks*, *Merlins*, *Gorfalcons*, *Tierulo*, *Goss-hawks* and *Lanners*. All the Nobles also keep several for Hunting, to which the *Persians* are inclin'd from their Youth, and even several of the common People; for every body has the liberty of Hawking,

Shooting, and Hunting. One may see all the Year round, in the City and in the Country, the Falconers going backwards and forwards with a Hawk on their Hand: And as the King often presents Birds of Prey to his chief Officers, especially to the Governors of Provinces; one may then see the Officers seven or eight Days together combing, stroaking, and continually commending the Beauty and Cunning of the Bird. They put on his Head a Hood set with Precious Stones, and little Golden Bells about his Feet. The Nobles have also Gloves made on purpose to wear when they hold their Birds, that are set round with Precious Stones; they dress likewise their Birds with *Jesses* and Golden *Vervels*. The *Persians* call the Bird-House *Baskané* and *Cuchskané*, *i. e.* a House of Deceitful Birds. There they keep a Register-Book of all the Birds presented to and by the King, where the Persons, Names, and Time, is set down, and where the Bird is described. The Birds of Prey are very Chargable in that Kingdom, being fed with Flesh, and nothing else; and some are fed with Fowls Flesh all Day long.

¶ I must not pass by a Bird of Prey which comes from *Muscovy*, much bigger than that I have spoken of, being almost as big as an *Eagle*. Those Birds are very rare, and the King has all those that are in his Kingdom, none being allow'd to have any but himself. It being usual in *Persia* to set a Value on the Presents made to the King: Without any Deduction, those Birds are set down at a hundred *Tomans* a Piece, which amount to fifteen hundred Crowns. And if any of them die by the way, the Embassador brings his Majesty the Head and the Wings of it, and he is allowed the Value of the Bird, as if it was alive. They say that Bird builds its Nest in the Snow, which it melts to the Ground with the heat of its Body, tho' it be a Fathom high: That when the Young ones are ready to fly away, the Old one pushes them before her to the Hole side; and if they want Strength to go over, and tumble in, the Old Bird flies over it, fills the Hole full of Snow, and stifles them as a degenerate Brood. They affirm almost the very same thing of the *Muscovian* Hawks, excepting, that sometimes out of a whole Brood, one young one only is strong enough to raise its self out of that deep Nest. 'Tis upon that Account that the *Muscovite Hawks*, and the *Hawks* of *Mount Caucasus*, are so much valued.

¶ They teach those Birds by setting them at Cranes, or other Birds, that are Hood-wink'd, that they may not know where to go, and how to fly; then they use those Birds thus taught, to take, *First*, all passing Birds *Eagles*, *Cranes*, *Wild-Ducks*, *Geese*, *Partridges* and *Guails*. *Secondly*, the *Rabbit*, and the *Hare*; they teach them likewise to hold any Wild Beast, except the *Wild Boar*; and the Way to teach them, is, by tying a Bit of

Flesh to the Head of one of those flea'd Beasts and stuff'd with Straw, which they lay on four Wheels, and keep moving as the Bird is eating, to use him to it. After those Birds are taught, they carry them a Hunting in this Manner; *First*, they hunt the Beast, till it is tired, then they let the Bird go; he sits on it's Head, beats the Eyes of it with his Wings, and pricks it with his Tallons, and with his Bill, which so stuns the timorous Beast, that it falls down, and gives the Hunters time to come to it. When 'tis a large Beast, they let go several Birds, which Torment it one after another. They set no Bird at the Wild Boar, because it is not fearful, but on the contrary Furious, and would tear the Bird to Pieces. Some have been taught to assault Men; that was common in the beginning of the last Age; and they say, that there are still such Birds in the King's Bird-House. I have not seen any of them, but I hear'd that *Aly-couly-can*, Governour of *Tauris*, whom I was particularly acquainted with, could not forbear diverting himself with that dangerous and cruel Sport, tho' with the loss of his Friends. It happen'd one Day that a Bird was let go on a Gentleman, and put out his Eyes, not being taken off in time, so that he died of the Fright, and the Pain. The King being acquainted with it, was so incens'd against the Governour, that a little after for that Fault, and some other Misdemeanor, he turn'd him out of his Favour. That Bird assaults Men, as well as Beasts. He lights on the Head, and strikes and tears the Face with his Wings and Beak, if he be not soon taken off; for at that time, he hears neither Voice nor Drum, and pulls the Face in Pieces in spight of any Body. All Swords-Men being Hunts-Men, usually carry at their Saddle-bow, a small Kettle-Drum, about nine Inches Diameter, to call the Bird back, which they call *Tavelabas*.

¶ In great Hunting Matches, they use wild Beasts, that have been taught, such as *Lions*, *Leopards*, *Tigers*, and *Panthers*. The *Persians* call those taught Beasts, *Yourze*. They hurt no Man. A Horseman carries one of them behind him, Hood-winkt with a Cloth Roll, and tied with a Chain, and stands in the Way of the Chased Beast, as close to it as may be; when the Horsemen sees any coming, he pulls off the Beast's Hood, and turns his Head towards the Prey; if he sees it, he gives a Shriek, leaps down, falls on the Beast, and pulls it down, if he misses it, he is commonly discouraged, and stops; the Master goes to him, comforts him, makes Much of him, and tells him it is not his Fault, and that he had not been set directly before the Beast. They say he understands that Excuse, and is satisfied with it. I have seen that sort of Sport in *Hircania*, in the Year 1666; and they told me, that the King had some of those Beasts bred up to Hunting; which because they were too big to carry on Horseback, were carry'd in Iron

Cages, on an Elephant without the Hood; that the Keeper had his Hand always on the Cage-Door, in order, when he perceived the Prey, and gave a Shriek, to let him out immediately. Some of those taught Beasts hunt cunningly, creeping on their Bellies under the Bushes and Hedges, till they be within reach of the Prey, then they rush upon it.

¶ In a Royal Hunting-Match, and in all great Hunting Bouts, they lay a Net round a little Valley, or a Plain, and chase Beasts from fifteen to twenty Leagues distance, round about the Country, which'some thousands of Country People range over. When there is a great Number of Beasts in the Net, and they are all hedg'd in by Troops of Horse-men, the King comes in with his Company, then every one falls on what's next to him, *Stags*, *Boars*, *Lions*, *Wolves*, and *Foxes*, and they make a horrid Slaughter of them, commonly amounting to the Number of about eight hundred Beasts. They say, that in some of those Hunting-Matches they have kill'd to the Number of fourteen thousand Beasts. In the common Hunting Bouts, when a Beast is taken, they stay till the best Man of the Company comes, who shoots an Arrow at him, then every Man falls on.

¶ The *Persians* are not unacquainted with Dog-hunting, the King has Hounds, and some Nobles likewise; but they are scarce, because that Creature is look'd upon by the *Persians* as the most impure, and therefore, is an Abomination to them. The Bird is likewise good for the Water, and will fetch and carry like a Dog.

¶ Hunting the wild Goat is curious Sport; those Beasts being light Footed, and hard to come at; they shoot them with a Musket in this Manner; they teach the Camel to follow that Creature slowly, and come up to it; the Hunts-man hides himself behind the Camel, and when he is within reach of the Goat shoots it, the Camel runs after it; and when it falls he stays by it, if he comes back, 'tis a Sign the Marks-man has mist his Aim.

CHAPTER X

OF THE FISH

THERE are two sorts of Fish, Sea-Fish, and Fresh-water Fish. The *Caspian* Sea, which belongs to *Persia*, is very full of Fish; they export the dried Fish into all Parts, especially the *Sturgeon*, the *Salmon*, and a kind of large *Carps*, call'd *Despitch*, which is a very good Fish. But there is not, I believe, in all the World, a Place so full of Fish as the *Persian* Gulph; they Fish twice a Day along the Shore, and take all the Sorts of Fish which *Europe* affords; but it is much better, more delicious, and in greater Plenty; the Fishermen sell it by the Sea-side, and what they have left at ten a-Clock in the Morning, or at Sun-setting, they throw it into the Sea again. They bring on the Coasts of that Gulph, some Fish, the Flesh whereof is red, which weighs between two and three hundred Pound; they take it on the Coast of *Arabia*, and Salt it like Beef; but it doth not keep long, because the Salt of that Place is corroding, and eats up every Thing; that's the Reason they Salt no Fish, but dry in the Sun, or in the Smoke, what they design to keep. Fresh-water Fish is not so plentiful, because there are but few Rivers in *Persia*, and they take abundance of Water out of them, so that very little Fish can breed there. We must except out of that Rule the River *Kur*, which is very full of Fish, and runs into *Iberia*. There are three sorts of Fresh-water Fish in that large Empire; that of Lakes, that of Rivers, and that of Kerises, or Subterraneous Canals. Those of Lakes are, amongst others, *Trouts*, *Carps* and *Shads*: *Trouts* are only to be found in *Armenia*; they are red, as large and good as in any part of the World. The most common River Fish is the *Barbel*, which breeds also in the Canals. The Canal Fish is very common, some of them are very large, but they are not wholsome, and the Spawn of them especially is dangerous, being a certain and a violent Vomit, by Reason that the Sun never shines on that Fish, and that it breeds in raw Waters; or because they take it with the *Nux Vomica*, or the Vomiting Nut. There are abundance of Crabs in the River of *Ispahan*; they crawl up the Trees, and live upon them, among the Boughs, Night and Day, where they go and take them, being a delicious Food.

CHAPTER XI

OF THE TEMPER, MANNERS, AND CUSTOMS OF THE PERSIANS

THE *Persian* Blood is naturally thick; it may be seen by the *Guebres*, who are the remainder of the ancient *Persians*; they are homely, ill shap'd, dull, and have a rough Skin, and an Olive Complexion. The same Thing is observ'd also in the Provinces next the *Indus*, whereof the Inhabitants are little better shap'd than the *Guebres*, because they marry only amongst them: But in the other Parts of the Kingdom, the *Persian* Blood is now grown clearer, by the mixture of the *Georgian* and *Circassian* Blood, which is certainly the People of the World, which Nature favours most, both upon the Account of the Shape and Complexion, and of the *Boldness* and *Courage*; they are likewise *Sprightly, Courtly* and *Amorous.* There is scarce a Gentleman in *Persia,* whose Mother is not a *Georgian,* or a *Circassian* Woman; to begin with the King, who commonly is a *Georgian,* or a *Circassian* by the Mother's side; and whereas, that Mixture begun above a hundred Years ago, the Female kind is grown fairer, as well as the other, and the *Persian* Women are now very *handsome,* and very well *shap'd,* tho' they are still inferior to the *Georgians*: As to the Men, they are commonly *Tall, Straight, Ruddy, Vigorous,* have a good Air, and a pleasant Countenance. The Temperateness of their Climate, and the Temperance they are brought up in, do not a little contribute to their Shape and Beauty. Had it not been for the Alliance before mention'd, the Nobility of *Persia* had been the ugliest Men in the World; for they originally came from those Countries between *China* and the *Caspian* Sea, call'd *Tartary*; the Inhabitants whereof being the homeliest Men of *Asia,* are short and thick, have their Eyes and Nose like the *Chinese,* their Face flat and broad, and their Complexion yellow, mix'd with black.

¶ As to the Natural Parts, the *Persians* have them as beautiful as their Bodies; their Fancy is lively, quick and fruitful; their Memory easy and copious; they have a ready disposition to Sciences, and to the *Liberal* and *Mechanick Arts,* and to *War* also; they love *Glory,* or rather *Vanity,* which is only the Shadow of it; they are of a tractable and complying Temper, of an easy and plodding Wit; they are *courtly, civil, complisant,* and *well-bred*; they have naturally an eager bent to *Voluptuousness, Luxury, Extravagancy,* and *Profuseness*; for which Reason, they are ignorant both of Frugality and Trade. In a Word, they are born with as good natural Parts as any other People, but few abuse them so much as they do.

¶ They are true Philosophers on the account of Riches, and the Misfortunes of the World, and on the Hope and Fear of a Future State; they are little guilty of Covetousness, and are only desirous of getting, that they may spend it; they love to enjoy the Present, and deny themselves nothing that they are able to procure, taking no Thought for the Morrow, and relying wholy on Providence, and their own Fate; they firmly believe it to be sure and unalterable, and carry themselves honestly in that respect; so when any Misfortune happens to them, they are not cast down, as most Men are, they only say quietly, *Mek toub est, i. e.* That is written, or, it is ordained, that that should happen.

¶ Twenty Years ago, it was the Opinion of several People in *Europe,* and of the most Noted and most Understanding Men, that the *Persians* would embrace the fair Opportunity of the *Turks* great Defeat to recover *Babylon* from them; and that they would declare War with the *Sultan,* now they saw him so low, beaten every where, and losing such large Countries. And I always said on the contrary; That I was sure they would take no Notice of it, because 'tis the Humour of the *Persians*, above all things, to value Life, and to enjoy it. They have lay'd by their Warlike Temper, and have given themselves up to Wantonness, which they don't suppose can be found in a great Bustle, and in dubious and laborious Undertakings.

¶ Those Men are the most lavish Men in the World, and the most careless of the Morrow, as I said just now. They cannot keep Money; and whatever Riches fall to them, they waste all in a very little time. Let, for Instance, the King give fifty or a hundred thousand Livres to any Man, he lays it out in less than a Fortnight, in buying Slaves of both Sexes; in hiring handsome Wives; in setting up a noble Equipage; in furnishing a House, or cloathing himself richly: And so spends the whole Sum so fast, without any regard to the Time to come, that unless some new Supplies intervene in two or three Months time, our Gentleman will be forced to sell again his whole Equipage by Piece-meal, beginning with his Horses; then his needless Servants; then his Concubines and Slaves; and lastly, even his own Cloaths. I have seen a thousand Instances of that Kind, one of them amongst the rest is very strange; An Eunuch who had been long Lord High Chamberlain, and for two Years the declared Favourite, the power of disposing of all Posts and Employments, and commanding as if himself had been King, and who consequently had frequent and favourable Opportunities of heaping up vast Riches, was turn'd out of Favour, but however not out of his Estate. Two Months were scarce elaps'd, but he was forc'd to borrow Money upon Pawns, his Credit was at an End, as well as his Money; not but that he had acquired vast Riches, but he wasted them as fast as he got them.

¶ The most commendable Property of the Manners of the *Persians*, is their kindness to Strangers; the Reception and Protection they afford them, and their Universal Hospitality, and Toleration, in regard to Religion, except the Clergy of the Country, who, as in all other Places, hate to a furious Degree, all those that differ from their Opinions. The *Persians* are very civil, and very honest in Matters of Religion; so far that they allow those who have embraced theirs, to recant, and resume their former Opinion; whereof, the *Cedre*, or *Priest*, gives them an Authentick Certificate for Safety sake, in which he calls them by the Name of *Apostat*, which amongst them is the highest Affront. They believe that all Men's Prayers are good and prevalent; therefore, in their Illnesses, and in other Wants, they admit of, and even desire the Prayers of different Religions: I have seen it practis'd a thousand Times. This is not to be imputed to their Religious Principles, tho' it allows all sorts of Worship; but I impute it to the sweet Temper of that Nation, who are naturally averse to Contest and Cruelty.

¶ The *Persians* having the Character of *Wanton* and *Profuse*; one may easily believe them to be *Lazy* also; those two Properties being inseperable. Their Aversion to Labour is the most common Occasion of their Poverty. The *Persians* call the Lazy, and Unactive Men, *Serguerdan*, i. e. turning the Head this Way, and that Way. Their Language is full of those Circumlocutions; as for Instance, to express a Man reduced to a Mendicant State, they say, *Gouch Negui Micoret*, he eats his Hunger.

¶ The *Persians* never Fight; all their *Anger*, being not blustering and passionate, as in our Country, goes off with ill Language; and what's very Praiseworthy, is, that, what Passion soever they be in, and among whatever profligate Wretches they may light, still they Reverence God's Name, and he is never blasphemed. That Nation cannot conceive how the *Europeans*, when they are in a Passion can disown God; tho' they themselves are very often guilty of taking his Name in vain, without any Need or Provocation; their usual Oaths are, *By the Name of God*; *By the Spirits of the Prophets*; *By the Spirits*, or the *Genius of the Dead*; as the *Romans* swore, *By the Genius of the Living*. The Gentlemen and Courtiers commonly swear, *By the King's Sacred Hand*, which is the most inviolable Oath. The common Affirmations are, *Upon my Head, Upon my Eyes*.

¶ Two opposite Customs are commonly practis'd by the *Persians*; that of praising God continually, and talking of his Attributes, and that of uttering Curses, and obscene Talk. Whether you see them at Home, or meet them in the Streets, going about Business or a Walking; you still hear them uttering some Blessing or Prayer, such as, *O most great God*; *O God most praiseworthy*; *O merciful God*; *O nursing Father of Mankind*; *O God forgive me*, or, *help me*. The least Thing they set their Hand to do, they say, *In the Name of God*; and they never speak of doing any thing, without adding, *If it pleases God*. Lastly, they are the most devout, and most constant Worshippers of the God-head; and at the same time, come out of the same Men's Mouths a thousand obscene Expressions. All Ranks of Men are infected with this odious Vice. Their Bawdy talk is taken from Arse, and C----t, which Modesty forbids one to Name; and when they intend to abuse one another, they invent some nasty Trick of one another's Wives, tho' they never saw or heard of them; or wish they may commit some Nastiness. 'Tis so among the Women, and when they have spent their Stock of bawdy Names, they begin to call one another *Atheists, Idolaters, Jews, Christians*; and to say to one another, *The Christians*

Dogs are better than thou, may'st thou serve for an Offering to the Dogs of the Franks.

¶ Men of all Ranks, as is beforemention'd, are observ'd to use such filthy Expressions, but not so common, and to that degree; for I must confess, that the Mobb is generally infected with it. The first time I waited on the Lord Steward of the King's Household, in the Year 1666, the *Persian* Court being in *Hircania*, a Man of Distinction came to him about some Business, the Lord Steward said to him, why don't you go to the first Minister, to whom I have already sent you back; the Man Answer'd very Modestly; *My Lord, I have been there, and he told me, that your Majesty* (they give that Title to the Nobles as well as to the King) *is to determine the Matter*; *Gaumicoret*, answer'd he, *I wonder'd to hear the Lord Steward speak in that Manner of the first Minister*; for the Word *Gau*, signifies a Turd, and *Micoret*, he eats: That's the usual Expression amongst them, to intimate a wrong or false Answer.

¶ That's one of the least Faults of the *Persians*; they are besides, Dissemblers, Cheats, and the basest and most impudent Flatterers in the World. They understand Flattering very well; and tho' they do it with Modesty, yet they do it with Art, and Insinuation. You would say, that they intend as they speak, and would swear to it: Nevertheless, as soon as the Occasion is over, such as a Prospect of Interest, or a Regard of Compliance, you plainly see that all their Compliments were very far from being sincere. They take an Opportunity of praising Men, when they come out of a House, or pass by them, so that they may be heard; and they speak so seasonably, that the Praise seems to come naturally from them, and carries no Air of Flattery along with it. Besides those Vices which the *Persians* are generally adicted to, they are Lyers in the highest Degree; they speak, swear, and make false Depositions upon the least Consideration; they borrow and pay not; and if they can Cheat, they seldom lose the Opportunity; they are not to be trusted in Service, nor in all other Engagements; without Honesty in their Trading, wherein they overreach one so ingeniously, that one cannot help being bubbl'd; greedy of Riches, and of vain Glory, of Respect and Reputation, which they endeavour to gain by all Means possible. Being void of true Virtue, they affect the Shew of it, whether out of a Design to impose on themselves, or the better to attain the Ends of their vain *Glory*, their *Ambition*, and their *Wantonness*. Hypocrisy is the common Disguise they appear in; they would turn a League out of the Way, to avoid a Bodily Pollution; such as brushing as they go by a Man of a different Religion, and receiving one in their House in Rainy Weather, because the Wet of his Cloaths pollutes whatever touches them, whether Persons or Goods: They walk gravely, make their Prayers and Purgations at set Times, and with the greatest Shew of Devotion; they hold the Wisest and Godliest Conversation possible, discoursing constantly of God's Glory, and of his Greatness, in the Nobelest Terms, and with all the outward Shew of the most fervent Faith. Altho' they be naturally dispos'd to good Nature, Hospitality, Pitty, Contempt of the World, and of its Riches, they affect them nevertheless, that they may appear to be possest of a larger Share of them than they really are. Whoever sees them only passing by, or in a Visit, will always give them the best Character in the World; but he that deals with them, and pries into their Affairs, will find that there is little Honesty in them; and that most of them are *Whited Sepulcres*, according to our Saviours Expression, which I think the more proper here, because the *Persians* study particularly a strict Observation of the Law. That is the Character of the Generality of the *Persians*: But there is without doubt, an Exception to that general Depravation; for among some of the *Persians*, there is as much Justice, Sincerity, Virtue and Piety to be found, as among those who profess the best Religions. But the more one Converses with that Nation, the fewer one finds included in the Exception, the Number of Truly, Honest and Courteous *Persians* being very small.

¶ After what I have been saying, one will hardly be perswaded, that the *Persians* are so careful of the Education of Youth as they really are; which is very true, notwithstanding. The Nobility, *i. e.* Men of Distinction, and substantial Housekeepers Children, (for among the *Persians* there is no Nobility strictly so called) are very well brought up. They commonly take in Eunuchs to look after them, who are instead of Governors, and have them always in their Sight, keeping them very strictly, and carrying them out only to visit their Relations, or to see the Exercises performed, or the Solemnity of Feasts. And because they might not be spoiled at School, or at the College, they are not sent thither, but have Masters at Home. They are likewise very careful that they don't converse with the Servants, lest they should hear or see an immodest thing; and that the Servants carry themselves before them respectfully and Discreetly. The Common People bring up likewise their Children carefully; they don't suffer them to ramble about the Streets, to take ill Courses, to learn to Game, and to Quarrel, and learn rogueish Tricks. They are sent twice a Day to School, and when they come back, their Parents keep them by them, to initiate them in their Profession, and in the Business they are designed for: The Youth do not begin to come abroad into the World 'till they be past twenty, except they be marry'd before; for in that Case they are sooner set at Liberty, and left to themselves. By the word married, I mean joined to a Wife, or a Spouse by Contract; for at sixteen or seventeen, they give them a Bed-fellow, if they be Amorous. They appear, at their entrance into the World, Wise, Well-bred, Obliging, Shame-fac'd, little Talkers, Grave, Mindful, and Chaste in their Life and Conversation: But most of them take to ill Courses soon, and give themselves up to Luxury; and for want of an Estate or Income to indulge their Inclinations, they fall to unlawful Practices, which offer themselves every Minute, and appear very plausible.

¶ The *Persians* are the most Civiliz'd People of the *East*, and the greatest Complimenters in the World. The Polite Men amongst them, are upon a level with the Politest Men of *Europe*. Their Air, their Countenance, is very well composed, Lovely, Grave, Majestical, and as Fond as may be; they never fail complimenting one another about the Precedency, either going out or coming into a House, or when they meet, but 'tis over presently. They look upon two Things in our Manners, as very ridiculous, *viz.* Contending so long, as we do, who shall go first; and covering our Head, to do Honour to any Man, which amongst them is a want of Respect, or a Liberty which no body takes but with his Inferiors or familiar Friends: They observe the right and the left Hand, but our Left is their Right, and so 'tis all over the *East*. They say, that *Cyrus* began first to place Men on his left Hand, out of respect to them, because that side is the weaker part of the Body, and the most exposed to Danger.

¶ They visit one another regularly on all occasions of Mirth and Sadness, and at solemn Feasts, the rich wait then for the Visits of inferior People, which they return afterwards. The Courtiers go and pay their Compliments Night and Morning to the Ministers, and wait upon them from their Palace to Court. They are led into large Halls, where they set Tobacco and Coffee before them, till the Lord, who is still on the Woman's side, comes out. As soon as they see him, every one rises, and stands up in his own Place; he goes by, bows his Head to the Company, and the Company to him again, but much lower; then he goes and sits down in his usual Place: He beckons to the Company to sit down; and when he is ready to go, he rises, goes out first, and every one follows him. The Rich receive also in that manner their Inferiors, but they use more Ceremony with their Equals, and their Superiors: They wish them well come before they sit down, and mind to sit down but after they are sat, and to rise after them when they go out. The Master of the House sits always at the upper end: And when he is willing to shew any Body some particular Respect, he beckons him to come and sit down by him; he does not offer him his

Place, for the Person he offers it to, would look upon it as an Affront, but out of an extraordinary respect to him, and goes and sits down beside the Stranger below him.

¶ When the Person visited is in his Hall, and is an Eminent Person, they behave themselves in this manner: The Visiter goes in softly, steps to the next empty Seat where he stands with his Feet close to one another, his Hands over one another in his Girdle, stooping a little with his Head, with his Eyes fix'd, and a grave and thoughtful Countenance, till the Master of the House beckons to him to sit down, which he never fails to do presently, either with his Hand, or with his Head. When a Man receives a Visit from his Superior, he rises as soon as he sees him come in, and offers to meet him half way. If he is visited by his Equal, he rises half way. If by an Inferior somewhat deserving, he only makes a motion of rising. Visiters seldom rise if any Body comes into the Room, except the Master of the House doth it, or any body has some particular Reason of shewing that respect to him that comes in. There is beside much more Ceremony observed in *Persia* at sitting down. Before Men to whom Respect is due, a Man sits presently on his Heels, with his knees and Feet close to one another: Before his Equals, he sits easier, that is, he sits on his Breech, his Legs a-cross, and his Body upright. They call that Posture *Tehazanou*, *i. e.* sitting on four Knees, because the Knees and Ancles lie flat on the Ground: Friends and familiar Acquaintance say presently *Sit down easy*, i. e. cross your Legs as you please; but unless they have sat half a Day in the same Place, they don't shift their Situation. The *Eastern* People are not near so restless, and so uneasy as we; they sit gravely and soberly, make no motion with their Body, or very seldom, except it be to ease themselves, but they never make any to help their Discourse; our way upon that account surprizes them strangely; for they don't believe, that a Man that is in his Wits, can be so full of Action as we are. 'Tis also amongst them a great piece of Rudeness for a Man to shew his Toes when he sits, he must hide them under his Gown. That the Reader may the better understand how they sit in *Persia*, I have caused two [*sic*] Figures to be set on the other side, where the Posture is exactly represented. Their usual way of Saluting is with a Nod, or laying their Right-hand on their Mouth, which is the way among Friends after a long Absence. Lastly, they also Kiss one another, and give a short Embrace, after a return from a long Journey, and on extraordinary Occasions.

¶ Those are the usual Manners relating to Action; those relating to Discourse are yet smoother, and more obliging. They receive their Visitors pleasantly with a *Koc-homedy*, *i. e.* you are come in good; *Safa a crudy*, you purge us with your Presence; *Giachuma calibut*; the Place you use to sit in at my House, has been empty; otherwise nobody has been here deserving the Honour, to supply your Absence, and such like Compliments; which are multiplied and repeated every foot, according to the Respect they have for the Visitors. I'll repeat it once more; The *Persians* are the most kind People in the World; they have the most moving and the most engaging Ways, the most complying Tempers, the smoothest

Persian in usual sitting position.

and the most flattering Tongues, avoiding in their Conversation, Relations or Expressions which may occasion Melancholy Thoughts: And when the Discourse or Occasion obliges them to it, they use Circumlocutions to avoid at least the Tragical Terms; for Instance, if they would say that a Man is dead, they say, *Amrekodber chuma bakchid*, i. e. he has made you a Gift of the Share of Life which he had, otherwise, he might have liv'd still many Years; but out of the Love he has for you, he has joined them to those you have yet to run. I remember upon that Account, a short and ingenious Story of the General of the Musketiers, in the time of *Abas* the

Second; That Prince, who was a Man of bright Parts, had given that General a White *Bear* to keep, which had been brought him from *Muscovy*, supposing that he would take more Care of it than they would in the Park of wild Beasts: However, the *Bear* did not live long, the King being acquainted with it some time after, desired to know what he died of, and asked the General, *What's become of my white Bear? Sir*, Answer'd he, *he has made you a Gift of the share of Life he had.* The King smiling said to him, *You are a Bear your self, for wishing that the Years of a Beast be added to mine.* They tell another Story pretty like that of the same General, which I insert here, with a Design to acquaint the Reader with the *Persian* Expressions. The King was Walking a short League off of *Ispahan*, along the Hill *Rousopha*, a thick Cloud lighting on the Point of a Rock, the King said to the General, *Look at that black Cloud, on the Point of that Rock, it is like the Hats of the Franks.* The *Eastern* Nations give that Name to the *European Christians. That's true, Sir*, answer'd the General, *and God grant you may Conquer them all; How is it possible*, Reply'd the King Smiling, *that I should Conquer them all, who are two thousand Leagues off me, when I can't Conquer the Turks, who are my nearest Neighbours?* They condole in these Terms, *Sercuma Salamet bachet*, i. e. *May your Head be safe and sound*; otherwise, *Your Life is so dear to me, that I care little who dies, so you do but live*; or *your Preservation is my only Concern.*

¶ The Compliments observ'd in Letters, Memoiers, and Petitions, are still longer and exacter than the Verbal ones, which are spoken in the Presence of Friends: But seeing I shall have an Occasion to discourse of them elsewhere, I shall only say here, that they have a Book on Purpose, containing the Titles to be given to all Orders of Men, from the King to the Cobler. That Book is call'd *Tenassour*, i. e. Method or Rule. Men of Business have it by Heart. I shall give no Abstracts of them, because the Stile of them may be seen in the Letters I have Inserted in my Journey from *Paris* to *Ispahan*, and in several Petitions, which one may read hereafter. One of their Politenesses in Discourse, is to speak always in the Third Person, both when they speak to others, and speak of themselves, much in the same Manner as the *Germans* do.

¶ As civil as that Nation is, they never Act out of Generosity; 'tis a Property they are Strangers to in the East, their Bodies and Estates being Subject to a Despotick and Arbitrary Power, their Minds and Hearts are so likewise; They do nothing but out of a Principle of *Interest*, that is to say, out of *Hope* or *Fear*: And they cannot conceive that there should be such a Country where People will do their Duty from a Motive of *Virtue only*, without any other *Recompence*. It is quite the Contrary with them;

they are paid for every thing, and before Hand too. One can ask nothing of 'em, but with a Present in one's Hand; and they have thereupon this Proverb, *That one comes back from a Judge, as one went to him*; As much as to say, that if one goes there with an empty Hand, one comes back without having any Justice done one. The poorest and most miserable People never appear before a Great Man, or one from whom they would ask some Favour, but at the same time they offer a Present, which is never refus'd, even by the greatest Lords of the Kingdom, such as *Fruit, Fouls, Lamb*, &c. Every one gives of that which he is possest of most, and of the Profession which he is of, and those who have no Profession give Money. It is accounted an Honour to receive these sorts of Presents; they make 'em Publickly, and generally take that time when there is most Company. This is the general Custom throughout all the *East*; and it may be, one of the Ancientest in the World. As this seems very *Mean* and *Dishonest* with the *Europeans*, I shall not add, that it is neither perhaps the most *Reasonable*, and I shall not take upon me to defend it. I shall only say, that the *Persians* do the Service always for which they take the Present, and that they do it Instantly, or the first Opportunity that offers. They likewise make Presents to their Patrons and Benefactors, upon Festivals, and other such like solemn Occasions, without asking any particular Favour of them.

¶ The *Persians* neither love walking Abroad, nor Travelling. As to that of walking Abroad, they look upon that Custom of ours to be very Absurd; and they look upon the walking in the Alley, as Actions only proper for a Madman. They ask very gravely for what one goes to the End of the Alley, and why one does not stand still, if one has Business to go there. This proceeds no doubt from their living in a Climate that is more even than ours. They are not so Sanguine as we are *Northward*, nor so Fiery. The most Spirituous part of their Blood perspiring more than it does with us, which is the Reason that they are not so subject to the Motions of the Body, which look so like Lightness and Disquietude, and which go often to Extravagence, and even to Madness. They don't know such a Remedy in *Persia*, as that which we call *Exercise*; they are much better sitting or leaning, than walking. The *Women* and the *Eunuchs* generally Speaking, use no Exercise, and are always sitting or lying, without prejudicing the Health: For the Men, they ride on Horseback, but never walk, and their Exercises are only for Pleasure, and not for Health. The Climate of each People is always, as I believe, the principal Effect of the Inclinations and Customs of the Men, which are no more different among them, than that of the Temper of the Air is different from one Place to another. As for what relates to travelling, those Journeys that are made out of pure Curiosity,

are still more inconceivable to the *Persians*, than walking Abroad. They
have no Taste of the Pleasure we enjoy in seeing different Manners from
ours, and hearing of a Language which we do not Understand. When the
French Company in the *East-Indies* sent Deputies to the King of *Persia*, the
King of *France* sent two likewise, but without any Character, Nam'd
Lalain, and *Boullaye*; and the Credential Letter imported, *That these
Gentlemen having an Inclination to Travel, and joining with these French Merchants,
who are the Deputies, in order to see the World; the King made use of this Opportunity to write to his* Persian *Majesty to recommend this Company of* French
Merchants *to him*. I came to the Court of *Persia* when these Gentlemen
were solliciting their Affairs, concerning which the Minister talk'd with
me very often, and I found immediately, that this Letter was not at all
pleasing to them upon many Accounts; as among others, because it was
Occasionally sent. The Ministers ask'd me, if we had no more Regard for
the Great Kings in our part of the World, than to send Letters to 'em by
People not Deputed on Purpose: But they hung mightily upon those
Words, *Gentlemen who have a mind to Travel*, which could not be put into
their Language, without an Air of Absurdity, being a thing not practis'd,
or even so much as known. They ask'd me if it was possible that there
should be such People amongst us, who would travel two or three thousand
Leagues with so much Danger, and Inconveniency, only to see *how they
were made, and what they did in Persia, and upon no other Design*. These People
are of Opinion, as I have observ'd, that one cannot better attain to Virtue,
nor have a fuller Taste of Pleasure than by resting and dwelling at Home,
and that it is not good to Travel, but to acquire Riches. They believe likewise, that every Stranger is a Spy if he be not a Merchant, or a Handi-
crafts-Man, and the People of Quality look upon it to be a Crime against
the State to receive 'em among them, or to Visit them. It is from this
Spirit of theirs no doubt, that the *Persians* are so grosly Ignorant of the
present State of other Nations of the World, and that they do not so much
as understand *Geography*, and have no Maps; which comes from this, that
having no Curiosity to see other Countries, they never mind the Distance,
nor Roads, by which they might go thither. They have no such thing
among 'em as Accounts of Foreign Countries, neither *Gazetts*, *News
A-la-main*, nor *Offices* of *Intelligence*. This would seem very strange to People
who pass their time in asking after News, and whose Health and Rest in
a Manner, are Interested in it, as well as to those who apply themselves
with so much care to the Study of the Maps and other Accounts; but this
is however very true; and as I have represented the *Persians*, it is plain,
that all that Knowledge is not requisite for the Pleasure and Tranquility

of the Mind. The Ministers of State generally Speaking, know no more what passes in *Europe*, than in the World of the Moon. The greatest Part, even have but a confus'd Idea of *Europe*, which they look upon to be some little Island in the *North* Seas, where there is nothing to be found that is either Good or Handsome; *from whence it comes*, say they, *that the Europeans go all over the World, in search of fine Things, and of those which are Necessary, as being destitute of them.*

¶ Yet notwithstanding what I have been saying, it is certainly true, that there is not that Country in the World, which is less dangerous to travel in from the Security of the Roads, for which they provide with a great deal of Care; neither is it less Expensive any where, by Reason of the great Number of publick Buildings, which they keep for Travellers, in all Parts of the Empire, as well in the Cities, as in the Country. They lodge in those Houses without being put to any Charge; besides which, there are Bridges and Causways, in all the Places where the Roads are too bad, which are made for the Sake of the Caravans, and of all those who travel from a motive of Gain.

¶ The Custom of the *Persians* who Traffick, or are in Business, is, that when they have got a Sum of Money together, they employ it first of all in Purchasing a House, which they never buy quite built, but rebuild it to the Size which they would have it; making use of a Proverb, *That a House which a Man buy's quite built, is no more proper for his Family, than a Garment that he buy's ready made is fit for his Body.* There are few People in *Persia* who Rent Houses. The poorest sort are generally the Owners of the Houses wherein they dwell. This proceeds from two Causes, *First*, That the *Persians* have not a Genius naturally bent upon Traffick. And the *Second* is, That their Religion forbids them taking any Interest for lending of Money, which is the Reason why every one avoids paying of Rent, but chooseth rather to buy a House, because he does not know how to employ his Money better. The next Purchase to this which the *Persians* make, is what they call *Bazarga*, or Market-place, which is a Gallery of Shops from one End to the other, most commonly Vaulted over, which they cause to be built near their House, or which they buy as Occasion offers. That generally is the first Land Estate which they buy. They afterwards purchase a Bath, then a *Caravanseray* or Inn. One might perhaps imagine that these Estates pay 'em a Yearly or Quarterly Rent, as they do with us; but one shall be surprized to find that they lett those Places by the Day, and oblige them to pay their Rents every Night, not so much as trusting 'em till next Morning; which is the Reason why those who acquire Estates and build upon 'em, cause the Buildings to be close to their Gates, that their Servants may the more commodiously receive their Rent. This however respects only the meaner sort of People, the others paying by the Week or the Month. But as they have no great Moveables in the *East*, that they neither make use of Tables, nor Chairs, nor Bedsteads, nor Cabinets, nor near so many Utensils for the Kitchin, a Lodger may much easier run away from them than with us. The richest among 'em, after having amass'd a great Estate for themselves and Children, set themselves about Publick Edifices, as Colleges, with Foundations for so many Students; after that, *Caravanseray's* or Inns upon the great Roads, for the reception of those who travel that way, without costing them any thing; then Bridges; and they end with Mosques, with a Revenue to entertain Priests, and something to distribute to Charities. The *Persians*, who call these Foundations *Sonab a caret*, as much as to say Merit for the future Life, say likewise, that these Beneficences are *kreir Jary*, as they speak it; that is to say, growing Goods; because, say they, the Prayers that are said in these Free Lodgings, and in these Temples, and when one actually makes use of the other Accommodations, turn to the advantage of the Founders, and are attributed to them.

¶ There are no other Carriages in *Persia* but Beasts for the Saddle, and great Tubs in the Nature of Cradles, cover'd and shut, wherein the Women of Quality Travel, two upon a Camel, of which I shall give a Description elsewhere. They have neither Coaches, Chariots, Litters, nor Chaises, whether because the Country is Mountainous, or that this is a Country broke off by Canals on every side, every body goes on Horseback, or upon a Mule, or upon those sort of Asses that Amble, and go nimble and easy. The Shop-keepers and Handy-crafts Men, have their Saddle-Beasts, and none but the poorest sort go on Foot. I leave it to the Reader, to make yet more Remarks on the Manners of the *Persians*, in the Series of my Relations, where I shall have occasion to speak of them.

¶ The Names which the *Persians* bear, are given 'em, either at their coming into the World, or when they are Circumcis'd, as they are to all the other *Mahometans*: And these Names are taken either from Eminent Persons of their Religion, from the *Old-Testament*, from their Histories, or they are Names of Power; for every one takes or gives himself a Name, according to his Mind; but they have no particular Sir-Names, or Names of the Family and Line; for their Sir-Names they take to themselves by way of Honour, the Proper Name of their Father, and sometimes that of their Son, in saying, such a one, the Father of such a one, or such a one, the Son of such a one; as for Example, *Abraham*, the Son of *Jacob*, and *Mahammed*, the Father of *Aly*. This is the Custom, time out of Mind, of naming themselves in the *East*. You may see it likewise in the *Old-Testament*, where one finds, for Example, the Kings of *Assyria* call'd *Ben Adad*, as much as to say Sons of *Adad*, and those of *Palestine* call'd *Abimelec*, that is to say, Son of *Melec*, a Term that signifies King. It is likewise very common among 'em to have several Sir-names, the one taken from the Name of his Father, and the other from his Son; and even to bear the Name of several of his Children, as the *Calif Abrachid*, the fifteenth *Calif* of the Race of the *Abassides*, who is sometimes named *Abon Jafer*, sometimes *Abon Mahammed*, which are the Names of his Sons. In short, it is very common with them to take for their Sir-name, the Calling that has been exercised, whether by the Father, or by his Ancestors, whether Liberal or Mechanick, by which they rais'd themselves in the World, *Mahammed Caian*, *Mahammed* the *Taylor*, *Soliman Atari*, *Soliman* the *Druggist*, *Jouacri*, the *Jeweller*, *Stanboni*, the *Constantinopolitan*, by Reason of his having got an Estate there; and what is Remarkable, as very Praise-worthy in my Opinion, that they are not ashamed of bearing these Sir-names after they become Rich, are raised to the highest Dignities, and are put into the greatest Employments. This is because they are rais'd by the Sciences, by their Employments, and especially by their Riches. There are but very few who are tied to it by Descent.

¶ As for Titles, they are not at all affected in the *East*, whether from Birth or Office. Every one fastens to his Name as he pleases, without the haughty Titles of Duke, Prince, and King: There are those which they never put after the Name, as the Title of *Mirza*, which signifies the Son of a Prince. This is to distinguish the Royal Personages from the rest of the World, who place these Titles before and after their Names quite another way, and contrary to others. One very strange Thing, and which one would scarce believe, is, that the *Persians* Glory in bearing the Title of Slaves. I speak of the People rais'd at Court, and who were born or bred up to Employments; they call themselves, by way of Honour, *Slaves of the King*, or *Slaves of the Saints*; for Example, The Duke Slave of *Ibrahim*, or of *Mahammed*, or of the King. These sort of Names, denote generally a Man in Offices, or one who aspires to 'em.

¶ When a Male Child is born into the World, it is the Custom for the Father to give every thing that he has upon him, to him who brings him the News. They come to him with their Turban off their Head, and say to him, *You have a Male Child born*; and he must strait make a Present for this good News, and as it were to buy his Clothes again, and what he has upon him.

CHAPTER XII

CONCERNING THE EXERCISES AND GAMES OF THE PERSIANS

I JOIN these two Actions together, because the *Persian* Term which signifies one, expresses likewise the other; and that the *Persians* call their Exercises honest Games, and the Games unlawful Exercises. In effect, the Exercises of the *Persians* are Games of Dexterity, the Design of 'em being to render the Body Supple and Vigorous, and learn 'em how to use and handle their Arms. But as the Body must be ready form'd, and strong for these Exercises, they seldom begin practising till they are eighteen or twenty Years of Age, the Youth till then being under the Correction of the Masters of the Sciences, and the Conduct of Eunuchs. Here are the principal Exercises in which the *Persians* occupy themselves.

¶ First of all, to bend the Bow, the Art of which consists in holding it right, bending of it, and letting the Cord go with ease, without letting the Left-hand which holds the Bow, and which is stretched out at length, nor the Right-hand, which handles the String, stir the least in the World. They teach 'em at first, to bend it easily, and then harder by Degrees. The Masters of these Exercises teach 'em to bend the Bow before 'em, behind 'em, and side-ways, up and down; and to be short, a hundred several ways; always quick and easy. They have Bows that are very difficult to bend; and to try their Strength, they hang them against a Wall to a Peg, and they tie Weights to the Cord of the Bow, at the Place where they put the notch of the Arrow: The stiffest of 'em will bear five hundred weight before they will bend. When they can handle an ordinary Bow, they give 'em others to bend, which they make heavy by putting a great many thick Rings of Iron upon the Cord: There are some of these Bows that weigh an hundred Weight; they handle them, they bend them, they unbend them, as I have said, as they are Jumping, Tossing and Tumbling, sometimes upon one Foot, sometimes on their Knees, and sometimes Running: The clattering of these Rings make a troublesome Noise: This is to get more Strength. They judge that they perform that exercise well, when, in holding the Bow in the Left-Hand stretch'd out very stiff, fast, and without shaking, they bring the Cord or String with the Thumb of the Right-hand to their Ear, as if they were to hang it upon it.

¶ For the better performing of this Exercise, they wear a Ring on their Thumb, an Inch wide within, and half as much without, upon which the Cord or String of the Bow bears: This Ring is made of Horn or Ivory, or of *Jadde*, which is a sort of Green Alabaster: The King has one of hard Bone and light, its natural Colours being Red and Yellow, which grows, as they say, like a Tuft upon the Head of a great Bird in the Isle of *Ceylon*. When they are very well skill'd in handling the Bow, their first Exercise is to let fly the Arrow in the Air, and who shall make it fly highest, they account him a clever Archer, and the Bow the best, that throws an Arrow to the elevation of forty-five Degrees, which is as far as the Bow will bear. The next Exercise is shooting at the Mark; and it is not only the shooting into it, but the Arrow must be thrown firm, and without shaking, into it. They afterwards learn to draw it with Strength and Weight. They Exercise themselves that way after this manner; They make about four Foot high, a Frame of about two Foot Diameter, sloping, about five or six Foot deep, fill'd with wet and fine Gravel, like the Frame of a Founder for Casting. They take their Bow and Arrow without Squares, and when they are ready to shoot, there comes a Servant with a great Flint-stone in his Hand, and strikes home just in the middle of the Frame, which is more to hinder them from taking Aim where to shoot, than to harden the Gravel. They shoot into it with all their Strength, and the Arrow generally sinks half-way into it. They draw it out, and shoot again into the Place, till such time as the Arrow is buried in it. They succeed in that Exercise according as they bury the Arrow at fewer or more times, and that falls out as they shoot strait to the same Point. These Exercises are to teach 'em to shoot the Arrow, the Art of which, in a Word, consists in shooting a great way, in shooting true, and in shooting stiff and strong, that the Arrow may enter and pierce through. They learn to say, at shooting the last Arrow, *Tir a ker derdil Omar*; *May the Arrow, this last Bout, enter the Heart of Omar*: And this is to keep up the aversion and hatred they have for the Sect of *Turks*, whereof *Omar* is the second Pontif after *Mahammed*. It is to be observ'd, that the Arrows for these Exercises, have a round piece of Iron, small and obtuse, whereas their Arrows for Battle have Iron like the point of a Lance, or like our Lancets.

¶ The second Exercise is to handle the *Sabre*; and as this Art consists in having a strong Wrist and very pliant, they teach the Youth to handle the *Sabre* with two Weights in their Hands, in turning them up and down, before and behind, quick and strong: And in order to make their Joints the more pliable, and the Nerves the more supple, they put, during the Exercise, two other Weights upon their Shoulders made like a Horse-shoe, that it may not hinder their Motion. This Exercise is good for Wrestling, as well as to make 'em use the *Sabre* well.

¶ The third Exercise is that of the Horse, which consists in Mounting well, to have a good Seat, to gallop with a loose Rein without stirring; to stop the Horse short in his Gallop, without moving one's self, and to be so light and active upon a Horse, as to tell, upon the Gallop, twenty Counters upon the Ground one after the other, and to take 'em up at their return, without slackening their Speed. There are People in *Persia* that sit so Firm and Light upon a Horse, that they stand strait on their Feet upon the Saddle, and make the Horse Gallop in that manner with a loose Rein. The *Persians* ride a little Side-ways, because they turn themselves so in performing their Exercises on Horse-back, which are of three Sorts, to play at the Mall, to draw the Bow, and to throw the Javelin. Their Play at the Mall is perform'd in a very great Place, at the end of which are Pillars near each other, which serve for the Ball to pass thro'. They throw the Ball in the middle of the Place, and the Players with a Mall-stick in their Hand, gallop after it to strike it: As the Mall-stick is short, they must stoop below the Saddle-bow to strike it, and by the Rules of the Game, they must take their Aim gallopping. They win their Match, when they have made the Ball pass between the Pillars. They play at this Game, having fifteen or twenty on a side. The Exercise of the Bow on Horse-back is perform'd by shooting at a Bowl or Cup behind one, put upon the end of a Mast or Pole about twenty-six Foot high, where they get up by little Ribs of Wood nailed to it, and which serve as Steps. The Gentleman takes his Career towards the Pole with his Bow and Arrow in his Hand, and when he is gone by it, he bends himself backwards either to the Right, or Left; for they must know how to do it both Ways, and lets fly his Arrow.

¶ This Exercise is common to all the Towns of *Persia*. Even the Kings, Exercise themselves that way. King *Sephy*, Grand Father of the King now Reigning, excell'd in it; he always brought down the Cup at the first or second Time. King *Abas* his Son was as Dextrous likewise at it. *Soliman*, who succeeded him, took less delight in it than his Predecessors. The *Javelin*, which they use in these Exercises, and is call'd *Gerid*, as much as to say, the Bough of a *Palm-Tree*, because it is made of the Boughs of a dry *Palm-Tree*, is much longer than a *Partizan*, and very heavy, insomuch, that it requires a very strong Arm to dart, or throw it. There are People in *Persia* so well made, and so Skilful at this Exercise, that they will throw a *Dart* or *Javelin*, six or seven hundred Paces. I shall have Occasion else-where to speak more particularly how they Act in these Exercises, which are the Carousals of the *Persians*.

¶ Wrestling is the Exercise of People in a lower Condition; and generally Speaking, only of People who are Indigent. They call the Place where they Show themselves to *Wrestle, Zour Kone,* that is to say, *The House of Force.* They have of 'em in all the Houses of their great Lords, and especially those of the Governours of Provinces, to Exercise their People. Every Town has besides Companies of those Wrestlers for Show.

¶ They call the *Wrestlers Pehelvon,* a Word which signifies Brave, Intrepid. They perform their Exercises to divert People; for this is a Show, as I have said, and thus it is, They strip themselves Naked, only with their Shoes on, made of Leather, that fit them very exactly, oil'd and greas'd, and a Linnen Cloth about their Wast greas'd and oil'd likewise. This is, that the Adversary may have less to take hold of, because if he should touch there, his Hand would slip, and he would lose his Strength. The two Wrestlers being Present upon an even Sand, a little Tabour, that always plays during the time of Wrestling, to animate them, gives the Signal. They begin, by making a thousand Bravadoes and Rodomontades; then they promise each other fair Play, and shake Hands. That being done, they strike at each others Buttocks, Hips, and Thighs, keeping time with the little Tabour; then they shake Hands again, and strike at each other as before, three times together. This is as if it were for the Ladies, and to recover their Breath; after that, they close, making a great Out-cry, and strive with all their Might to overthrow their Man. The Victory is never judg'd to signifie any thing, till the Man be laid flat upon his Belly, stretch'd all along upon the Ground.

¶ *Fencing,* is another Exercise for the Publick Show and Diversion. The Fencers being upon the Spot, in sight of the Spectators, lay their Arms upon the Ground at their Feet. These are a straight *Sabre,* and a *Buckler,* they kneel down, and kiss them with their Mouth, and with their Forehead; then they get up again, taking them in their Hand; at the Sound of the Tabour, they dance and skip about, making a thousand Postures and Motions with their Arms very dexterously; then they begin, and reach one another several Strokes with the Sword, which they receive upon their *Buckler:* They always strike with the Edge, if they do not come too near each other, for then they present the Point. These Fencers are sometimes in good Earnest, and draw Blood; but if the Combate becomes too hot, they are parted.

¶ Besides these Exercises which are for the Diversion of the *Persians,* they have of those who Dance upon the Ropes, *Poppet-Shows,* and doing Feats of Activity as adroit and nimble as in any Country whatever. They dance upon the Rope bare-Foot. They draw a Cord from the Top of a Tower thirty or forty Toises high, quite down, and pretty stiff; they go up it, and afterwards come down, which they don't do by crawling down upon the Belly, as they do elsewhere, but they come down backwards, holding by their Toes, which they fasten in the Rope, which of consequence cannot be very big. One cannot well see it without having a dread upon one, especially when the Rope-Dancer to show his Strength and Activity, carries a Child upon his Shoulders, one Leg on one side, and the other on the other, that holds by the Forehead. They don't dance upon a strait Rope, as the Rope-Dancers in *Europe* do; but they make Leaps and Turns. Their finest Turn is this, They give the Rope-Dancer two hollow Basons, like Soop Dishes; he puts them upon the Rope, the bottom of the Basons being one against the other, and he sits in that Bason which is uppermost, having his Backside in the hollow of the Bason; he takes two Turns, backward and forward; then at the second Turn, he causes the undermost Bason to fall dexterously, and rest upon that which is uppermost, upon which he again takes two Turns, and then makes it fall again, and he himself is astride upon the Rope. There are of 'em that dance upon a Chain instead of a Rope.

¶ Besides these Dancers, there are Vaulters, who leap with a surprising Activity. They jump thro' a Hoop trim'd with the Points of a Poignard, between the Spaces, which are not at a Foot distance, but are put thro' in such a Manner as to bend so easily, that the Body causes 'em to give way going through. They likewise leap through a Rope which two Men hold fast in a Square, from sixteen, to eighteen Inches only, which they hold about five Foot from the Ground. One can scarce get a Child thro' it, but those who hold it, know how to enlarge it so dexterously, that it cannot be perceiv'd.

¶ Their *Vaulters* take their turn with *Flambeaux* in their Hands lighted at both Ends, which they every Moment pass over their Faces without burning themselves. They will cause a Spade red-hot to be hammered upon an Anvel plac'd upon their naked Belly, keeping themselves bent backwards upon their Hands and Feet, about five or six Inches from the Ground, after having caus'd a Poignard to be put under their Back, the point not above an Inch from it, to shew that the Stroaks of the Hammerer don't move 'em, for if they had, the Poignard must have stuck in their Back. The *Vaulter* or *Tumbler* keeps himself in that Posture till the two Hammerers have finish'd the Spade. When that turn is accomplish'd, there comes another *Vaulter*, who puts himself in the same Place and Posture, upon whose Belly they put an Apple or a Melon, which a Man comes and cuts in two with one Stroke of a *Sabre*, taking his Aim very high, without so much as touching the Skin.

¶ Their *Juglers* make use of Eggs instead of Balls under their Cups to play their Tricks withal: They put about seven or eight Eggs in a Bag, which they have stamp'd upon before-hand, and which they cause to be done by those of the Spectators, who have a mind to it; and in a moment afterwards they will cause these Eggs to become *Pidgeons* or *Pullets*. Then they will give you the Bag to see and handle, which is their Pouch, and when they are sufficiently convinc'd that there is nothing in it, they put it upon the Ground in the middle of the Place, and in a Minute's time they take it in their Hand, and pull out all the Utensils of a Kitchin.

¶ The *Puppet-shows* and *Juglers* ask no Money at the Door as they do in our Country, for they play openly in the publick Places, and those give 'em that will. They intermingle Farce, and Juggling, with a thousand Stories and Buffooneries, which they do sometimes Mask'd, and sometimes Un-mask'd, and this lasts two or three Hours: And when they have done, they go round to the Spectators and ask something; and when they perceive any one to be stealing off before they go to ask him for any thing, the Master of the Company cries out with a loud Voice, and in an Emphatical manner, *That he who steals away, is an Enemy to Ali*. As who should say among us, *An Enemy to God and his Saints*. For two Crowns the Juglers will come to their House. They call these sort of Diversions *Mascare*, that is to say *Play, Pleasantry, Raillerie, Representation*; from whence comes our Word *Masquerade*.

¶ Besides the *Persian Juglers*, of which there are in all the Towns of the Kingdom, as I have been saying, there are Companies of *Indian Juglers* in the great Cities, especially at *Ispahan*, but who don't know any more than those of the Country. I admire at the Credulity of many Travellers, who have seriously reported that these *Juglers* know how to produce in a Moment, such and such a Tree loaden with Flowers and with Fruit; make Eggs hatch upon the Spot, and a thousand other wonderful things of that Kind. Mr. *Taverner* among others, puts it plainly in his Relations, tho' from the manner of his telling it, he must needs discover enough of the Cheat. I knew that they were so from the first time that I saw them perform'd, because that from my Mistrust, I observ'd 'em narrowly. The *Juglers* show their Tricks in this manner; They spread a Cloth, round or square, according to the Court or Garden where they are made to Play, and they always spread it at a little Distance from the Spectators: When all their Pieces are ready, they open the Cloth in the Presence of the People; then they take a Stone or Kernel of some Fruit in Season, and with their usual Affectation, Strutting, and abundance of Stories of their Conjuring-Book, fit only to dazle the Sight of the Silly or Ignorant, they plant it in the Ground in the middle of their Tent, then water it, and afterwards close it up again: That done, they plant themselves between the Tent and the Spectators, and play other Tricks of *Pass, &c.* During which time, one of the Company slips cleverly under the Cloth, and plants in the Ground, just where the Kernel or Stone was, a little green Bough of that kind of Tree which they had promised. In the mean time every one is attentive to their other Tricks; which when they had been at about a quarter of an Hour, they open the Tent before the Company, and with great Exclamations show this Sucker-Plant. One of them, the more to impose upon the Foolish, lies at that time upon it and sprinkles it with his Blood, cutting himself for that purpose under the Arm-pit, or elsewhere. All the rest begin their Invocations, and sham Wonder, then they let fall the Cloth again, and fall to their other Tricks as before. This Diversion lasts, by five or six Fits, or Intervals, an Hour or two, and till such time as they have shown this Young Plant four or five Foot high, with some Fruit upon it. This is their Miracle; at the sight of which, the Servants, and all those who are so foolish to believe it, stand in great Admiration. The first time I saw this Trick, I would willingly have come nearer the Tent, the better to have seen it done: These *Juglers* oppos'd it: I bid 'em not to come near it themselves, and to show it at some distance; still that could not be done, that was to disturb and hinder their Operation. I then let them alone to do it; but I caus'd them to be watch'd by two Servants, who saw all their Play; and I discover'd 'em my self by my Attention. I saw this Trick of the Tree in several Places, and it was still the same thing. I have heard it affirm'd, that some of 'em perform this Trick with counter-feit Wood. The *Indian* and *Persian* Tricks are all the same, which certainly much surpass ours in Ingenuity and Nimbleness, and they make their Matter very dexterously, and with a wonderful deal of Art. I have seen at *Colconda* four Women stand strait on end upon one another's Shoulders; the fourth had a Child in her Arms, and she who bore or carry'd the others, ran; for she went, as they call it, *faster than a foot pace.* The second jump'd upon the shoulders of the first: The other two got up by a Tree. I have heard told to the late Mr. *Carron,* (one of the Ablest Men that the *Indies* and Trade had ever form'd) some of the best Tricks which the *Chinese* and those of *Japan* perform, in speaking of those of the highest Form; They assure ye, that there are of 'em that take a Child, throw it into the Air, and make 'em fall Limb by Limb, first one Leg, then another, and so of all the rest, the last of which is the Head: That those *Juglers* join the Parts again upon the Ground; after which, the Child gets up and appears as it was before. There is no possibility of being made sensible of this Story or Fable, this is without doubt a Trick that there is no way to comprehend, unless as a Trick of Dexterity, which is perform'd by the quickness of the Operation in changing the Objects, and thereby deceiving the Eyes of the Spectators. I should never have done, were I to set down every thing I have heard told concerning these *Indian* and *Chinese Juglers*, where they would make me believe there are Impostures or Witchcrafts; in a Word, that the Devil was in it. I try'd all I could to see the like, but to no purpose always, the *Magick* Whitening as I came near it: And I found my self continually oblig'd to acknowledge the Cheat.

⁋ The *Persians* call the Games of Chance, *Taoum*: Their Religion forbids 'em, and the Polity authorises that Prohibition, by imposing Fines on those who Play. The *Michel darbachi*, which is one of the great Officers of the Court, to which is annex'd that of Inspector over the Publick Women, and who takes their Tribute, is established likewise over the Play, and receives the Fines. One may see how easy it is to forbear Play, when one resolves against it, in that the *Persians* do not Play, generally speaking, tho' they look upon the sin of Play to be Light and Venial, whereas the use of Wine is common enough among them, though their Religion forbids it more strictly. There are even Doctors who hold, that the Games of *Hazard* are not forbid; but when they play for Mony, and not when they don't play for any; but the one is a Consequence of the other, seeing that they can never play at Games of Chance but for something. The meaner sort of People have Cards, which they call *Ganjaphé:* They are of Wood very well Painted: The Pack has fourscore and ten Cards in it, with eight Suits: They play very aukwardly, and without any Invention. They have, again, the *Totum*-Dice, *Bowling*, *Tennis*, *Chuck*; but there is not one Man in a hundred that plays there; and those that do play are the very Vulgar sort of People. They play at Tables in the Coffee-Houses, and at a Game with Shells, which the *Turks* have mightily in Use: And these Games have been carry'd out of *Europe* into *Persia* by the *Armenians*. It is the same thing with the Play of the Eggs, which is very common towards the New-Year. They make 'em of all Colours, Painted and Gilt, that are worth a Pistol or two a Piece. There are some, the Shells whereof are harder than your ordinary Eggs, they having a Secret to harden them. Some People of Quality, but very few, play at *Chess*. They hold this Game forbid among the rest; but they don't look upon it to be Dishonest like the others. This Game has been the Subject of many Learned Disputes concerning its Origin, and the Etymology of its Terms: The *Persians* maintain that it is an Invention of their Ancestors, and the Terms of the Game are in effect, Originally from the Ancient *Persians:* They call it *Sedreng*; which implies a hundred Thoughts or Cares, because one's

Thoughts must be wholly employ'd upon it: Others will have it from *Chetreng*, which is almost the same thing; for in *Persia* the Letter *S*, and the Letters *Ch*, are clos'd the same way; *Chetreng* signifies the Grief or Anguish of the King, by Reason of the Extremity to which the King of *Chess* is reduc'd. *Chec* and *Mate*, come from *Cheic* or *Chamat*, which is the most considerable Term of this Game, which they make use of to express that the King is near being taken, and signifies that the King is under a Consternation, or amaz'd. The *Persians* esteem this Game mightily, saying, that *he who knows how to play well at a Game of Chess, is fit to govern the World*. They say likewise, that to play well at it, *one must make a Party hold out three Days*.

¶ I shall speak of *Singing* and *Dancing* in the following Discourse, in the Chapter of *Musick*; but I shall conclude this with the Description of a very solemn Diversion in *Persia*, which is the Feast of the *Chatir*, or Footman of the King. This is, when the Overseer of the Foot-men has a mind to be receiv'd into the King's Service. He must go from the Gate of the Palace to a Pillar, which is a *French* League and a half from the Palace, and fetch twelve Arrows from thence one after the other, between the two Suns. He is not receiv'd as the King's Footman till after that Trial. When King *Soliman* was mounted on his Throne, they show'd him some things in his State; and as they spoke very much concerning the Feast of the *Chatir*, he order'd that it should be solemniz'd with all the Pomp imaginable, and that they should spare no Cost; and this is that which was perform'd the 26th Day of *May*, 1667; a Day set a-part by the *Astrologers*, who judg'd that to be the most Auspicious for this Festival. The General of the Musketeers who was, at that time, the Favourite, had brought a *Chatir* the Day before to the King, who promis'd to take him, if he accomplish'd his Course, and gave him a *Caloat* or entire Habit, with Permission to begin at four a Clock in the Morning, this was granting him a Favour of nigh an Hour; for the Order, as I have said, is for them to do it between the two Suns, as they call it: And they immediately give Orders for opening the Houses, setting out the Shops, and watering the Streets all along the Ways: That was done to a nicety; and the next Day every thing was set out, adorn'd and fitted. The Place Royal of *Ispahan* was emptied and made clean, like a great Room for a Ball: Before the Great Gate there was a Tent built fourscore Foot long, about thirty wide, and high in Proportion, born upon gilt Pillars, and stretch'd sloping, so that it was open upon the Gate, and the Corner of the Place by which the Runner came: The Tent was lin'd with fine Tabby, and with Brocard; the Bottom was cover'd with a Rich Carpet, all of a-piece, having squares of Brocard: At the Pillars of the Tent hung Plumes of *Herons*, and of all other sorts of Feathers, from Top to Bottom, which the King's Footmen wear on their Heads and Girdles, with little Bells, which they tie round 'em likewise, to keep themselves in Action. At one Corner there was a Beufet of Vessels of Gold and Precious Stones, with several Liquors; and in another, twenty Basons of Gold of all sorts of *March-panes*, and dry and wet Sweet-Meats. Ten or twelve of the King's Footmen richly clad, each in different Colours, and differently trimm'd; for in *Persia* they don't know what a Livery is, did the Honours of the Tent, to whoever was pleas'd to come and see it, who was of sufficient Quality to enter it, as being the Masters of the Feast. The Ushers of the King's Guard being at the Doors of the Tent, and the Body Guard making a Lane in the Place at all the Avenues. Over against the Great Gate of the Palace were nine Elephants ranged in Order, covered with rich Housings, and set out with so many Chains and Fetters, with other Ornaments, all of Massy Silver, which another Beast would have sunk under the Weight of. Each Elephant had his Manager clad after the *Indian* manner, very well set out. The biggest Elephant was Harness'd and ready to receive the Prince upon a cover'd Throne placed upon his Back, instead of a Saddle. This Throne was big enough for him to lie at length. Arms, as the *Bow*, *Buckler*, and *Arrows*, are always hung at one of the two Staffs that support the upper part of the Throne: And after that you see, at the South End of the Place, in one part, the Wild Beasts train'd up for Hunting, as the *Lion*, the *Panther*, the *Tiger*, and others; and in another Place *Indian* Chariots, drawn by beautiful Oxen all White: And the Beasts for Combat, as the *Bufflers*, *Bulls*, *Wolfs* and *Rams*, each with a Collar furnished with little Baggs filled with Amulets or written Papers, to serve as a Preservative. The *Mahometans* hang of these Amulets, not only to the Necks of these Beasts, but likewise of all others; to the Necks of their Wives and Children. They even hang them to Inanimate things: You will sometimes find them quite cover'd over with them. The other End of the Place, which is to the North, had likewise its Companies for Diversion, and for Shew; these were the Rope Dancers, Companies of Women Dancers, Companies of Footmen ready to Dance; Bodies of *Jugglers* for a thousand several sorts of Tricks, such as *Legar-de-Main*, *Fencers*, *Puppet shows*, *&c.* and at a distance from them, Companies of Players upon all sorts of Instruments. The right *Chatirs* or Footmen, know how to Dance or Vault, especially those of the Great Men, and they make them Dance for their Diversion; for in the *East*, Dancing is reckon'd Dishonest, or if you will, Infamous; and there are none but the Publick Women who Dance. Hereupon I remember, that in the Minority of the King of *France*, there came a *Persian* to *Paris*, whom the King of *Persia* had sent into *Europe* with a *French* Merchant, settled at *Ispahan*, to sell Silks, and bring from thence some curious Merchandizes of *Europe*. They show'd Every thing to the *Persian*, who did not understand a Word of any *European* Language. They brought him amongst other Places, to a Ball where the King Danc'd; and when His Majesty Danc'd, they bid him take Notice of Him: And they afterwards asked him, whether or no the King did not Dance well? *By the Name of God*, replied he, *He is an excellent Chatir*.

¶ In this manner the Grand Place was disposed and set out. The Streets through which he that Runs must pass, which for the greatest part were cover'd Markets, were likewise wonderfully set out; the Shops were spread with rich Stuffs, and some were set out with Arms like the great Room of an Arsenal, with a great many Colours intermix'd.

¶ The Way was water'd every time he that Run came to go by it, the Moment before he came, and they strewed it with Flowers. The Suburbs were spread with Pavillions, and the City likewise, to the turn where he fetch'd the Arrows. A Body of *Indians* to the number of two or three Thousand, were there in one Place. That of the like Number of *Armenians*, in another. The *Ignicoles*, or Worshippers of Fire, in one Place, the *Jews* in another; every Body as well plac'd as he could to please the King, who had desir'd it. At the Gates of the Greatest Lords who were in the way, were Tables covered with Perfume-Pots, Sweet-Waters, and Basons with Sweet-meats: In short, all the Way was as it were border'd with Instruments of *Musick*, with *Kettle-Drums* and *Trumpets*, who play'd in Companies, as soon as they perceived him who Run, was coming.

¶ He was in his Shirt with a single Roll of Cloth pretty thin, with a Silver Ground, which cover'd his Breech: He carried a Linnen Cloth in several Doubles folded upon his Stomach in a St. *Andrew*'s Cross, which kept his Breasts up very close, and was tied to his Waste: And he had another Linnen Cloth that went between his Legs well bound: His Arms, Legs, and Thighs, were rubed with an Ointment of a dark Yellow Colour made up with a mixture of *Oil of Roses* and an *Oil of Nutmegs* and *Cinamon*: He had Footmens Shoes on upon his bare Feet, which is a Shooing peculiar to them: And though he had no Stockings on, as I have said, he had Garters. In short, he had a Cap upon his Head which came almost to the bottom of his Ears, adorn'd with three or four little Feathers, as light as Wind. Upon his Bonnet, Neck, Arms, and upon his Stomach, you see *Amuletts*, hung as I have been representing to you but just now.

¶ In this Manner the Footman was fitted out. He always run his Course with a great many in Company; sixteen or twenty Footmen belonging to great Lords, run on Foot before him, and by his Sides, at the Rate he went at, relieving one another. They were preceded by a Number of Gentlemen, five and twenty, or thirty in Number, among whom there were moreover, some of the greatest Lords, who run two hundred Spaces before, more out of State, than to make Way. A Courier on Purpose, nam'd by the King, follows him each Course, to be a Witness of it. They refresh his Face at every Turn, with sweet Waters, and they throw some all along upon his Thighs, Arms, and Legs, to refresh them. They continually Fan him, both behind and on his Sides; and all that with so much Dexterity and Nimbleness, tho' the Way was always cover'd with People, both Foot and Horse; there is never any Body before him. Every one resounded his Praises, and made a thousand Vows for him, calling upon God, and imploring the Saints with Cries, that rent the Air; and the great Lords, who met him in his Course, promis'd him Wealth and Honours, by which his Swiftness, Courage, and Strength were Animated. He could not do it, but from being Spirited, and rais'd to a degree of Inchantment, by the agreeable Noise that is made about him.

¶ I forgot to tell you, that upon the Pillar that marks the End of his Course, and where the Arrows which he goes to fetch, are pass'd thro' a Scarf; there is a *Pavillion* built half as big as that which I have describ'd before the Gate of the Palace, which was Adorn'd after the same Manner, and furnish'd with several Entertainments. When he who runs, goes the first time before the Gate, he sets forward by leaping and capering, and moving his Arms, as if he had a mind to Fence, and show Postures. This was to put himself in Wind; he does this the first Course, without Resting, either going or coming; but in the other Courses, he stops a little to take Breath. When he enter'd the Tent where the Arrows were, two of the strongest Footmen took him by the Strength of their Arms, or main Force, set him down upon a Carpet, where during the Space of a *Pater*, or *Pater-Noster*, they put some *Sherbet*, or other Cordial to his Mouth, and hold *Perfumes* to his Nose; and at the same time another Footman, took an Arrow out of one of the King's Officer's Hands, and there put it thro' his Back. These Arrows are about a Foot long, and not thicker than a large Writing Quill, having a little sort of a Streamer at the End of it, like that which is put to the *Consecrated Bread*. The Foot-man perform'd his six first Courses in six Hours, for the others, he took a little more time. The greatest Lords of the Court, as I have said, all Accompanied him, one after the other in his Courses. *Cheic-Aly Can*, Governour of the most

important Province in *Persia*, and at that time, mightily in Favour, tho'
he was sixty eight Years of Age, rode six Courses with him, changing his
Horse so many times. The first Minister, almost as old as the other, rode
three Courses. The *Nazir*, or High Steward, a Lord of very near the same
Age, perform'd but two Courses, being call'd elsewhere, upon the King's
Service: But the better to make his Court to the King, he made his only
Son, a Youth of about two and twenty Years of Age, well made, and
charmingly handsom, perform the twelve Courses intire, he continu'd
running, without any Intermission, from four of the Clock in the Morning,
till six at Night, in the midst of all this hurly-burly, and terrible Noise,
and without any Refreshment, but a little *Cordial*. The King had order'd,
that twelve Principal Workmen belonging to the Palace, should run each
of them a Course with the Footman, which was accordingly done.
I follow'd him all the seventh Course, in which he began to slacken his
Pace, by Reason of the Heat of the Sun, and the Sand he pass'd; nevertheless he always put me to the Gallop. When he came into the Palace
Royal, there was such Hollowing, Shouting, Musick playing, and above
all, upon certain Kettle-Drums, carry'd upon Carts, which were bigger
than Tunns. I never heard such a Noise in all my Life: And I learnt
afterwards, that they heard it a League off. At the sixth Course, the King
came to the Door of the Tent, to see him who run, come in, and to encourage him. At the eighth Course, the Tent was serv'd with thirty
Basons of Massiff Gold, full of good Meat, to regale the Foot-men; and
at three in the Afternoon, the King appear'd at the Windows of the
Pavillions, which were upon the Place, before the great Gate, then began
all the Diversions which had been prepar'd for that Purpose, each before
him, without any Regard to the Spectators; the Beasts to Fight, the Men
and Women Dancers to Dance, each Company apart; the Rope-Dancers
to fly about, the Jugglers to play their Tricks, the Wrestlers to Engage.
This Confusion of Exercises and Sports, where one did not know which
to fix ones Eyes upon, was the most whimsical Sight in the World; but
every one almost was intent upon the Fighting of the wild Beasts, which is
one of the most ravishing Sights among the *Persians*: Among the rest, that
of the *Lion* or *Panther*, with the *Bulls*; and upon the Fight of the *Buffler*,
the *Rams*, *Wolfs*, and of the *Cocks*. These Horn'd Beasts don't Fight with
one another after equal Manner; for these *Bufflers* rush upon, and take
hold of one another's Horns; they push at one another and never quit,
till one or other is overcome, and fled out of the List: But the *Rams* rush
upon one another at ten or twelve Yards distance, and meet each other
with such a dreadful Shock, that one may hear the Stroak at fifty Yards

distance; after that, they retire quick, running backwards to about the same distance, when they return to the Charge, and run against one another again, and so on, till one or t'other be laid upon his Back, or that the Blood gush out of his Head: As for the *Wolfs*, they stand upon their Feet, and take hold of one another's Bodies: As this Beast is heavy, they must make him Angry before he will Fight; and they do it after this Manner, they tye him fast by one Foot to a long Cord or Rope, then they show him a Child, or little Boy in the Place, and they let him go at him; he runs hard at him, thinking to glut himself; but when he is just ready to throw himself upon the Child, they gather in the Cord, and draw him back, then they let go a little, upon which he warms, stands up upon his Feet, and roars, to which they stir him up, by irritating him, till he was grown as furious as they would have him. I say nothing here concerning the Fights of the wild Beasts, because I shall have Occasion to mention them elsewhere. To conclude this Relation of the Feast of the *Chatir*, I shall say, that the King gets on Horseback at Five a-Clock, and going before him, he meets him again at the Gate of the Suburbs: When he understood the King came, he took a little Child, which he found in a Shop, and put it upon his Shoulders, to let him see that he was not Spent; and this redoubl'd their Shouts and Acclamations of Joy. The King call'd to him as he was going by, and told him, he would give him the *Calaat*, or *Royal Garment*, from Head to Foot, 500 *Tomans*, which is 22000, 500 *Livres*, and make him Chief or Head of the *Chatirs*, which is a considerable Trust, in respect to the Income. All the Grandees sent him likewise Presents. Yet it was said that he had not run well, because he had not brought the twelve Arrows in twelve Hours, but had taken near fourteen to do it in. They say that a Foot-man in the Reign of *Chasefy*, did it in that Time. It is a fine Foot-Course, to run six and thirty Leagues in twelve Hours.

CHAPTER XIII

OF THE CLOATHS, AND HOUSEHOLD-GOODS

THE Cloaths of the *Eastern* People are no wise subject to Mode; they are always made after the same Fashion, and if the Wisdom of one Nation appears in a constant Custom for their Dress, as has been said, the *Persians* ought to be mightily commended for their Prudence; for they never alter in their Dress, and they are no more addicted to change in their Colour; their Shadowings and Make of the

Stuffs. I have seen some Cloaths that *Tamerlain* wore, which they keep in the Treasury at *Ispahan*; they are cut just in the same Manner as those that are made at this time of Day, without the least difference.

⁋ I have plac'd on the side several Pictures of Men and Women, dress'd after the *Persian* Manner, to the End that you may have a more distinct and quick Idea of their Dress, than by a Description. The Men wear no Breeches, only a pair of Drawers lin'd, which hang down to their Ancles, but which have no Feet; they are not open before, but must be undone when they have occasion to make Water. You must take Notice, that the Men put themselves all in the same Posture with the Women, when they are doing the Works of Nature, and in that Posture they untie their Drawers, and pull 'em down, tho' but a little way, and after they have done their Occasions, they get up and tie 'em again. The Shirt is long, and covers their Knees, passing over their Drawers, instead of being put into them. It is open on the right Side, upon the Pap, to the Stomach, and on the Sides below, as ours are, having no Neck to it, only stitch'd as the Shifts of our Women are in *Europe*. The Women, who are rich, and sometimes the Men, new border the Neck of the Shirt or Shift, with an Embroidery of *Pearl*, about a Fingers breadth, upon solemn Occasions. Neither the Men, nor the Women in *Persia*, wear any thing at their Necks. The Men put a *Cotton* Wastcoat, which they fasten before, upon their Stomachs, and falls down to their Hams, and over it a Robe, which they call *Cabai*, as wide as a Woman's Petticoat, but very strait above, passing twice over the Stomach, and is fasten'd under their Arms, the first round under the left Arm, and the other which is uppermost, under the right Arm. This Gown is cut sloaping, in the Manner you see it in the Figure, which is on the Side. The Sleeves are narrow, but as they are much longer than they should be, they Plait 'em at the Top of the Arm, and button 'em at the Wrist. The Gentlemen likewise wear the *Cabai* after the *Georgian* Manner, which are not different from others, only that they are open upon the Stomach, with Buttons and Loops: Tho' this Wastcoat be very well fitted to the Back, yet they tie two or three Sashes upon it, folded double, about four Fingers wide, Rich and Genteel, which makes 'em a wide and strong Pocket, to put what they have in, with greater Security than in our Breeches Pockets. They put over the Robe a short, or close-bodied Coat, and without Sleeves, which they call *Courdy*; or a long one, and with Sleeves, which they call *Cadabi*, according to the Season. These close-bodied Coats are cut like the Robes, that is to say, they are wide at Bottom, and narrow at Top, like Bells; they are made of Cloth, or Gold Brocade, or a thick Sattin, and they daub them all over

Persian Costumes

with Gold or Silver-Lace, or Galloon, or they Embroider them; they are Furr'd, some with *Sable-Skins*, and others with the Skins of the Sheep of *Tartary*, and *Bactriana*, the Hair of which, is finer than that of the *Horses*, and of no longer Curl than the *Gold-Sand*. There is no better *Fur*, nor warmer than those *Sheep-Skins*. The close-bodied *Fur-Coats* have a Facing of the same *Fur*, that is in the inside, which comes from the Neck to the Breast, like a *Tippet*; and next to it, underneath, there is a row of Buttons, quite down, which are more for Ornament than Service, for they seldom button their close-bodied Coats. The Stockins are of *Cloth*, and all of a Piece, as I have said, that is, they are cut like a Sack, and not according to the Shape of the Leg; they come but just up to the Knees, below which they tie them; they put a Piece of red Leather, very well stitch'd, to the Heel of them, to hinder the Heel of the Shoe, which is sharp, from doing it any harm, and piercing thro', which it would do in three or four Days time. It is only since the *Persians* traded with the *Europeans*, as well by the Means of their *Armenian* Subjects, as of the *European* Companies, that they have worn *Cloth-Stockins* in *Persia*. No body wore them before that time; and the King himself covered his Legs, as the Soldiers, Carriers, Foot-men, Country People, and abundance of the common People do to this very Day, by wrapping a coarse *Linnen Cloth* round their Legs, about six Fingers wide, and about three or four Ells long, just as if they were swadling a Child. This way of covering their Legs and Feet is very commodious and proper for Servants; they make them light or thick, according to the Season of the Year: It keeps the Leg tight, and when it is wet or dirty, they dry or clean it in a Moment. In the Winter time, they wrap the Feet round as well as the Legs; and in the Summer, they put their Shoes on their Feet Naked. The Shoes are of different Sorts or Fashions in *Persia*; but they are all without Ears, and not a bit open on the Sides; they are nail'd quite under the Heel, and they trim the Sole of the Shoe with little Nails, at the Place where the Bottom of the Foot bears, to make it last the longer. You see in the Figure the Fashion of the Shoes, which the People of Quality wear, which are made like the Womens Slippers, that they may throw them off the easier, when they are got into their Houses; because their Floors are cover'd with Carpets. These Shoes are of *Green Shagreen*, or some other Colours; the Sole, which is always a single one, is as thin as a Past-board, but it is the best Leather in the World. None but those sort of Shoes have Heels, the rest are flat. Some have Leather at Top, the others are of Cotton, knit as our Stockins are, but much stronger; they are exactly shod with these Shoes, which they call Shoes of a Foot-Boy, or Lackey; and the Foot never turns in them; but they cannot put them on without a strong Horn; from whence it is, that you always see a Lackey have one of Iron or Box at his Girdle. They climb and run to a Miracle, with those Shoes and Stockings on. The poor People make the Soles of their Shoes of *Camels* Leather, because it lasts much longer than any other; but it is a soft Leather, that takes in the Water like a Spunge. The *Peasants* make the Soles of their Shoes with Rags and Shreds of *Linnen Cloth*, threaded a breast, and very close. These Soles, tho' they are thick, yet are very light, and they can never wear them out; they call them *Pabouch Quive, i. e.* Shoes made of Rags.

¶ The *Persian Turban*, which they call *Dulbend*, that is to say, a Band that goes round, and which is the finest part of their Dress, is a Piece so heavy, that it is a Wonder how they wear it; there are of them so heavy, as to weigh twelve or fifteen Pound; the lightest of them weigh half as much. I had much ado at first to wear this *Turban*; I sunk under the Weight, and I pull'd it off, in all Places where I durst take that Liberty; for it is look'd upon in *Persia* to be the same thing as with us in *Europe*, to pull of one's *Peruke*: But by Accustoming my self to it, I came in time to wear it very well.

¶ These *Turbans* are made of coarse white Cloth, which they use to shape it, and they cover it with a fine rich Silk Stuff, or of Silk and Gold. These Stuffs of the *Turban*, have the Ends richly Woven with Flowers, and about six or seven Inches in breadth, which they tie in a Knot, in the middle of the *Turban*, like a Plume of Feathers, as you see in the Figure, which I have given you. Tho' this Dress for the Head is so heavy, they wear nevertheless under the *Turban*, a *Chalot*, or Leather Cap, stuff'd with Cotton, and stitch'd, and sometimes a Cloth one. You must believe that the Climate of *Persia* requires that one's Head should be very well cover'd; for there is nothing, generally speaking, practis'd in any Place, but there is a very good and proper Reason to be given for it; The constant and perpetual Custom is not a bit the Effect of this Odness and Caprice; the Climate, if I may so say, is certainly the Inventer of it, as well as the Cause of all which we see is peculiar in the Carriage of the People, and perhaps, even in their Manners, which I shall not fail to observe. They cover in *Persia*, generally speaking, the Stomach more than the Back, yet it is quite otherwise in the *Indies*, where they cover the Back most, and particularly the Nape of the Neck.

¶ The Stuffs they make their Cloaths of are Silk and Cotton; the Shirts and Drawers are of Silk; the Vests and Robes are lined with a thin Cloth, and stuffed with Cotton between to make them the warmer; the Lining also must be coarse and thin, like a Buckram, that the Cotton may keep and stick to it the better.

¶ They wear no Black in the *East*, especially in *Persia*; this is an unlucky and odious Colour, which they cannot regard; they call it the Devil's Colour: They Dress indifferently in all Colours at all Ages; and it is a very diverting Sight, to see when one walks out, or in the publick Places, a vast number of People, all in Party-colours, clothed in Stuffs glittering with the Gold, the Lustre, and Vivacity of the Colours.

¶ The *Persians*, for the most part, let the Beard grow on the Chin, and all over the Face, but short, and which only covers the Skin; but the Ecclesiasticks and Devots wear it longer: Their Rule is to take the Chin in their Hand, and cut off that which is below it. The Soldiers likewise are excepted, and the old Cavaliers, who wear no other Beard but two great and thick Whiskers, which they suffer to grow to such a length that they can tuck it behind their Ears, and keep it there like a Crotchet. *Abas* the Great, call'd Whiskers the Ornament of the Face, and gave more or less Pay to the Soldiers according to the length of their Whiskers. As for the long Beards which they wear in *Turky*, they are held in Abhorrence by the *Persians*, they call them Brooms for a Privy, or House of Office. In this manner the *Persian* Habit is made, which seems to be the same with that, which, as it is said, *Cyrus* gave to the *Persians*, consisting in long Robes and a Turban.

¶ The Habit of the Women resembles, in a great many things that of the Men; the *Drawers* fall in the same manner down to their Ancles, but the Legs of them are straiter, longer, and thicker, because the Women wear no Stockings. They cover their Feet with a Buskin, which reaches four Fingers above the Ancle, and which is either Embroider'd or of the richest Stuff. The Shift which they call *Comis*, from whence, perhaps, the Word *Chemise* or Shift comes, is open before down to the Navel: Their Vests are longer, and hang almost down upon their Heels: Their Girdle is small, and not above an Inch wide: Their Head is very well cloath'd, and over it they have a Vail that falls down to their Shoulders, and covers their Neck and Bosom before. When they go out, they put over all, a great white Vail, which covers them from Head to Foot, not suffering any thing to appear, in several Countries, but the Balls of their Eyes. The Women wear four Vails in all; two of which they wear at Home, and two more when they go Abroad. The first of these Vails is made like a Kerchief, falling down behind the Body, by way of Ornament: The second passes under the Chin, and covers the Bosom: The third, is the White Vail, which covers all the Body: And the fourth is a sort of Handkerchief, which goes over the Face, and is fasten'd to the Temples. This Handkerchief or Vail, has a sort of Net-work, like old Point, or Lace, for them to see through. The *Armenians*, contrary to the *Mahometans*, have even at home, their Faces vail'd down to their Nose, if they are Marry'd. This is that their nearest Relations, nor their Priests, who have the Liberty to Visit them, may only see part of their Face: But their Daughters don't wear this Vail but just to their Mouth, for the quite contrary Reason, which is, that they may see enough to make a Judgment of their Beauty, and make a Report of it. The Custom of these Vails for the Women, is the most ancient of any thing which their Histories speak of: But it is difficult to know, whether it was Pride, Vain-glory, or Modesty, which induc'd them to wear 'em first; or whether it was the Jealousy of their Husbands. Neither the Women nor Men wear Gloves; they don't know what it is to put on Gloves in the *East*.

¶ The Head-dress of the Women is plain; their Hair is all drawn behind the Head, and put in a great many Wefts; and the Beauty of that Head-dress consists in having those Wefts thick, and falling down to their Heels; and if the Hair be not long enough, they tie Wefts of Silk to lengthen them: They trim the Ends of these Wefts with Pearls, and a Knot of Jewels, or Ornaments of Gold and Silver. The Head is no otherwise dress'd under the Vail or Kerchief, but from the End of a Fillet, cut or hollow'd Triangularwise; and this is the Point that covers the Head, being kept upon the top of the Fore-head by a little Fillet, or String about an Inch broad. This Head-band or Fillet, which is made of several Colours, is small and light: The little Fillet is Embroider'd, in Imitation of Needle-work, or cover'd with Jewels, according to the Quality of the People. This is, in my Opinion, the ancient *Tiara* or Diadem of the Queens of *Persia*; none but the Married Women wear them; and this is a Mark whereby they are known to be under Authority. The Girls have little Caps instead of the Kerchief, or the *Tiara*.

¶ They wear no Vail in the House, but they cause Two tresses of their Hair to hang down upon their Cheeks. The Cap of young Women of Condition, is fasten'd with a Stay of Pearls. They don't shut up the young Women in *Persia*, till they are six or seven Years of Age; and before they come to that Age, they go out of the *Seraglio* sometimes with their Father, insomuch that one may see them. I have seen some of them prodigiously Handsom; one may see their Neck and Breast, than which nothing in Nature can be finer. The *Persian* Dress gives one the Liberty of seeing much more of the Waste than ours does.

¶ Black Hair is most in Esteem with the *Persians*, as well the Hair of the Head, as the Eye-brows and Beard: The thickest and largest Eye-brows are accounted the finest, especially when they are so large that they touch each other. The *Arabian* Women have the finest Eye-brows of this kind. Those of the *Persian* Women, who have not Hair of that Colour, dye and rub it over with Black to improve it: They make themselves likewise a black Patch or Lozenge, not so big as the Nail of one's little Finger, a little under the Eye-brows; and in the dimple of the Chin another little Purple one; but this never stirs, being made with the point of a Lancet. They likewise generally anoint their Hands and Feet with that Orange-colour'd Pomatom, which they call *Hanna*, which is made with the Seed or Leaves of *Woad* or *Pastel*, ground, as I have describ'd it above, and which they make use of to preserve the Skin against the heat of the Weather. Observe likewise, that among the Women, the smallest Wastes are the most esteem'd.

¶ The Ornaments of the *Persian* Women are very different; they dress their Head with Plumes of Jewels pass'd into the Fillet of the Fore-head; or with knots of Flowers instead of them: They fasten a Crotchet of Precious-Stones to the Fillet, which hangs down between their Eye-brows; a row of Pearl, which is fasten'd to the Top of the Ears, and goes under the Chin. The Women in several Provinces have a Ring pass'd through their Nostril, which hangs like an Ear-ring. This Ring is thin, and big enough to be put upon the middle Finger, and at the Bottom there are two round Pearls, and a round Ruby, between, set in it. The Women Slaves particularly, or those who are born Slaves, almost all wear these Rings; and they are so large in some Countries, that you may wear them upon your Thumb: But at *Ispahan* the Natural *Persians* don't bore their Nose at all. The Women of *Caramenia Desarta* do worse, they bore their Nose at the Top, and put a Ring through there, to which they fasten an inlay of Jewels, which covers all one side of their Nose. I have seen a great many dress'd in this manner at *Lar*, the chief City of that Province, and at *Ormus*. Besides the Jewels which the *Persian* Ladies wear at their Head, they wear Bracelets of Jewels, of the bigness of two, and almost three Fingers, and very loose round the Arm. The People of Quality wear Rows of Pearl: The young Girls have nothing commonly but little Manacles of Gold, about the thickness of a tagg'd Point, with a Precious Stone, at the Place where it shuts. Some of 'em likewise wear Fetters made like these Manacles, but that is not usual. Their Necklaces are either Chains of Gold or Pearl, which they hang to their Neck, and which fall below the Bosom, to which is fasten'd a large Box of Sweets. There are of these Boxes as big as one's Hand, the common ones are of Gold, the others are cover'd with Jewels; and all of them are bor'd through, fill'd with a black Paste very light, made of *Musk* and *Amber*, but of a very strong Smell. One lives and is reviv'd with Perfumes in the *East*, instead of being incommoded by them, as we are in these cold Countries. As for Rings, there is no People in the World wear so many as the Women in *Persia:* And to say it at once, they have their Fingers loaded with them.

¶ One may Dress after the *Persian* manner very reasonably, both Men and Women, yet there is not a Country where Luxury and Shew abound more in the Men as well as the Women: For what relates to the Men's Dress, a Right *Turban* can't be bought under fifty Crowns; the finest cost twelve or fifteen hundred Livres; and to be well dress'd, one must buy those of three or four hundred *Francs* or *Livres* a-piece. They wear 'em, it's true, a long time, but then they must have several for change: Besides, it is customary, every *New-Years Day*, to new Cloath throughout; and when their Relations marry, one may buy Robes handsome enough for twenty or five and twenty Crowns; but they change every Day: The People of Quality seldom wear one two Days together; and if there fall but the least drop upon it, let it be what it will, it is in their Opinion, a spoil'd Robe; another must be put on immediately: Their Sashes likewise cost very dear; they wear Brocaded ones, from twenty to an hundred Crowns Value, and one of Camel's Hair over it; The Workmanship of which is so fine and curious, that it costs almost as much: And if one will wear Sable, there is still another Reckoning to be made; for one can't have a handsome close-body'd Coat under three thousand Livres, and the finest under as much again. An Officer, whose Pay does not amount to above twelve or fifteen hundred Livres, puts on a new Dress which shall cost him more. This Luxury of the *Persians* is the Cause of their Ruin as much as any thing else; for though their Cloaths last a long time, yet they cost them abundance of Money at first. The Men of the Sword wear a Sword and Dagger by their Side, as well as every Body belonging to the Court; but the Ecclesiasticks, the Men of Letters and Lawyers, the Merchants and the Handycrafts wear none. The Princesses of the Blood-Royal have the Priviledge to wear a Dagger. They don't at all suppress this Luxury in *Persia*, but quite the contrary; they generally excite and encourage it. The *Persians* have a common Proverb, *Corbat Balabas*, Honour is according to the Habit.

¶ I come now to the Household-Goods, which are nothing near so expensive as they are with us in the *West*. The Floors are first of all cover'd with a great thick Felt, with a fine Carpet upon it, or two, according to the bigness of the Room. There are of their Carpets, that are three-score Foot long, and which two Men can't carry. Upon these Carpets, against the Wall, they spread quite round the Room Mattresses or Quilts, about three Foot wide, which they cover at Top with Coverlets, that are no thicker than a *Spanish* Cloth, made of Callicoe, stitch'd with white or colour'd Silk, or stitch'd with Gold, which cover the Mattresses, with a new Border of a Foot, or a little more; upon them are rang'd in Order all along the Wall large Cushions, to lean against. They put at the End of these fine Coverlets, which are the Beds of the Ancients, large Spitting-Boxes of Silver, at proper Distances, which serve likewise to keep them smooth by their Weight. These are the Chairs of the *East*, in a manner speaking, and whereon they sit, and when one has once cover'd a Room in this Manner, it lasts a Man's Life; for these Cushions are of good Velvet, or thick Brocade, and never wear as those who use the *Persian* Stuffs, in our Country can sufficiently testify; tho' our Air of *Europe* changes and destroys things more than that of *Persia*, beyond Comparison. They put no other Houshold Goods in the Rooms and Chambers of the *Persians*; no Beds nor Chairs as we have, no Looking-Glasses, no Tables nor Stands, no Cabinets nor Pictures. The *Persians* sit easier upon the Carpets than we do upon our Seats, at least, I was so well Accustom'd to 'em there, that I thought my self not half so easy in a Chair, and that it was of no use to me: In effect you see, that all the bottom of the Body is rested upon those Seats of the *Persians*; and the Legs as well as the Thighs; whereas, in our Chairs, the Legs are quite standing. That Posture likewise keeps one much warmer in cold Weather; but one must not for all this, try that Experiment with us; for the Moisture of our Air, which penetrates every thing, would prejudice our Legs and Thighs, when we sit thus upon the Ground. I have several times put my Hand under these Felts of the Chambers at *Ispahan*, and elsewhere, which are laid upon the Ground without any Floor, fancying that I must of necessity find the Ground damp, but I always found it very dry. If one should cover the Ground thus with Carpets in *Europe*, one should find them rotten at the Year's End, in most of the Countries.

¶ For the Beds which they lie upon, they are plain, like their other Moveables: They consist of Mattresses or Quilts, which they spread at Night upon the Carpet in the Chamber, and a Sheet which they spread over it, and a Coverlet stuff'd with Cotton, to cover them withal, and two Down Pillows. The fine Mattresses are of Velvet, and the Coverlets are of Brocaded Silk, or of Gold and Silver, of all Colours. In the Morning, they fold up every thing in a large Toilet of Tabby, which they put in the Wardrobe; these are the Beds of the *Eastern* People. They know nothing of Beds rais'd and built upon four Posts. They are Accustom'd to lie thus

upon the Ground; the goodness of the Air making them dispence with Bedsteads and Curtains, which are absolutely necessary in moist Countries. I can't help recounting again the Happiness these People enjoy, who live in a Climate that stands in need of so few things, in Comparison of ours; for the present Occasions being the Springs and Sources of Troubles which we endure, and the Occasion in like Manner of Vices and Passions, that disorder us. It is a great Happiness to live in a Country where these Wants are neither so many, nor so pressing.

¶ I have observ'd elsewhere, how they light their Houses, in which they seldom use Candles, but Lamps, in which they burn instead of Oil, clean Tallow, pure and fine, like Wax, and which does not smell a bit. They use sometimes Wax-Candles, and among others, those that are scented, which are of Wax, work'd up or needed with Oil of *Cinamon* or *Cloves*, or some other Aromatick.

CHAPTER XIV

OF THE LUXURY OF THE PERSIANS

THE Luxury or Profuseness of the *Persians* is particularly Remarkable in the Number of their Servants. It is true they have a great many more in the *Indies* than in *Persia*; but ten Servants in the *Indies* don't stand their Master in as much as three Servants do theirs in *Persia*. The great Lords have Domesticks in every Degree that the King has, and with the same Titles. This Crowd of Servants has been the Ruin of the Houses, for having most of them Wives, and their Wages, how great soever, not being sufficient to maintain their Families, they are forc'd to Cheat and Rob their Master.

¶ The Luxury of the *Persians* consists likewise in their Cloaths, Jewels, and Furniture of their Houses. I have spoken of the sumptuousness of their Dress: As to their Jewels, the Men wear abundance upon their Fingers, and almost as many as their Wives; you will see them sometimes with fifteen or sixteen Rings upon their Fingers, five or six upon one Finger only; yet they wear 'em but upon the three Fingers from the middle one. The Rings of the Men are set in Silver, with a very thin Hoop: This is to the end they may say their Prayers without pulling them off; for they find it is not decent to pray to God with so many Ornaments of Gold on, because they ought to present themselves before God in an humble and poor Condition, the better to move his Compassion, and draw down his

Blessings: In this manner they explain themselves; and they look upon themselves to be in that State when they have no Gold about them, tho' they have Jewels, which is however a most ridiculous Superstition. The sensible People likewise, who can't chime in with this Distinction, lay aside their Rings, and all their other Ornaments, when they would say their Prayers. The Women are not so Superstitious, for all the Rings which they wear are made of Gold. Besides the Rings which the Men wear upon their Fingers, the People who are Rich, wear a parcel of seven or eight Rings, and more, in their Bosoms, tied to a String which is round their Neck, to which their Seals are fasten'd, and a little Purse. All this goes together into their Bosom between their Vest and their Robe, and they pull it out when they would Sign any Writing, or divert themselves with the Sight, in looking upon their Jewels, or in shewing 'em to People: For they make a great shew with their Jewels, as the Women in our Country do with their Seals and little Jewels, which they hang at their Side with their Watches. The *Persians* wear, besides all that, Jewels at their Weapons, as at their Dagger and their Sword, which are Cover'd with them, if they have wherewithal, or else they are of Gold Enameled, as is likewise the Belt and Clasps. The Dagger goes into their Sash, and they tie it there with a String, putting a round of Jewels at the Place where the Knot is, which they call the *Rose of the Dagger*. Next, they wear Jewels upon their Head at their Caps of the *Sophy*, which they put on upon the Days of solemn Festivals. There are of these Caps which have five or six Plumes of Jewels in them, as you have seen in the fore-going Figures. No Body can put 'em upon a *Turban* but the King, excepting new-married People, who have the Liberty to wear them as long as their Wedding holds. After having talk'd so much of Jewels, I shall observe that the *Persians* have a particular Value for the colour'd Stones, and much more than they have in the *West*; which may proceed perhaps, from hence, that the thickness of our Air hinders them from having that Lustre, which they have in hot and dry Countries, as in *Persia*.

¶ The Trappings of the People of Condition, are either of Silver, Gold, or precious Stones; some of them fasten upon the Leather of their Trappings, instead of Goldsmiths Work, Gold Ducats all along, to avoid paying the Fashion. Their Saddles are enrich'd with Massif Gold before and behind: The Pad of the Saddle, which is not fasten'd to the Saddle, as it is with us, and borders five or six Inches upon the Horses Buttocks, like a little Housing, is Embroider'd; and some have them Embroider'd with Pearls. They put, besides all this, either for Show, or to preserve the Beast from Cold, a rich Housing, which hangs much lower down than ours.

¶ The great Profuseness of the *Persians* is in their *Seraglio*'s, which costs them a vast deal of Money, as well from the Number of Women which they entertain there, as from the Profuseness occasioned by their Love. Rich Cloaths are continually renewing there, Perfumes consum'd in abundance; and the Women being thus rais'd and entertain'd after the softest and most voluptuous manner, contrive all they can to procure those things which they delight in without considering the Expence.

¶ When a Man of Quality makes a Visit, he causes one or two léd Horses to go before, each led by a Servant on Horse-back; two, three, or four Footmen, more or less, according to his Condition, run before his Horse, and by his Side. There is moreover a Man behind him on Horse-back, who carries his bottle of Tobacco, another who carries an embroidered Toilet, wherein there is generally a close-body'd Coat and a Cap: And another Man who goes as a Companion: If he goes to walk abroad, he carries another Servant on Horse-back, with a *Yactan*, which are two little square Chests, wherein are put what will serve to make a light Collation, with a Carpet over it: When he stops in any Place, whether in a Garden, or by the Water-side, or any other Place, they spread a Carpet, upon which he sits and falls to smoking. If this Man of Quality goes a Hunting, a Falconer or two on Horse-back likewise, with the Hawk upon the Fist, join themselves to this Retinue; and in this manner the People of Quality in *Persia* go.

CHAPTER XV

CONCERNING THE FOOD OF THE PERSIANS

BEFORE I treat of the manner in which the *Persians* feed, I fancy my Reader would gladly know what the Eating and Drinking of all the *Asiaticks* in general is.

¶ I shall *First* observe, That the *Asiaticks* are nothing near so great Eaters as the *Europeans*. We are Wolves and Voracious Beasts, when compar'd with them: I don't attribute the Cause intirely to their Sobriety, in taking that to be the Virtue that subdues the Gluttony, there are much stronger Reasons to be given; for, *First* of all, they live in much hotter Climates than we do. *Secondly,* That their Climes have not the Nutriment, that is to say, neither the Variety nor Plenty of ours. In the *Third* Place, That they do not use bodily Exercise as much as we do, such as Walking, Dancing, Tennis, &c. they are as Sedentary as Recluses in comparison of us. A *Fourth* Reason is, The continual use of Tobacco, which yet damps the Stomach a great deal more, as every one knows, and they never have the Pipe from their Mouth. *Fifthly*, That Wine and strong Liquors likewise, that provoke the Appetite, are forbid them. A *Sixth* is, The immoderate use of *Opium*, and several sorts of cold and soporiferous Drinks. These and other such-like Reasons, are the Causes of this Temperance of the Eastern People. We often attribute this Custom to the Virtue of People, which, in Effect, proceeds from no other Cause but the Temper of the Clime.

¶ The *Turks*, the *Persians*, and generally speaking, all the People of *Asia*, who are *Mahometans*, to the farthest part of the *Indies*, eat of all sorts of Beasts which their Religion has not declar'd Impure, without any difference between one Country and another, than this, that the Climates breed more or less according to their Temper: The *Turks*, for Example, who dwell in a Country that is not so warm and more proper for Pasture, eat more Flesh, and are likewise accustomed to their *Chiorbas*, which are Soops of Grain and Roots, as we do with us: The *Persians* on the contrary, who inhabit a hotter Climate, and less Plentiful, I speak in General, use Fruit, Milk-meats, and Sweet-meats mightily.

¶ That which I say with Relation to these *Asiaticks* eating of all sorts of Lawful Beasts, must be understood of those which they can and do eat sometimes; for it is certain they are not admirers of Fish nor Wild-Fowl, nor Beef, nor Veal; I always speak in General. Their usual Food is *Mutton*, *Lamb*, *Kid*, and *Hens*; these are what they chiefly Value, and particularly the *Persians*, who commonly eat of 'em both Rich and Poor, and are what they like, and dress the best.

¶ The *Turks* make three Meals a Day, and all upon things that are Dress'd and Hot. The *Persians* make but two; for a Dish or two of Coffee, with a bit of Bread, very early in the Morning, is not look'd upon to be a Meal. The Reason for this difference, proceeds from nothing but the Climate, as I have said. The Cold in *Turky* locking up, as it were, the Natural Heat within, creates a better Stomach, and makes one eat more there; from whence it comes that the *Turks* eat more nourishing Meat, and in greater abundance: Besides that upon the same account of the Climate, the *Turks* use more Action, and employ themselves in more sorts of Exercises, whether on Foot or Horse-back. It is not the same thing with the *Persians*, the Heat and Drought of their Air benumbing their Bodies, and consequently is less nourishing to them.

¶ I have said that the *Persians* make but two Meals: The *First* is of *Fruits*, *Milks*, and *Sweet-meats:* They have *Melons* all the Year round, and *Grapes* eight Months of the Year: They are never without Cheese, Curds, Cream, and Sweet-meats, this is generally their Mess at Dinner, which is between the Hours of Ten and Twelve, except upon their Feast-Days, upon which they dress Meat. They Sup upon Soops made of Fruit and Herbs, Roast-meat, upon Meat bak'd in an Oven or Stove, upon Eggs, Roots, and Pilo, which is equally their most delicious Food, and Daily-Bread.

¶ As to their Manner of Cooking and getting ready, they cannot be enough commended for it, it being very plain. Regousts, Cocks-combs, Sweet-breads, &c. Sallets Pickl'd, and Salt-Meats, are Strangers to their Tables. They use nothing to whet their Appetites, but some Slices of Lemon, and a few strong Herbs, of which they put a little before every one, with a Radish or two; they are very moderate likewise in dressing of their Meats; they use no beaten Pepper, little Salt, little or no Garlick, in a Word, little or nothing of what we are so greedy of among us, and which we are so Prodigal of to provoke the Appetite. You shall never see 'em Pound their Pepper, nor other Spices; they say, that in Powder they are not wholsome; and they put them whole into their Meats, that they may have the Taste only, and not the Substance, which they look upon to be hard of Digestion.

¶ To speak now of the Service at Table; they are serv'd all at once, and it is the same thing with Respect even to the King's own Table. Whatever Entertainments they have, and of whatsoever Country their Guests are, the Meal does not last above half an Hour. I have admired at the Even-ness of their Tastes in eating: You will never hear any one complain of the Meats being too high, or too little Season'd; of it's sowerness, or sweet-ness of the Spice; of its being over or under done; they bring neither Pepper, Salt, Oil, nor Vinegar to Table; every one has a plain Taste, and loves the same Things; thus they live. I leave it to grave and wise Peoples Opinions, whether that plain and Temperate Food ought to yield or be preferr'd to that of *Europe*, where there is so great Variety and Profuseness.

¶ The *Eastern Christians*, dispers'd among the *Turks* and *Persians*, don't live altogether as they do, they being for the most Part lovers of wild Foul, Fish, Ragousts, and black Meats, whether it proceeds from the Wine and strong Waters which they drink often to Excess, whether from the severe and frequent Fasts, which they keep out of Custom, makes 'em greedy and Gluttons; or whether they get their daintiness in *Europe*, where they make long stays, by the Use of our Ragousts, and other Table Dishes.

¶ In the *Indies*, as up to *China* and *Ispahan*, whether in the Islands, or the Terra-firma, the Religions divide People in their Food, as well as in their Belief, and Worship; for all the Gentiles, generally Speaking, eat nothing that has had life, or could have had life, that has Seed or Leaven;

I say, generally speaking; for there are some Tribes or Sects, the *Portuguese* call them *Castes*, who are allow'd to eat any sort of Flesh. As for the *Indian Mahometans*, they eat Meat, but much less than elsewhere, upon Account of the Climate, as I have said. Kid and Hens are their ordinary Food, because they have less Blood, and digest better. Roots, Grain, Grapes and Herbs, are what they commonly eat. They correct the Crudities with Butter, which they mix with every thing, and from which they draw their best Substance, as well as the *Gentiles*.

¶ *India*, consider it throughout, is certainly one of the most Fruitful Countries in the World, abounding as much in large Cattel, Corn and Butter, as it is Barren, with Respect to Wild-Foul, Fish, and Fruit.

¶ Rice is the most common and best Esteem'd Food of all *Asia*, and is to be met with every where throughout the *East*. As it is light and cooling, they prefer it to Bread, and it even serves for Bread, in the most *Southern* Countries, where a good many People use it as their only Food. Rice is likewise very good in Illnesses. *Mathiole*, and other learned *European* Naturalists, have acknowledg'd all that I have said of this excellent Grain. They dress it a great many Ways, which I shall reduce to three. The *First*, is to boil the Rice in Water, without any other Seasoning, and then they dissolve it in boiling to make Broth for sick People, or they bake it dry, in using it for Bread. The *Second* way, is to make Soops with it, with Roots, Milk, or Meat. The *Third*, is to make *Pilo*, or *Kichery*, those exquisite Foods, so cry'd up by the *Eastern* People. I shall speak by and by, concerning the Manner of their dressing, this *Pilo*, and these rich Soops: I shall only speak here of the first way of dressing, and how it is done in the several Parts of the *Indies*, where it is most us'd.

¶ But you must observe beforehand, that the Rice of *Asia* is tenderer and more easie to boil, in Proportion as the Country where it grows is more or less *Southerly*. In the *Indies*, one Boil is sufficient for the Rice, and even there where it is the hardest; they wash it well, in rubbing it with their Hands, they shake it, and put it into the Pot, where it is presently done; and even in a great many Places in the *Indies*, they have no Occasion of Water to dress it; they do nothing but put a wet Cloath upon the Pot, under the Cover. I have seen it drest in a *Bamboo*, this is a thick sweet Cane, hollow and hard, that grows in the *Indies*, and of which there are some as thick as one's Leg; they have a little thin Skin, or Rind in the inside, which is more solid and hard than the Wood. When the Fire has Penetrated to that, they take the *Bamboo* half burnt from off the Fire, and they take out the Rice well done. I relate these little particulars, because our *Italian* Rice is so hard, and that one has so much trouble in boiling it. When I came to enquire into the Reason of this difference in the dressing of the Rice, which being the same, could not however be drest equally as soon every where: I found out, that the Water was the main Article in dressing; the one penetrating and dissolving sooner than the other; as well as that the one softens this Grain in the boiling; whereas the other Waters sensibly harden it: I don't well comprehend the Reason, but for all that don't, dissallow the Thing, being convinc'd by Experience of the Difference there is, in the Staining of the Callicoes, and *China*-Ware, in those Countries, which are more or less Beautiful, according to the Water which they use: I shall thereupon say by way of Digression, that the best Stain'd Callicoes are made on the Side of *Coromandel*; but there is a palpable Difference, to those who are Skill'd in 'em between that which is made in one Village, and that of another, especially in the Liveliness, a Thing which is always attributed to the Water, that their Callicoes are dipp'd in, which according as it is more or less Muddy, Brackish, or has a smoaky black Steam, dulls or preserves the Brightness of the Colours, in spreading it upon the Bed, where it keeps the Colours as the Painter had laid them. They tell the same thing with Respect to *China*, who say for the very same Reason, that the beautiful Varnish of that precious Earth, proceeds from the different Qualities of the Water; for which Reason, they make it but in few Places of *China* and *Japan*; upon which, they have affirm'd to me a Thing remarkable enough: It is, that they don't make their *China* where they prepare their Earth, but upon those Places where there is Water proper to preserve the brightness of the Paint, or Stain: So that they prepare the Earth in one part of the Kingdom, and make the *China* in another, at a great Distance. They say, that there is but one Place in all *Japan*, where they are allow'd to bake *China*: And to the end that the Manufacture may not be made worse than it should be, they are not allow'd to light the Ovens when they bake it, nor to open them but before a Magistrate.

⁋ To return to the *Rice* boil'd in Water, they make use of Plates for that which they prepare dry in their small Bread like the Peal of a Pastry-Cook: The meaner sort of People use the hollow Dishes, where every one takes a handful: They look upon it to be thoroughly ready, when it is so well boil'd that it melts in the Mouth, and yet so dry that it will fall Corn by Corn and not bruise, and that one does not soil one's Fingers in taking hold of it. It is us'd for Bread in the most Southern parts of the *Indies*, as I have said; and among all the *Europeans* Indianiz'd, as at *Fort St. George*, *Batavia*, and particularly at *Goa*. I have found, by Experience, from the long Stay I made in the *East*, that according as one is habituated to the Air of the Country, one accustoms one's self also to the use of *Rice*, and grows out of conceit with Bread. *Rice* indeed is a most delicious and wholsome Food; it is light, cooling, of a sweet Taste, and Digests very soon, and without trouble: It creates little Blood, and little Excrement, and does not cause Vapours: All that is mighty good in thick and hot Climates, as the *Indies*, but elsewhere, and in ours, it would not answer the End, the Air of *Europe* requiring solid, poignant, and juicy Food, a thing which I must repeat over again; because in my Opinion, from a right Observation of the different Climates, one may form a better Judgment of the Food, Cloaths, and Lodging of the several People of the World, as also of their Customs, Sciences, and their Industry; and, if one have a mind to it, of the False Religions which they follow. That which I esteem most in the *Rice*, is the Quality it has of tempering and purifying the Blood: In Agues and several other Distempers, they pound it, and cause it to be boil'd in a great deal of Water, with which they make a Broth more or less liquid, as they have a mind to it. When they are upon the Recovery, they put some Sugar, Milk of Almonds, and a little Cinnamon in that Broth, which makes it very delicious and nourishing. There is nothing easier, sooner made, and more reasonable. I generally Supp'd upon a Porringer of that Broth, and I found it always agreed with me very well.

❡ There is a sort of Rice in the *Indies*, which the *Portuguese* value very much, and which they call the *Sweet Rice:* The Grain of this *Rice*, have, for the most part, one or two little red Streaks upon the Skin, and they give a stronger and more agreeable Smell than the Common *Rice*; but it is in those Streaks only that the Perfume lies. I brought some of it into *Europe*, as well beaten as unbeaten; but both the one and the other had equally lost its fine smell. The *Persians* call this *Rice, Rice of a good Smell*, or *Fine Rice*. The grain of the *Indian Rice* is almost half as small again as that of *Persia* and *Turky*, and they do not look upon it to be near so cooling. As for the Price, it does not cost above a Half-penny *per* Pound at *Bengall*, and on the Coast of *Malabar*, which are the Countries that abound in it most. At *Surat*, which is the other End of the *Indies*, the best *Rice* is sold at a Penny *per* Pound, and the common sort at eight *Deniers*, or two thirds of a Penny.

❡ I must add besides, that the goodness of the *Rice* does not discover itself in the Sight nor Smell of it; the Proof lies in the Dressing of it, and consists in these three Things, That it boils quick; that the Grain remains intire; and that it swells. The New *Rice* is not so much valu'd as the Old, because it does not smell at all, but it must not be kept too long; for by the time it is four Years old, it has lost its Flavour.

¶ Wheat Bread is us'd throughout almost all *Asia*. I have cross'd *Turky* three times by different ways, and in every Place where I have been, they have eat Bread; for I don't reckon the Coasts on the *Black Sea*, from the Lake *Mæotis*, till you come to *Georgia* in *Turky*, where the People live upon a sort of Mill, and where Bread corn and *Rice*, are very scarce; seeing that the *Turks* have not taken Possession of those Countries, contenting themselves with drawing Contributions from them, and to Ravage 'em from time to time, to keep them the more under subjection. There are several Places in *Persia* where they eat very little Bread; whether it is from the great plenty of *Rice* as there is all along the *Caspian Sea*, or from the scarcity of Bread-corn, as upon the Coasts of the Ocean; yet there is Bread to be found every where. There is likewise Bread throughout the *Indies*, tho' they eat a great deal less than they do in *Turky* and *Persia*, and the Corn either grows upon the Place, or is brought from the Neighbourhood, but infinitely less in Quantity than the *Rice*, it being much more sought after, and more healthy in hot Countries, and where the Air is heavy. The Isles upon the Eastern Ocean, and the main Land, near the Line, bear no Corn as I know of. *Madagascar*, which stretches it self on this side of the Tropick, has none neither: It comes in the Blade, but not in the Ear, the heat of the Sun, burning it up before it grows to Seed. These Countries, as well as all those that have a Scarcity, are furnish'd by Traffick: They lade at *Surat* for *Java* and *Sumatra*, and in several other Places. The *Hollanders* provide themselves there for *Batavia*. There is likewise very little Corn in *Africa*, unless where there are *European* Colonies settl'd; and generally speaking, there is but little between the two Tropicks. The great Countries live upon nothing but *Millet*, others upon *Rice*, others upon *Dates*, others upon *Cassave* only; as in *America*, through the Industry of the *Hollanders*, there grows very good Corn at the *Cape of Good Hope*. The Natives Till nothing, out of perfect Laziness and aversion to Work. These People, whom they call *Hotentots*, are the nastyest, slothfullest, and most brutish *Barbarians* that I ever saw in all my Travels. As for the rest, the *Mahometans*, and the *Gentiles* generally, make their Bread without Leaven, which their Religion forbids.

¶ As to their way of making Bread, I shall speak first of all concerning that of the *Gentiles*, which is very plain; for they not only bake their Bread every Day, but they bake it that very Moment they design to eat it. After having wash'd their Bodies all over, according to the Precepts of their Religion, they take the Flower in a Bason of Wood or Metal, they knead it and cover it; they then make a little Fire between three Stones, upon which they put a Plate of Iron as thin as a Five-penny Piece round, and

a Foot Diameter, more or less, according to the quantity of Bread that
is to be laid upon it: It is not above sixteen or eighteen Inches from the
Ground: When it is hot, which it is very soon, they take the Dough again,
make a little Cask very little thicker than the Plate of Iron, and of the
same size, and lay it upon it: It bakes while they are getting another
ready; and after it is bak'd they take it out, and lean it against the Stones,
the uppermost part towards the Fire, that it may bake a little more.
A Man in less than an Hour's time, kneads and bakes as much Bread as
will serve a dozen People; for while he is getting one Cask ready, he keeps
another upon the Plate, and another against the Fire, and so in order,
which makes very quick Work, and without a great many Implements,
as you see. This is the common *Indian* Bread, upon which they always
throw some strong Grain, or they rub it with their *Hing*, which is *Assa-
fœtida*, a thing they love extreamly. The Rich among 'em seldom eat any
thing but their butter'd and sugar'd Cakes.

¶ I never saw *Musk* or *Ambergrease* made use of in the common Food, in
any Country of *Asia* where I have been: The *Turks* put it in their fine
Sherbets, and particularly in that which they call *Sultani*, as much as to
say Royal. The *Persians* neither put it in their Meat nor Drink, but they
use abundance of it in several sorts of their Sweet-meats and Confections
which are made, the one only to fortify or strengthen, the other to stir
up Love, and which the People of Condition seldom fail eating of both
before and after Meals, especially when they visit and enjoy one another:
Hereupon I have observ'd how much they have consum'd of it in their
perfum'd Pastes, of which the Women carry large flat Boxes at their
Stomach, hung at the Neck to Chains of Gold or Jewels, according to
their Quality, which hold, one with another, near three Ounces of Paste,
for it is very heavy. The *Persian* Women are, for the most part, very
Prodigal in Perfumes: They still use less *Amber* and *Musk* in their Nourish-
ments, by reason of the great Heat; but Men and Women are profuse in
it, as in other Places, and even more, their Bodies being weaker than in
cold Countries, and requiring a greater support for the Pleasures of Love.
I remember, that being at the Solemnity of the Marriage of the three
Royal Princesses of *Colconda*, in the Year 1679, that the King their Father,
who had no other Children but them marry'd upon the same Day; he
gave Perfumes to all that were invited; at their coming, they threw it
upon those who had white Cloth on; but they gave it into the Hands of
those who were Cloth'd in Colours, otherwise they would have spoil'd
their Cloaths by throwing it upon them; which was done in this manner:
They threw a Bottle of Rose-water upon the Body which held about half

a Pint, and another larger Bottle of Water colour'd with Saffron, so that the Vest was stain'd with it: Then they rubb'd the Arms and Body over with a liquid Perfume of *Labdamum* and *Ambergrease*, and they put upon his neck, a large String of *Jessamin*. They have Perfum'd me in the same manner (*Saffron* excepted) in many great Houses of that Country, and elsewere. This manner of caressing and doing of Honour, is universal among the Women, who have wherewithal to provide this Profuseness. In *Persia* and the *Indies*, they keep their *Sherbets* clear and in Syrup, by Reason of the heat of the Air, which would dry them too much, and make 'em as hard as a Stone: But in *Turky* they keep them in Powder like Sugar: That of *Alexandria*, which is the most esteem'd throughout this large Empire, and which they transport from thence every where, is almost all in Powder. They keep it in Pots and Boxes; and when they would use it, they put a Spoonful of it into a large glass of Water. It mixes of itself with the Water, without being forc'd to stir it, as we do our Syrups, and makes a most admirable Liquor. They make up the *Sherbet* throughout the *East*, like a Sugar-loaf; I have seen Loaves as light in *Persia*, that they have weigh'd but twelve Ounces, which have been as thick as Sugar-loaves of eight Pounds. The Sister of the late King *Abas* the Second, and Aunt of *Soliman* the Thirteenth, since Reigning, a most Bountiful Princess, with whom I transacted abundance of Affairs for four Years together, as I have related elsewhere, sent me from time to time, Regales of Sweet-meats, where there was always of these *Sherbets* in the Loaf, which were exquisitely and wonderfully good, as well as Sweet-meats. I shall observe by the bye, that in *Persia*, *Turky*, and the *Indies*, the Better sort of People make their Sugar at Home as well as the *Sherbet* and Sweet-meats. The *Sherbets* are generally made of Violets, Vinegar, and the Juice of *Pomegranates*, and particularly of *Citron-Juice*. The Word *Sherbet* in the *East* is taken for a mixt Potion or Drink.

¶ The *Eastern* People have another *Sherbet* which is more common: This is to mix in the Water with a little Sugar, or a little Salt, the juice of *Citron*, or the *Pomegranate*, or the juice of *Garlick* or *Onion*. They call that sort of *Sherbet Truahi*, as much as to say, somewhat Sower. They serve 'em, at all Meals, in large *China* Ware, with Wooden Spoons hollow'd, with a long Handle to them. These Liquors serve to whet the Stomach, as well as to quench the Thirst: They take it by Spoonfuls all the time of their Meal; during which time, it is not customary to Drink.

¶ They have often ask'd me, whether the abstaining from Flesh, or not abstaining, makes any difference in point of long Life among those who live under the same Clime? To which I answer'd in a Word, No. The

Banjans, who never eat Flesh, live no longer than the other *Indians*; and I remark'd moreover, that generally speaking, they don't spin the Thread of Life so long in the *East*, and especially in the *Indies*, as they do in *Europe*; which I attribute to their making use of Women too soon, and too much, and using Provocatives, notwithstanding the Heat of the Climate, which is extreme, as Sweet-meats, &c. which waste them, as well as give them, Animal Spirits. But it is certain, that in return for that, those that abstain from Flesh, are less liable to Distempers than the others: The great Debauches in Meat and Drink are grievous to the *Indians* for the little while they last; and this is the Reason that the *English* live there so little a while, the excessive eating of Beef, and the extravagant use of Brandy, Sugar, and Dates, pulls 'em down in a little time. The variety of Meats likewise carries off abundance of *Europeans*, or makes them droop away much. The different Quality of the Juices of so many sorts of Food, making as it were a War in the Stomach, which that part weaken'd by the dissipation of the Spirits, is not able to bear. The Illness that carries them off most in the end in the Indies, proves to be what I say, for it is commonly a *Diarrhæa*, or a looseness of the Belly, which degenerates immediately into a Bloody-Flux; an illness so fatal that very few People get over it. But it must be remark'd besides, that if the Eastern People enjoy a more constant State of Health than we do, by abstaining from Flesh, it hinders them on the other Hand, from being so Strong and Vigorous.

¶ I come now again to my Subject, which relates to the Food of the *Persians:* They are not great Eaters, and some think it proceeds from their Country's not being fruitful, nor abounding in Food; but I am not of that Opinion: I believe on the contrary, that the want of Plenty in their Country, is because they have not the People as we have. If their Frugality proceeded from the Scarcity of their Country, rather than from their Nature, there would be none but the meaner sort of People who would eat but little, whereas, generally speaking, 'tis every one; and they would more or less, in each Province, according to the fruitfulness of the Country; whereas the same Temperance governs the whole Kingdom. They make two Meals a Day, as I have already observ'd, one of Fruit, Milk-meats, and Sweet-meats, between ten and twelve of the Clock in the Morning, which they call *Hazeri*, as who should say, That which is ready; because as it is ready in a Moment's time, one may say, it is always ready; and one of Meat about Seven a-Clock at Night. This is their Supper and Grand Meal. In the Morning when they get up, they have their Coffee; and some of 'em eat a little Crust of Bread with it. As their Days are not so unequal as ours, they keep up to the Rule of Life with more ease. They go to Bed between Nine and Ten of the Clock at Night, all the Year round, and get up by break of Day. They dress Meat twice a-Day for the King, because that one Part of the great Seralio makes its Grand Meal in the Morning; but no Body eats Meat but once a Day, whether Noon or Night. The *Persians* provide nothing before Hand, generally speaking, but they buy every Day what they have occasion for that Day. This is the Reason that they pay a great deal dearer; but they find their Accompt in it, as they say in the End, because of the Waste which the Servants make of what is left in their keeping. They never likewise dress Meat a Day before Hand, nor keep any thing from one Day to another. They kill the Mutton and Lamb in a Morning, which they eat at Night; and they don't kill the Poultry till they have a Mind to put it into the Pot; the Flesh is not a bit tough as in cold Countries; and the *Persians* look upon that which is freshest kill'd to be the Best; they only dress as much as will serve one Meal, and if any is left, they give it to the Poor; there is not so much as a Crust of Bread, nor a Bit of Meat raw, or drest in the House, when they go to Bed.

¶ The Meats which they commonly use, are Lamb, and Kid, Capons, Hens, Pullets, and Eggs. This is their usual and regular Diet. They add to that, by way of Regalio, Pigeons, Fish, and Venison. There are however few but the King and some great Lords, who eat of 'em, because they don't care for 'em. The poor People in the cold Provinces, eat Beef and Veal, during Winter; but they kill so little, except among the *Christians*, and *Gubres*, that it would not be worth mentioning. Swines-Flesh is forbid them, the Hare, and all the other Animals that are forbid by the *Jewish* Religion. The *Persians* can't so much as hear a Hare nam'd, because it is subject to Fluxes, like the Women. They value Mutton above all Butchers Meat, saying, it has no ill Habit, and that consequently one can contract no ill Habit in eating of 'em; for their Physicians are unanimously of Opinion, that the Man becomes the same with the Animals, upon which he feeds. They commend themselves mightily for their way of living, saying, *that one has nothing to do but to look upon their Complexion, to judge how much it exceeds that of the* Christians, *who eat Beef and Swines Flesh, and who drink Wine.* In effect, the Complexion of the *Persians* is even; they have a fine beautiful and smooth Skin; whereas the Complexion of the *Armenians*, their Subjects, especially the Women, is rugged and full of Pimples, and their Bodies large, and excessive heavy. One might likewise attribute the Difference of the good Plight, between the *Persians* and the *Armenians*, to the unequality of the *Armenian's* Diet, who Fast for thirty or forty Days together, during which Time, they eat nothing but Herbs and Oil; and then for so long time, eat excessively of Eggs and Flesh; whereas the *Persians* have but one Fast of thirty Days, during which time, still they never change their Meats, but only eat less; and that during the rest of the Year, they live every Day after an even Manner. They have in *Persia*, from *February* to *May*, the Kid, which in my Opinion is the most delicious Meat that can be eaten; and from *March* to *July*, the Lamb, which has likewise a most excellent Taste.

¶ The *Persian* Bread is generally thin, and like their broad thin Casks. There are several sorts of it. The ordinary Bread is bak'd in round Ovens, made in the Ground, like a Hole about four or five Foot deep, and two Foot Diameter. They put the Bread against the Oven, and as the Bread is not so thick as one's Finger, especially in the Middle, it is bak'd in less than a quarter of an Hour. They have again another sort of Bread, which they call *Lavach*, which they make round, as large as a hollow Plate, and as thin as Parchment, which they bake upon a round Copper Plate; and another sort which they call *Senguck*, that is to say Flint-bread, because it is bak'd in Ovens made as ours are, the Bottoms whereof are cover'd with large Flint Stones, as big as a Wall-Nut and two Fingers high. This Bread is not thicker than the ordinary Bread; it is made long-ways, and weighs about a Pound and a half. The Bakers bake it upon Flint-stones, to save Wood; these Stones taking and keeping Fire the best, and heating the Dough sooner; but that Bread is more bak'd in some Places than others. The Bread is generally white, and good in *Persia*, and all made without Leaven. In Substantial Houses, they bake Bread twice a-Day: It is the Business of the Slaves to grind the Corn, and knead the Dough, and put it to the Fire. One may see in *Herodotus*, that this was the Custom in the first Age of the World. They strew generally upon all the Bread, excepting that which is in Leaf, some sleepy Grain, as the Seed of *Poppies*. Seed of *Sesame*, or *Turkish* Corn, of that which they call the Seed of *Mielle*, which the *Botanists* call *Nard*, or Pepperwort; that inclines them to Sleep, which is what they would have it do in the *East*, where they generally lie down after their Meal, as well in the Morning as at Night. Ancient Histories inform us, that they always us'd after their Meals in the *East*, the white Poppy-seed, roasted for the same End. Others strew Anis-seed, or Fennel-seed in the Room of it.

¶ The People of mean Condition are serv'd in the Morning with one of these Loaves, in a Wooden Bason, Painted and Varnish'd, putting at one End of the Loaf a quarter of a Pound of Cheese, and on the side of the Loaf, two *China* Cups, one with Sower Milk, curdl'd, the other with this sower Milk, curdl'd and diluted with Water, which serves for Drink, and some Fruit, especially the Melon: If he have Company with him, each has a Bason set before him, furnish'd after the same Manner. The Cheese in *Persia* is not made up in a solid Mass or Lump; they keep it in Goats-Skins, as we keep our Butter in Potts, and they cut and serve it up as small almost as Dust; they generally mix it with their sower Milk, and especially during the hot Seasons, with Fennel, with the Seed of Turpentine, and sometimes with their small Grapes that have the Taste of the Thistle; they serve the Milk in Ice, as well as the Water, which they give them to drink after eating; and this is the Dinner of the common People. The People in a higher Station, are serv'd, besides these light Messes, with Resine, or bak'd Meat, with Paloude, which is a sort of Starch, bak'd with Sugar, several sorts of Fruits, Sweet-meats, little Biskets, and sometimes petty Pattees, or Harsh-meats; but it is seldom practis'd, excepting at Weddings, and Festivals, to give Meat in a Morning, and when that is done, they serve up likewise Soops of several Sorts of Gousts, with Meat in 'em cut small: As to what remains, no Body rises from his Place to go and place himself at Table; they serve the Eating before every one in the same Place where he sits; and this is practis'd as well among the Great as little ones; they bring this Bason before you in the Place where you are, without either Table, Cloth, or Napkin; they use no Napkin at Dinner time, but at Feasts, because they then make use of more Plates, and Porringers, or Cups, than can be kept upon a Bason, and that some of these Meats may grease.

¶ They sup upon Soops, with Hash'd Meat, mingl'd with Peas, and other Roots; then with *Pilo*, which is Rice bak'd with Meat; and because the Rice serves instead of Bread, they seldom give any thing at Supper, but the Bread in Leaf, which serves as a Plate or a Cover, except at Feasts, where they give three or four several sorts of Bread.

¶ They serve every one with two or three sorts of the Leaf-bread, and an handful of strong Herbs upon it, to serve as a Sallet; sometimes they give a little Saltsellar, but this is done in very few Places. They feed themselves with their Fingers; they pull the Meat to pieces too with their Fingers; they cover the Meat with Rice like a Ball; they put a little Salt upon it with their Thumb, and they carry this large Morsel to their Mouth, which they swallow without chewing it, as we do Soops. This is eaten quick, and is very nourishing, and so the Repast is soon over; and this so much the more, in that they rarely Talk in Eating. They serve with the Meat Cups of *Sherbets*, with a wooden Spoon each a Foot long, as I have said, that they may carry it the more easily to their Mouth. This is their Drink at

Supper, they give 'em no other during the Repast. At the conclusion they bring 'em hot Water to wash the Grease off their Hands, which every one wipes upon his Handkerchief, and then they give a Glass of Water to whoever asks for it.

¶ As *Pilo* is the grand Mess with the *Persians*, I shall tell you how they Dress it. It is properly Rice boil'd in Broth with meat, or in Butter, in such sort that the Seeds or Grains remain whole without cracking, and likewise without being hard or dry, but so well done, that in putting it into one's Mouth, or pressing it between the Fingers, they make a Paste of it. They make above twenty sorts of this *Pilo*, with Mutton, Lamb, Pullets, *&c.* The Generality Season and make it thus; they boil six or seven Pound of Mutton in pieces, of about a quarter of a Pound each, with a Hen or two; then they take all the Broth and Meat out of the Pot; then they take some Butter and put at the bottom, which they fry very well; and they there put a lay of Rice, about an Inch thick; they put Onions slic'd, Almonds peel'd and cut in two, dry Pease fry'd in a Pan, cut likewise in two, some of the small Grapes, which they call *Kikmiche*, which has no Stone; some whole Pepper, Cloves and Cinnamon, with some Garden-Cresses for the Seasoning; upon that they put the Meat, and then they fill up the Pot with Rice, and throw in the Broth there, till it runs over: The Rice boils in a quarter of an Hour; and when it is boil'd and dry, and the Broth wasted away, they pour melted Butter scalding hot upon this Rice: Then they cover the Pot close with a Cloth dipp'd in hot Water and put under the Lid of the Pot, to keep the Rice moist, and they let it soak thus; after which they Dish it up. As the Butter is the chief Ingredient in the *Pilo*, they use the best for that purpose, and take abundance of Care in getting of it. The Butter in *Persia* is made with Cow's Milk, and the Milk of Sheep put together, which they esteem much more than any other. They don't use Fresh-Butter in that Country, nor do they eat any upon Bread: They keep it liquid in Vessels like Oil, and it is very nigh the same Colour: There is of that sort which smells like a Violet, and another Perfume which is very agreeable, which makes People very desirous to eat it. They season their other *Pilo*'s one with Fennel cut small; others with the juice of Cherries, Mulberries, or Pomegranates; others with Saffron and Sugar; others with Tamarins. They dress Rice dry, which they cover with Mince-meat, or Amuletts, or Eggs poach'd upon fry'd Onions, or upon Lettices fry'd; or upon fresh or salt Fish, and several other ways; in all which the *Pilo* is exquisite eating. One of the most delicious ways which they dress it, is that of baking it under the Spit, the Fat of a Lamb or Kid, and Hens, falling by degrees upon the Rice, it imbibes it, and gives it a most agreeable Taste. As for the Rice, as we dress it almost reduc'd to a Pap, the *Asiaticks* don't love it at all: They look upon it to be insipid and sick Food: They boil it so likewise in pure Water with whole Pepper and a little Cinnamon, as I have already observ'd, and they give 'em of this to eat. The Pease which I have said they put in the *Pilo*, are parch'd, and these Pease are a Ragoo, especially when they are done with Salt: Their way of parching them is this; they take a Pan, as if it were to make Sweet-meats; they fill it half full with very fine Sand, and they put it over a little Fire; when the Sand is hot, they put the Peas in it and stir it; and as the Sand is heavy, the Peas are always at the Top, and are parch'd without changing their former Colour: They roast the Almonds thus, as well as the Grain, which they call the cold Seeds, and the *Pistacho-Nuts*, and afterwards they throw some Salt upon them in the Pan, giving them thus another Tincture or Impression, which makes these Fruits very agreeable, and whetting to the Appetite.

❡ The meaner sort of People dress nothing at Home, especially in a Countŕy where Wood is scarce, as at *Ispahan*, and several other Places, but as soon as they shut up Shop, they go to the Cooks and buy *Pilo*, or whatever they have a mind to for Supper: There are an infinite Number of Cooks throughout the whole City, each of which sells a particular Meat: Their Kitchin is in the nature of a Shop: You will see, in the fore part, two or three Kettles of about thirty Inches Diameter, boiling upon Stoves; and behind the Shop, which is divided from it by a Curtain, one or two little Places, which you go up to by two or three Steps cover'd with Carpets, where they sit down to eat. The Fire of these Stoves is very rarely made of Wood or Charcoal, that being too dear a Commodity in the greatest part of *Persia:* They make their Fire generally with Heath and dry'd Leaves. The common People use a sort of Turf made of the Dung of a Beast and Earth put together, which the Peasants who make them and use in abundance, bring to Town to sell. When the Meat is dress'd, they keep it hot, by putting two or three Wicks under the Pot, according to its bigness, as they do in a Lamp: They light these Wicks, and they feed them with the fat of the Pot. This turns one's Stomach mightily at first, but Custom makes it familiar to one: One may easily judge that these Cooks being at so little Expence, sell very good Pennyworths.

❡ That which I have admir'd very much in the way of Living of the *Persians*, besides their Sobriety, is their Hospitality: When they Eat, far from shutting the Door, they give to every one about them, who happens to come at that time, and oftentimes to the Servants who hold the Horse at the Gate. Let who will come at their Dinner or Supper-time, they are not in the least put out of their way; as they eat but little, there is always enough. The *Persians* speaking in praise of Hospitality, say, that *Abraham* never eat without Guests; and that that happy Rencounter with the three Angels, which is mention'd in Scripture, happen'd to him one Day, when having no Company to Dine with him, he went out of his Pavillion, to see if he could meet no one of his Acquaintance, or whom he thought proper to invite. They likewise eat up all, as I have observ'd, without laying by any thing for another time; and if any thing is left, they give it to the Poor.

¶ The *Persians* who are pretty well to pass, seldom eat the Entrails, Feet, or the Heads of Beasts, it goes against their Stomachs. The poorest sort of People only eat them, buying 'em in the Shops that dress nothing else. They call the Cooks that dress them, *Guende paikon*, as who should say, *Cooks for the rotten Pieces*. But this Name might be given more properly to those Cooks who put stinking Meat in their Ragoos, and which they had already put in two or three Sauces, without being able to sell it: Those Cooks hash or mince it, and season it with Herbs and sower Juices. They call these Hashes *Ach Truch*, that is to say, *sowerish Soops*. They likewise make another sort of Jelly-Broth, where the Flesh is as it were dissolv'd in boiling, or in a liquid Paste. The *Armenians* especially are great lovers of it, tho' this Broth is sometimes made of the Flesh of a Horse, Camel, or Ass: They even say it cannot be made of any other Flesh, by reason no other sort of Flesh is solid enough. Among their excellent Messes, there is a sort of Broth which they call *Bourani*, a Name which they say, had its Original from a Daughter of *Almaimon*, Calif of *Babylon*, who invented it. It is made with Fowl and peel'd Barley, made into broth with several sorts of Herbs.

¶ To say somewhat of their Roast-meat; They dress their large Meat either in an Oven, or a Stove: And I shall first of all observe, That they have a way of roasting their Sheep, Lambs, and Kids, whole in their own Gravy, which is delicious Eating. Their roasting it at the Oven is done thus. I have said, that their Ovens are Holes in the Ground: They hang up a Mutton or Lamb whole in the Oven, hung by the Neck to an Iron Spit, which is at the Mouth of the oven, putting an Earthen Pan under it for it to drop in: The Beast roasts equally on all Sides without scorching: The Stoves at which they roast them are like your Preserving Stoves; and every thing roasted after this manner eats very well. The *Armenians* have a way of roasting the Mutton and Lamb in their own Skin upon the Coals, as they do Chest-Nuts. When the Mutton is dress'd, they put the

Skin again upon it, and sow it up well, and then they put it on the Coals and cover it: The Mutton is all Night a doing, and it is not over and above good when it is done.

¶ As for the Meat which they roast upon a Spit, it is dry and good for nothing: They likewise very seldom roast any great Pieces that way, their Flesh-meat being not full enough of Gravy to be put upon a Spit. Their Roast meat is generally little bits of Mutton or Lamb dipp'd in Vinegar, with Salt and an Onion, spitted as they do Larks: This is the best of their *Ragoos*, and this is what they generally roast upon a Spit.

¶ I shall say nothing in this Place concerning the Feasts of the *Persians*, having describ'd a great many throughout the whole course of this Work: I shall only say, that those which the King makes are generaly at One a-Clock in the Afternoon; whereas those which other People make are at Supper-time: However, those who are invited don't fail of coming at Nine or Ten a-Clock in the Morning, and they generally make an Apology at their entring the House, for their coming so late, laying the fault upon some unforeseen Accident. This is because the Feasts in the *East* last all the Day long; they pass their time away in taking Tobacco, in Discourse, in Sleeping after Dinner, in praying to God together, in Reading and hearing People Read, in repeating Verses, and hearing People Sing well, in the nature of a Chorus, the Actions of the Kings of *Persia*, in Heroick Poems, like that of *Homer*. The Graver sort of People keep to that, and give no other Diversion; but the Beaux and Gentlemen of the Sword, have Companies of Dancers, who Dance and Sing in the Nature of an Opera, where every thing tends to stir up Love; and where, towards the Conclusion, they act the Delights of Love with too great a Freedom. These Dancers are Harlots, who will do any thing for Money: Each brings her Servant with her; and those whom it is not convenient to meddle with, upon account of their Monthly Issues, wear a pair of Drawers of black Taffaty: This is to prevent any one's thinking of 'em and more especially that they may not meddle with 'em, as being in a State of Legal Pollution; at which time they eat apart. When Supper is serv'd up, they put the large Messes before the chief Guest; after which, the Master of the House looks upon him and says in a low Tone, and making of Signs, *Sir, that is at your disposal.* He answers with the same Signs, that he desires *the whole Company may partake of it.* I shall yet observe two things upon this Subject: The *First* is, That the Son or Relation of the Master of the House does the Office of Master, and serves every one at the Feast. The *Second* is, That the Children of the House never sit at the Feast till they are Marry'd, which generally comes to pass before they are twenty

Years of Age. The *Persians* call the Feasts *Mageles*, as much as to say *Assembly*.

¶ They use abundance of *Ice* in *Persia*, as I have been observing; in Summer especially every one drinks with *Ice*: But that which is most remarkable, is, That tho' at *Ispahan*, and even at *Tauris*, which is further North, the Cold is dry and penetrating more than it is in any part of *France* or *England*, yet the greatest part of the People drink with *Ice* as well in the Winter as the Summer. *Ice* is sold in the out-parts of the City in open places: Their way of making it is thus; they make a deep Hole, at the farther end of the Cellar towards the North, and before it, they dig deep Squares of sixteen or twenty Inches, like so many little Basons; they fill 'em with Water over Night, when it begins to freeze, and in the Morning, when all is frozen, they break it to Bits, and put all these Pieces together in the Hole, where they break 'em again into little Bits, as well as they can; for the more the Ice is broken, the better it is; then they fill the square Holes with fresh Water, as they had done the Day before, and at Night, they go and Water with your Gourd Bottles, with Handles to them, these Pieces of Ice, which are broke in the Hole, to the End, that they may hold the better together. In less than eight Days Working after this Manner, they have Pieces of Ice five or six Foot thick; and then they gather the People of that Quarter together, who with loud Shouts of Joy, and Fires lighted upon the Edges of the Hole, and with the Sound of Instruments to Animate them, go down into it, and lay these Lumps of Ice one upon the other, which they call *Codrouc*, as much as to say, Basis or Foundation, and throw Water between, to make them hold together the better.

¶ It falls out so, that in six Weeks time, an Ice-house of a Fathom or more deep, and as broad and long as one will, is fill'd up to the very top with Ice. The Snow hinders the Work mightily, and causes a great deal of Trouble; but when that happens, they sweep it, and throw it out with a great deal of Care, because that when that melts, it would likewise melt the Ice: When the Ice-house is full, they cover it with a sort of Sea-Rush, which they call *Bazour*, which they find in *Persia*, by the Water-side. In the Summer when they go to open the Ice-House, it is another Festival for that Quarter. They sell the Ice by Ass-loads, at eighteen Pence a Load, which is two Pieces of Ice, each weighing threescore Pounds. This is about two Deniers a Pound. The Bits and Pieces of the Ice that are cut, fall to the Lot of the People of that Quarter, who help to make it, and every one comes in the Morning to take his Share: What is very Remarkable, as well as Agreeable in their Ice, is its beauty and clearness; you can't see the least Dirt, nor gloominess; Rock-water is not clearer, nor more transparent than it is. They keep Snow likewise in the Places where they can do it with Conveniency, tho' there is Ice in abundance; this is out of Delicacy, because they find their Drink much more Agreeable with Snow than with Ice, especially the Sherbet.

CHAPTER XVI

OF THE STRONG AND SMALL LIQUORS

THEY drink nothing for the Generality in *Persia*, but *Coffee* and Water; their Treat for Drink is Sherbet, and Waters of Fruit and Flowers. They make an admirable Sherbet of the Citron, Mulberries, Cherries, and Pomgranates; they use abundance of the Water of the brown Willow-Tree, made of Buds, which the Tree produces in Spring-time, which they give of to Sick People as much as they will, especially to those who are troubled with Agues, and other Waters agreeable to their Taste, than which, nothing is more refreshing. They drink likewise Water of Roses, mingled with Water; the Rose-water is very agreeable in *Persia*; it does not smell a bit like a Drug, as it does with us; Whether it is from its being Distill'd without Water, which is contrary to our Method, or that it proceeds from the Nature of the Flower; they Transport it throughout all the East, and they Freight whole Vessels with it for the *Indies*. They extract it very easily after this Manner, they put the Roses into a great Kettle, and take another large Kettle for the Receipient, put in the Ground, and fill'd with Water, and cover'd with a Wooden Cover, which they stop up well with the Substance of Roses squeez'd; the Pipe that passes out of one into the other is nothing but a dry'd Cane; they put two Pounds of Water, to three Pound of Roses, and they extract about two Pound and a half of Rose-water; they draw likewise an excellent Spirit from the Sallow Water, which they use in Perfumes, and in rubbing of their Body; and an Essence of Roses, of which they draw a Quarter from a Pound of Roses: They draw moreover an Oil of Roses, which they call *Atre*, and is a wonderful Quintessence, if I may so say, and is very dear; for from forty Pound Weight of Essence of Rose-water, it is difficult to draw a Drachm of this Oil; they put for this Purpose the Essence of Roses four and twenty Hours in the Air, in a cover'd Tub, in which time, there rises upon the Superficies, a Grease of a brown Colour, which is this Oil, which they gather together with a Straw; the *Persians* prefer the smell of this to Ambergrease prepar'd, and the *Indians* do the same, calling it *Rougangulab*, as much as to say, Butter and Oil of Rose-water: It is likewise a great deal dearer than *Ambergrease*, and a great deal scarcer; an Ounce of it is sometimes worth two hundred Crowns in the *Indies*.

❡ As for Coffee, its a Liquor too well known to require much to be said of it. I have given an Account in my Travels from *Paris* to *Ispahan*, what the Effects of it are. I refer the Reader then, or rather I would have him refer himself to a little Treatise, Entitl'd, concerning *Tea*, *Coffee*, and *Chocolate*, compos'd by one of my Illustrious and most intimate Friends, Mr. *du Four* of *Lyons*, a Man, who is an Honour to Commerce, by his Application to all curious Knowledge, and especially that which regards the East; and by another excellent Work of his, which he has publish'd, Entitled, *Advice of a Father to a Son*; but as I have not as yet made mention of the Houses where they drink their Tea and Coffee in *Persia*, I shall tell you in this Place how they are made.

❡ These Houses, which are spacious and large Rooms, and rais'd in different Figures, are generally in the finest Parts of the Cities, because there is the Rendezvous, and place of Diversion for the Inhabitants. There are many, where there are Basons of Water in the Middle, especially in the great Towns. These great Rooms have Estrades, or Galleries, quite round about, three Foot high, and three or four Foot deep, more or less according to the bigness of the Place, made of Wood or Stone to sit upon after the Eastern Manner; they open them at Day-break, and it is then, and in the Evening, that they have the most Company; they serve you very exactly there with Coffee, very quick, and with abundance of Respect; there they converse; for there is the Place for News, and where the Politicians criticise upon the Government, with all the Freedom in the World, and without being disturb'd: The Government not troubling it self with what the World says: Here they play at those innocent Games I have been speaking of, which are like Draughts, or Chests; and besides this, there are your Repeaters in Verse and Prose, which the *Mollas*, *Derviches*, or Poets, take their Turns to Perform. The Discourses of the *Mollas*, or *Derviches*, are upon Moral Subjects, and like our Sermons; but it is not look'd upon to be scandalous not to be attentive to them; no Body is oblig'd to quit his Game or Conversation for that. A *Molla* stands up in the Middle, or at one End of the *Cahue kahne*, or Coffee-House, and begins to preach with a loud Voice; or else a *Dervich* comes in all at once, and harangues the whole Company, concerning the Vanity, Riches, and Honours of the World: It often happens, that two or three are talking all at a Time, one at one End, and one at another, and sometimes one shall be a Preacher, and the other a Repeater of Romances: In short, with Regard to that, there is the greatest Liberty taken in the World; the serious Man dares not say a Merry Thing; each makes his own Harangue, and listens to what he likes. The Discourses generally end in saying; There is enough said, go in the Name of God about your Business; then those who have held these Discourses, ask somewhat of the Auditory, which they do very Modestly, and without any Importunity; for if they should do otherwise, the Master of the Coffee-Room would not suffer them to come in again, so that those give them who will. These Houses were heretofore very infamous Places; they were serv'd and entertain'd by beautiful *Georgian* Boys, from ten to sixteen Years of Age, dress'd after a Lewd Manner, having their Hair ty'd in Wefts, like the Women; they make 'em Dance there, and Act and say a thousand immodest Things, to move the Beholders, who caus'd these Boys to be carry'd, every one where he thought Proper; and this fell to the Lot of those who were the most beautiful and engaging; in such sort, that these Coffee-Houses were nothing else in Reality, but Shops for Sodomy, which was very terrible to Wise and Virtuous People. *Calif Sultan*, Primier Minister of *Abas* the Second in the fiftieth Year of the last Age, brought the King, as debauch'd as he was himself, to Abolish these vile Practices, which he did, and since that time, there has been nothing of that to be seen in those Places.

¶ Wine and intoxicating Liquors are forbid the *Mahometans*; yet there is scarce any one that does not drink of some sort of strong Liquor. The Courtiers, Gentlemen, and Rakes, drink Wine, and as they all use it, as a Remedy against Sorrow, and that one Part drink it to put them to Sleep, and the other to warm and make them Merry; they generally drink the Strongest, and most Heady, and if it does not make them presently Drunk, they say, *what Wine is this? Damagne dared?* It does not cause Mirth. Nevertheless, as they are not us'd to drink Wine, they make Faces in drinking of it, as if they were taking a Medicine, and till they are heated, the Wine is too cool for 'em, they must have some Brandy, and the Stronger it is, the better they like it.

¶ They make Wine throughout all *Persia*, except in the Places where no Body is permitted to drink it as in the Countries where neither *Christians*, *Jews*, nor *Guebres*, who are the *Persian Heathen*, live. They make excellent Wine every where, where the People know in the least how to make it; the Use of it is forbid by the *Mahometan* Law, as I have been saying; the Toleration which they have, therefore depends upon the good Will of the Sovereign, and the Caprice, or rather Covetousness of the Governours, and this is what hinders them from learning to make Wine well, and that they have not the proper Impliments.

¶ They make the best in *Georgia*, in *Armenia*, in *Media*, in *East-Hircania*, at *Chiras*, and at *Yezd*, the Capital City of *Caramania*. The Wine of *Ispahan* was the worst of all, before the nice *Europeans* pretended to make it, which they did about twenty Years ago: It was made of that small sweet Grape without Stones, above mentioned, and was very Heady, Rough, and cold in the Stomach, as they say. The *Armenians*, in immitation of the *Franks*, mix it with large Grapes, and make a very good Wine of it, which bears mixing with Water, very well. They do not put up their Wine in Hogsheads as we do; the heat of the Air would shrink them, and the Wine would be spilled; but into Jarrs, or *Pitarres*, which are Oval Earthen Pitchers, four Foot high, which contain commonly above two hundred and fifty Quarts; there are some which hold about a Barrel; some are Glazed within, others are Plain, but the latter are done with a Grease made of Sheeps Suèt, Clarified, to hinder the Wine from soaking into the Clay; they keep those Jarrs in a cool Cellar, as we do our Hogsheads, and also bury in the Ground up to the Top, those that are to be kept last. I have heard, that they have in the Province of *Poitou* in *France*, some of those Jarrs, or Pitarres, which are called, *Pones*; the *Persians* call 'em *Komr*, an *Arabick* Word, which signifies Wine, and comes from a Verb, that signifies, turn topsy turvy, because Wine mixes, and turns the Brain topsy turvy. The *Arabians*, to make amends, give an honourable Name to the Wine, which they call *Keram*, i. e. Liberal, because the Juice of it inclines those who drink it, to Liberality, and to noble Exploits. The Wine keeps a long time in those Vessels, but none can tell how long it might be kept, because they never keep it very long, for fear of the *Mahometans*, who when the Humour takes 'em, order the Wine-Jarrs to be broke every where, without Respect of Persons; but if one may give Credit to *Strabo*, the Wine keeps in them for three Generations, which is as much as to say, almost for ever. 'Tis usually transported in Bottels, and in pitch'd Leathern-Jacks; the *Mahometans* liking the Strongest best, as I have already said; they put in the Wine that's made for them, *Nux-vomica*, *Hempseed*, and *Lime*, to make it the more Heady, and the more Intoxicating.

¶ As for Grave Men, that abstain from Wine, as forbidden and unlawful of it self, they warm and elivate themselves with Seed of Poppies, tho' it be more inebriating, and more fatal than Wine; they prepare that Drug several ways: It was first brought up in behalf of Men in great Places, to alay the Uneasiness of troublesome Affairs. The *First*, is the Juice it self of the Poppy, which they take ready made up into Pills, of the bigness of a Pins-Head at first, then gradually, and successively to the bigness of a Pea, and stop there, for a greater Quantity would kill them. That Drug is pretty well known in our Country to be Narcotick in the highest Degree, and a true Poison. The *Persians* find that it entertains their Fancies with pleasant Visions, and a kind of Rapture; those who take it, begin to feel the Effects of it an Hour after; they grow Merry, then Swoon away with Laughing, and say, and do afterwards a thousand Extravagant Things, like Jack-Puddings, and Merry-Andrews; it has that Effect, especially upon those who have a peculiar Disposition to Jesting; the Operation of that dangerous Drug lasts more or less, according to the Dose, but commonly it lasts four or five Hours, tho' not with the same Violence; After the Operation is over, the Body grows Cold, Pensive and Heavy, and remains in that Manner, Indolent and Drowsy, till the Pill is repeated. A Superior of the *Missionary Carmelites* of *Ispahan*, call'd Father *Ange* of St. *Joseph*, a Man Skilful in Physick, as well as in many other Sciences, being desirous to understand more particularly the Effect of that renowned Juice, took a Pill of it at the Time of my being in that City, and told us afterwards, that he found that it did dispose him against his Will, to Laugh, and utter a thousand Idle Stories; that he saw *Phantoms* and *Chimeras* pass by before him, which look'd very Comical, and wonderfully Diverting, and had no ill Effect upon him afterwards: But as little soever as one Accustoms himself to those Poppy Pills, one must constantly use them, and if one misses taking them but one Day, it is discern'd in ones Face and Body, which is cast into such a languishing State, as would move any one to Pity. It fares a great deal worse with those, in whom is rooted the Habit of taking that Poison, for if they forbear it, they endanger their Lives by it. They tell a Story upon that Account, of a Man, who had been used to it for several Years, that went out a Walking but five Miles from his House, without his Pill Box, the usual Time of taking them being come, and missing his Box, he mounts his Horse immediately, and Spurs him on a Gallop, to get the sooner to his House, but he fainted at half-way, and died. The Government has endeavour'd several times to prevent the Use of that Drug, upon the Account of the fatal Effects it has throughout the whole Kingdom, but it could never Compass it, for it is so general a Disease, that out of ten Persons, you shall not find one clear from that ill Habit: Wine-drinkers are however to be excepted. They say that nothing but Wine can answer the Properties of Opium, when one is us'd to it; therefore, when they would bring one off of that dangerous Drug, they present him Wine; but as it usually happens that they are not satisfied with it, because Wine does not work so Powerfully with them, they must return to the Drug, saying, that without it, they can enjoy no Pleasure in the World, and had rather go out of it: It is certain, that if one should leave off Opium suddenly, he would die for Want of it; those who are adicted to it, never attain to old Age; and besides, they are at the Age of Fifty, troubled with Pains in their Sinews, and Bones, bred in them by the Malignancy of that Slow Poison; their Spirits are moreover so low, that they dare only appear when the Drug affects them. Men, who have a Mind to destroy themselves, take a Piece of it as big as ones Thumb, and drink a Glass of Vinegar after it, there is no way to save them after that, and no Antidote is effectual, they die without Pain, and go out of the World as Merry-Andrews goes off of the Stage, *viz.* Laughing; therefore 'tis their common Expression when they are driven to the last Shift, *I will take some Asium*; the Name which the *Persians* give to that Drug, and from which we have derived that of Opium; signifies Originally, weakned in his Sence, because the immoderate use of that Juice, weakens the Brain, and the Senses; they call it likewise *Teriac, i. e.* Cordial; and those who use it, *Jeraki*, which is an Affront among the *Persians*, as is among us the Word, Drunkard.

¶ There is a Decoction of the Shell, and of the Seed of Poppies, which they call, *Locguenor*, and sell Publickly in all their Cities, as they do Coffee. 'Tis good Sport to be in those Decoction houses, among those that drink of them, and to observe them before the Operation, and after, during the Time of the Operation. When they come into the Decoction house, they are Dull, Pale, and Languishing, and soon after they have drunk two or three Cups of that Liquor, they are Peevish, and like Mad-Men, nothing Pleases them; they find Fault with any thing, and Quarrel together, but afterwards they are Friends again, and every Man giving up himself to his Predominant Inclination, the Amorous entertains with Love-stories to his Angel; another between Sleeping and Waking, laughs in his Sleeve; another Swaggers like a Hector; another tells a Story of a Cock and a Bull, in a Word, you would think you are really in a Mad-house. A sort of Drowsiness and Lethargy succeeds that uneven and immoderate Mirth: But the *Persians*, instead of calling it by its deserv'd Name, call it a Rapture, and maintain, that there is a Supernatural, and a Divine Impulse, in that Frame of Mind. As soon as the Operation of the Decoction abates, every one withdraws, and goes to his own House.

¶ There is an infusion of Seed of Poppies, mixed with some Hempseed, and *Nux-vomica*, they call that Infusion, *Bueng* and *Poust*; it is much Stronger than the others; according to the Quantity, they take of it, it casts them into a Ludicrous and merry Phrensy, and a little after, it takes their Senses quite away; therefore it is directly forbidden by their Religion. The *Indians* use it with their State-Criminals, when they wont take their Life away, in order to deprive them of their Senses; and with the King's Children, when they intend to Incapacitate them for Reigning. They say, that that Way is less Barbarous than to kill them, as they do in *Turky*, or to Blind them, as in *Persia*. The *Yusbecks* have found out a way to take the Smoak of that Seed, mixed with Tobacco; and they have brought the Mode of it into *Persia*; it is not so prejudicial in that Manner.

⁋ The *Indian Buing* is plainer than that I speak of; yet it has as fatal Effects: It is nothing but pure Hempseed, and the Skin and Leaves of Hemp, beaten and infused together, without Seed of Poppies. Oftentimes they put in nothing but the Leaves, and then 'tis soon ready, for they only beat the Leaves in a Wooden Mortar, with a little Water, and when 'tis beaten to Powder, and the Water is thick, they drink it. The *Mahometans* only use it, and some Sects among the *Indians*; the *Banjans* continuing to forbid the Use of it, by Reason of its pernicious Effects on the Brain: But in all Sects, none but the Scum of the People drink of it, especially the Beggars, and Mumpers; they never miss taking of it once a Day, except upon a Journey, for then they take it three or four times a Day, and by the Virtue of that Drink, they walk more Briskly and Nimbly. I just now told you, that in *Persia* they sell that Drink in Publick-houses, as they do Coffee; but they seldom resort thither in a Morning; between three and four a-Clock in the Afternoon you see them full of Men, who seek in that infatuating Liquor some Relief to their Troubles, and some abatement to their Misery; the Use of it becomes Mortal in Time, like that of Opium, especially in the cold Countries, where its mischievous Property sinks the Spirits so much the more; the constant Use of it alters their Complexions, and weakeneth wonderfully both the Body and the Head; and when the Operation is over, he who before kept on Laughing, Jesting, and playing the Jack-Pudding, falls down on the Ground suddenly, and looks like a dying Man; about an Hour after he recovers by Degrees. The Habitual Use of that Stuff is also as dangerous as that of Opium; those who have once contracted an Habit of that Drink, being no longer able to live without it, and being so knit to it, that they would die for Want of it.

⁋ The Seed of Hemp has more Virtue than the Leaf, and the Skin has more than either.

⁋ In the Year 1678, being at *Surat*, two *English* Ladies looking out of the Window, saw a *Sakirer* Beggar pounding some of those intoxicating Leaves, which they had a Fancy to taste, enticed, either by the Colour of the Leaf, which was of a charming Green, or by one of those fantastical Whims, which possess Women some times; one of their Servants brought each of them a small Glass full of it, and to allay the Strength of the Plant, he put in it some Sugar, and some beaten Cinamon, about four Hours after, they begun to be affected with that mad and comical Drunkenness, which is the infalible Effect of that Potion, then they were taken with a Laughing Fit, and with a Humour of Dancing, and telling Stories, without either Head or Tail, till the Potion had perform'd its Operation. ¶ There is another inebriating Decoction, which is also forbidden by the *Mahometan* Religion, and even stricter than the rest, because the Consequences of it are still more Prejudicial, and more sudden than the Potions of the Poppy. The *Persians* call it, *Tchorie*, it is made of a Flower, like that of the Hemp.

¶ The *Persian* Vinegar is not made of Wine, for Wine is forbidden, but it is made of Grapes, of Pomgranat-Juice, of Willow-Water, and of Palm-Tree Water, in the Places where that Tree grows, *Iracon*-Oil, in the Number of Liquors; there are several sorts of it in *Persia*. *First*, there is Olive-Oil, which is scarce, because it is only made in the Province of *Hircania*, and is good for little, because it is ill-made, and spoils also in the Carriage, which makes it thick, and brackish. The Olive-Trees of that Province are extraordinary large, the Reason of which is this; when the Inhabitants plant them, they usually plant three or four together, which in time join close, and grow together, and make but one Stock; that Invention came from *Mesopotamia*, where they set in that Manner several young Olive-Trees, twisted round, which grow together, and make but one Tree, of a prodigious bigness. The *Persians* do not care for Olive-Oil, having several other sorts at a very easy Rate, that are very good. The most delicious, is that they call *Ardé*, it is very sweet, very clear, and of the finest yellow Colour in the World: It is made of a Seed call'd, *Koucheek*, the Flower whereof is of an Orange Colour, and it is supposed to be the Wild-Saffron, the Oil of *Chirbac* is more common, but is not so good, as that of *Ardé*, and grows Strong in few Days; they draw it out of a Seed call'd, *Gongeth*, which some fancy to be the *Sesame*: Besides those Eating-Oils, they have Lamp-Oils, *viz.* Walnut-Oil, and the Oil of a Seed like a small Bean, which the *Persians* call, *Kechak*, and *Bedingil*, which they say is the *Ricinus*, or *Ricinum Ameticanum*, or the *Palma Christi Silici*. The Name of *Kechak*, which the *Persians* give it, is probably the same as ·*Kike*, which *Herodotus* says the *Egyptians* gave to the Seed, whereof they made that sort of Oil; which he says likewise, the *Grecians* call *Pria*. All *Asia* is full of that sort of Bean, which grows on a Plant, commonly a Foot high; but in the Territory of *Ispahan*, twice as high, and where whole Fields are full of it: It is of a light Grey, stained with Blackish Spots and Streaks, which make the Leaf of it like a Parsly Leaf; the Skin of that Kidney-Bean is as thin as the Skin of a Wall-Nut, and splits in two, like other Beans, and like Almonds. Diascorides, and his Commentators say, that that Seed grows on a Tree; but it is a great Mistake, as well as what some of our Books of Travels tell us, that they draw the Oil from it with boiling of it. For they draw it with a Mill turn'd round by a Horse or an Ox: The Mill is made of two Wheels less than ours, of three Foot Diameter only: The upper Wheel has a Hole in it, wherein they throw the Beans one by one; and the under Wheel has a small Pipe or Tube to let out the Liquor: That Oil of *Ricinum* is thick and blackish, and in the burning stinks and is full of Smoak: That may perhaps be the Reason why the *Portuguese* call it *Flower of Hell*: None but Poor People use it.

¶ Lastly, They have in *Persia* the Oil of *Naphte*, which the *French* call *Tear of Mastick*; the *Persians* burn it and use it in Painting, and in Varnish, as the *French* do: The best comes out of *Hircania* and the Northern *Media*, on the Bank of the *Caspian Sea*. That Oil drops from the Rocks as clear and as liquid as Water, and thickens afterwards and keeps its clearness more or less, according as the Rocks are more or less exposed to the *East* and *North*, for the Oil of these Rocks is always White; whereas, the Oil of other Rocks grows Brown in time.

CHAPTER XVII

OF MECHANICK ARTS AND TRADES

BEFORE I treat of the *Arts* and *Trades* in particular, I'll make five general Observations with regard to the Subject; Three on the Genius of the *Eastern* People, to shew what they understand and are capable of understanding, in all that relates to Arts and Man's Industry; afterwards another on the Method of the *Eastern* Artificers; and lastly, another on the Polity of the *Persian* Artificers.

¶ The first is, That the *Eastern* People are naturally Soft and Lazy, they work for, and desire only necessary things. All those beautiful Pieces of Painting, Carving, Turning, and so many others, whose Beauty consists in an exact and plain imitation of Nature, are not Valu'd among those *Asiaticks*: They think, that because those Pieces are of no use for the occasions of the Body, they do not therefore deserve our Notice: In a

Word, they make no account of the making of good Pieces; they take notice only of the Matter, which is the Reason that their Arts are so little improved; for as to the rest, they are Men of good Parts, have a penetrating Wit, are Patient and Sincere, and would make very skilful Workmen, were they paid liberally.

¶ The second Observation is, That they are not desirous of new Inventions and Discoveries; they think they enjoy all the Necessaries and Conveniencies of Life, and rest Contented, choosing rather to buy Goods from Strangers, than to learn the Art of making them: 'Tis well known how much Money the *Turks* and *Persians* lay out in Watch-work, especially the *Turks*, who lay out at least a hundred and fifty thousand Crowns a Year, to my certain Knowledge; yet the *Turks* do not go about to learn that Trade which they see so Profitable, nor Paper-making, tho' absolutely Necessary; nor many such-like Trades. Neither is there in *Persia* one single Native that knows well, how to mend a Watch. They have desired a hundred times to have Printing-Houses; they acknowledge the Usefulness and Necessity of them; they see the Advantage and the Profit of them; yet no body undertakes to set up one. The Brother of the Great Master, who was a very Learned Man, and the King's Favourite, would have engaged me, in the Year 1676, to send for Workmen to teach them that Ingenious Art: He shewed His Majesty the *Arabick* and *Persian* Printed Books I had given him; whereupon a Contract was made; but when they should have laid down the Money, all was broke off. In the *Indies* likewise great Guns are much in use; all the Strong Holds are stored with them; all their Armies carry some into the Field; even great Retinues have some Ordnance with them, both Iron and Brass; yet the Casting Trade is still a Secret among them, and they had rather send into *Europe* for Guns, than employ both *Europeans* and *Turks*, who offer their Service every Day to cast some.

¶ The third Observation is, That the hot Climates enervate the Mind as well as the Body, lay the quickness of the Fancy, necessary for the invention and improvement of Arts. In those Climates the Men are not capable of Night Watchings, and of a close Application, which brings forth the valuable Works of the Liberal, and of the Mechanick Arts. 'Tis by the same Reason likewise, that the Knowledge of the *Asiaticks* is so restrained that it consists only in learning and repeating what is contain'd in the Books of the Ancients; and that their Industry lies Fallow and Untill'd, if I may so express my self. 'Tis in the North only we must look for the highest improvement and the greatest perfection of the Arts and Sciences.

¶ The next Observation I am to make on the Method of the Eastern

Artificers, is, That they need but few Tools about their Work. 'Tis certainly an incredible thing, in our Country, to hear how easily and conveniently these Workmen set themselves up and Work at their Trade: Most of them have neither Shop nor Shop-Bench; they go and work wherever they are sent for; they sit on the bare Ground, or on an old Carpet in the corner of a Room, and in a Moment you see the Board up and the Workman at Work sitting on his Breech, holding his Work with his Feet, and working with his Hands: The tinners of Kettles and Pans, for Instance, who use so many things in *Europe* about their Work, go to People's Houses in *Persia*, and work there for the very same Charge: The Master, with his little Apprentice, brings his whole Shop with him, consisting in a Sack of Coal, a pair of Bellows, a little Solder, some *Sal Armoniack*, and some bits of Pewter in his Pocket. When he is come, he sets up his Shop wherever you please, in the corner of the Yard, or of the Garden, or Kitchin, without any occasion for a Chimney: He makes his Fire against a Wall, that he may set up his Pans against it when he warms them; he lays his Bellows on the Ground, and covers the Pipe of them with a little soft Clay shaped like a Vault, then sits to his Work as well contented as if he was in the largest and convenientest Shop. The Gold and Silver Smiths, as well as the rest, go likewise and work at People's Houses, tho' one would think their Tools are less ramageable, and not so easily removed; they carry a Clay Anvil shaped almost like a Chafing dish, but a little higher: Their Bellows is but a plain Kid-Skin, with two bits of Stick at one end of it, to stop the Hole that draws in the Air; and when they would blow it, they tie a small Pipe at the other End of it, which they run into a Forge, and blow with the left Hand: They take those Bellows drawn up like a Bag, out of a Leathern Bag, which serves them instead of a Filing-Skin, in which they lay up also a pair of Pincers, an Ingot-Mold, a Wiredrawing Iron, an Anvil, a Hammer, some Files, and other small Tools: The Master carries the Bag, and the Apprentice the Forge, and you see them go in that manner wherever they are sent for, and go back at Night with their Shop under their Arm. When the Workman is going to melt some Metal he makes his Crucibles as he wants them; and when he sets himself to work, he fastens the Skin to the Forge, and sets the Anvil down by him, and works in his Cap. The Reason why they have their Work done at Home, is because they won't trust the Workmen, and would see whether things be done according to their Mind.

¶ As to the Polity of the *Persian* Tradesmen, which is my fifth *Observation*, I will inform you of one thing only, That the Trades have every one a Head to the Company elected out of their Body, who is appointed by the King;

and that's all their Government. Yet strictly speaking, they do not form a regular Body, for they never meet. They have neither Guards, nor Visitors, but some few Customs only, which the Head of the Trade Causes to be observed; as for Example; That there be always a due Distance between the Shops and Tradesmen of the same Trade, except in the Places which are particularly designed for one sort of Work. Whoever is about to set up a Shop in any Trade, goes to the Head of the Trade, gives his Name and Place of Abode to be set down in the *Register*, and pays some small Fee for it. The Head never enquires of what Country the Tradesman is, nor who was his Master, nor whether he understands his Trade. The Trades likewise have no Restrictions, to hinder one from incroaching upon another. A *Tinker* makes Silver Basons, if they are bespoke; every one undertakes what he pleases, and they never Sue one another upon that account. There is likewise no binding of Apprentices among them, and they learn their Trades for nothing: Far from it; the Boys that are put out 'Prentices with a Master, have Wages the very first Day they go to him. The Parents make an Agreement between the Master and 'Prentice for so much *per* Day the first Year; a Half-penny, or a Penny a Day, according to the Age of the 'Prentice, and the Hardship of the Trade; and the Wages encrease now and then, according to the 'Prentices's Improvement. The thing is still without any mutual Confinement, with respect to Time, as I have said; the Master having always the Liberty to turn away his 'Prentice, and the 'Prentice to leave his Master. There it is indeed that Knowledge must be stolen; for the Master thinking on the Profit he may reap by his 'Prentice, more than on teaching him his Trade, doth not trouble himself much with him, but employs him only in those things that relate to his Profit. The Trades are bound to the King's Average, *i. e.* to do the King's Work when they are order'd; and the Trades which are not employ'd in that Work, as the Shoe-makers, the Cap makers, the Drawer-makers, pay a Tax to the Place call'd *Cargh Padcha*, i. e. the King's Expence.

¶ I come now to Arts and Trades in Particular, and shall begin with *Husbandry*. I have already observed the Saying of the Young *Cyrus*, That the *Kingdom of* Persia *is of so large an Extent, that Winter and Summer happen there at the same time.* So that you will easily believe what I am going to say, *viz.* That they Sow and Reap at the same time. And what is observable again, you may see that great Variety in sixscore Leagues riding only. I observed at leisure, that wonderful Variety in the Year 1669, coming from the *Persian Gulph* to *Ispahan* in the Month of *February*. After three or four Days Journey from *Ormus* to *Laar* in *Caramenia*, I found them

Reaping; as I went on further, I saw the Corn grow every Day greener: And lastly, twenty Days ride beyond, I saw them Sowing of it. Harvest begins in *June* at *Ispahan*, which is about the Center of the Kingdom; but the fruitfulness of the Soil depending chiefly on the Water throughout the whole Kingdom, I shall tell you before I go any further, how the *Persians* get it, and how they convey it from one Place to another.

¶ They divide, in *Persia*, the Water into four several sorts; two on the Ground, which are the River Water and Spring Water; and two under Ground, *viz.* That of Wells, and that of subterraneous Conduits. They dig at the foot of Hills for Water, and when they have found a Spring, they guide it in subterraneous Conduits to ten Leagues distance, and sometimes further, down Hill all the Way, that it may run the swifter. No People in the World know better how to Husband Water than the *Persians*. Those Conduits or Channels, are sometimes near fifteen Fathom deep; and I have seen some of them of that depth: They are easily measured, for at every ten Fathom distance, there are Vent-holes, the Diameter whereof is as big as that of our Wells. One of my Neighbours at *Ispahan*, Son of the Visier of *Corasson*, *alias* the Ancient *Bactriana*, has often told me, that his father had found in the Register-Books of the Province, that there had been formerly forty-two Thousand *Kenses*, and that some of the Wells were unfathomable; and that by report, they were seven hundred and fifty *Gueze*'s deep. The *Gueze* is the *Persian* Ell, which is four and thirty Inches long: At that rate, they would be three hundred and fifty four Fathom deep, which is incredible. However it may be inferr'd from thence what numbers of Conduits there is all over the Kingdom, and their wonderful Art in making of them. I was told also in *Media*, that in the space of sixty Years only, the number of those underground Conveyances was grown less by four Hundred than it was. There is certainly no Nation in the World that understands so well the way of Undermining, and making Conveyances under Ground, as the *Persians*. Those subterraneous Ways are usually about nine Foot deep, and three Foot broad.

¶ Besides the River and Canal Water, they have Well-Water almost throughout the whole Kingdom: They draw the Water with Oxen in great Leathern Pails, which commonly hold near two hundred and fifty pound weight: The Pail has at the bottom a Leathern Pipe about three Foot long, and half a Foot Diameter, which is turned up with a Cord tied at the top of the Well, to hinder the Water from running out: The Ox draws up the Pail by a thick Rope, which turns round a Wheel three Foot Diameter, fastned at the top of the Well like a Pully, and brings it to a Bason hard by, wherein it empties itself out of the Pipe, then the Water afterwards branches out into the Lands. *Note*, that they make the Ox draw down a Descent about thirty Degrees below the Horizon, the Gardiner sitting on the Rope to ease himself, and the Ox likewise; so that the Contrivance, tho' a Rustick one, is easy both in the Performance, and in the Expence, requiring one Man only to manage it.

¶ As to the distribution of the River and Spring Water, it is made Weekly or Monthly, as occasion requires, in this manner: They lay on the Canal, which conveys the Water into the Field, a Brass Bowl round and thin, with a little Hole in the Center of it, whereat the Water comes in by Degrees and when the Bowl sinks the Measure is full, and they begin again, till the quantity of Water agreed upon, be all run into the Field. The Cup is commonly near three Hours before it sinks. They make use likewise of that Contrivance in the *East*, to measure the Time by: 'Tis the only Clock and Sun-Dial they have in several Parts of the *Indies*, especially in Forts, and in Noblemens Houses, where a Guard is set. The Gardens pay so much a Year for Water so many times a Month; the Water never misses coming on the Day appointed; then every one opens the Canal of his Garden, to let in the Water: As they water a great part of a Garden at once, it would be very easy to let in more Water into one's Garden than one ought to do, and so keep it out of another's; but that kind of Cheat, is strictly forbidden, and the guilt of it is severely punished. The better to understand how the Water is distributed, you must know that every Province has an Officer appointed over the Water of the said Province, who is called *Mirab*, i. e. *Prince of the Water*, and orders the distribution of it every where very exactly, his Men attending constantly at the Brooks and Streams, to let it into the Lands and the Fields, according to his Order. It is a very profitable Office: The Officer of *Ispahan*, for Instance, gets by his Place four Thousand *Tomans per Ann.* or sixty Thousand Crowns of *French* Money, without reckoning his Deputy's Profits. The Land and Gardens of that Royal City, and of the Neighbouring Parts, pay twenty Pence a Year to the King by *Girib*, which is their common Land Measure, and is less than an Acre, for River or Spring Water, for the other Water is free. Besides the constant Duty of Twentypence *per Girib*, there are the ordinary and extraordinary Presents made to the *Mirab*; for Instance: When any Body wants Water, he must go and complain to him: He usually answers, that there is no Water in the Country: But as soon as one has made him a Present (for no Body fails doing it, lest the Fruits and the Corn should be spoiled) the Water comes in plentifully. River Water and Spring Water, differ in the Rate, the latter being cheaper than the other, because it is neither so muddy nor so sweet.

⁋ They Plough with a Share drawn by lean Oxen (for the *Persian* Oxen do not grow fat as ours do) Yoked, not by their Horns, but with an Arch and a Breast-Leather. The Plough-share is very small, and the Coulter doth but scratch the Ground as it were: As fast as the Ground is turned up, the Ploughmen break the Clots with great wooden Mallets, and with a small Harrow; then with a Spade they smooth the Ground, and mark it out into Squares, like the Grass-Plots in a Garden, and make the borders of them a Foot high, more or less, according to the quantity of Water it requires. The Rule they observe in watering the Squares, is to let it be high enough for a Duck to swim in; and that is the way of watering their Gardens every Week.

⁋ The most common Corn in *Persia* is *Wheat*; which is very good, and very clean; and *Barley*, *Rice*, and *Millet*, whereof they make Bread in some Places, as in *Courdestan*, when their Corn happens to be spent before Harvest. They sow neither *Oats* nor *Rye*, except, in the Places Inhabited by the *Armenians*: Their *Rye* is sown for some particular Occasions in Lent. *Rice* is the most general Food of the Country, and the most delicious, as has been already observ'd. The *Persians* Wonder our Noblemen do not eat it, and say, that *God has kept from us the wholsomest and pleasantest Food in Nature.* That Corn grows up in three Months time, tho' they transplant it after it is Bolled: For at first they sow it as they do other Corn, then they remove it one Stalk after another into a well soak'd and muddy Ground; for it must be kept constantly water'd; and that's it that makes the Air so unwholsome where it grows because there breed abundance of Insects in that muddy Water, such as Toads, and others: And when they would have the *Rice* to ripen, they turn away the Water and drain the Field; then the Insects die and infect the Air. The *Rice* ripens after it is laid dry, in eight Days time.

⁋ Besides the way of watering the Land, used by the *Persians*, they have likewise the way of Storcoration, so much esteemed formerly by the *Romans* in Husbandry. That is it where with they improve their Land in *Persia*, instead of Horse-Dung, which they use to litter their Horses with, as has been said. The Country-men heap up together all the Filth and Dirt of the Streets, fill Sacks with it, and carry it Home on their Asses, which doth not cost them much, for otherwise they would go back empty. The *Persian* Towns have no common Sewers, every House has one near it, or instead of it, a hole in the Ground a foot deep, which is also their House of Office. The goers and commers do not perceive it at first, the dryness of the Air dispelling the ill smell. You see the Countrymen, as soon as they have unloaded their Asses or Mules in the Market, clear the

Privies, and load their Beasts with the Filth. The Houses which have not a Sink-hole in the Street, let, as it were, their Dung by the Year to some trusty Countrymen, who present the Master every Year with some Fruit, for allowing them a free egress and regress to the House. They come to them constantly every Week, especially to the great Houses, where they had rather load their Beasts than elsewhere. The *Melons* and *Cucumbers*, which require very hot Dung, they warm with Pidgeon and Man's Dung. The Countrymen say, there is a remarkable difference in the Fruit, that grows in the Beds dung'd, with the Excrements of great Flesh-eaters, and Wine-drinkers, as the *Europeans* are; they do not lay that Dung on the Land as it is, lest it would scorch it with its heat; they throw it into a great Pit in their Yard, all the Summer long, and when the Pit is half full, they fill it up with Moulds, the Rain and Snow that falls on it incorporates them together, they let it lie so for the space of two Years, then use it. They reckon three different sorts of Dung; that which they gather up higgledy piggledy; that which the Countrymen get out of Sinks and Privies, and is unmix'd, and the Pidgeon Dung.

¶ With the help of that Manure, the Land, whether Sandy, Stony, or Clay, is made capable of all sorts of Seeds; and there is some Land that bears Barley twice a Year. In the Neighbour-hood of great Cities, the Land never lies Fallow; as soon as one sort of Fruit is gathered, they set another. Two or three Years after the Land has been Dunged, it grows dry; but they Dung it again presently, and Water it, and then it recovers its former Fruitfulness.

¶ They do not Thrash the Corn with Flails in Barns, as we do, but they take it out of the Stalk in this Manner, They gather up the Stalks into round Heaps of about forty Foot Diameter, not fearing (as we do) either Thieves or Storms, then they lay down part of them with Forks, and draw over them small Sledges with Iron Wheels; the Sledge is about three Foot long, and two broad; the top of it being higher than the bottom, is, as it were, a Seat for the Cartman, the Bottom, which is made of four Pieces of Wood, laid square, has across them three round Sticks, and sometimes four, which are instead of Axle-Trees; those round Sticks are like our Pastry Cooks Rouling Pins, and go in some Iron Wheels, made something like the Wheels of our Jacks, but that they are dented sharp, most like the Teeth of a Saw; they put any Beast to that Cart, either a Horse, an Ass, an Ox, or a Mule, and set on him a little Boy, who puts him to a full Trot; those Wheels break and cut the Straw, and squeze the Corn out of the Ears, without breaking it, because it slips between the Teeth; some Men, who stand by, thrust the Straw under the Sledges, and the Corn being the heavier remains at the bottom, as I have already observ'd; they draw seven or eight Sledges one after another, over one Heap, according to the bigness of it, and each Beast runs round it, three or four Hours together, then they take it out of the Sledge, and without covering him, he sweats; they unhood-wink him, and Fodder him, putting another Beast to the Sledge, in the Room of him; when the Straw is cut in that Manner, it serves for Fodder to all Carriage Beasts: For in *Persia*, there is no Hay, the Country is too dry, and too hot, to bring any; besides, that Straw is better and cooler for them. In some Countries, the Horses, Oxen, and Mules, run round the Heap, and tread the Corn out of the Ears.

¶ Rice is not so easily shell'd; Men who have a great many Slaves, make them beat it in a Wooden Mortar, but they commonly make use of a Machine, or great Beam, which falls on the Rice that lies in a Hole, made in the Ground, laid with Bricks, about three Foot Diameter, and three Foot Deep; the Beam is four Foot long, one of the Ends of it holds by an Hinge, being fasten'd like an Axle-Tree, at the other End is a thick Iron-Ring, half sharp, of about four Inches Diameter; a Man raises the Beam with treading on the Breech, and the End of it falls on the Rice, thro' the Iron Ring, which breaks the Shell of the Corn; the Art consists in saving the Corn, and not breaking it. The Whitest Rice being the most valued, they rub it after it is shell'd with Flower and Salt, mixed together.

¶ What I found most Observable in their Husbandry, is the way of dressing Vines in *Armenia*, in *Media*, and in their adjacent Parts; the Winter being there very sharp and long they lay their Vines in the Ground all Winter long, and in the Spring they uncover them. That Art might perhaps succeed very well in *England*, and in all other cold Countries in *Europe*. I have observ'd in my Travels from *Paris* to *Ispahan*, that in *Georgia*, and in the *Eastern Hercania*, they do not dress their Vines; they grow round great high Trees, and bear for all that, the most delicious Grape of which the best Wine in the World is made. Take Notice here, that throughout the Kingdom they do not prop their Vines, because the Stocks of them are very large, being about eight Inches Diameter. The Grapes that grow at *Casbin* are the biggest I ever saw, and the best in the World; they grow in a very hot and scorching Climate, yet after the Vine hath Blossom'd it doth not Rain one Drop on it, neither is it Water'd.

¶ When they find an Ant walk, or some other Insects, that go to gnaw the Stock, or eat the Fruit, they scrape the Foot of it, and lay some new Mould round it, and that turns away the Insects from it.

¶ Their way of Rearing Melons is likewise very Curious; therefore they have the best Melons in the World, except perhaps those of *Balk*, and of other Places of little *Tartary*, which some Men like better; they Rear 'em up in the open Air, and never in Gardens, finding they are smother'd there; that is very far from covering them with Glaz'd Frames, and with Bells, as we do. They sow the Melons in Mould, mix'd with Pidgeons Dung, and as soon as they are knit, they lift up the Shanks of them, and lay them on Beds, that the Water that runs into the Field may not touch them; when they begin to be as big as a Walnut, they take from the Stalk the most backward and smallest of them, and suck off with their Tongue a kind of Down, that grows on the Rind, which holding the Dust, that the Wind and Sun raise upon it, makes in Time a caustick Skin, which wasts the Moisture of the Fruit, stops its Growth, and takes away its Sweetness. When the Melons are grown as big as Apples, they lift up the Stalks of them again, and lay them on a little Bank, that they may be the more exposed to the Air, and the better secured from Wett; they now and then uncover the Roots of them, about three Inches deep, and lay about them some Pidgeons Dung, which they cover again with Mould, and then Water them; they do it to quicken the Root. Their Melons have all of them a fine smooth Skin, not divided into Ridges, as ours are.

¶ The Rearing up of the Palm-Tree is also remarkable; when that Tree is four Years old, which is a very tender Age for a Tree that lives two Ages, as I have observ'd elsewhere; they dig a Hole close by the Tree, but not so close as to uncover the Root of it, and after they have dug near thirty Foot deep, slanting, they throw into that Hole a great deal of Pidgeons Dung, and other Dung, and fill it up; the Intent of it, is to make the Tree bear good Fruit; when the Trees are grown big enough to bear Fruit, they take in Blossom time, Sprigs of the Male Palm-Tree Blossoms, and Graft them on the Top of the Female Palm-Trees, just where they Bud, and as it were in their Womb: It has the same Effect as Seed, and they say that without it, the Fruit would be but small and dry.

¶ I come now to the *Persian* Architecture, I mean their way of Building.

¶ The *Persian* Houses are not built of Stone, not because Stone is scarce, but because it is not a proper Material to build with in hot Countries; neither are they built of Timber, except the Ceilings of great Houses, and the Columns and Pilasters that bear 'em up; the Material is Brick, either hardned in the Sun, or burnt in the Fire; and forasmuch as their Houses are but Plaister'd over, they are very far from affording so noble a Prospect as ours do; but within they are very Convenient, and look very Airy; they seldom make stately Porches, or outward Ornaments to them. The way of the Country is very contrary to those Pieces of Architecture, made for Shew: Far from that, you see in most Houses, about six Foot within the Entry of the House, a Wall, as high and as broad as the Entry, which is, as it were, a Skreen, to hinder the Goers and Comers from looking into the Yard. The Houses have commonly no Rooms, but Ground Rooms, those which have Upper-Stories, have but one, and their Ground Rooms are so much the lower Roofed: 'Tis the way of all the *Eastern* Countries, and it would very likely be the way of ours, had not the Dampness of our Climate obliged us to remove from the Ground; whereas, they scruple not in the *East*, and especially in *Persia*, to build low, and even to build under Ground, as it is practised in the cold Parts of the Kingdom, because the Air being clear and dry, the Low Rooms are consequently as wholsome as the Upper Rooms. Our constant Custom of Lodging in the first and second Floors incapacitates us to judge of the Inconveniency of going up and down continually, and was it not for that, we would find that Inconveniency as troublesome as it seems to be to the Easterlings: But it is time you should be a little acquainted with the Materials us'd among them, in the Construction of their Edifices.

¶ The Tiles or Claybricks, are made in thin Wooden-Moulds, eight Inches long, six Inches broad, and two Inches and a half thick. The Brick-makers tread the Clay with their Feet, they usually blend it with pounded Straw, cut small, to make it stick the better, and that the Bricks and Tiles which are made of it be not brittle, and may last longer; they draw afterwards their Hand over them, to smooth them, after they have dipt them in a Tub of Water, mixed with Straw cut smaller than the first; they take out the Mould, and set the Tile a drying, which is done in three Hours time, then they take them up, and lay them one against another, where they make an end of drying. Those Tiles cost but eight or nine Pence a Hundred at the Place where they make them, but if you have them made at Home, and find Materials, you give but about three Pence a Hundred. The poor People make their Tiles without Straw, except a little on the top of them.

¶ As to the burnt Bricks, they are made of two Parts Clay, and one Part Ashes, well work'd together in Wooden-Moulds, bigger than the Tile-Mould; they lay them several Days in the Sun a drying, then they set 'em in a great Kiln, sometimes twenty Cubits high, one against another, at some distance, which distance is filled up with Plaster; they stop the Oven, and keep Fire in it three Days, and three Nights together. Those Bricks are red and hard, and cost about a Crown a Hundred.

¶ Their Plaster, which is call'd *Guetch*, is not like ours in every Respect, it is neither so fine, nor so white, how well soever it may be prepared;

they fetch it not from the Places where it is made, as we do, for they have none amongst them, they take it out of the Mountains in large Stones, and in great Plenty; they burn it, then pound it, or bruise it with a great Grinding-stone, thicker than a Mill-stone, but not so broad by two Thirds of the Diameter, it turns round on its Back, and a Man always stands by, with a Shovel, to throw the Plaster under the Grinding-stone. The Countrymen bring Plaister, especially in Winter, because then they have little to do at Home, and want Dung for their Land. They have also Plenty of Lime, and they bruise it with their Feet, without being burnt: Besides Lime, they have also a white Earth, which they get in the Stone Quarries, in small Bits, like Plaster; that Earth dissolves in Water as soon as 'tis put into it; they Whiten Houses with it, and it does incomparably better than the Plaster. The Houses of the common People are Painted with a brown Colour, made with a sort of Earth call'd, *Zerd guill*, i. e. yellow Earth.

❡ Before I go on any further, I will speak two Words concerning the Soil, such as 'tis in the Province of *Parthia*. *First*, it is hard and close in the Surface, three Foot deep; you find reddish and blackish Streaks, and Veins near three Fingers broad; a little deeper, the Earth is partly Gravel, partly Clay, and under that is quick Sand; next to it you find a solid and hard Soil, and if you dig deeper, you come to a Layer of Flints; beyond which, *viz.* twenty Foot in all from the Surface, you find the Water; the Wells are seldom deeper than five and twenty Foot.

❡ At *Ispahan*, which is the Metropolis of the Empire, the Soil is naturaly Clay, and as weighty as a Rock, so that if the Place where they build be Virgin Ground, which was never dug up, the *Persians* build upon it without any Foundation at all; but if the Ground has been broken up before, they dig sometimes three Cubits deep, before they come to hard Ground, and they fill the Foundation with Clay Bricks, laying between every Layer of Brick a Layer of Plaister; those Bricks are made of the same Clay which is dug out of the Foundations; then they begin to build the Wall with those Clay Bricks, which they do over with Clay, mixed with *Straw*, and *Kaguil*, i. e. Mud and Straw, made of the same Material as the Bricks; the Wall is built by Layers, which they let dry, before they lay a new one on, and it is built so, that the higher it rises, the narrower it grows; the top of the Wall is cover'd with a Layer of red Bricks, to keep out Water the better, or else it is overlaid with those Tiles bak'd in the Sun, laid close at the Top, and hollow at the Bottom, that the Water may run off. All their Walls are very thick, yet more or less, according to their height; the Foundation of the most substantial Houses are of red Brick, a Foot above the Surface of the Ground: In that Manner are built the Walls of Yards, Gardens, and of all sorts of Inclosures; those Houses are overlaid with Lime and Plaister, well mix'd and beaten together, which makes a wonderful hard Cement, because the Plaister is a little Stony, even when it is beaten, but it is not so white as ours. I have not seen in any Part of the World higher Walls than in *Persia*; they outdo those of the most private Monasteries, especially the Walls that inclose great Mens Houses, and that's the usual Token whereby they know the Palaces in this Kingdom.

¶ The Top, or Covering of a House, is always vaulted, they cannot build it otherwise, unless they build it of a Timber Ceiling: That's it that has made the *Persian* Bricklayers so Skilful in making of Vaults and Domes. There is no Country in the World where they make Domes, both so high and so stately; their Skill in that sort of Work appears in that they use no Scafolds, to make the small Arches and the little Domes, as they do in *Europe*. The Vaults of the Houses are built low, and flat, because they commonly make Terraces on the top, by filling the space between the Cupolas, and levelling of it, that they may take the fresh Air, and lie there: But in Houses of the common People, they let the Vaults lie as they are, and don't fill the space between them, without they are overcast with Mortar, like the ordinary Walls, or done with Brick, the better to keep them against Snow and Rain. They set round the Terraces of all substantial Mens Houses, Rails, about three Foot and half high to lean on: As for the House-Floors, they are made either of plain Earth, or of Brick, or of Plaister; but commonly they are made of Earth only.

¶ The Shell of the House being finished, they set about the inside of it; they overcast it first with the Mortar, call'd *Kaguil*, then put on a Layer of fine Plaister, then they whiten it, or do it over with beaten Talcum, which is a Dust of the Stone Talcum, blended with Lime, that gives a fine Gloss to the Walls, Vaults, and other Things that are overcast with it, for you would think that those Walls are Silver'd over; therefore the *Persians* call that Dust *Zer, varac*, i. e. Leaf Silver.

¶ As to the Ornaments, the most common are those of Painting, which I have treated of before. They seldom have any Carv'd-work, and what they have is only Flowers, and Foliage, which they rough Carve in the Plaister, with the Chisel; the Rais'd-work being pretty flat, remains white, and the Ground is greyish; they Paint that rough Carving, and afterwards lay Gold and Blue on it, which much set off those Ornaments. I have already observ'd, that the Moresk-work, done on the Houses, is very Beautiful, and looks Charmingly; the clearness of the Air contributes much to it; for it hinders the Colours, which of themselves are already wonderfully bright from fading: I have seen Colours no where so fine as in *Persia*, for the Beautifulness, Duration and Thickness, both of the Natural and Artificial Colours. The dampness of the *European* Climates spreads a Mist over the Colours, which deadens and dulls them; so that it may be said, that those who have never visited the *Eastern* Countries, are Strangers to the shining and bright Part of Nature.

¶ As to the inward Shape and Contrivance of the Houses, the Noblest are commonly raised between two and four Foot above the Surface of the Ground, with four Fronts, that Face the four Cardinal Winds. A Bank about eight Foot deep, encompasses the Body of the House, which contains commonly a small Parlour in the Middle, with four large Parlours round it, open at the Top, which look like great Porches or Portico's, in which from thirty to forty Persons, and sometimes a hundred, may sit round on a Line. Those great Porches are parted from the little Parlour but by Sashes, or thin Doors, which are likewise instead of Windows, reaching from the Ground to the Vault. Take Notice, that the Arch begins commonly at half the height of the Wall; the Houses are all open in Front, or only shut in with Sashes; at the Corners of the Porches are little low Rooms or Closets, made of bare Walls, without Windows, the Light coming in at the Doors, which are wide and open, with two Leaves, that fold over one another, like Window-Shutters. The Stateliness of the *Persian* Houses consists in being so open at the Top, that one sitting within side of the House, may sit as cool as if he sat without Doors. That Manner of Building looks very handsome, and very convenient in *Persia*, where the Winter is short, and the Air is dry, hot, and clear; but it would not agree with us *Europeans*; the dampness of the Air would soon have ruin'd those Clay-Houses; they make in the Parlours, or Winter Porches, and in the Rooms adjoining, small Chimneys, the Mantle-Trees whereof are but about three Foot high, and about two Foot broad, in the Shape of a Semi-Circle, and which reaches down low enough to keep in the Smoke; they burn the Wood upright in them; they make the Chimneys so small, both because Wood is pretty scarce in *Persia*, and because they usually warm themselves in a sort of Chafing-dish or Furnace, in this Manner; they make a great Hole in the Floor of those Parlours, and of the Winter Rooms, near twenty Inches deep, and eight Foot Diameter, according to the wideness of the Room; those Holes are cover'd over in Summer with Boards, under the Carpets, and are not seen; in Winter they uncover them, and set over them a Wooden Table, a Foot high, and a Foot wider than the Hole on which it stands, and they spread on the

Table one or two stitch'd Coverlets, which hang down half a Yard round the Table; when they have Occasion to use the Furnace, they put in a few Coals, well lighted, and strewed over with a few Ashes, to make them last the longer, then they draw near the Table close to the Hole, and lay the end of the Coverlet in their Laps, as high as their Waste; there they sit very warm, and very easy, and the Heat inclines them insensibly to a sweet Slumber; and they eat in the Winter over that Fire, and lie round it; the *Persians* call it, *Coursi*, i. e. Seat, because that Table looks like a Seat. In the Houses belonging to the common People, the Windows, which are like our Lattices, are made of the Plain Tree, which is a very fine sort of Wood: But in Noble Men's Houses, they are all Sashes, whereof the Squares are made of a thick waved Glass, to hinder People looking in, and are of all Colours irregularly, and without order, some Red, some Green, some Yellow, and so on; they make also a kind of Windows the Glass whereof is set in Plaster, in the Figure of Birds, or of Flower-Pots, and the rest is of bits of Glass of all Colours, in imitation of the natural Colours of what is there represented.

❡ In all Houses, and even in the meanest, there are Basons of Water, the Make whereof is very strong, built with Bricks, overcast with a Cement call'd, *Ahacsia*, i. e. black Lime, which in process of time, becomes harder than Marble; they make that Cement with very fine Ashes, taken out of the Hearths of Baths, mix'd with half the Quantity of quick Lime, and with a kind of Down beaten very well together for a whole Day, as tho' they would make an Amalgamation; that Down grows on the top of some Reeds, and is so light, that it is carry'd away with a Breath; it is call'd, *Louy*, some say, 'tis the Tipha of the Herbalists: Some Bricklayers bind that Mortar with very fine Flocks, or small Kid-hair; both those Materials are a sure Proof against the Water, and the Fire also; but the Frost cracks them, and makes them scale off; that Mischief is prevented, by draining those Basons in the Winter, and filling them with Tree Leaves, and afterwards covering them with Matts or Carpets: All this is meant of the Basons in the common Peoples Houses; for in rich Mens Houses, the Basons are built of a very hard Freestone, Edged all round with white Marble.

❡ The Wood-work of Houses consists only in Doors and Sashes, which are fixed without Hinges, or any other Iron-work, in this Manner; They leave at the top and bottom of the Door a round Piece of Wood, and they make a Hole at the top in the Corner of the Lintel, and one at the bottom in the Threshold, where the Pieces of Wood are to go in, and serve instead of Hinges for the Door to turn on, and in that Manner, they hang all the

Doors in the *East*, and even in Palaces, as well as other Houses: There were no other sorts of Doors in the famous Buildings of *Solomon*. Thus the Houses in those Countries are built without Smiths as well as without Carpenters; no Iron-work is to be seen in their Edifices, but a Pin with a hole in it, and a Chain and Padlock to fasten the Door with; the *Persians* do not use Iron Locks, their Locks are made of Wood, and so are their Keys, but very different from ours; for the Lock is like a little Harrow, that goes half way into a Wooden Staple, and the Key is a Wooden Handle, at the End whereof are some Wooden Points, also set, which they thrust in at the top of the Staple, and with them lift up the little Harrow. There is no Lead us'd, neither in the Building of the Houses, every thing, and even the Spouts being made of Wood. The Sashes are made either of Squares of Glass, or of Oil'd Cloth, Painted, and very fine and transparent. I forgot to tell you, that they make in the thick Walls, as has been said, Niches a Foot deep, which serve as Shells and Cupboards; they are contriv'd in several Shapes, and Painted afterwards of the Colour of the Wall; they are very convenient to set either Flower Pots, Perfuming Pots, Books, or any such like Things on them.

¶ As I have just now described the *Persian* Buildings, it may easily be inferr'd, that they are not subject to Fire; the *Persians* have no Apprehension of it, and if it catches any where, which happens very seldom, it can but at the worst, consume what is in the same Room; they are sure, that it will go no further; and will be put out; but then on the other Hand, those Houses are much troubled with Water, and if it should soak but three Days in a Foundation, it would cause it to tumble; so that to take all the Forts in the Country, one would need but overflow them for a Week; but that is no easy Matter in that Country, where the Water is scarce, and where the Rivers may be turn'd in an Instant out of their natural Channels; therefore 'tis upon that Account, that the *Persians* are very careful of their Terraces or Coverings of the Houses, as the chief Part, whereon depends their Preservation. Their Care about them, is to keep always the Rain-Spouts clear, at the bottom, and to sweep the Snow off of the Terrace, when it falls very thick. 'Tis a Sport for the Mob to throw the Snow off of the Houses, and they run up chearfully to the House-top. The young Men of the Ward go up into all the Terraces, one after another, and clear them in a Moment; and to encourage them the more to it, the Musick waits on them all the time. The Bricklayers work with a kind of a Tone, and what's Remarkable in their work is, that when they hand the Tiles or Bricks to one another they put on Gloves, that they may not sully the Bricks with the Sweat of their Hands. I must not forget to tell you also, that they strew Salt on the Beams, Rafters, Ceiling, and other Pieces of Timber, to keep the Worms from them.

¶ The Houses last as long as they are pleased to repair them, the dry and clear Air contributing to their Preservation; but as I have observ'd else-where, the *Persians* do not like their Parents Houses, they love to build some fit for themselves, which is very rational; for, as they say, there is the same difference, between building a House fit for one's Family, or taking one ready built, as between making oneself a Suit of Cloaths, or buying one ready made.

¶ The Reason of it is perhaps, because they build very cheap; for they build as it were, a House, with what is taken out of the Foundation; and the Poor People, who can make Shift with the Shell of the House only, have soon finish'd it. The *Persians* Rate their Houses according to the height and thickness of the Walls, which they measure by the Yard, as they do Stuffs. The King has no Right in the Sale of Houses, but the Surveyor, who is call'd, *Mamar bachi*, i. e. head of the Bricklayers, hath two *per Cent.* for Lots and Sales; but 'tis very seldom they pay him the full Sums, every one compounding with him according to his Credit or Employment. That Officer has also five *per Cent.* upon every House the King orders to be built; they appraise them when they are finish'd, and the Surveying Officer, who inspected it, receives for his Fee and Salary, the fifth Part of what the House cost in Building.

¶ I shall observe three Things more, concerning the *Persian* Buildings; The *First* is, that they Line the Walls with Earthen Tiles, as the *Dutch* do their Chimneys; The *Second* is, that in the Country, several of their Doors are made of one large Stone, turning upon its Hinges, like the Wooden ones; The *Third* is, that the *Persian* Houses cost very little in Building, in Comparison of ours.

¶ They reckon when they Build, that one third Part of the Charge goes for Brick; another third Part for Plaister; and the last third Part, for Wood-work, including the Doors and Windows.

¶ The *Persians* have but indifferent Carpenters; the Reason of it is, because, of the little Wood there is in *Persia*, and of the little Timber they commonly use in Building; 'tis not so with the Joyners; they are very skilful, and very ingenious in composing all sorts of Inlaid-work and Mosaick-work, and they make noble Ceilings in that Kind; they fit them all on the Ground, and when they are done, they raise them up over the top of the Building, on the Columns, that are to bear them up: I have seen a whole one of fourscore Foot Diameter, rear'd up, with the help of a Machine, like the Draught I present you with on the other side, not

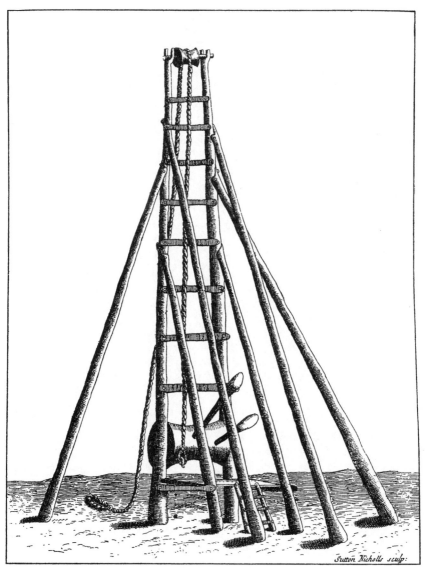

Wooden Crane

knowing whether our *European* Workmen have any such; the *Persians* use no other, and they raise every thing with a Pully; they make also Lattices and Rails very well. The Joyners sit on the Ground at their Work, their Plains are not like ours, for they thrust the Shavings out of the Sides, and not out of the Top, which seems to be a more expeditious way; their ordinary Wood is a white Wood, very soft, and without Knots; and therefore very easy to be wrought; they have an excellent Wood, that comes out of *Hercania*, in long Boards, like the *Norway* Deal Boards.

¶ Not knowing very well what Method to set the other Trades in, I shall divide them into two Classes. The first, of those which the *Persians* understand best, and the other of those they understand least.

¶ *Embroidery* is one of the Mechanick Arts they are best vers'd in; they do all sorts of Embroidery very well, especially the Gold and Silver Embroidery, either on Cloth, Silk, or Leather. They exceed us in that Art, and the *Turks* likewise, whose Stitching and Embroidery on Leather we so much admire: Their Leather Seams, as well as those of Horse-Trappings among the rest, is so smooth and so neat, that you would take it for Embroidery. Their Leather Pails are also very well sewed, tho' with Thongs of Sheep-skin very indifferently Tann'd. The Gold and Silver Thread they use, is so well twisted, that they would take it for Wire when 'tis wrought, the Silk not appearing in the least.

¶ The Enamel Ware, or *China* Ware, as they call it, is likewise one of the curiousest Manufactures; they make it all over *Persia*: The finest is made at *Chiras*, the Metropolis of *Persia*; at *Metched*, the Capital of *Bactriana*; at *Yezd* and *Kirman* in *Caramania*, and especially in a Village of *Caramania*, call'd *Zorende*. The Earth whereof that Ware is made, is pure Enamel, both within and without, like the *China Ware*: The Grain of it is as fine and transparent as that is; whereby it happens that one is often deceived in that Earthen *Ware*, and that one cannot distinguish it from *China Ware*: Nay, you meet sometimes with some *Persian Ware* that exceeds the *China Ware*, so beautiful and lively is the Varnish of it: I speak still of the new *China Ware*, and not of the old. In the Year 1666, an Embassador of the *Dutch* Company, called, *Hubert de Laresse*, having brought the King a Present of a great many valuable things, and amongst the rest, six and fifty pieces of old *China Ware*, the King, as soon as he saw it, began to Smile, and ask'd scornfully, what it was. They say that the *Dutch* mix that *Persian Ware* with the *China Ware*, and import it into *Holland*. 'Tis certain that the *Dutch* have improved themselves much in *Persia*, in the way of making *Earthen Ware*, and they would make it still better had they the same clear Water, and the same clear Air they have in *Persia*. The skilful Workmen in *Enamel Ware*, ascribe to the Water the gloss of the Colour, as has been already observed, and say, that there are some Waters that dissolve the Colours and make them spread, whereas there are others that contract and fix them. The Pieces which the *Persian* Potters called *Cacoiper*, or *Earthen Ware Bakers*, make best, are the Enamel Tiles painted and cut out in imitation of *Moresk Work*. Indeed nothing can be seen livelier and brighter in that Kind, or drawn finer and more regular. The *Persian Earthen Ware* is Fire-proof; so that they not only boil Water in it without breaking, but they even make *Pilo*-Pots of them. It is hard enough also to make Mortars to grind Colours and other Materials in, and Bullet-Molds. The Matter of that fine Enamel is Glass, and little River Pebbles pounded very small, together with a little Mould mixed with them. There is no *Earthen Ware* made in the *Indies*; all that is used there, is Imported either from *Persia*, *Japan*, or *China*, and other Kingdoms between *China* and *Pegu*. There is a Story that the Potters of the Town of *Yezd* in *Caramania*, sent once, by way of Chalenge, to the Potters of *Ispahan*, an Earthen Dish that held twelve Pound weight of Water, and weighed itself but a Dram; and the Potters of *Ispahan* sent them back a Dish of the same bigness and form, which held but a Drachm of Water, and weigh'd twelve Pound weight. There are some Tradesmen in *Persia* whose Employment is to mend *Earthen Ware* and *Glass*, they join the Pieces together, and sew them with very small Tin Wire, and rub the seam over with a kind of Chalk or smal Lime: A Dish so mended, holds Water as well as before.

❡ The *Gold Wire-Drawers* and *Thread-Twisters*, are very dextrous Workmen. They draw an Ingot, weighing a *Mescal*, or Drachm, nine hundred *Guezes*, or *Persian* Ells long, each *Gueze* being five and thirty Inches long. Their Tools of several sizes, are like our *Wire-drawing* Irons: they wind on Bobins and Drums, and buy at the Mint, the small *Wire* of the bigness of a Pin: Their Thread is the best and the smoothest that can be imagined. All the Art they use to give it that lively and lasting Colour, is to guild the *Wire* very fine and very thick.

❡ I must bring in next the Tanning of *Hides*, especially that of *Shagreen* and of all sorts of *Turkey* Leather: Abundance of it is made in *Persia*, and is exported to the *Indies*, to *Turkey*, and to other neighbouring Kingdoms. *Shagreen* is made of an Asse's Rump, and of a Seed called in *Persian*, *Tochm Casbini*, i. e. Seed of *Casbin*, which is black, hard, and bigger than the Mustard-seed, which they use for want of the *Casbin* Seed. The same *Persian* Word signifies Egg and Seed, because the Egg and the Seed are, as it were the same thing. The Name of *Shagreen*, whereby we call all those rough Hide, comes without doubt, from the *Persian* Word *Sagri, i. e.* Buttocks. They call by that Name the Rump of any Beast they ride on: And they give that Name to that sort of Hide, because it is made of an Asse's Rump, as I have said. The Tanners dress coarse Hides, and dress them with Lime. They use no Bark, but use Salt and Galls instead of it; and that's enough in their Country, the Air being hot and dry.

⁋ The *Turner's* Trade is also one of the Mechanick Arts, which the *Persians* understand very well. They have no Frame for Turning, as we have; their way consists only in a Trendle, to which they fasten whatever they intend to Turn, a Thong that goes twice round the Trendle, and which a Boy holds with both Hands, pulling now one end of it, then another end, turns the Piece about. But when they have but small Pieces to Turn, the Workman needs no help, for with one Hand he stirs the Axis with a Bow, and with the other Hand he holds the piece of Wood. They use no Wimbles as we do, but they use Gimblets of several Sizes, which are instead of them, and which they turn with the same Instrument as they do Wood; 'Tis a piece of Iron flat and sharp at the End, shaped like a Rib, that it may cut the better, hafted in a round Handle filled with Lead to make it weighty, about which they put a Strop that goes quite round it, they hold fast the Gimblet with the Left Hand, on the piece of Wood they intend to bore, and turn it with the Right Hand. That is their Mechanick way of Turning and Boring. They lay on Lacker very neatly; the violent Motion of the turning Instrument melting it without the help of Fire: They spread it with a Palm tree Stick, because that Wood is porous, and then with a piece of coarse Cloth and a little Oil, they give a wonderful Lustre to their Work, which never goes off: That Lacker likewise is never subject to scaling. Among other things, they make Childrens Cradles extraordinary well. They turn Metals as well as Wood, but they are very far from attaining to the Skill of our Workmen. They have brought several times to *Persia* and the *Indies*, some of those curious Ivory works turned with an exquisite Nicety; but because they were of no use, and fit only to draw Admiration and Respect on the Workman, they made no account of them. The *Orientalists* are not Nice enough to apply their Minds to the Ingenuity we admire in them, far from it, they value it very little by reason of the unusefulness of the Work. Moreover, the *Persian* Turners, are unskill'd in the turning of an Oval; 'tis a Figure, the working whereof they are utterly unacquainted with.

⁋ Next to the Turners I set the *Tinkers* and *Tinmen*, who work very neatly in that Country, both with the Hammer, File, and turning Instrument: Our Silversmiths do not work better than those Tinkers; the

Reason of it, I think, is because the Table Utensils and Kitchin Implements are commonly made of Copper; they use no Iron, Brass, nor
Pewter in their Kitchin Utensils; they are all of tinn'd Copper; their
Tin-work is fine, white, and as neat as Silver: The *English* Pewter is not so
bright: 'Tis true, they are forced every six or eight Months, to Tin it over
again, but then it is done very quick and very cheap, a Plate being Tinn'd
both within and without for a Penny Charge, and the rest in proportion:
They set about it a very different way from our Workmen. *First,* They
boil the Utensil in grey *Kalt,* then give it the 'Prentice to scower with
Sand, which he does with his bare Feet standing on it, and turning it this
way and that way, till it be very clean. Then they set it a heating on a
Charcoal Fire, with the hollow side to the Fire, and when the Utensil
begins to be red hot, the Workman with one hand takes hold of the
Utensil with a pair of Pincers, and with the other Hand takes a little fine
Cotton well beaten, which he dips in *Salt Armoniack,* and rubs the Vessel
well with it; after that he takes a small Ingot of fine Pewter, and holds
it fast against the bottom of the Utensil, to melt it upon it, and spreads
the Pewter all over with the Cotton, cover'd over with *Salt Armoniack*; and
when the Piece is Tinn'd over, he throws it into cold Water, from whence it
comes out as white and as bright as burnish'd Silver. The *Salt Armoniack,*
which they use in tinning, is purified over the Fire with some Water,
which they let waste all away till the Salt be reduced to Powder. They
are singularly handy about that Business, and their Copper Furniture
tinn'd over, have that Advantage above ours, that they are lighter, and
never melt nor bruise. The *Persians* have Copper in their Country, as
I have said, but they do not value it so much as the *Japaneze* or *Swedish*
Copper. I forgot to tell you that they have their Pewter from the *Indies.*
As to Lamps, Candlesticks, and other cast Pieces, the *Persian* Workmen
turn them over two Puppets with a Strap.

❡ The *Gunsmiths* make very good Weapons, especially Bows and Swords.
The *Persian* Bows are the most valued of all the *East*: The Matter whereof
they are made is Wood and Horn laid over one another, and cover'd over
with Sinews, and over that with the Skin of a Tree very sleek and smooth;
they Paint them afterwards, and Varnish them so admirably well, that
one may see one's self in those Bows, and the colour of them is as bright
as possible. The Goodness of a Bow, as the *Persians* say, consists in this,
viz. That a Bow be hard to bend till the Arrow be half laid over it, and
then that it be soft and easy, till the end of the Arrow be fixed in the
String: The Bow-strings are of twisted Silk of the bigness of a first Quill:
The Quivers are made of Leather Embroider'd with Gold or Silk: Their

Cimiters are very well Damask'd, and exceed all that the *Europeans* can do, because I suppose our Steel is not so full of Veins as the *Indian* Steel, which they use most commonly. They have in their Country plenty of Steel, but they do not prize it so much as that, and ours less still than theirs; yet their Steel is eager and very brittle: They forge their Blades cold, and before they dip them, they rub them with Tallow, Oil, or Butter, to hinder them from breaking: Then they temper them with Vinegar and Coperas, which being of a corroding Nature, shews those Streaks or Veins, which they call Damask Work; and that is it likewise which they call Damask Steel, because that Town was the most celebrated Place of the Manufacture of those curious Cimeter-Blades that were made of the Steel which was imported from the *Indies* by the *Red-Sea*, in the late Ages. The *Persians* make also very well, the Barrels of Fire-Arms, and Damask them as they do the Blades, but they make them very heavy, and cannot avoid it: They bore and scower them with a Wheel, as we do, and forge and bore them so even that they almost never burst. They make them alike strong and thick all along, saying, that the Mouth of the Gun being weak, the Report shakes it, and communicates the wavering Motion to the Bullet. That's the Reason, that if their Guns be thicker, they therefore carry the Shot further and straighter, they Soder the Breech of the Barrel with the heat of the Fire, and reject Screws, saying, that a Screw Breach going in without Stress, may be thrust out by the Violence of the Powder, and is not to be rely'd on. They do not understand very well how to make Locks or Springs; those they put to their Fire-Arms, are very unlike ours; for they have no Steel, the Pan is very fast, being all of a Piece with the Barrel, the which moves along a small rough Iron Branch, that comes out of the Inside of the Gun, and moves backward, that is toward the But-End, on the Pan, but quite contrary to it; the Pan is usually no bigger than the little Finger Nail, without Snap-haunce; and most Pans are rough within, like a File, that the Prime may stick the better to it. They do not understand how to Mount Fire-Arms, and do not observe the Rules of Staticks, but make the But-End small and light, which is the Reason that their Guns are light at the Breech, and heavy at the Muzzle. ¶ The Workmen in Iron and Steel are also very well vers'd in their Trade; they Hammer both Iron and Steel cold, and succeed very well in it, with Respect to several sorts of Tools, and Instruments, as among others, Iron Plates, whereon they bake the Bread, call'd, *Lavatche*, no thicker than Parchment, and Country Ovens, which are shap'd like two Semi-cones, or Semispheres, cut thro' the top, and fasten'd together with great Iron-Hooks; the Diameter of them is two Foot and a half, and the height from three to four Foot; there stick out in the Inside of those Cones, large Pins, about four Fingers long, and as big, with flat Heads, as broad as half a Crown. When they have Occasion to use those Ovens, they overcast both the Inside and Outside of them, with Clay, which sticks to the Nails-head, and make as it were, a Wall of it, to which they stick the Bread; those Ovens are call'd *Tendour*, as are also the common Ovens, which are of the same Shape, being dug in the Ground, and like Pitts, round about which they stick also the Bread, which is easily done, that sort of Bread being no thicker than a Fingers breadth. When they intend to remove those Ovens, they break off the Clay, and lay the two Semi-cones on a Horse's Back, one Part on each side of the Horse; the Iron and Steel Tools they make best also, are among other Saws, which are made of Steel, as smooth and as bright as a Looking-Glass; the Razors, which are but half as big as at the Handles, yet are as broad at the End, shave excellently well; the Sizors, which they make hollow on the Inside, like Gutters, saying, that being so shap'd, the Edge of the two Blades joins closer, and cuts better. Almost all their Looking-Glasses are Convex, some few are Concave, like the Burning-Glasses. The Air being very dry in *Persia*, as I have observ'd it over and over, the brightness of those Looking-Glasses doth not grow Dull, and they never Rust. The *Eastern* People use likewise Glass Looking-Glasses, and even abundance of them, tho' not near so many as Metal ones, and that they do upon two Accounts, the first is, because those Metal Looking-Glasses are more lasting, and do not break with falling; the second Reason is, because, when the Glass Looking-Glasses are once unsilver'd, they become useless, the way of Silvering Glass being unknown in all the *Eastern* Parts, and the Quick-silver that is on the Backside of the Looking-Glasses coming off easier there than in *Europe*, by Reason of the great dryness of the Air, and in the *Indies* quite contrary, by Reason of its great dampness. The Orienta-lists have used Glass Looking-Glasses, but since their Trade with the *Europeans*. Note, that they Polish their Metal-Glasses with fine Emeril, pounded to Powder, as fine as Dust, having no *Venetian Tripoli*, or having so little, that one may say, it is not used among them.

¶ The other Mechanick Arts, wherein the *Persians* are pretty well vers'd, are those that follow; The Art of making Fire-Works, wherein their Workmen equal, and perhaps exceed those of all other Parts of the World.

¶ The Art of dressing Beasts, of setting out their Meats very Neatly. The *Persians* believe, that those who exercise that Trade are Polluted with the Blood they handle; yet the Butchers are dispers'd here and there in all the Streets of Cities, and have no fixed Shambles as in our Countries. When the Butchers intend to kill a Beast, they carry it to a Corner of their Shop, and there make a little Hole to receive the Blood of it, then they cast down the Beast, turn the Head of it towards *Mecca*, and themselves too, they cut the Throat of it with a Knife, kept for that Purpose, only both to keep it clean, and to avoid the Danger of cutting any forbidden Thing, or of touching any Unclean Thing; at Night when they shut up Shop, they strew Salt on the Block whereon they chop their Meat, lest the Dogs should lick it, and so make it Unclean.

¶ The Art of Lapidaries, who understand pretty well the Grinding of soft Stones, and the Cutting of them. The *Persian* Lapidaries make their Wheels of two Parts of Emeril, and one Part of Lave. They find, that there is a great deal of Care required in making the Wheels; for the Composition must be extraordinary well work'd together, and be allow'd such a due Proportion of Heat, that the Clamminess, which they call *Chire*, i. e. Milk or Cream, be not dried up; they turn those Wheels hafted on a round Chuck, with a Bow, which they hold in one Hand, and the Stone in the other: It is difficult to make very straight a Stone that way; but to make amends, the cutting of it is easy and cheap; when they intend to Polish the Stone, they set in the Room of that Wheel another Wheel, made with red *Willow*, on which they strew Calcined Pewter, or some Tripoly. The Seal Engravers use the Bow, and a very small Copper Wheel, with Emeril; they have *Persian* and *Indian* Emeril, which is of a very different Nature; for the *Indian* Emeril grinds better, the smaller it is, and the other is quite contrary.

¶ The Art of Dying, which seems to have been more improved in *Persia* than in *Europe*, their Colours being much more solid and bright, and not fading so soon; but the Honour of it is not so much to be ascribed to their Art, as to their Air and Climate, which being dry and clear, causes the Liveliness of the Colours, as also to the Strength of the Dying Ingredients, which growing most of them in the Country, are used when they are Green, and full of Sap. Their Dying and Painting Colours are the Bole, or red Earth, the *Rounat*, or *Oppoponax*, which are two common Ingredients in *Persia*; the *Brazil*-Wood, which is Imported amongst them from *Europe*; the *Japan*-Wood, and the Indigo, which they fetch from the *Indies*. They use moreover in Dying, several Herbs, and Simples of their own Growth, and Gums, and Skins of Trees, and Fruits, and of Walnuts, and Pomgranats, and the Juice of Lemon; the *Lapis Lazuli*, which they call *Lagsverd*, from whence comes the *French* Word, *Azure*, is got in their Neighbourhood, in the Country of the *Yusbecks*, but *Persia* is the general Store-house for it.

❡ The Mistery of Shaving, which they are perfect Masters of; they shave with a wonderful Dexterity, you can scarce feel them, especially when they shave your Head; they begin at the Top, and draw the Razor downwards, as if they only run it over your Head, and your Head is shaved in a Moment; but before they set the Razor to it, they rub it a great while, then they wet it; 'tis in my Opinion, that long Friction that Facilitates the shaving, so that 'tis scarce felt; they use no hot Water for shaving, but cold, and set no Bason under your Chin; their Bason is a Cup, no bigger than a Parrot Cup; they wet their Hands in the Water that's in it, then wet the Face with it; they are likewise very cleanly in their Trade; for when they shave the Head, they throw all the Hair into one Place; they wipe the Razor on the Hair unshaved, so they never use a Razor Cloth, and never wipe it but with their Finger: I am perswaded, that the heat and dryness of the Climate are a great help to the Barbers in shaving: 'Tis their way after they have shaved one to cut also the Nails, both of his Hands and Feet, with a sharp Iron, like that Instrument, which the Chirurgeons call a Fleam; then they draw your Fingers and Arms, and handle your Head, and your Body, especially your Shoulders, to see, as it were, if every Limb be in its right Place, which affords much Ease and Pleasure; the Barbers go every Morning to their Customers, to hold the Glass before them, which is commonly four Inches Diameter, with a Handle to it, they are not paid for that, but when they shave the Face and Head, they have three or four Pence given them; those who give them five Pence pay them Nobly.

❡ The Art of Standish making; they make their common Standishes six Inches long, and two Inches both broad and high, of the thickness of a Tester, one Piece within another, like a Chest of Drawers, they make them in an Iron Mould, with Sheets of Paper pasted over one another, rubbing the last Sheet with Mutton Suet, and laying over it a curious Varnish, that is a Fence against Rain; the Inside of the Standish is lined with Leather, which makes it a solid Body, as hard, and harder than Wood: The Paste they use is not made of Flower, but of a Root, beaten to Powder, call'd *Senchon*; it is bruised between two Grinding Stones, as the Corn is, but is no finer than Saw-Dust, they dilute it in cold Water, where it swells presently, and sticks wonderful fast.

❡ The Taylors Trade; they work very neatly, and cut Cloaths so exactly, that they set without the least Wrinkle: As for the Sowing Part, they exceed us certainly, none can be made finer, or more even; they seldom sow the Outside of the Cloth as we do, but the Inside, and their most common Seam is what we call the Back-stitch; they make Carpets,

Cushions, Door-hangings, and other Felt Furniture, like Garden Knots, and Mosaick-Work, representing what they please, and all of it so neatly sowed, that you would think the Figures are Painted, tho' 'tis all of it but Patch'd-Work; the Seam of them is not seen if you look at it never so near, they are drawn so curiously fine.

¶ Those are the Arts and Trades which the *Persians* understand tolerably well: Those they do not understand are as follows.

¶ The Art of Glass-making; there are Glass Houses all over *Persia*, but most of the Glass is full of Flaws, and Bladders, and is Greyish, upon the Account doubtless, that the Fire lasts but three or four Days, and that their *Deremne*, as they call it, which is a sort of a Broom, which they use to make it, doth not bear heat so well as ours. The Glass of *Chiras* is the finest in the Country; that of *Ispahan*, on the contrary, is the sorriest, because it is only Glass melted again; they make it commonly in Spring. They do not understand to Silver their Glass over, as I have observ'd already; therefore their Glass Looking-Glasses, their Sash-Glass, and their Snuff-Bottles are brought to them from *Venice*. Moreover, the Art of Glass-making was brought into *Persia*, within these four score Years. A Beggarly and Covetous *Italian* taught it at *Chiras*, for the Sum of fifty Crowns. Had not I been certainly informed of the Matter, I should have thought they had been beholden to the *Portugueze* for their Skill, in so noble and so useful an Art. I ought not to forget to acquaint you with the *Persian* Art of Sowing Glass together very ingeniously, as I have hinted above; for provided the Pieces be not smaller than ones Nail, they sow them together with Wyre, and rub the Seam over with a white Lead, or with calcined Lime, mix'd with the Whites of Eggs, which hinders the Water from soaking thro.

¶ Among their Sentences, there is a Godly one, relating to the ingenious Piece of Work just mentioned: *If broken Glass be restored again, how much more may Man be restored again after his Dissolution in the Grave?*

¶ Paper making, which is perform'd very rudely in *Persia*, because they use nothing but Calico, either Dyed or Painted; therefore their Paper is brownish, foul, ragged, and over-limber; they use a great deal of *European* Paper after they have prepared it; but they fetch some from little *Tartary*, which they prefer before it; they prepare their Paper with a little Soap, which they rub over it, then they smooth it with a sleek Stone, to the intent their Ink may run more freely.

¶ The Trunk-makers Work is likewise perform'd very Slovenly; their Trunks, which stand on four Feet of white Wood, are very light, and are overlaid with black Skins, both within and without, the Fore-Part of them is adorn'd with Figures, cut out in Leather of several Colours; they put them in Sacks of Goats Hair, the bottom whereof is lin'd with Leather, and so load their Horses easily with them. All their Trunks are Padlock Trunks, for they have no other Locks.

¶ The Book-binders work also very Clumsily, and one thing you'll hardly believe, is, that they cannot make a Book Cover all of one Piece; they make it of two Pieces, Pasted together on the Back of the Book, which is always flat, because they know not how to make it round; and altho' they paste those two Pieces very neatly, yet the Patching appears plain in time.

¶ The *Persian* Soap is made with Mutton-Suet, and the Ashes of strong Herbs; it is soft and close, not Whiten'd well, but it is very cheap. The *Persians* send into *Turkey* for some, and especially to *Aleppo*, where the best in all the *Eastern* Parts is made, and may be in all the World, being white, fine, and much harder than that of *Europe*, which must be imputed to the goodness of the Ashes of *Aleppo*, where all the *Europeans* stock themselves with them, to make Soap. Those Ashes are made of a sort of Plant, that grows in the Desarts, and in Sandy and dry Places; they burn it in *Syria* and *Egypt*, under their Baths. Ashes mixed with Lime and Olive Oil, is the Composition whereof Soap is made; Oil is also very good, and very Plentiful at *Aleppo*. The *Persian* Soap is not made with Oil, but with Beef, Mutton, and Goat Suet. They do not use so much Soap in *Persia* by far, as they do in *Europe*, for several Reasons, and among others, because most of their Linnen is Dy'd, and is made of Silk, such as Shirts, Drawers, Handkerchiefs; because there is no Linnen but *Calico*, which is washed in cold Water; and because the Air, and the Sun, and cold Water perform a wash without much Soap, and much trouble; they rub the Linnen a little, then spread it on the Grass, and Water it every quarter of an Hour, for near four Hours time, according as the Sun shines hot, which makes it whiter than Snow. I have kept for ten Years Linnen wash'd in the *Indies* with cold Water, and without Soap, and when we sat our Linnen by it, we found that *European* Linnen look'd but dark and brown in comparison of it; and one may judge how much of its whiteness it had lost with lying so long in a Trunk.

¶ The Goldsmiths Trade, that curious Art, so much spread Abroad, is very little understood by the *Persians*; they know nothing of Enamelling, what they do best is the Filligreen-work, they Engrave pretty well, especially Emboss'd-work, and make Stone-Rings tolerably; those are the particular Things they are best Skill'd in, in that Art.

¶ As to the Watch-making Trade, it is still unknown among the *Persians*.

When I was there, they had but three or four *European* Watch-makers: I guess'd the Reason of it to be this, *viz.* their living in a Climate where the Days are not so different in their length, and where the Air is always Clear and Serene, they can guess by the Sun at the Time of the Day, without the help of Clocks; they use no Sundials neither.

CHAPTER XVIII

OF MANUFACTURES

HAVING Discours'd of the Mechanick Arts of the *Persians*, I must treat at the same time of their *Manufactures*. They have very good ones in *Cotton*, in *Goats* and *Camels Hair*, in *Yarn*, and especially in *Silk*, it being a plentiful and common Commodity in *Persia*; the Natives have addicted themselves particularly to the well-working of it; and 'tis the thing they are best skill'd in, and in which they have the most considerable Manufactures of all their Country. Their Workmen have Reels, Spindles, and Winding-wheels, to wind Silk on, very much like ours. They keep their raw and unwrought Silks in damp Places, which they water sometimes to continue the weight of them, because they sell it by weight; and for the same Reason, they keep that which is wound up in Leathern Bags. I shall pass by several sorts of Stuffs of all Silk, such as Taffeties, Tabbies, Sattins, Turbants, Sashes, Handkerchiefs, and Silk-Stuffs mixed with Cotton-Thread, or with Camel or Goats-hair, which are made all over *Persia*. I shall only speak of their Brocade. They call Brocade *Zerbafe*, *i. e.* Gold Tissue. There is the single Brocade, whereof there are a hundred Sorts; and the double Brocade, which is called *D'ouroye*, i. e. with two Faces, because it had no wrong side, and the *Machmely Zerbafe*, or Gold Velvet. They make Gold Brocades which cost fifty *Tomans* the *Gueze* or Ell, which being two Foot and half a Quarter long by the *French* Measure, comes to about thirty Crowns the Inch, or eleven hundred Crowns the Ell. No part of the World affords so dear a Silk. They employ six Men together about the Loom to make it, who use about thirty several Shuttles to weave it, whereas they commonly use but two. Notwithstanding the extraordinary rate of that precious Brocade, the Workmen employ'd in it, do not earn above fifteen or sixteen Pence a Day at it, and can make but the thickness of a Half-crown Piece of it. Those dear Brocades are bought for Curtains and Door-Hangings, which are generally used, and are the most common Furniture of a House, and for

Cushions. The Gold Velvet that's wrought in *Persia* is very charming, especially the curl'd Velvet and all those rich Stuffs, have that admirable Property, that they last for Ever as it were, and the Gold and Silver does not wear off whilst the Work lasts, and keeps still its Colour and brightness: 'Tis true the Silver tarnishes at length, after twenty or thirty Years; yet then it doth not come off, which I think ought to be imputed to the clearness of the Air, as much as to the goodness of the Work. The finest Looms for those Stuffs, are at *Yezd*, at *Cashan*, and likewise at *Ispahan*; those for Carpets are in the Province of *Kirman*, and especially at *Sistan*. Those are the Carpets we commonly call in Europe, *Turky* Carpets, because they brought them through *Turky* before they traded with the *Persians* by the Ocean. The *Persians* Rule to know good Carpets, and to Rate them by, is to lay their Thumb on the edge of the Carpet and to tell the Threads in a Thumb's breadth, for the more there are, the dearer the Work is: The most Threads there are in an Inch breadth is fourteen or fifteen.

¶ The *Camel hair* Stuffs are wrought especially at *Yezd*, and at *Kirman* in *Caramania*: They call that Camel-wool, *Teftick*, and also *Kourk*; it is almost as fine as Beaver-wool, extraordinary soft and smooth in one's Hand, but they can make nothing that's substantial or strong with it. There are also *Camlets*, *Stamines*, and Silk and Worsted *Druggets* made in these Towns. In the Country of *Mougan* they make the coarse and thick *Serges* for the Common People.

¶ The best *Goats-hair* Stuffs are woven in *Hircania*; they are like *Barracan*; but the finest are made along the *Persian* Gulf at *Dourack*. From thence come those sort of Mantles called *Habbé*, which are Cassocks with Sleeves no longer than a Jacket Sleeve, and all of a Piece, without any Seam; some of them are very fine, and commonly striped.

¶ The *Persians* do not understand to make Cloth, but they make very fine and very light Felt Tufts, that are warmer than Cloth, and are a better fence against Rain; they work the Wool of it as the Hatters do the Cony-wool, and make of it Cloaks for rainy Weather for the Mobb: they use it instead of oiled Cloth: They spread it over Floors, either upon the Carpets, to lie the softer on them, or under them, to keep them from the Damp.

¶ They make also *Calico Cloth* very reasonable; but they make none fine, because they have it cheaper out of the *Indies* than they can make it. They call that Cloth *Kerbez*, as if one should say, Ass's Webb: From that Word came probably, the Word *Carbasson*, and the Word *Carbæsius*, used by the *Greeks* and *Latins*, to signify coarse Linnen Cloth. They understand also the painting of Linnen, but not so well as the *Indians*, because they buy in the *Indies* the finest painted Linnen so cheap, that they would get nothing by improving themselves in that Manufacture. A work they understand very well is overlaying with Gold and Silver Linnen Cloth, Taffety, and Sattin; they do it with Moulds, and represent on them what they please, *viz.* Letters, Flowers, and Figures; and they Stamp them so neatly, that you would think 'tis Gold or Silver Embroidery. They print with Gum-water.

¶ They make also Matts and Ozier hand Baskets, which fold together, or roll up very neatly. There can be no finer Matts seen than theirs. The best Manufacture is at *Siston*, because the Rushes are first brought thither. Those Rushes grow in Fens near the River *Tigris*, and the River *Euphrates*.

CHAPTER XIX

OF THE COMMERCE OR TRADE; AND ALSO OF THE WEIGHTS, THE MEASURES, AND COIN

TRADING is a very honourable. Profession in the *East*, as being the best of those that have any Stability, and are not so liable to change. 'Tis not to be wonder'd at, for it cannot be otherwise in Kingdoms, where on the one hand there is no Title of Nobility, and therefore little Authority annexed to the Birth; and where on the other Hand, the form of Government being altogether Despotick and Arbitrary, the Authority annexed to Places and Employments cannot last longer than the Employments themselves, which are likewise precarious; for which Reason Trading is much set by in that part of the World, as a lasting and independent Station. Another Reason why it is valu'd is, because the Noblemen profess it, and the Kings also; they have their Deputies as the Merchants have, and under the same Denomination: They have most of them their Trading Ships, and their Store-Houses. The King of *Persia*, for Instance, sells and sends to the Neighbouring Kingdoms, Silk, Brocades, and other rich Goods, Carpets and Precious Stones. The Name of Merchant, is a Name much respected in the *East*, and is not allowed to Shop-keepers or Dealers in trifling Goods; nor to those who Trade not in foreign Countries: 'Tis allow'd only to such as employ Deputies or Factors in the remotest Countries: And those Men are sometimes rais'd to the highest Ranks, and are usually employed in Embassies. There are Merchants in *Persia* who have Deputies in all parts of the World: And when those Deputies are returned Home, they wait on their Master, under no better Denomination than that of a Servant, standing up always before them, and waiting at Table, tho' some of those Deputies are worth above threescore thousand Crowns. In the *Indies* the Laws are still more favourable to Traders, for tho' they are much more numerous than in *Persia*, they are nevertheless more set by. The Reason of this additional Respect, is, because in the *East*, Traders are Sacred Persons, who are never molested even in time of War; and are allowed a free Passage, they and their Effects, through the middle of Armies: 'Tis upon their account especially that the Roads are so safe all over *Asia*, and especially in *Persia*. The *Persians* call a Trader *Saudaguer*, *i. e.* Gain-Monger.

¶ The Eastern Merchants affect Grandure in Trading, notwithstanding they send their Deputies into all Parts, and stay at Home themselves, as in the Center of their grand Concern; they make no Bargains themselves directly, there is no publick place of Exchange in their Towns; the Trade is carried on by Stock-jobbers, who are the subtilest, the cunningest, the slyest, the complaisantest, the patientest, and the most intriguing Men of the whole Society, having a valuable and insinuating Tongue beyond Expression: They are called *Delal*, which answers to Great Talkers, that Word being of a contrary Signification to *Lal*, *i. e.* Dumb. The *Mahometans* have a Proverb alluding to the Name of those Men, viz. That at the last Day, *Delal Lal*, the Stock-jobbers, or Talkers, will be Dumb; intimating that they will have nothing to say for themselves. 'Tis very curious to see them make Bargains: After they have Argued and Discoursed a while before the Seller, and commonly at his own House, they agree with their Fingers about the Price: They take hold of one another's right Hand under a Cloak or Handkerchief, and entertain one another in that manner; the strait Finger stands for Ten, the bent Finger for Five; the Finger end for One; the whole Hand for a Hundred; and the Fist for a Thousand. Thus they denote Pounds, Pence, and Farthings, with a Motion of their Fingers: While they bargain they put on such a grave and steady Countenance, that 'tis impossible to know in the least either what they think or say.

¶ However, the *Mahometans* are not the greatest Traders in *Asia*, tho' they be dispers'd almost in every Part of it; and tho' their Religion bears sway in the larger part of it. Some of them are too Effeminate, and some too severe to apply themselves to Trade, especially foreign Trading. Wherefore in *Turky*, the *Christians* and *Jews* carry on the main foreign Trade: And in *Persia* the *Christians* and *Indian Gentiles*. As to the *Persians* they Trade with their own Countrymen, one Province with another, and most of them Trade with the *Indians*. The *Armenians* manage alone the whole European Trade; the Reason whereof is, because the *Mahometans* cannot strictly observe their Religion among the *Christians*, with relation to the outward Purity it requires of them; for Instance, Their Law forbids them to eat Flesh either Dress'd or Kill'd by a Man of a different Religion, and likewise to drink in the same Cup with such a one; It forbids to call upon God in a Place adorned with Figures; it even forbids in some Cases, the touching Persons of a contrary Opinion, which is a thing almost impossible to keep among the *Christians*.

¶ Another hindrance there is to the *Mahometan* improvement of Trade, *viz*. The forbidding Usury and Interest without any distinction. *Mahammed* broached his Religion in a Country whereof the whole Riches and Trade consisted in Cattle and breeds of Horses, where little Money was seen, and where the Trade was managed by way of Exchange, as in former times: And as it appears by a thousand things of the *Alcoran*, that he did not foresee that it would be propagated throughout the World, he perceived no inconveniency in forbidding to lend Money upon Interest. The old Commentators of his Institution, have not explained that Prohibition; so that it has remained in force to this Day. Thus their Law allows no Interest; but it allows Changes, especially Maritime Changes, upon any Advantage whatsoever, as thirty and forty *per Cent*. Profit, or more: As to Interest, the Parties have the way of eluding the Law just as they please. They go to the Judge and borrower, holding in their Hand a Bag of Money; one saith there is in it such a Sum, tho' the Interest agreed on be wanting in it, the Judge without any further Enquiry, orders the Writing to be drawn up; 'Tis even enough, without so much Precaution, to own before Witnesses, that one has received so much (altho' less) to make the Debt Authentick.

¶ *Silk* is the Staple Commodity of *Persia*. They get some in the Province of *Georgia*, of *Corasson*, and *Caramania*, but especially in *Guilan*, and *Mezanderan*, which is *Hircania*. They compute that *Persia* brings Yearly two and twenty thousand Bales of *Silk*, each Bale weighing two hundred and seventy six Pound Weight; the *Guilan*, ten thousand; the *Mezanderan*, two thousand; *Media*, and *Bactria*, three thousand a piece; that Part of *Caramania*, call'd *Caraback*, and *Georgia*, each of them two thousand; and that Account increases every Year, because *Silk* improves continually. There are four sorts of *Silk*; the First, and the worst, is call'd *Chirvani*, because it comes chiefly from *Chirvan*, a Town of *Media*, near the *Caspian* Sea, it is a thick and rough *Silk*, and the coursest Thread of the Shell; It is that they call *Ardache* in *Europe*. The Second, which is a Size better, is call'd *Karvari*, i. e. an Ass-load, to denote that sort of *Silk*, which the Unskilful buy: We call it *Legia*, in our Country, probably from the Word *Legian*, a small Town of *Guilan*, on the Sea, where none but such a sort of Silk is made. The Third, is call'd *Ketcoda Pesend*, as tho' one should say, the Citizen sort, which Name the *Persians* give to all things of a middling Character. The Fourth, is call'd *Charbaffe*, i. e. *Brocade-Silk*; because the best *Silk* is used for those rich Goods. The Abundance of the *Persian Silk* Exported is too well known, to say much of it. The *Dutch* Import of it into *Europe*, to the Value of near six hundred thousand Livres Yearly, by the *Indian* Sea; and all the *Europeans* who Trade in *Turkey*, Import nothing more valuable than the *Persian Silks*, which they buy of the *Armenians*. The *Muscovites* Import it likewise.

¶ Some Foreigners Trade with the *Persians* for *Camels Hair*, call'd *Testick*, as has been said; and some *Europeans* for *Kids Wool*. They use it in *Europe* in making of Hats. The best *Wool* of that sort, comes from *Caramania*, and from *Casbin*, a famous City of *Parthia*.

¶ *Persia* Exports to the *Indies* abundance of *Tobacco*, all sorts of Fruit dry'd, Pickel'd in Vinegar, and preserv'd, especially Dates, Marmelad, Wines, Distill'd Water, Horses, *Persian* Ware, Feathers, *Turky* Leather of all Colours, a great deal whereof is Exported to *Muscovy*, and other *European* Countries. It Exports to *Turky*, towards *Babylon*, and *Nineveh*, Tobacco, Galls, Thread, coarse Goats-Hair Stuffs, Matts, and all sorts of Box-work, and many other things. The Exportation of Steel and Iron is forbidden in the Kingdom, but it is Exported notwithstanding: The *Persians* Export likewise to *Muscovy*, all sorts of *Silks* and *Stuffs*, and *Sheep-Furrs*.

¶ 'Tis not to be supposed however, that the *Persians* manage the Trade with the same Method and Rules we use, or with half our Skill: For Instance, Trading by Commission, and the way of Change by Letters, is little used; but as I have observ'd it, every one goes to sell his own Goods himself, or sends his Deputy's, or Children to do it; there are some *Persian* Traders who have Deputies in all Parts of the World, as far as *Sweden* on the one side, and *China* on the other side; that's the Method of all the Orientalists; and it was that of the whole World, before *Europe* was so stock'd with People, and Towns, that in some Places they lay as it were a top of one another, in comparison with those of *Asia*; and there was no longer need of going oneself, or sending Expresses, but one might reach to one another, and hand Things from one Place to another safely.

¶ Besides, *Europe* is so chargeable a Country, with comparison to the *East*, especially in Travelling, and Trade is there so necessary, and so generally carried on, that if one went oneself to carry one's Goods from one Place to another, it would happen that whole Towns would Travel as it were; they have no Posts neither in the *East*, because the Trade is not spread far enough, and is not manag'd with so much Activity; because the Towns are too distant, and because Messengers are hired at a very easy Rate; for they send an Express a thirty Days Journey for thirty Livres, and he performs that Journey, which may amount to three hundred *French* Leagues, in eighteen or twenty Days time, and sometimes in fifteen. In the *Indies* they may hire one for half the Money. I have sometimes sent Expresses a forty Days Journey, for five Crowns. When those Expresses who are the Meanest and Wretchedest of Men, are hired to go a Journey; they run presently from Place to Place, and give Notice of their intended Journey, in order to get some Letters to carry, which they carry for as little as you please; they bow four times to the Ground to thank you for fifteen Pence, for carrying a Packet of Letters of three Ounce weight; they call those Expresses *Chatir*, which is the Name of Running Footmen, and of all those who can run well, and walk roundly; they are known in the Road by a Bottle of Water, and a Satchel they have at their Back, instead of a Knapsack, to carry Provision for thirty or forty Hours time, and to make the more Speed, they leave the High-Road, and cross the Country: They are known also by their Shoes and some Bells, like our Waggon Horses *Bells*, which stick to their Girdle to keep them Awake. They are bred up to that Business, and it goes on from Father to Son; they are taught to walk at a good round Rate with the same Breath at eight Year old. In the *Indies*, the King's Packets are carried by two Expresses on Horse-back, riding full Gallop, who are relieved every two Leagues; they carry the Packet openly on their Head; one may hear them coming by their *Bells*, as well as a Post-Boy by his *Horn*, and when they have lighted off their Horse, they throw themselves flat on the Ground, and two Men standing ready, take the Packet, and carry it away in the same Manner

¶ I have observ'd elsewhere, that in *Persia*, they sign no Bills, Bonds, or other Writings; but that instead of it they set their Seal to them; at the top of the Paper they write their Name, and their Sirname, which is always the Father's proper Name, and then Seal it at the bottom, as I have said, in the Presence of Witnesses, who attest it with their Seals also: In that Manner do the Merchants make their Writings; and altho' in most Cases the Contracts made without due Form of Law be void, yet amongst Merchants they remain in full Force, the Secular Power ratifies them. The Use of Sureties is very common amongst them, they call it in their

Language, *putting oneself in the Room of the Person Bound*. When they ask a Poor Man for a Bail, and he is not able to give one, he answers, *Iman rezza*, or such like Saint, who comes next in their Head, is my Bail.

¶ All Payments are made in Silver, Gold is not Current in Trade. Their Money Bags hold fifty *Tomans* a-Piece, which come to two thousand five hundred *Abassis*, or eighteen Penny Pieces of *French* Money, without any Mixture of the Rinds; those Silver Bags are long and narrow, and made of Leather, for the Conveniency of Carriage; they do not tell their Silver, but weigh it by the Weight of a *Toman*, worth fifty *Abassis*, or eighteen Penny Pieces; thus they never miss-reckon; for they lay the weighed Pieces by one another, five *Tomans* in a Heap, or ten in a Heap, so that 'tis impossible to Mistake, as you see. I was mightily taken with that Method, because 'tis safe, and saves time, but chiefly, because it prevents taking of bad Money; for if there be a Clipt or false Piece in the Bag, 'tis certainly found out by the Weight in that Manner; they take the light Parcel of the value of fifty *Tomans*, as has been said, and put it in the Scales, five and twenty *Tomans* in each Scale, then they divide again into two Parts, the light Half, laying twelve Pieces in each Scale, and the odd Piece by it-self, then they divide the light Parcel again into six, then into three, till they have found the naughty Piece, which is an infallible way, as you see, and they do it presently.

¶ I have observ'd in another Place, that the *Persians* never tear the Paper, after the return of a *Bond*, or any other Instrument; they take off the Seal with a Penknife, then dip it in Water, and make a little *Ball* of it, which they stuff into a Hole, where it wears out, and turns to Dust.

¶ I add to this Chapter the Description of Weights and Measures, and of the *Persian* Coins.

¶ The common Weight is of two sorts, the *Civil Weight*, and the *Legal Weight*; the *Legal Weight*, which they call *Cheray*, and which is like the *Weight* of the *Sanctuary*, according to the Use of the *Hebrews*, weighs commonly double the *Civil Weight*. They have like us, different *Weights* for *Physick*, and Precious Stones, from the *Common Weights*; their *Civil Weight* is also of two sorts, the *King's Weight* and the *Tauris Weight*, as they call it; the *King's Weight*, or the *Great Weight*, weighs exactly as much more as the other; they call their *Common Weight* as we say a Pound, *Man*, and also *Batman*; the small *Weight-Man*, comes to five Pound fourteen Ounces, of *Paris-Weight*; their way of dividing it is as follows, The Ratel, which is the sixth Part of a *Man*, and like our *Pound Weight*, and the *Derham*, or Drachm, which is the fiftieth Part of a Pound, the *Mescal*, which is half a *Derham*, the *Dung*, which is the sixth Part of a *Mescal*, and comes to eight Grains of *Carat Weight*; and the Barley-Corn, which is the fourth Part of a *Dung*. The *Eastern Weights* are all reduced to the Barley-Corn, which is probably the first *Weight* of the World. One finds in their Books a *Weight* call'd *Vakie*, which should be an Ounce, such as ours is, and another bigger *Weight*, call'd *Sab Cheray*, containing eleven hundred and seventy *Derhem*; 'tis by that *Weight* they pay the Tythes, and Alms of Precept. You must Note, that the Word *Dung*, signifies not only a *Weight*, but also a Piece of Money, which weighs twelve Grains only.

⁋ I shall take Notice here, that the *Persians* have several Names of *Weights* like ours; which perswades me, that both they and we have borrowed them of the *Arabians*: *Ratel* is the *Weight* call'd in *Latin*, *Rofulus*; *Dinar* in *Persian*, and *Denier* in *French*, are of the same Value. The *Persian* Word, *Derhem*, which is the third Part of an Ounce, is near the same thing as *Drachme* in *French*, which is the eighth Part of it. Note also, that *Derhem* in the *Persian* Books is taken for a Piece of Silver worth thirty *Deniers*.

⁋ There are two sorts of *Ells*, the *Royal Ell*, which is three Foot long, wanting an Inch, and the *Short Ell*, or *Guezemoukesser*, as they call it, which is but as long as two thirds of the other. The *Geometrical* Measure is call'd *Girib*; the Land is Measur'd by no other Measure; and the *Girib* contains a thousand and sixty six *Square Ells*, each *Ell* containing thirty five Royal Inches; that is, that the side of the *Girib* is two and thirty *Guezes* long, and two thirds. The Carpets that are sold by the *Ell* are measur'd also by the *Square Ells*, Multiplying the Length by the Breadth, which the *Persians* call *Ell* by *Ell*: For Instance, if a Floor Carpet is twelve *Ells* long, and three broad, they say, three times twelve is six and thirty; they reckon so in several Parts of *Europe*, and probably that Method came out of the *East*, with the Manufacture of Carpets.

⁋ The *Persians* have no Measure for dry Goods, such as a Bushel, because they sell every Thing by *Weight*, even Liquors they have no Measure, neither for Time and Use, neither Clocks nor Sun-dials, as I have said already; they divide the Day into eight Parts, most of which the *Mahometan* Priests give Notice of in Towns, by calling People to Prayer.

⁋ The *Persian* League is called *Fars Seng*, i. e. *Persian Stone*; which *Herodotus*, and other *Greek* Authors, who have writ the *Persian* History, call *Parasanga*, which is no great Alteration. The Pronunciation of the *f* and the *p*, being most Unison. It appears from the signification of the Word *fars seng*, that formerly the Leagues were mark'd with great and high Stones, both in the *East* and *West*: All Learned Men know, that in the Latin Tongue, the Word *Stone* is always used instead of the Word *League*, *Ad primum vel secundum Lapidem*, i. e. to the first or second League. *Herodotus* saith, that the *Parasangue* contains thirty Furlongs long, which would come to two *French* Leagues, at the rate of twelve thousand Foot in a League. The *Persians* make it six thousand Paces long, or *Endaze*, which is the *Persian* Word for Pace: That word signifies likewise Cast, to intimate that a Pace is made by casting the Body forward. The *fars seng*, or *Parasangue*, is mostly the same throughout the whole *Persian* Empire.

¶ As to the *Persian* Money, the *Persians* call all sorts of Coins *Zer*, which signifies properly Gold; for *Zim*, in their Language, is the word they call Silver by. They distinguish the Silver Money by the word *Dirhem*, or *Drachm*, and the Gold Money by the word *Dinar* or *Denier*. They reckon by *Dinar Bisty*, and *Tomans*, tho' they have no Coin so called, they being only Denominations. By the word *Dinar* is understood Silver in General. *Dinar* in a particular Signification, is equivalent to a *French Denier*; and doubtless the word *Denier*, which occurs in most of our *European* Tongues, in *Greek* and *Latin*, comes from the word *Dinar*, which is a Term found in all the *Eastern* Dialects, as far as the Indies, as I observed just now. There is the common *Dinar*, and the legal *Dinar*, or *Cheray*, as I have explained it above: And the *Dinar Cheray*, signifies the Weight and Value of a *Ducat*, or of the Gold Crown Piece: They use the *legal Denier* but in Books of Accompts. One *Bisty* makes ten *Dinars* or *Deniers*; and one *Toman* makes ten thousand *Dinars*. Their current Coins are of Silver, which is, or ought to be, according to the Standard of *Spanish* Silver. The *Chayé*, which is the lowest Silver Coin, is worth four Pence Half-penny of *French* Money. The *Mamondy*, which is worth two *Chayés*, is worth Nine-pence. The *Abassi* is worth four *Chayez*, and the *Toman* is worth fifty *Abassis*, or ten thousand *Dinars*. *Toman* is a word of the *Yusbeck* Language, which signifies ten Thousand, being equivalent to the Term *Myriades* among the *Greeks*. The *Tartars* reckon their Forces by ten Thousands, as we do by Battalions: Their Camp is therefore divided into ten Thousand effective Men bearing Arms, and they express the Grandure of a Prince, by the Number of *Tomans* he keeps under him. The Town which *Xerxes* built in *Syria*, and call'd by the Name of *Mynandra*, had its Denomination, upon the Account of its prodigious Armies, which they reckon'd by ten thousands, as they do now by Battalions, and Squadrons. They have also other Brass Coins, *viz.* the *Casbequi*, a Word compounded of *Ras*, Money, from whence came *Kasne*, a Treasure; and of *Becklord*, as tho' one said, the King's Coin, and that Piece is the tenth Part of a *Chayé*; but they have no Gold Money; for these Pieces of Gold, Stampt with the King's Effigie, and coined at his Accession to the Throne, and on New-Years Day, which are of the same Weight as the *German Duckat*, are not current among the People any more than Counters are current in *France*; besides, those Pieces of Gold have no proper Name; the *Persians* call them commonly *Tela*, i. e. Pieces of Gold; they are call'd also *Cherrasis*, i. e. Nobles, by Reason of their Value.

¶ Formerly there was no other Coin in the Kingdom but Silver *Bestis*, which are worth two and twenty *Deniers*, and those four Pence half-Penny Pieces, which they call'd *Chayé*, i. e. Royal. But afterwards, and in the time of the Sultan *Mahmoud*, about four hundred Years ago, the Money encreasing, they Coined Double *Chayez*, called *Maymondys*, from the Name of the Sovereign. *Abas the Great* being inaugurated King, and *Persia* abounding with Silver and Trade, he order'd Double *Maymondys* to be Coined, which were called by his Name, *Abasts and Mamondys and half*; which they call *Abassis* of five *Chayez*: They Coin sometimes Pieces of Double five *Chayez*, and Pieces of five *Abassis*, but 'tis only out of Curiosity; they are not current in Trade. There is a Coin all along the *Persian* Gulf, called *Larins*, which is the most common in Trade. *Larins* signifies Coin of *Lar*, which is the Capital of *Caramania Deserta*; which was a distinct Kingdom before *Abas* the Great, King of *Persia*, who Conquer'd it, join'd it to his Kingdom about sixscore Years ago. That piece of Money is of good Silver, and is worth two *Chayez* and half, which comes to eleven Pence and three *Deniers* of *French* Money: The mark of it is very extraordinary, being a round Wire of the bigness of a Quill folded in two, and an Inch long, with a small Mark on it, which is the Prince's Stamp. None having been Coined since that Conquest, is the reason they are now very scarce. They do nevertheless reckon by that Coin in all that Country, and in the *Indies*, along the Gulf of *Gambay*, and in the Neighbouring Parts. They say, that formerly it was current throughout all the *East*. The *Persian* Money is made with a Hammer, they are not acquainted with the Mill. The Money weighs exactly the same alike in all Parts. There are coining-Houses; the charge of coining is greater than in any other part of the World, for it amounts to seven and a half *per Cent*. The Stamp of the Money, like that of the Great Seal of the Kingdom, represents in the middle of one of the Sides, the *Persian* Belief in these Words; *There is no God, but God. Mahammed is God's Prophet; Aly is God's Vicegerent,* and the Names of the twelve *Imans* round it; and on the other side the Name of the King, of the Place and of the Year. The Copper Money has on one side the *Persian* Hyerogliphick, *viz.* A *Lyon* with a *rising Sun* on his Back; and on the other side, the Time and the Name of the Place where the Money was coined.

FINIS